KODANSHA COMICS TRADE PAPERBACK ORIGINAL

Q HOLDER! VOLUME 7 COPYRIGHT © 2015 KEN AKAMATSU
NGLISH TRANSLATION COPYRIGHT © 2016 KEN AKAMATSU

UBLISHED IN THE UNITED STATES BY KODANSHA COMICS, AN IMPRINT OF ODANSHA USA PUBLISHING, LLC, NEW YORK.

UBLICATION RIGHTS FOR THIS ENGLISH EDITION ARRANGED THROUGH ODANSHA LTD., TOKYO.

RST PUBLISHED IN JAPAN IN 2015 BY KODANSHA LTD., TOKYO.

SBN 978-1-63236-209-4

RINTED IN THE UNITED STATES OF AMERICA.

WW.KODANSHACOMICS.COM

8 7 6 5 4 3 2 1

DITING: LAUREN SCANLAN
RANSLATOR: ALETHEA NIBLEY AND ATHENA NIBLEY
ETTERING: JAMES DASHIELL

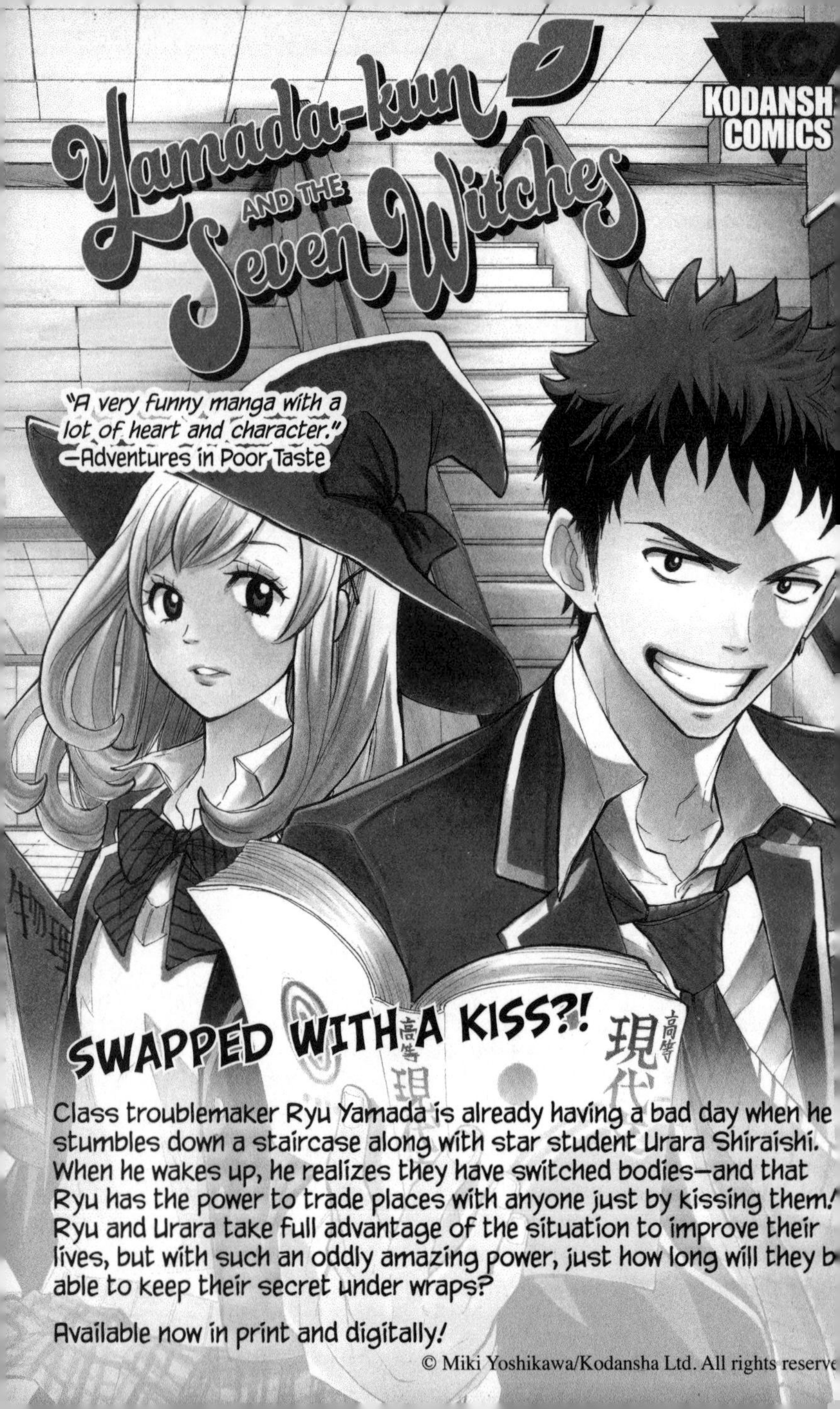
Yamada-kun AND THE Seven Witches
KODANSH COMICS
"A very funny manga with a lot of heart and character."
—Adventures in Poor Taste
SWAPPED WITH A KISS?!
Class troublemaker Ryu Yamada is already having a bad day when he stumbles down a staircase along with star student Urara Shiraishi. When he wakes up, he realizes they have switched bodies—and that Ryu has the power to trade places with anyone just by kissing them! Ryu and Urara take full advantage of the situation to improve their lives, but with such an oddly amazing power, just how long will they b able to keep their secret under wraps?
Available now in print and digitally!
© Miki Yoshikawa/Kodansha Ltd. All rights reserve

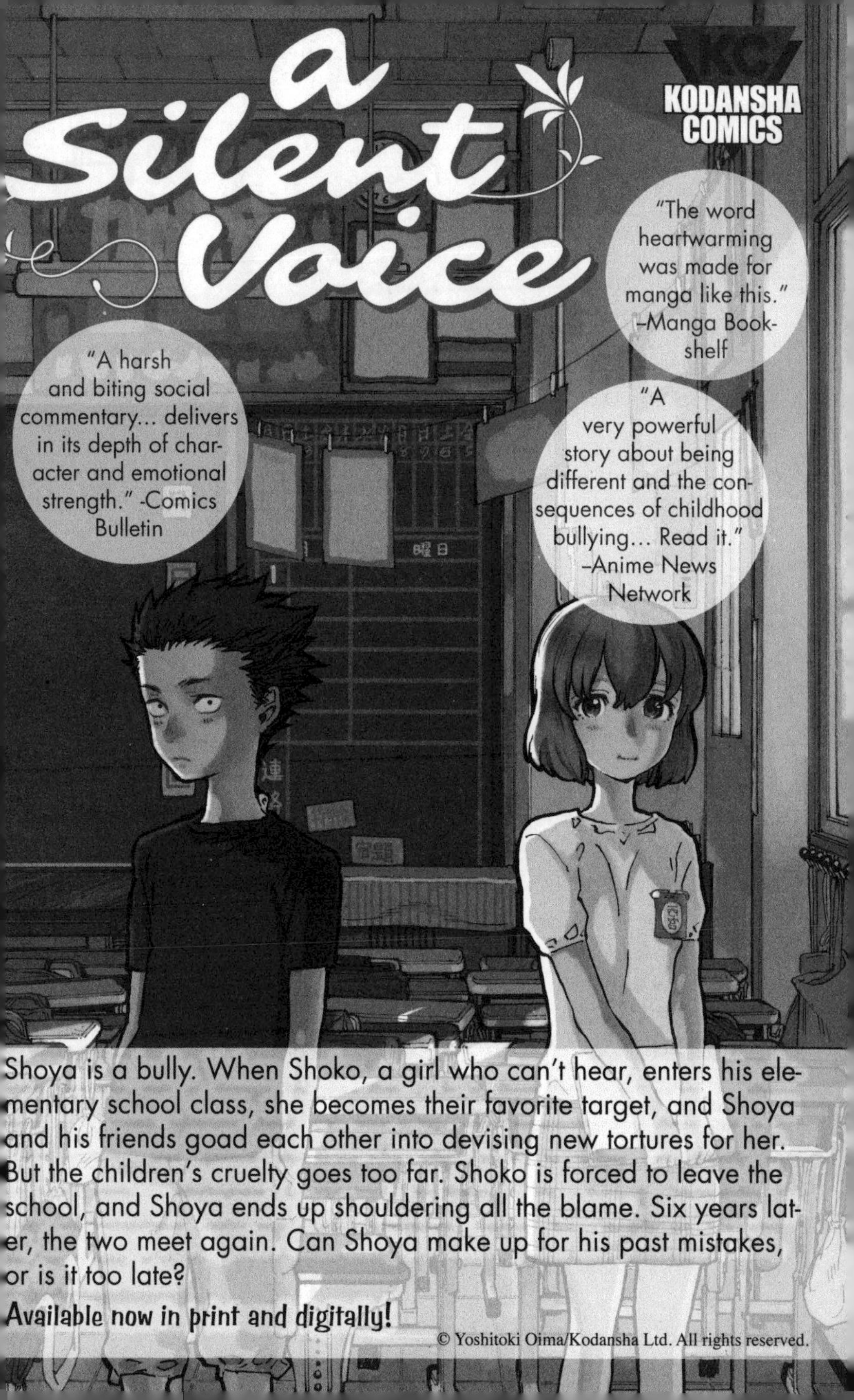
a Silent Voice
KODANSHA COMICS
"The word heartwarming was made for manga like this." –Manga Bookshelf
"A harsh and biting social commentary... delivers in its depth of character and emotional strength." -Comics Bulletin
"A very powerful story about being different and the consequences of childhood bullying… Read it." –Anime News Network
Shoya is a bully. When Shoko, a girl who can't hear, enters his elementary school class, she becomes their favorite target, and Shoya and his friends goad each other into devising new tortures for her. But the children's cruelty goes too far. Shoko is forced to leave the school, and Shoya ends up shouldering all the blame. Six years later, the two meet again. Can Shoya make up for his past mistakes, or is it too late?
Available now in print and digitally!
© Yoshitoki Oima/Kodansha Ltd. All rights reserved.

NO.6

A PERFECT LIFE
IN A PERFECT CITY

For Shion, an elite student in the technologically sophisticated city No. 6, life is carefully choreographed. One fateful day, he takes a misstep, sheltering a fugitive his age from a typhoon. Helping this boy throws Shion's life down a path to discovering the appalling secrets behind the "perfection" of No. 6.

KC
KODAN
COMI

UQ HOLDER!

KEN AKAMATSU

vol.7

CHARACTERS

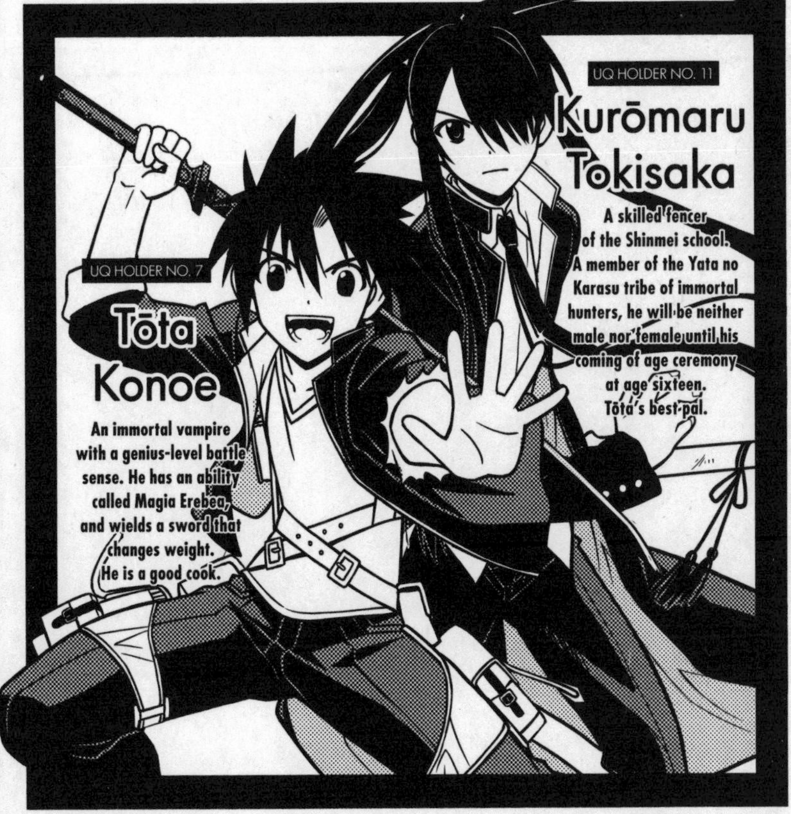
UQ HOLDER NO. 11
Kurōmaru Tokisaka
A skilled fencer of the Shinmei school. A member of the Yata no Karasu tribe of immortal hunters, he will be neither male nor female until his coming of age ceremony at age sixteen. Tōta's best pal.
UQ HOLDER NO. 7
Tōta Konoe
An immortal vampire with a genius-level battle sense. He has an ability called Magia Erebea, and wields a sword that changes weight. He is a good cook.

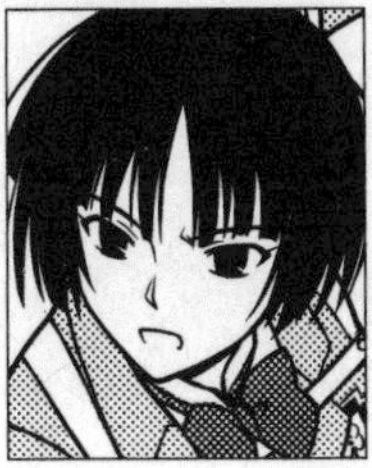

UQ HOLDER NO. 4

KARIN

Cool-headed and ruthless. Her immortality is S-class. Also known as the Saintess of Steel. Loves Eva.

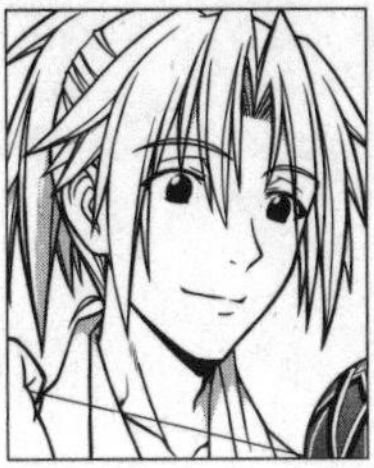

UQ HOLDER NO. 10

IKKŪ AMEYA

Looks young but is an 85-year-old full-body cyborg. Very good with his hands. ♡

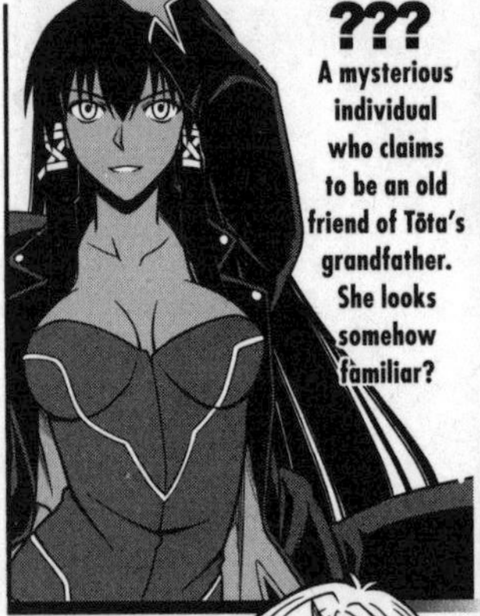
???
A mysterious individual who claims to be an old friend of Tōta's grandfather. She looks somehow familiar?

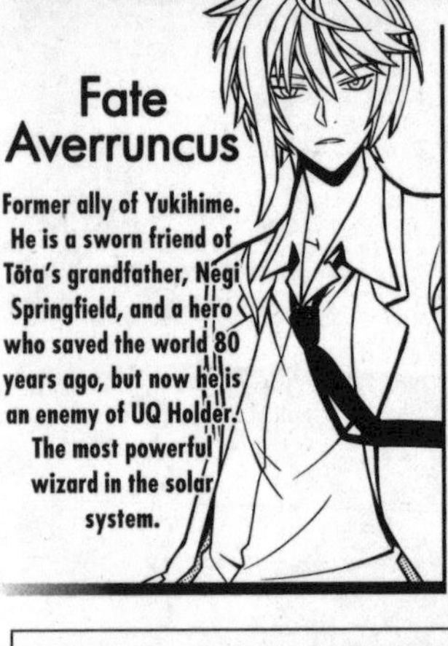
Fate Averruncus
Former ally of Yukihime. He is a sworn friend of Tōta's grandfather, Negi Springfield, and a hero who saved the world 80 years ago, but now he is an enemy of UQ Holder. The most powerful wizard in the solar system.

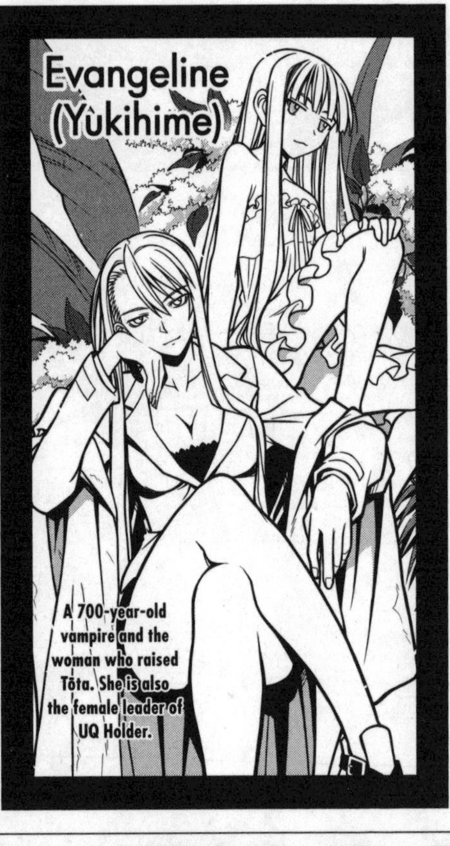
Evangeline (Yùkihime)
A 700-year-old vampire and the woman who raised Tōta. She is also the female leader of UQ Holder.

UQ HOLDER NUMBERS

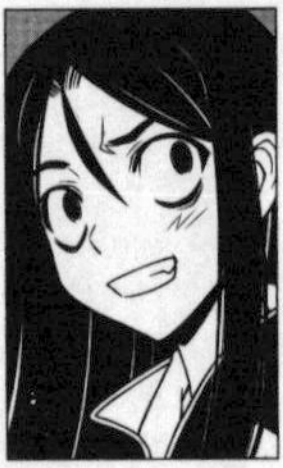

UQ HOLDER NO. 12

SANTA SASAKI

After a tormented past as the victim of bullying, he became a shut-in. He thought he was alive, but is actually a ghost. Because of that, he can use multiple abilities.

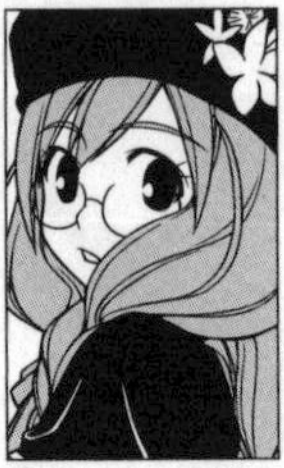

UQ HOLDER NO. 9

KIRIË SAKURAME

The greatest financial contributor to UQ Holder, and constantly calls Tōta incompetent. Her ability is called Reset & Restart.

THE STORY SO FAR

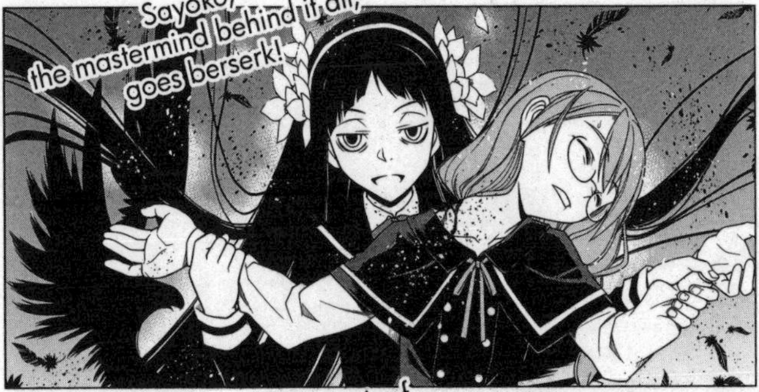
Sayoko, the mastermind behind it all, goes berserk!

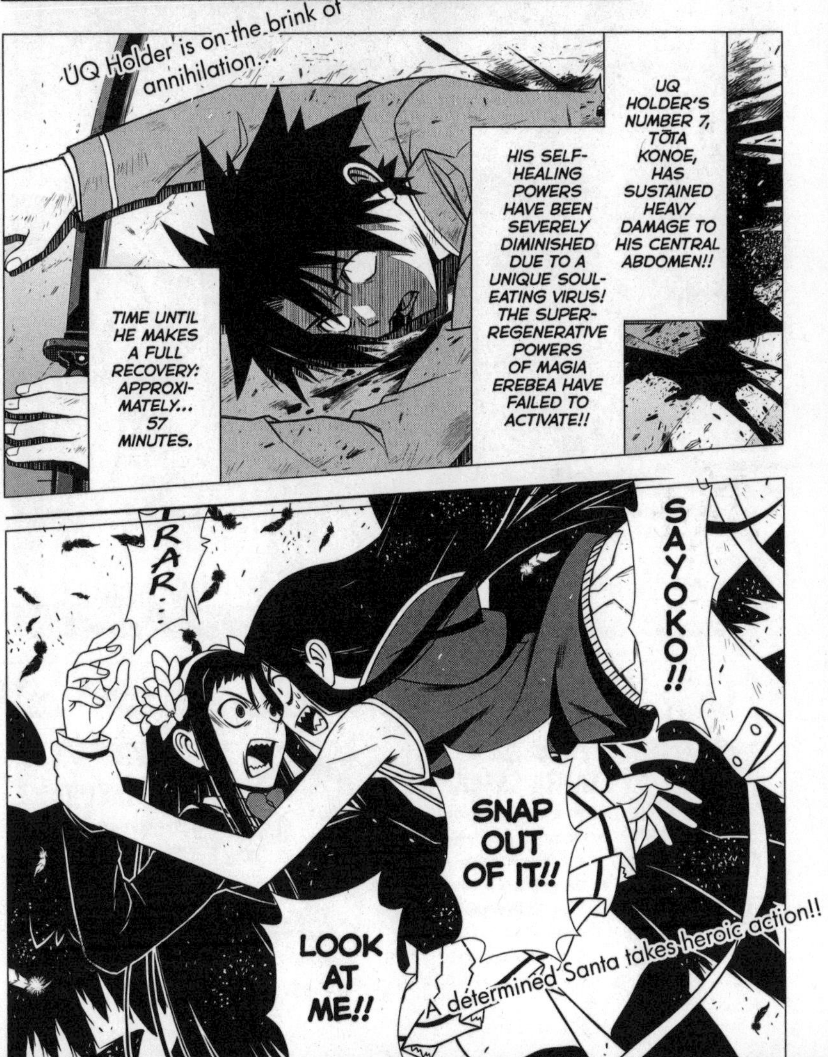
UQ Holder is on the brink of annihilation...
UQ HOLDER'S NUMBER 7, TŌTA KONOE, HAS SUSTAINED HEAVY DAMAGE TO HIS CENTRAL ABDOMEN!!
HIS SELF-HEALING POWERS HAVE BEEN SEVERELY DIMINISHED DUE TO A UNIQUE SOUL-EATING VIRUS! THE SUPER-REGENERATIVE POWERS OF MAGIA EREBEA HAVE FAILED TO ACTIVATE!!
TIME UNTIL HE MAKES A FULL RECOVERY: APPROXIMATELY... 57 MINUTES.
SAYOKO!!
RAR...
SNAP OUT OF IT!!
LOOK AT ME!!
A determined Santa takes heroic action!!

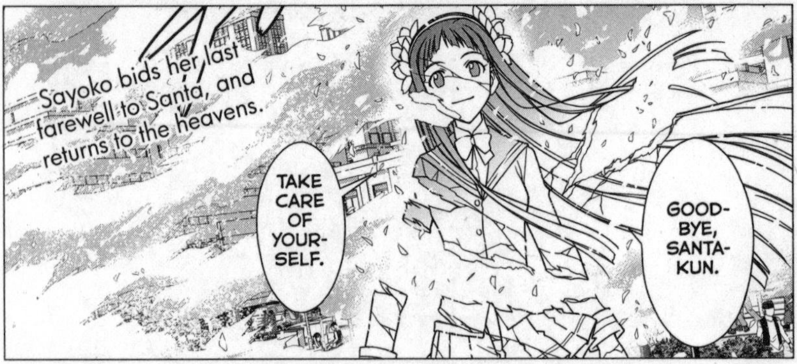
Sayoko bids her last farewell to Santa, and returns to the heavens.
GOOD-BYE, SANTA-KUN.
TAKE CARE OF YOURSELF.

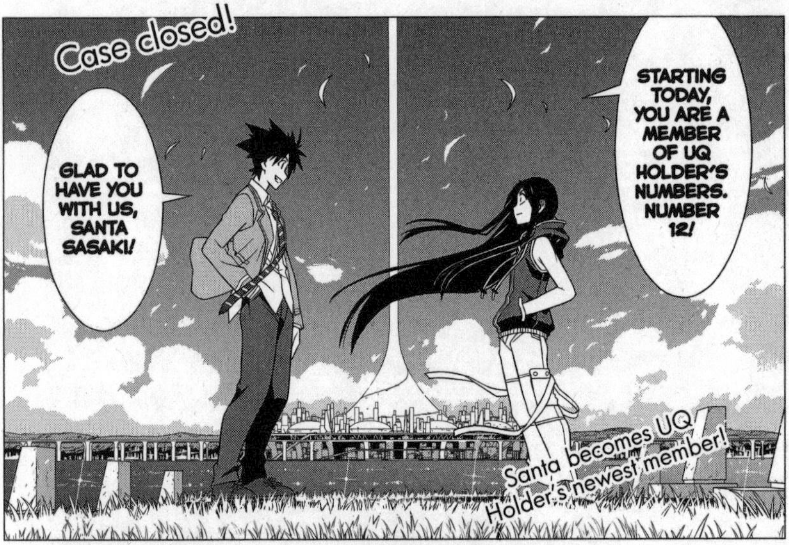
STARTING TODAY, YOU ARE A MEMBER OF UQ HOLDER'S NUMBERS. NUMBER 12!
Santa becomes UQ Holder's newest member!
Case closed!
GLAD TO HAVE YOU WITH US, SANTA SASAKI!

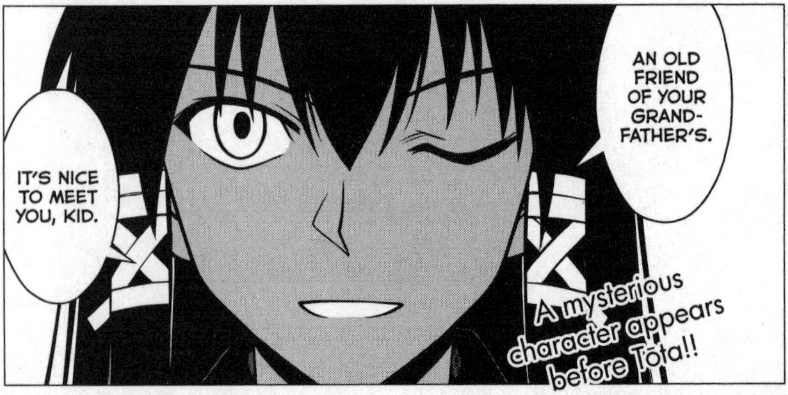
AN OLD FRIEND OF YOUR GRAND-FATHER'S.
IT'S NICE TO MEET YOU, KID.
A mysterious character appears before Tōta!!

CONTENTS

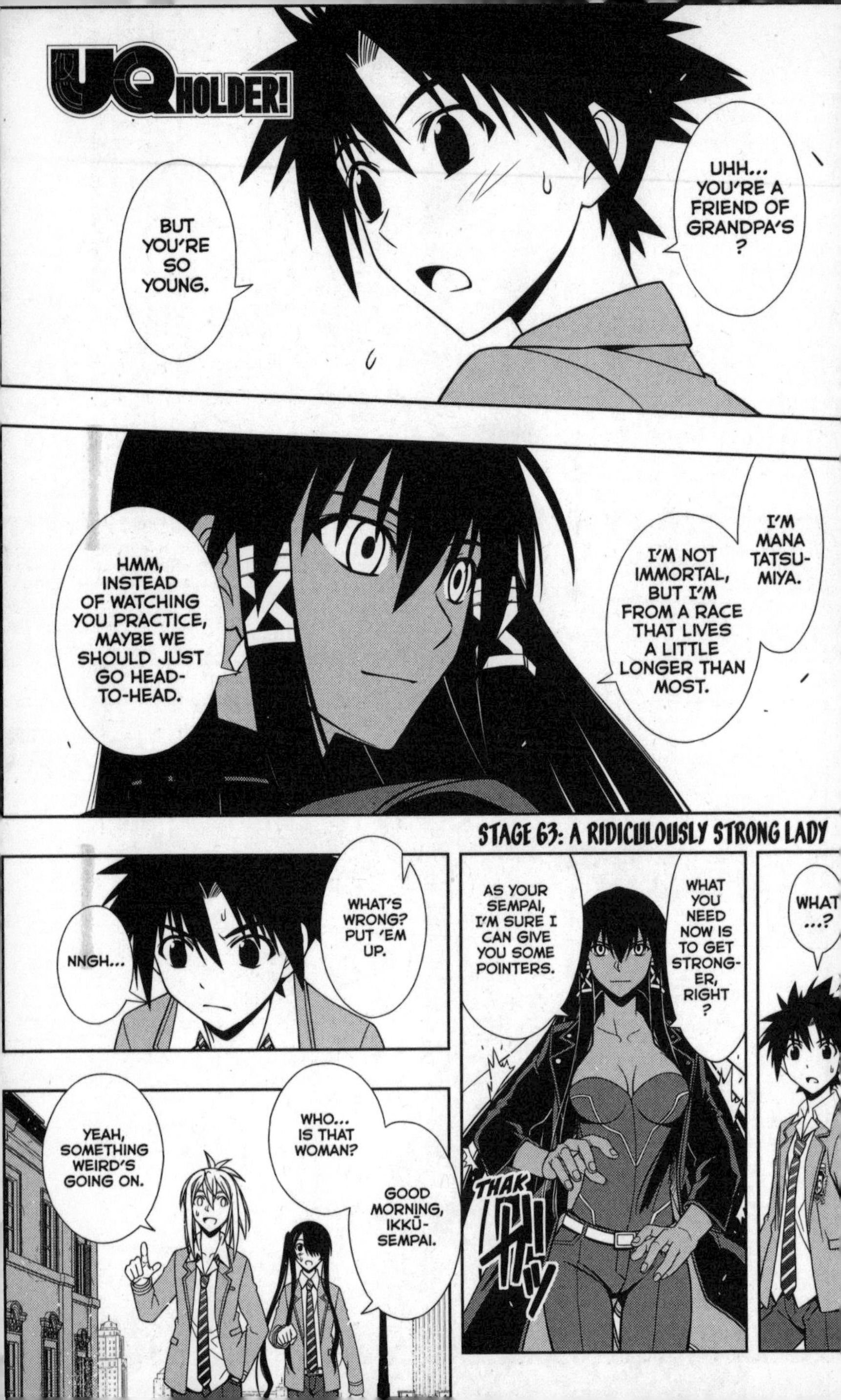
UQ HOLDER!
UHH... YOU'RE A FRIEND OF GRANDPA'S?
BUT YOU'RE SO YOUNG.
I'M MANA TATSUMIYA.
I'M NOT IMMORTAL, BUT I'M FROM A RACE THAT LIVES A LITTLE LONGER THAN MOST.
HMM, INSTEAD OF WATCHING YOU PRACTICE, MAYBE WE SHOULD JUST GO HEAD-TO-HEAD.
STAGE 63: A RIDICULOUSLY STRONG LADY
WHAT...?
WHAT YOU NEED NOW IS TO GET STRONGER, RIGHT?
AS YOUR SEMPAI, I'M SURE I CAN GIVE YOU SOME POINTERS.
THAK
WHAT'S WRONG? PUT 'EM UP.
NNGH...
WHO... IS THAT WOMAN?
GOOD MORNING, IKKŪ-SEMPAI.
YEAH, SOMETHING WEIRD'S GOING ON.

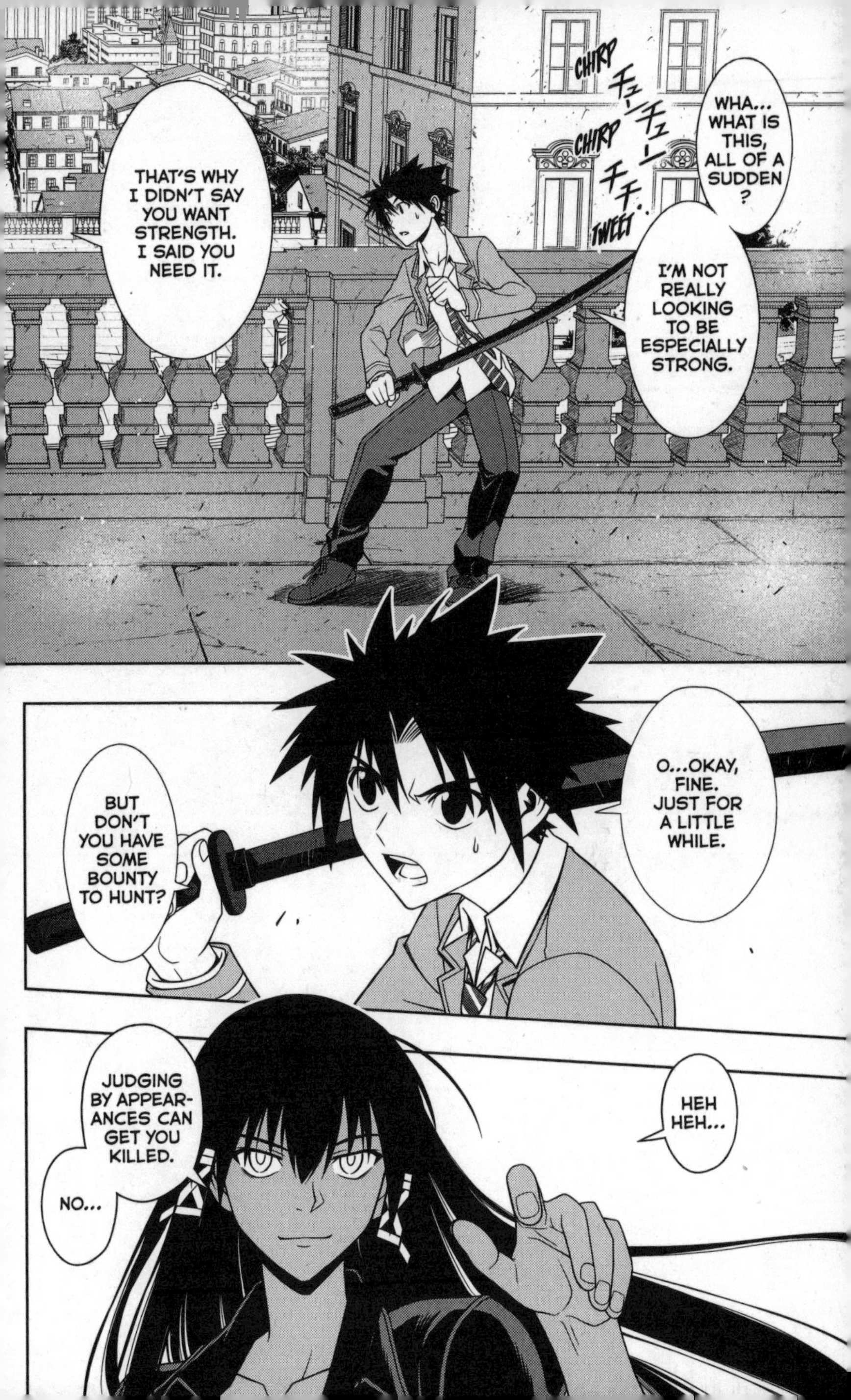
WHA... WHAT IS THIS, ALL OF A SUDDEN?
CHIRP
CHIRP
TWEET
I'M NOT REALLY LOOKING TO BE ESPECIALLY STRONG.
THAT'S WHY I DIDN'T SAY YOU WANT STRENGTH. I SAID YOU NEED IT.
O...OKAY, FINE. JUST FOR A LITTLE WHILE.
BUT DON'T YOU HAVE SOME BOUNTY TO HUNT?
HEH HEH...
JUDGING BY APPEARANCES CAN GET YOU KILLED.
NO...

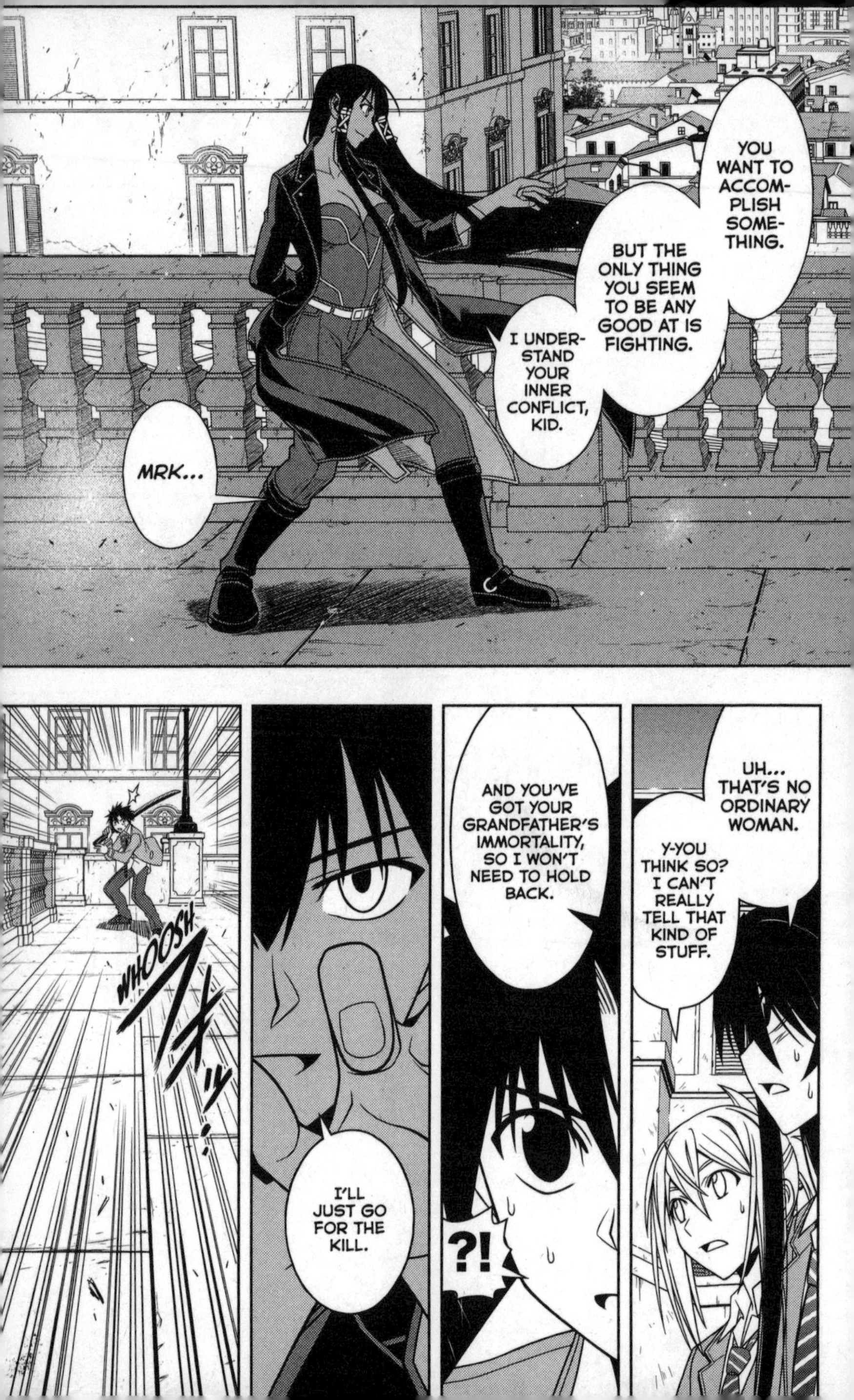
YOU WANT TO ACCOMPLISH SOMETHING.
BUT THE ONLY THING YOU SEEM TO BE ANY GOOD AT IS FIGHTING.
I UNDERSTAND YOUR INNER CONFLICT, KID.
MRK...
UH... THAT'S NO ORDINARY WOMAN.
Y-YOU THINK SO? I CAN'T REALLY TELL THAT KIND OF STUFF.
AND YOU'VE GOT YOUR GRANDFATHER'S IMMORTALITY, SO I WON'T NEED TO HOLD BACK.
?!
I'LL JUST GO FOR THE KILL.
WHOOSH

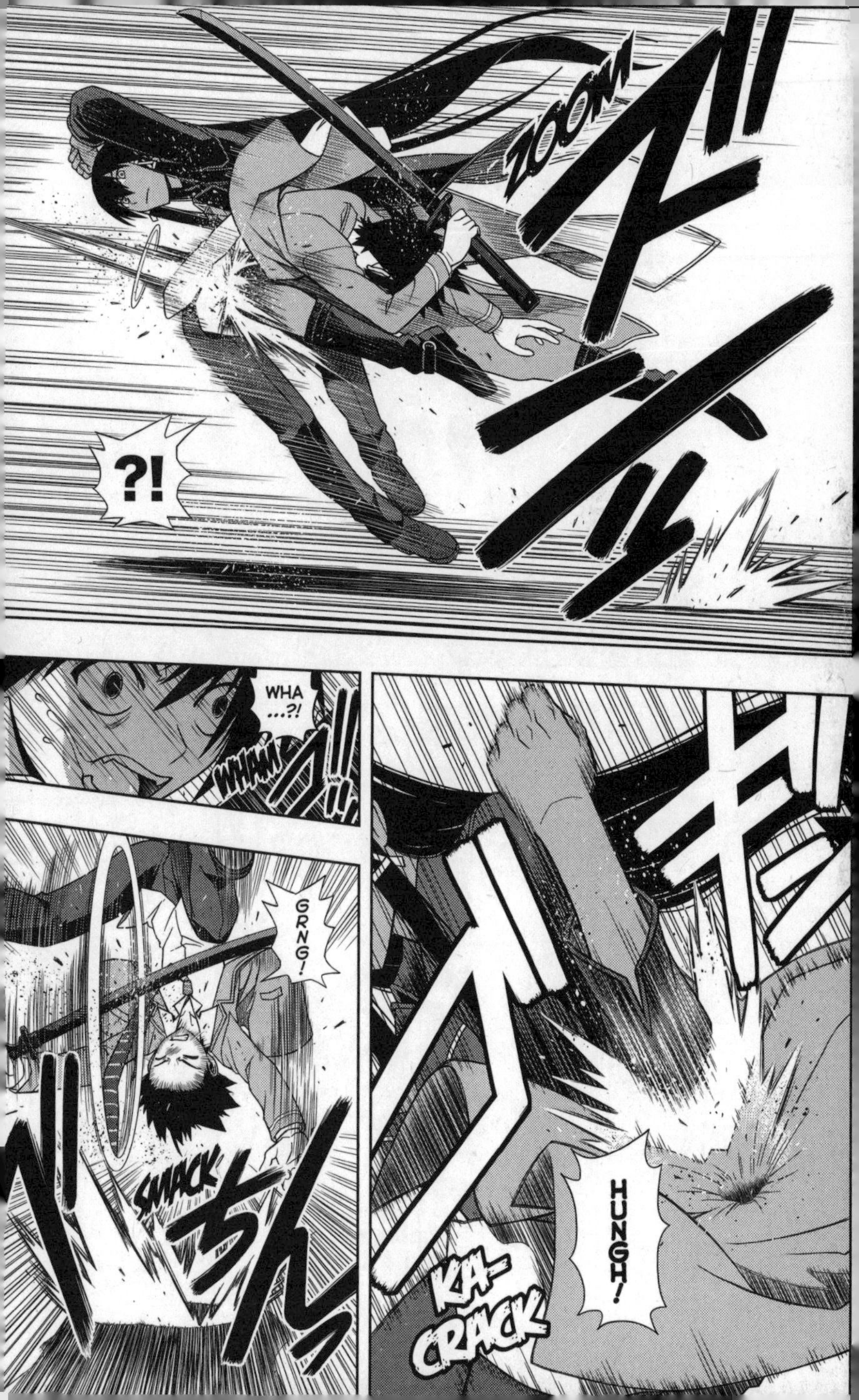
ZOOM
?!
HUNGH!
KA-CRACK
WHA ...?!
WHAM
GRNG!
SMACK

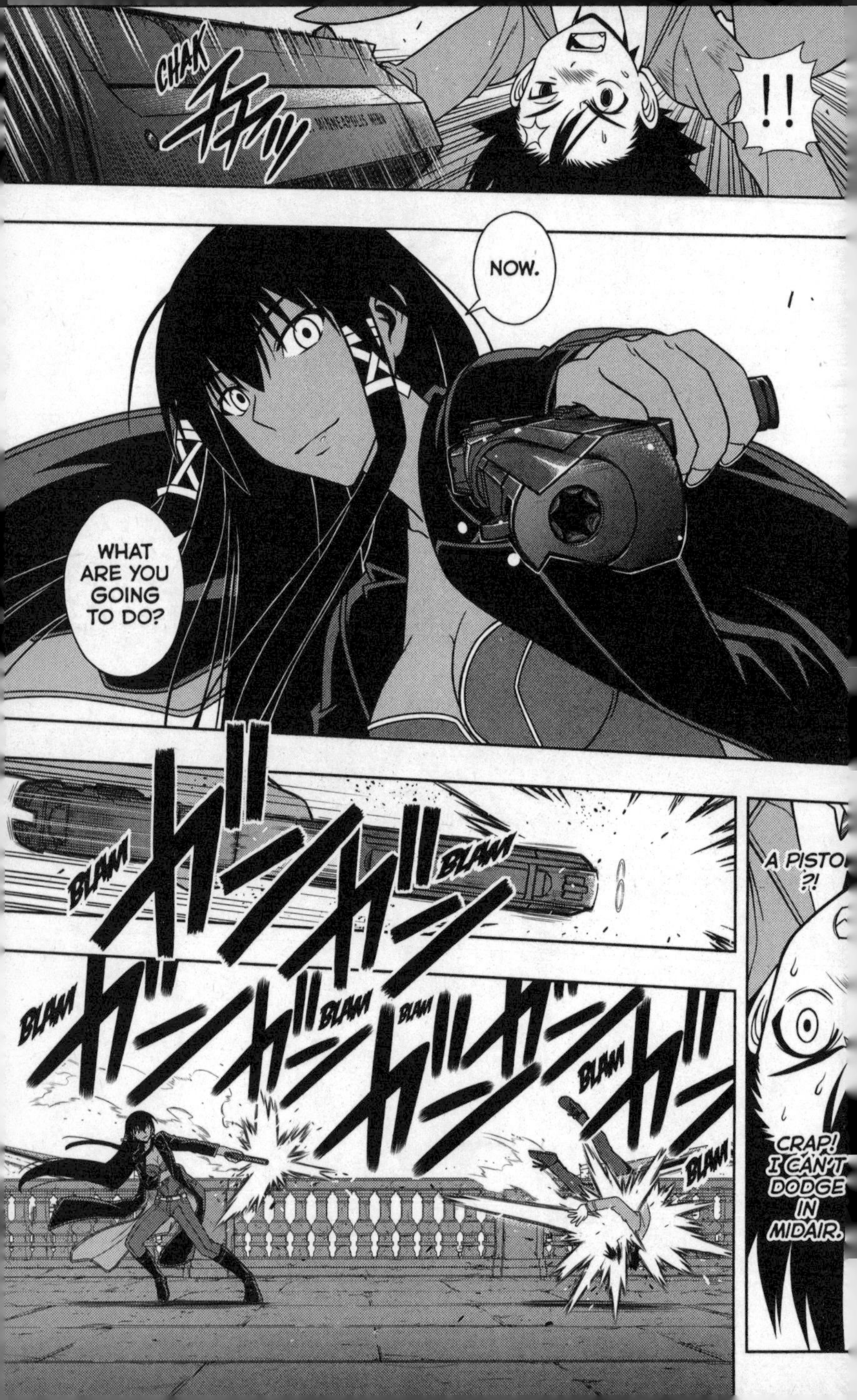

CHAK
!!
NOW.
WHAT ARE YOU GOING TO DO?
A PISTO ?!
CRAP! I CAN'T DODGE IN MIDAIR.
BLAM
BLAM
BLAM
BLAM
BLAM
BLAM
BLAM

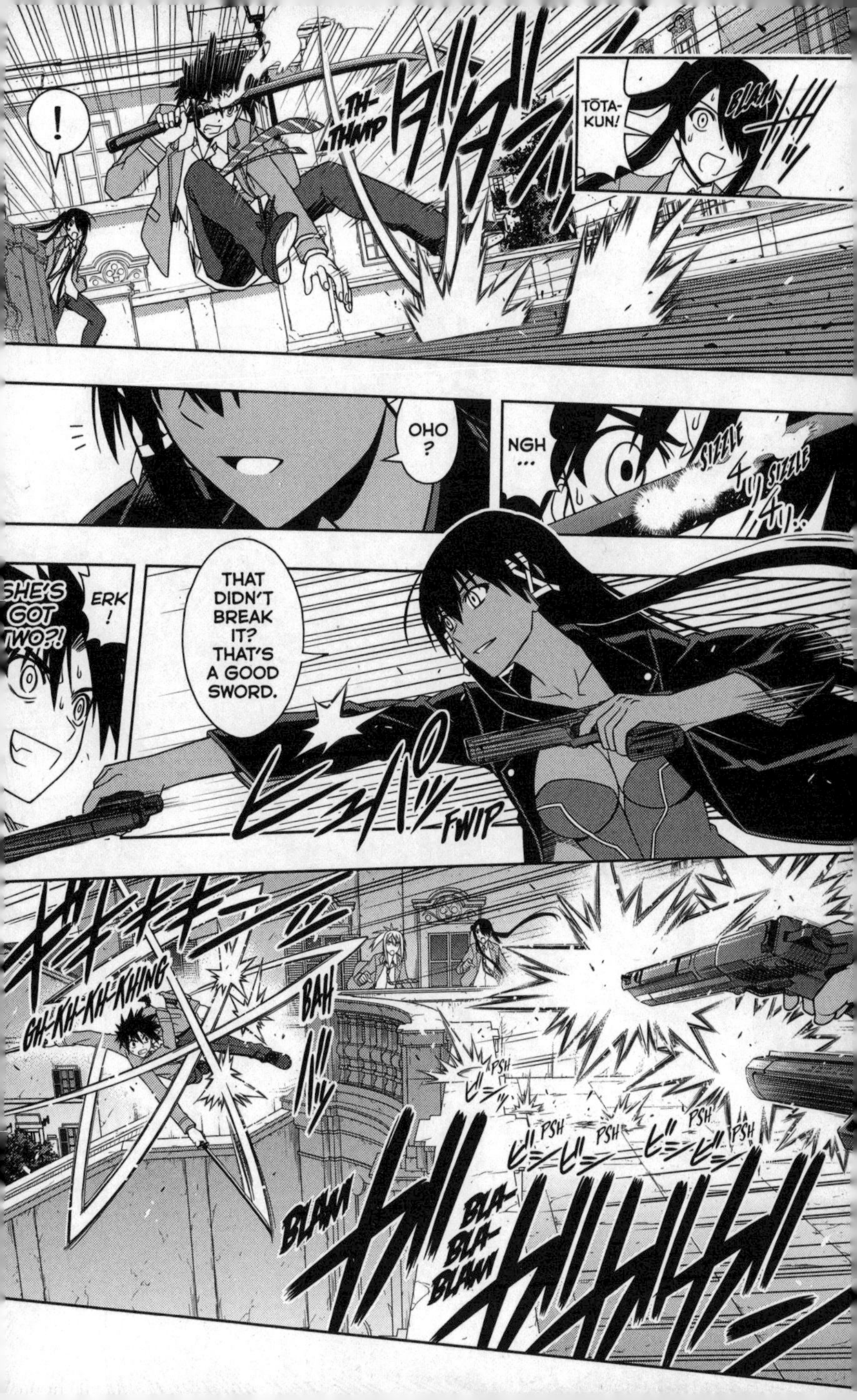
TŌTA-KUN!
BLAM
TH-THAMP
!
NGH ...
SIZZLE
SIZZLE
OHO ?
THAT DIDN'T BREAK IT? THAT'S A GOOD SWORD.
FWIP
ERK !
SHE'S GOT TWO?!
PSH
PSH
PSH
PSH
PSH
BAH
GH-KA-KA-KHING
BLA-BLA-BLAM
BLAM

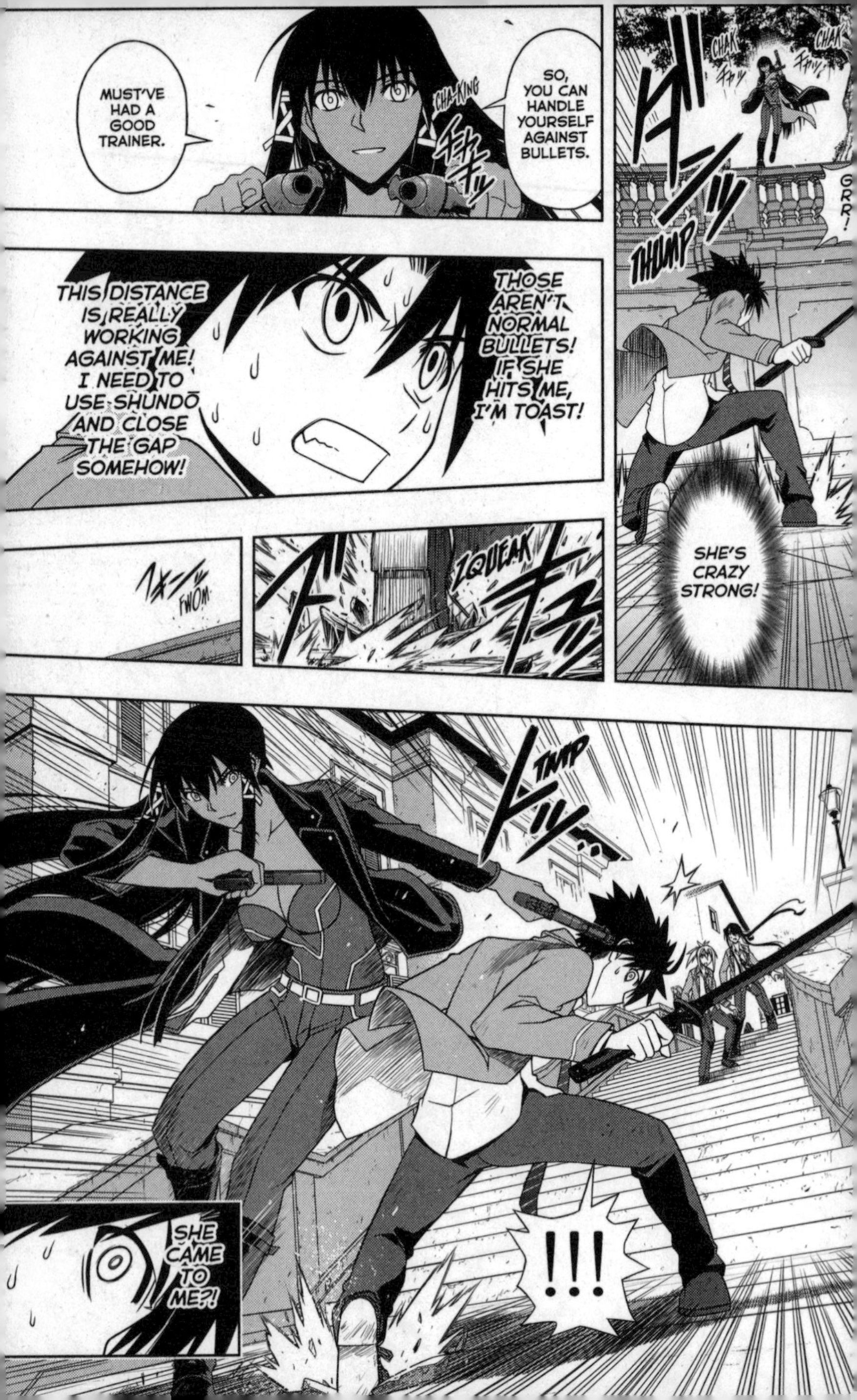
CHAK
CHAK
GRR!
THUMP
SHE'S CRAZY STRONG!
SO, YOU CAN HANDLE YOURSELF AGAINST BULLETS.
CHA-KING
MUST'VE HAD A GOOD TRAINER.
THOSE AREN'T NORMAL BULLETS! IF SHE HITS ME, I'M TOAST!
THIS DISTANCE IS REALLY WORKING AGAINST ME! I NEED TO USE SHUNDŌ AND CLOSE THE GAP SOMEHOW!
ZQUEAK
FWOM
TMP
!!!
SHE CAME TO ME?!

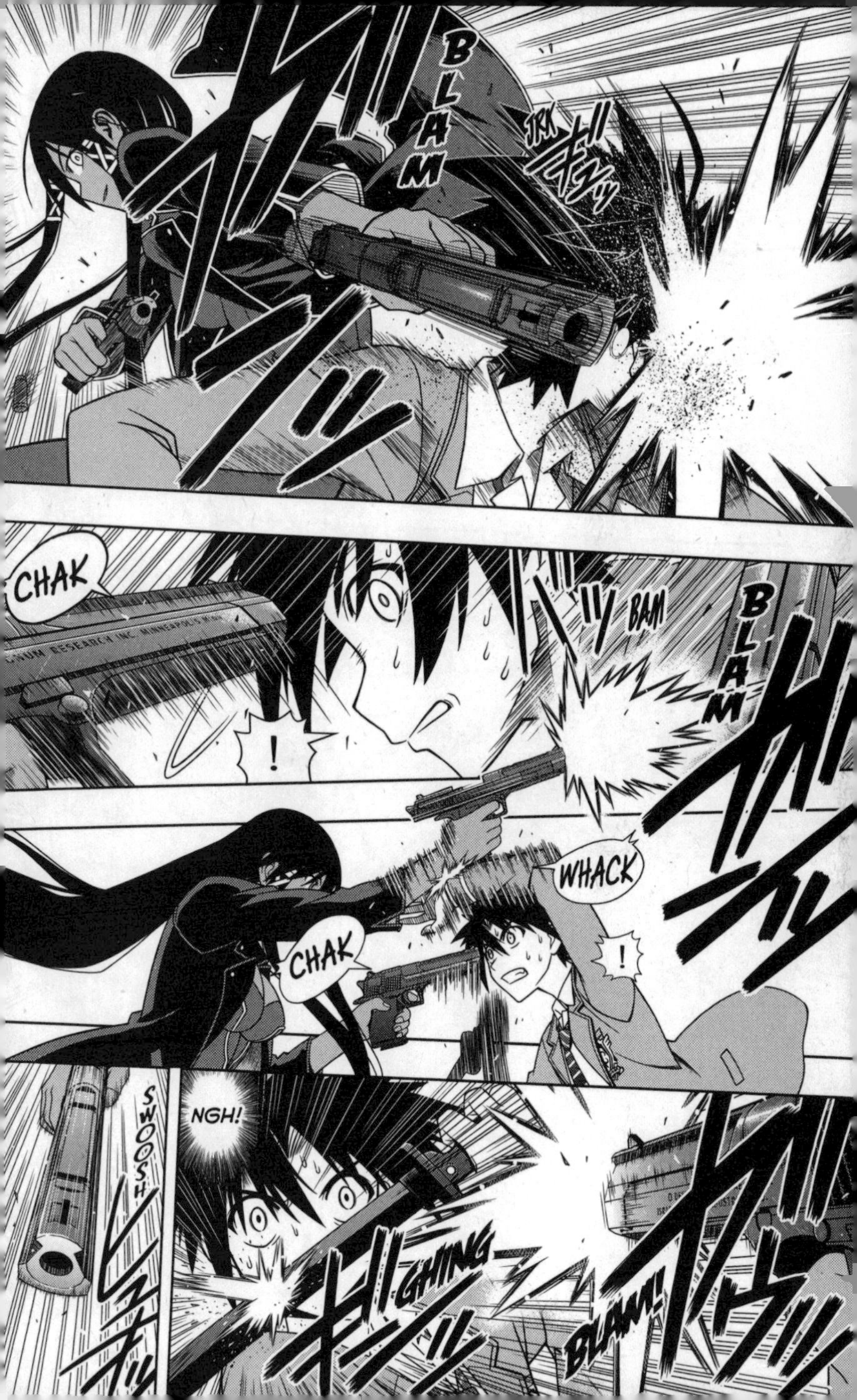
BLAM
JRK
BLAM
BAM
CHAK
!
WHACK
!
CHAK
BLAM!
GHING
NGH!
SWOOSH

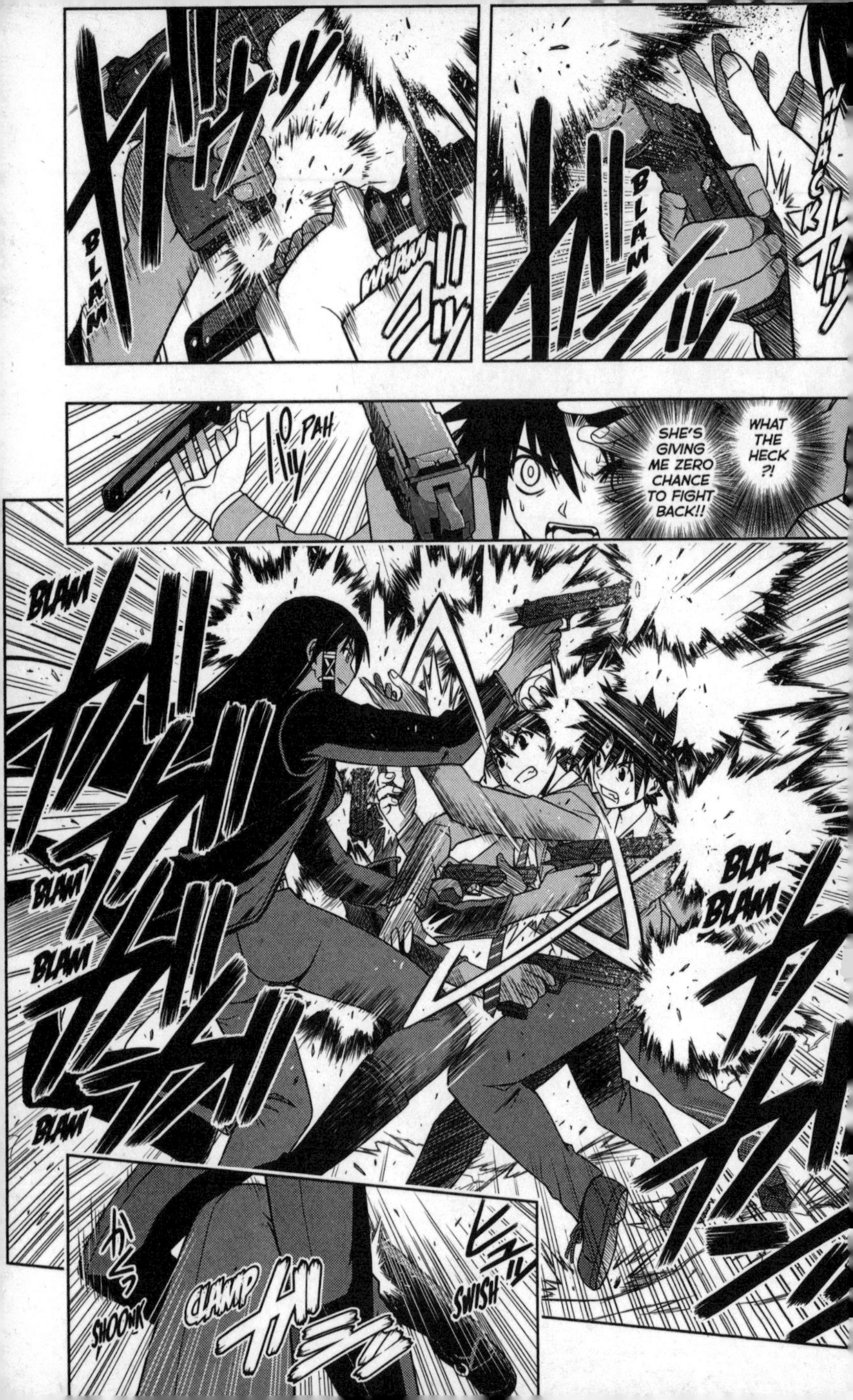
WHACK
BLAM
WHAM
BLAM
WHAT THE HECK?!
SHE'S GIVING ME ZERO CHANCE TO FIGHT BACK!!
PAH
BLA-BLAM
BLAM
BLAM
BLAM
BLAM
SWISH
CLAMP
SHOONK

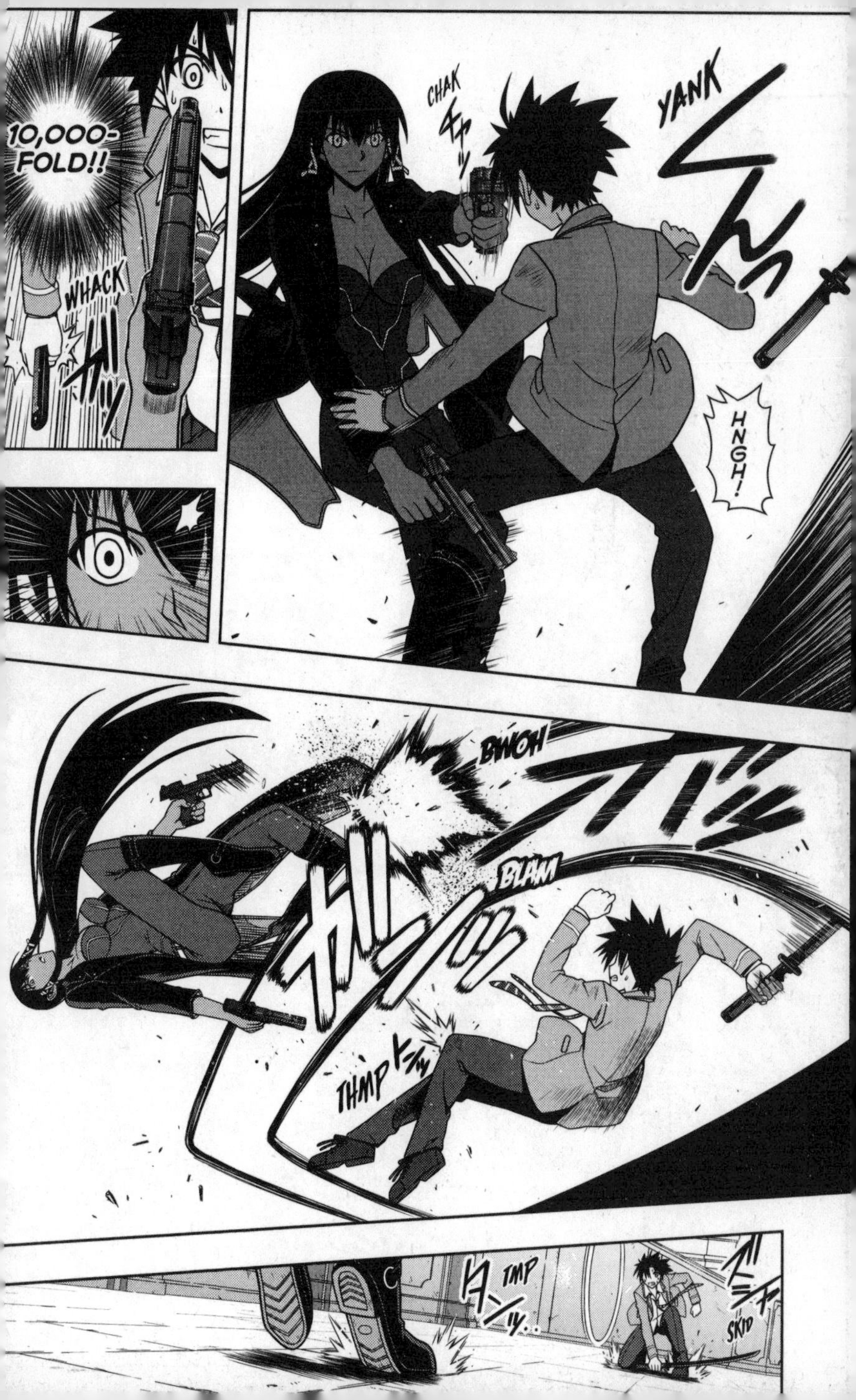

YANK
CHAK
HNGH!
10,000-FOLD!!
WHACK
BWOH
BLAM
THMP
SKID
TMP

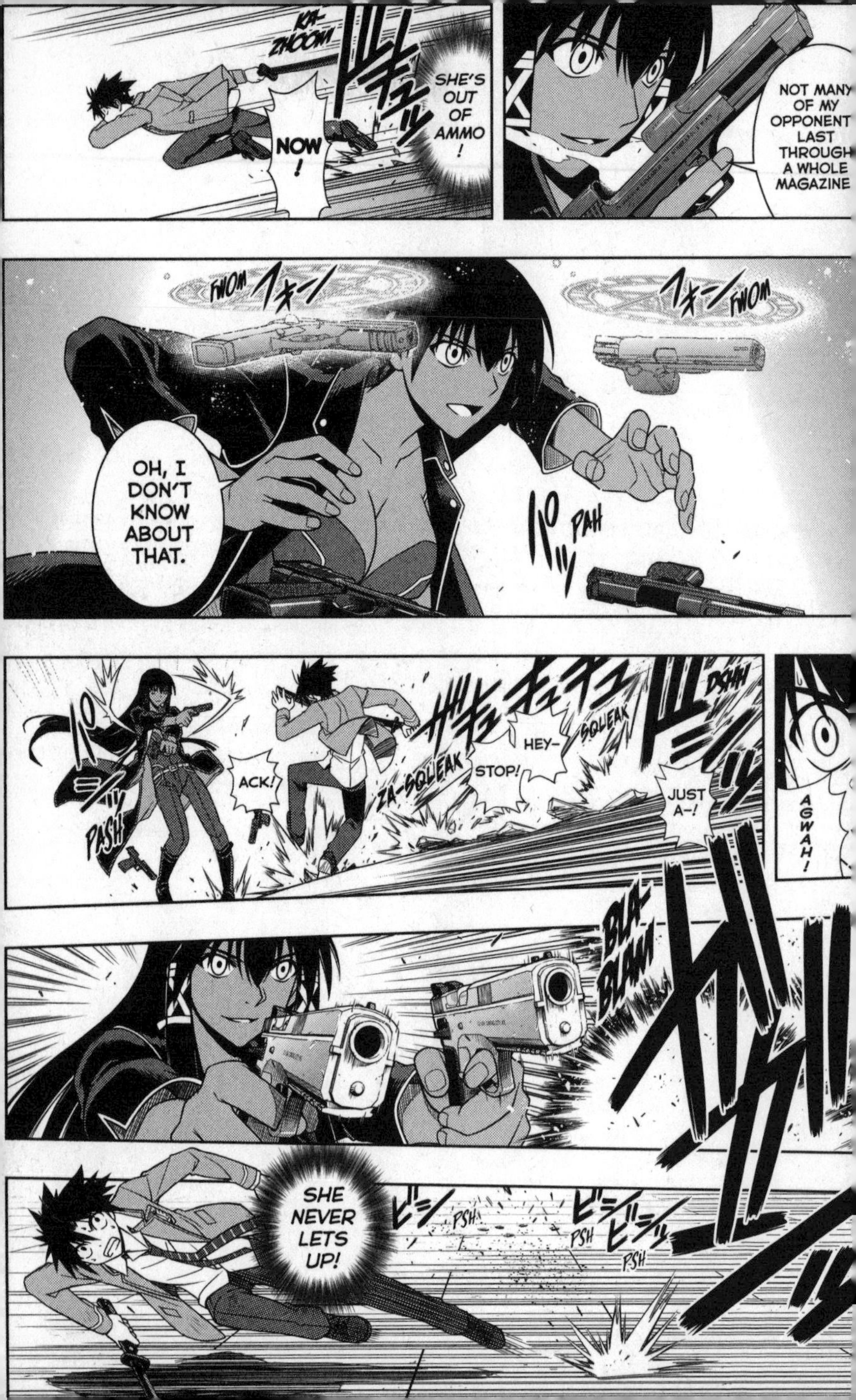
NOT MANY OF MY OPPONENT LAST THROUGH A WHOLE MAGAZINE
KA-ZHOOM
SHE'S OUT OF AMMO!
NOW!
FWOM
FWOM
OH, I DON'T KNOW ABOUT THAT.
PAH
AGWAH!
DSHH
JUST A-!
SQUEAK
HEY-
STOP!
ZA-SQUEAK
ACK!
PASH
BLA-BLAM
SHE NEVER LETS UP!
PSH
PSH
PSH

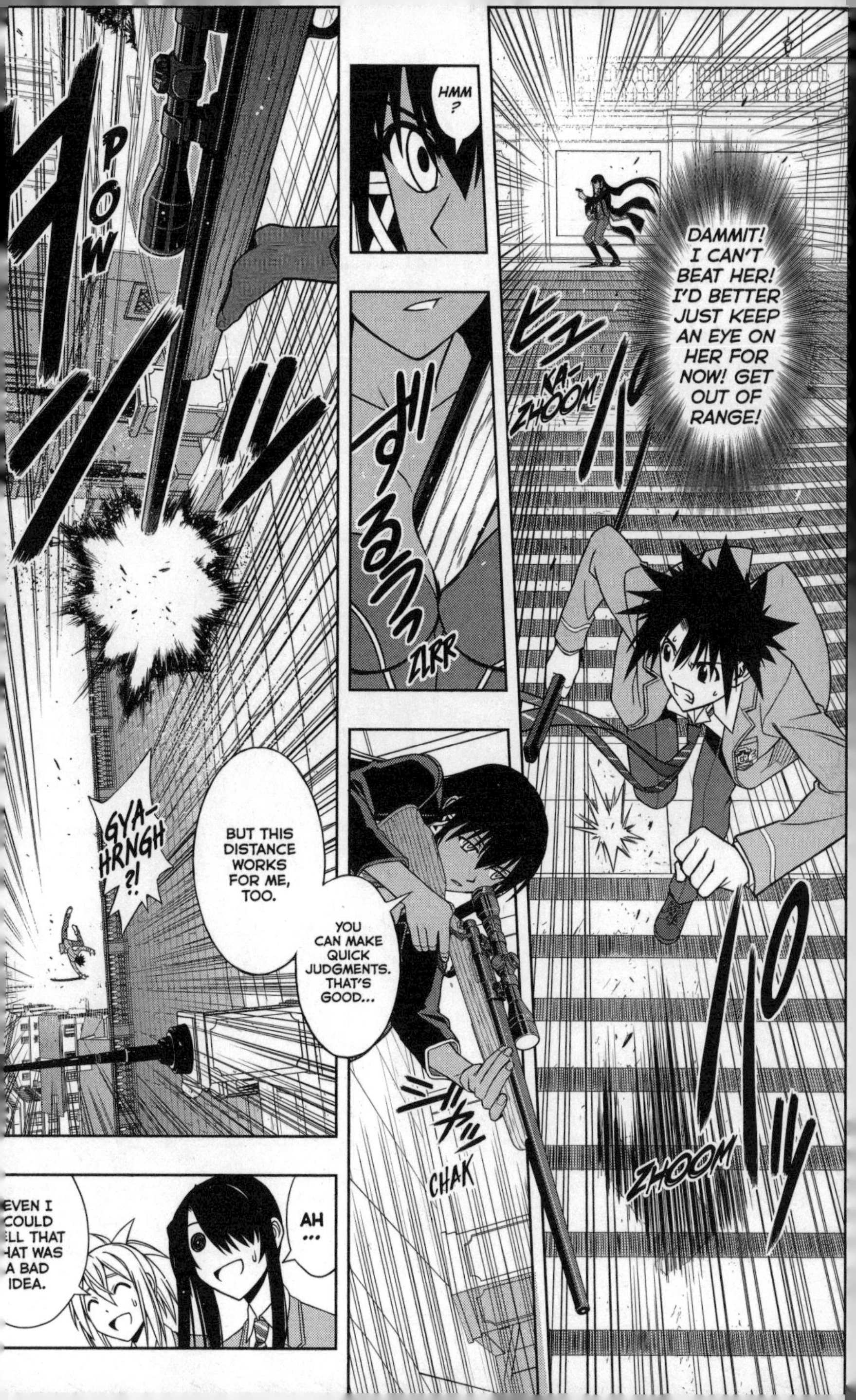
DAMMIT! I CAN'T BEAT HER! I'D BETTER JUST KEEP AN EYE ON HER FOR NOW! GET OUT OF RANGE!
KA-ZHOOM
ZHOOM
HMM ?
ZLRR
BUT THIS DISTANCE WORKS FOR ME, TOO.
YOU CAN MAKE QUICK JUDGMENTS. THAT'S GOOD...
CHAK
POW
GYA-HRNGH ?!
AH ...
EVEN I COULD ELL THAT HAT WAS A BAD IDEA.

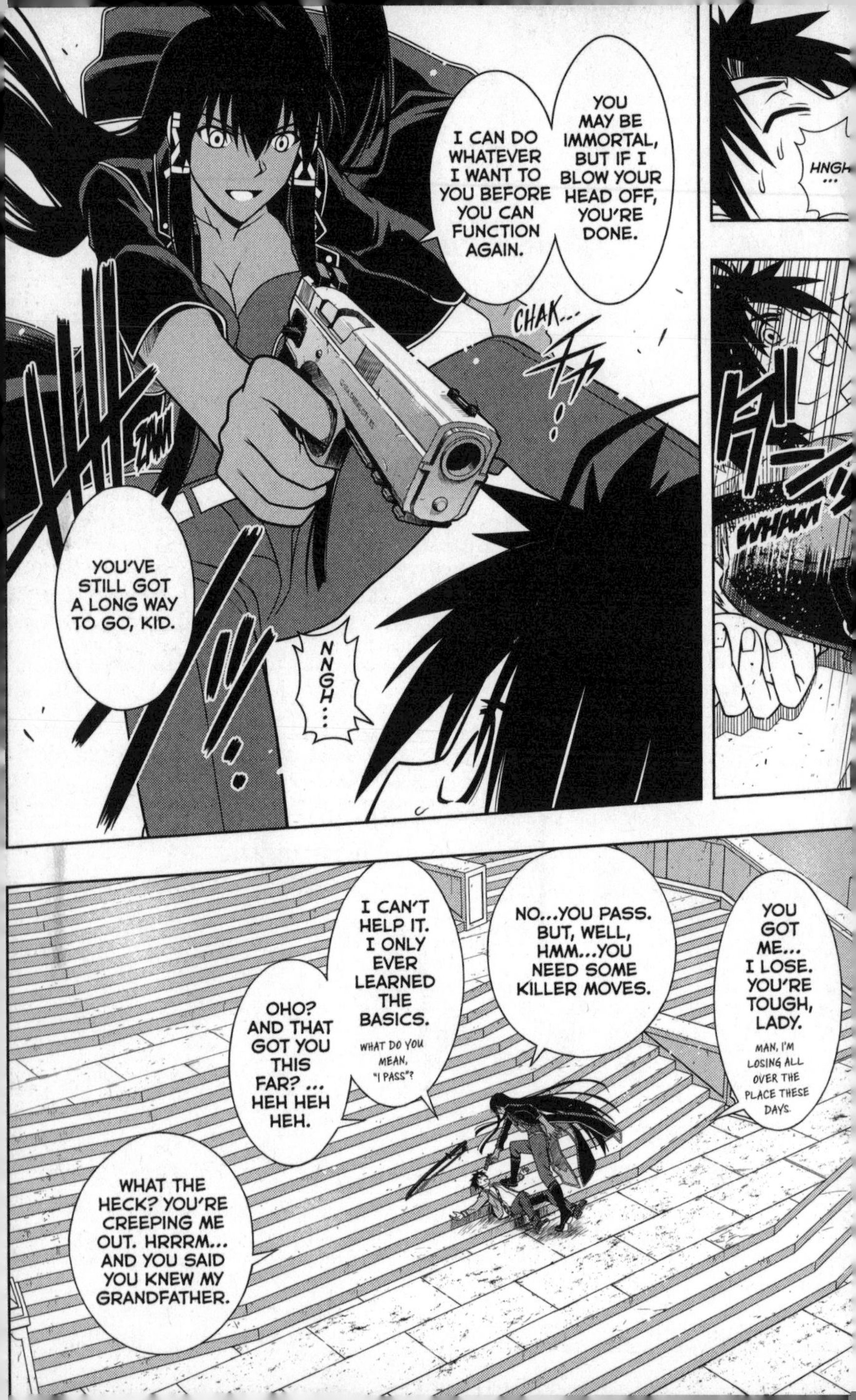

HNGH...
WHAM
YOU MAY BE IMMORTAL, BUT IF I BLOW YOUR HEAD OFF, YOU'RE DONE.
I CAN DO WHATEVER I WANT TO YOU BEFORE YOU CAN FUNCTION AGAIN.
CHAK...
NNGH...
YOU'VE STILL GOT A LONG WAY TO GO, KID.
YOU GOT ME... I LOSE. YOU'RE TOUGH, LADY.
MAN, I'M LOSING ALL OVER THE PLACE THESE DAYS.
NO...YOU PASS. BUT, WELL, HMM...YOU NEED SOME KILLER MOVES.
I CAN'T HELP IT. I ONLY EVER LEARNED THE BASICS.
WHAT DO YOU MEAN, "I PASS"?
OHO? AND THAT GOT YOU THIS FAR? ... HEH HEH HEH.
WHAT THE HECK? YOU'RE CREEPING ME OUT. HRRRM... AND YOU SAID YOU KNEW MY GRANDFATHER.

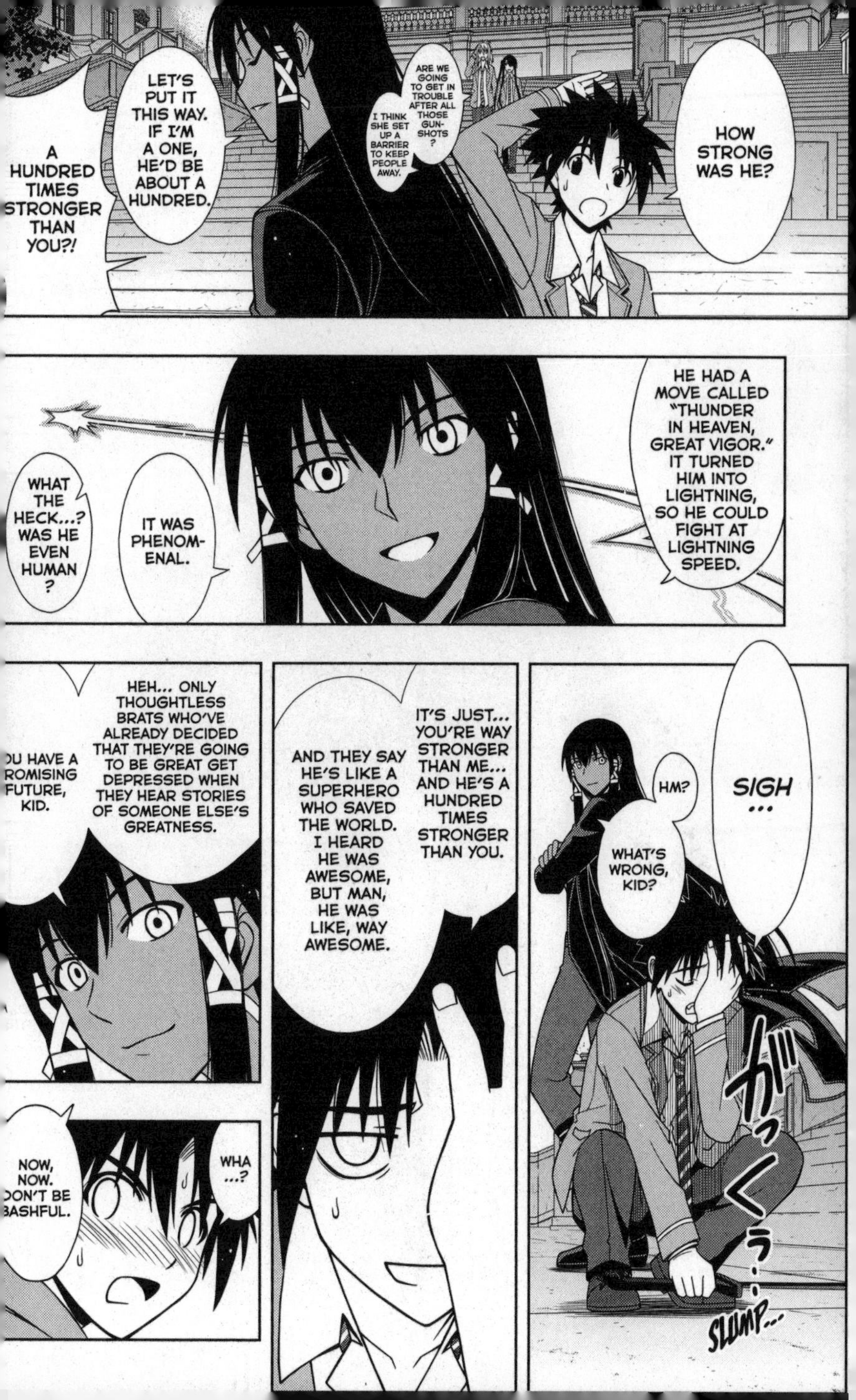
HOW STRONG WAS HE?
ARE WE GOING TO GET IN TROUBLE AFTER ALL THOSE GUN-SHOTS?
I THINK SHE SET UP A BARRIER TO KEEP PEOPLE AWAY.
LET'S PUT IT THIS WAY. IF I'M A ONE, HE'D BE ABOUT A HUNDRED.
A HUNDRED TIMES STRONGER THAN YOU?!
HE HAD A MOVE CALLED "THUNDER IN HEAVEN, GREAT VIGOR." IT TURNED HIM INTO LIGHTNING, SO HE COULD FIGHT AT LIGHTNING SPEED.
IT WAS PHENOM-ENAL.
WHAT THE HECK...? WAS HE EVEN HUMAN?
SIGH...
HM?
WHAT'S WRONG, KID?
SLUMP...
IT'S JUST... YOU'RE WAY STRONGER THAN ME... AND HE'S A HUNDRED TIMES STRONGER THAN YOU.
AND THEY SAY HE'S LIKE A SUPERHERO WHO SAVED THE WORLD. I HEARD HE WAS AWESOME, BUT MAN, HE WAS LIKE, WAY AWESOME.
HEH... ONLY THOUGHTLESS BRATS WHO'VE ALREADY DECIDED THAT THEY'RE GOING TO BE GREAT GET DEPRESSED WHEN THEY HEAR STORIES OF SOMEONE ELSE'S GREATNESS.
OU HAVE A ROMISING FUTURE, KID.
WHA...?
NOW, NOW. ON'T BE ASHFUL.

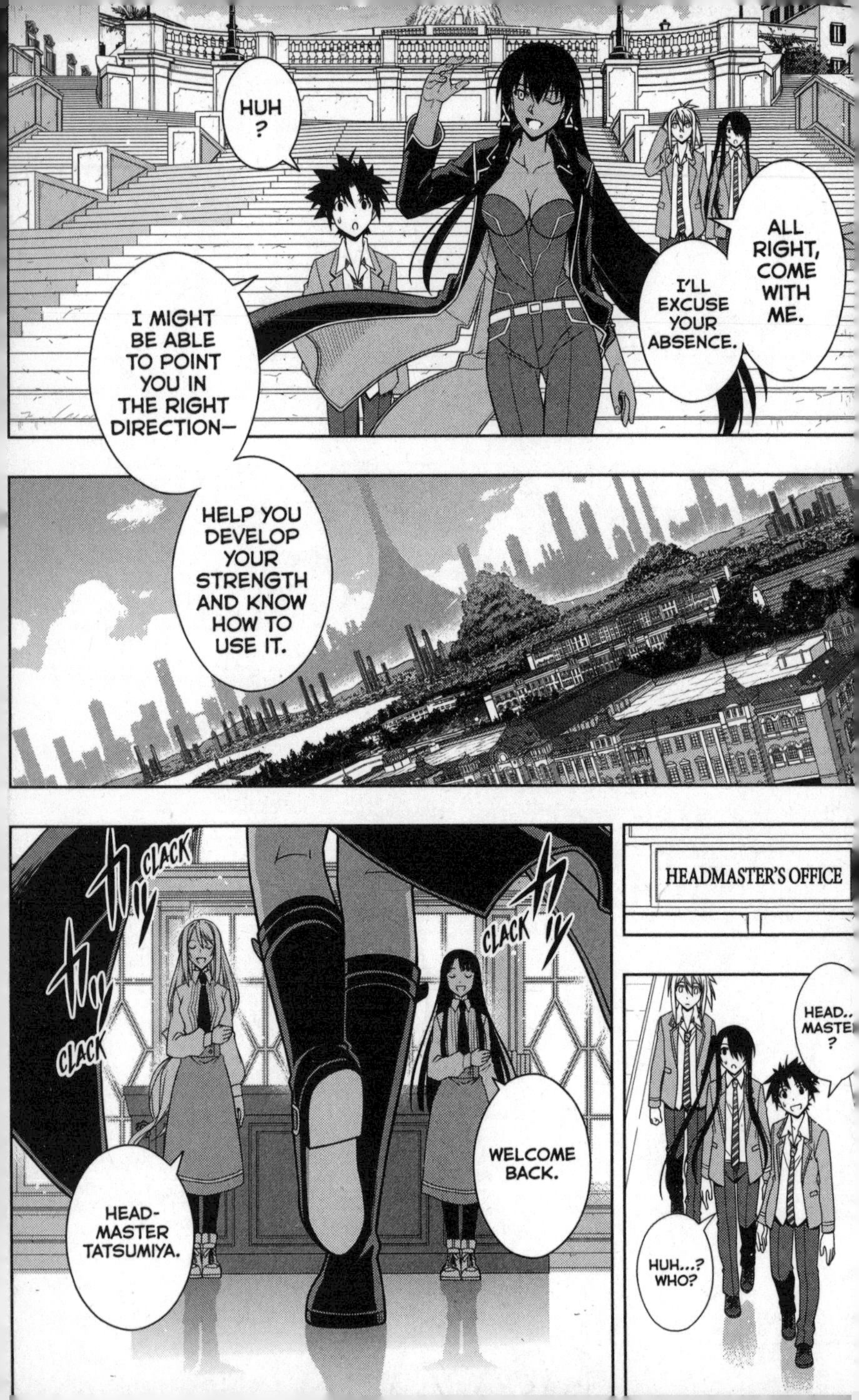
ALL RIGHT, COME WITH ME.
I'LL EXCUSE YOUR ABSENCE.
HUH?
I MIGHT BE ABLE TO POINT YOU IN THE RIGHT DIRECTION—
HELP YOU DEVELOP YOUR STRENGTH AND KNOW HOW TO USE IT.
HEADMASTER'S OFFICE
HEAD.. MASTE ?
HUH...? WHO?
CLACK
CLACK
CLACK
WELCOME BACK.
HEAD-MASTER TATSUMIYA.

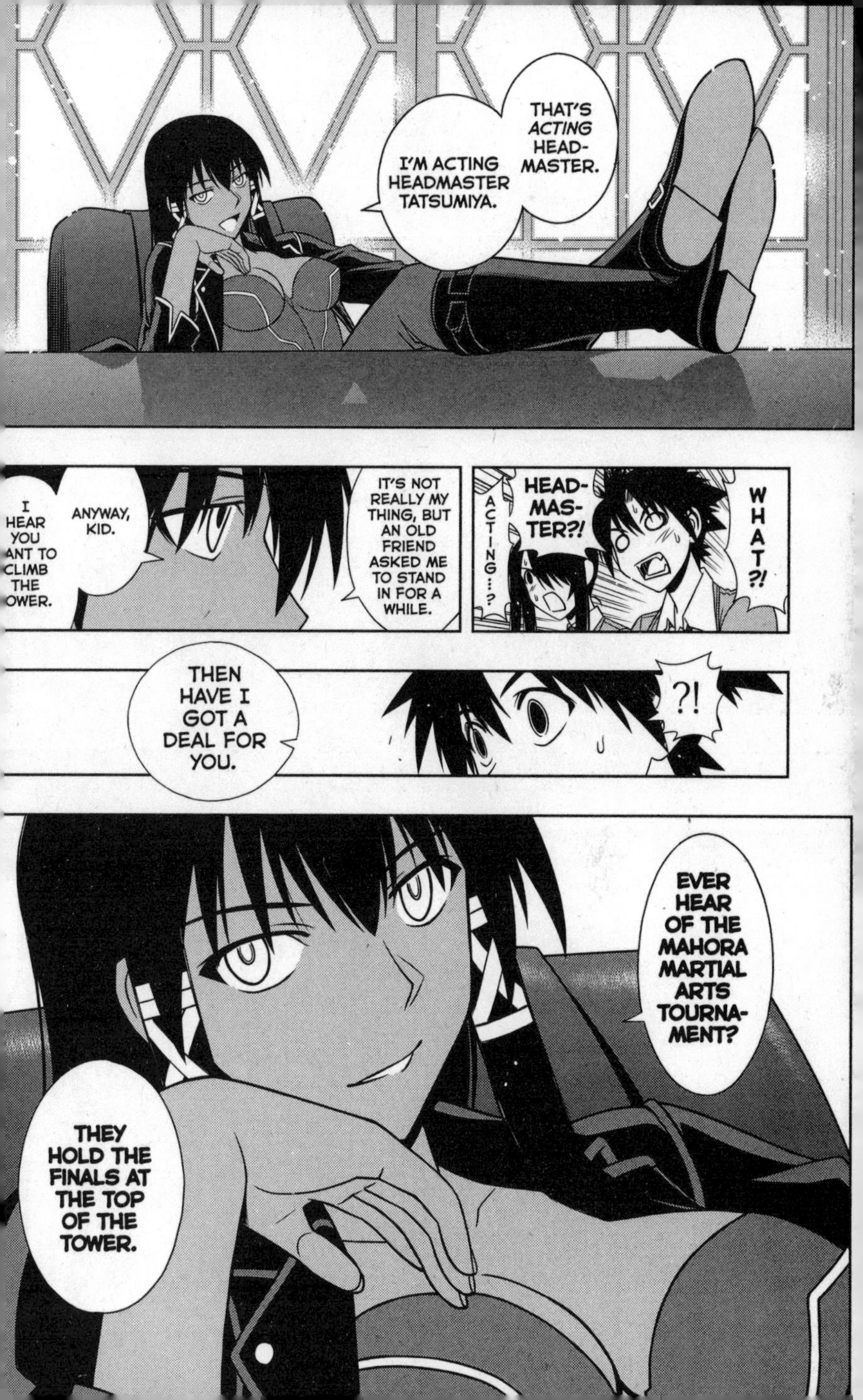
THAT'S *ACTING* HEAD-MASTER.
I'M ACTING HEADMASTER TATSUMIYA.
WHAT?!
HEAD-MAS-TER?!
ACTING...?
IT'S NOT REALLY MY THING, BUT AN OLD FRIEND ASKED ME TO STAND IN FOR A WHILE.
ANYWAY, KID.
I HEAR YOU ANT TO CLIMB THE OWER.
?!
THEN HAVE I GOT A DEAL FOR YOU.
EVER HEAR OF THE MAHORA MARTIAL ARTS TOURNA-MENT?
THEY HOLD THE FINALS AT THE TOP OF THE TOWER.

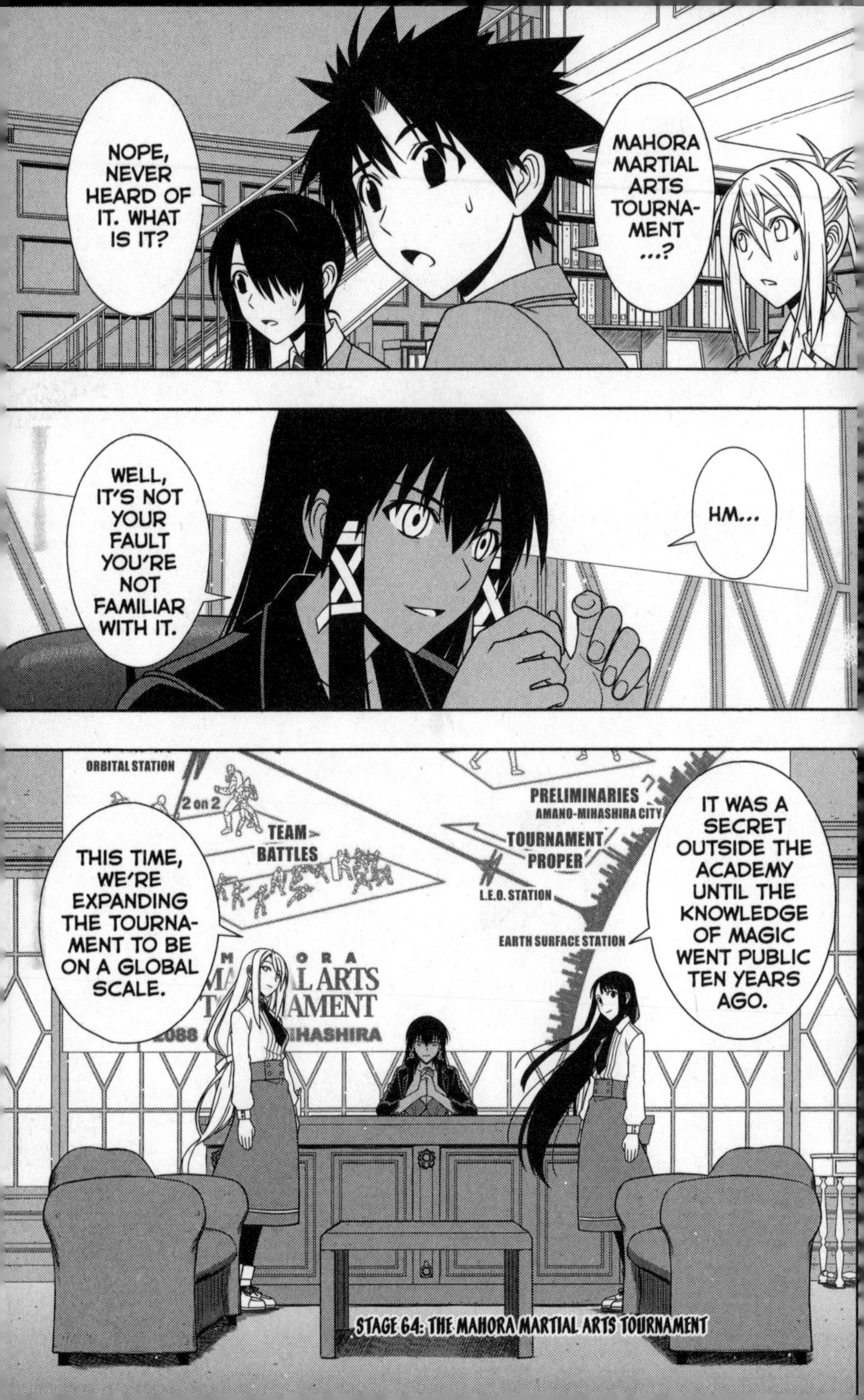
MAHORA MARTIAL ARTS TOURNAMENT ...?
NOPE, NEVER HEARD OF IT. WHAT IS IT?
HM...
WELL, IT'S NOT YOUR FAULT YOU'RE NOT FAMILIAR WITH IT.
ORBITAL STATION
2 on 2
TEAM BATTLES
PRELIMINARIES
AMANO-MIHASHIRA CITY
TOURNAMENT PROPER
L.E.O. STATION
EARTH SURFACE STATION
IT WAS A SECRET OUTSIDE THE ACADEMY UNTIL THE KNOWLEDGE OF MAGIC WENT PUBLIC TEN YEARS AGO.
THIS TIME, WE'RE EXPANDING THE TOURNAMENT TO BE ON A GLOBAL SCALE.
STAGE 64: THE MAHORA MARTIAL ARTS TOURNAMENT

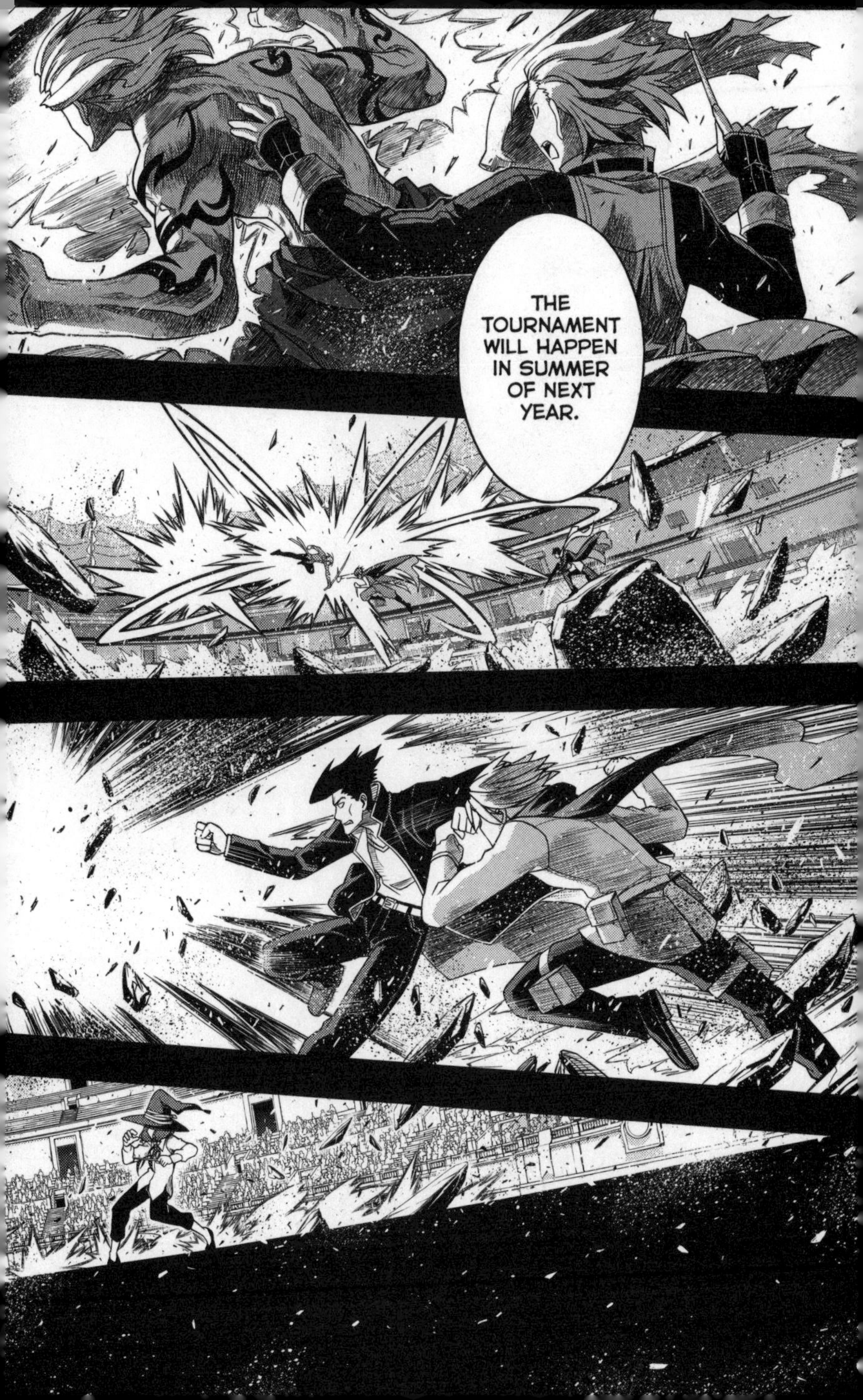
THE TOURNAMENT WILL HAPPEN IN SUMMER OF NEXT YEAR.

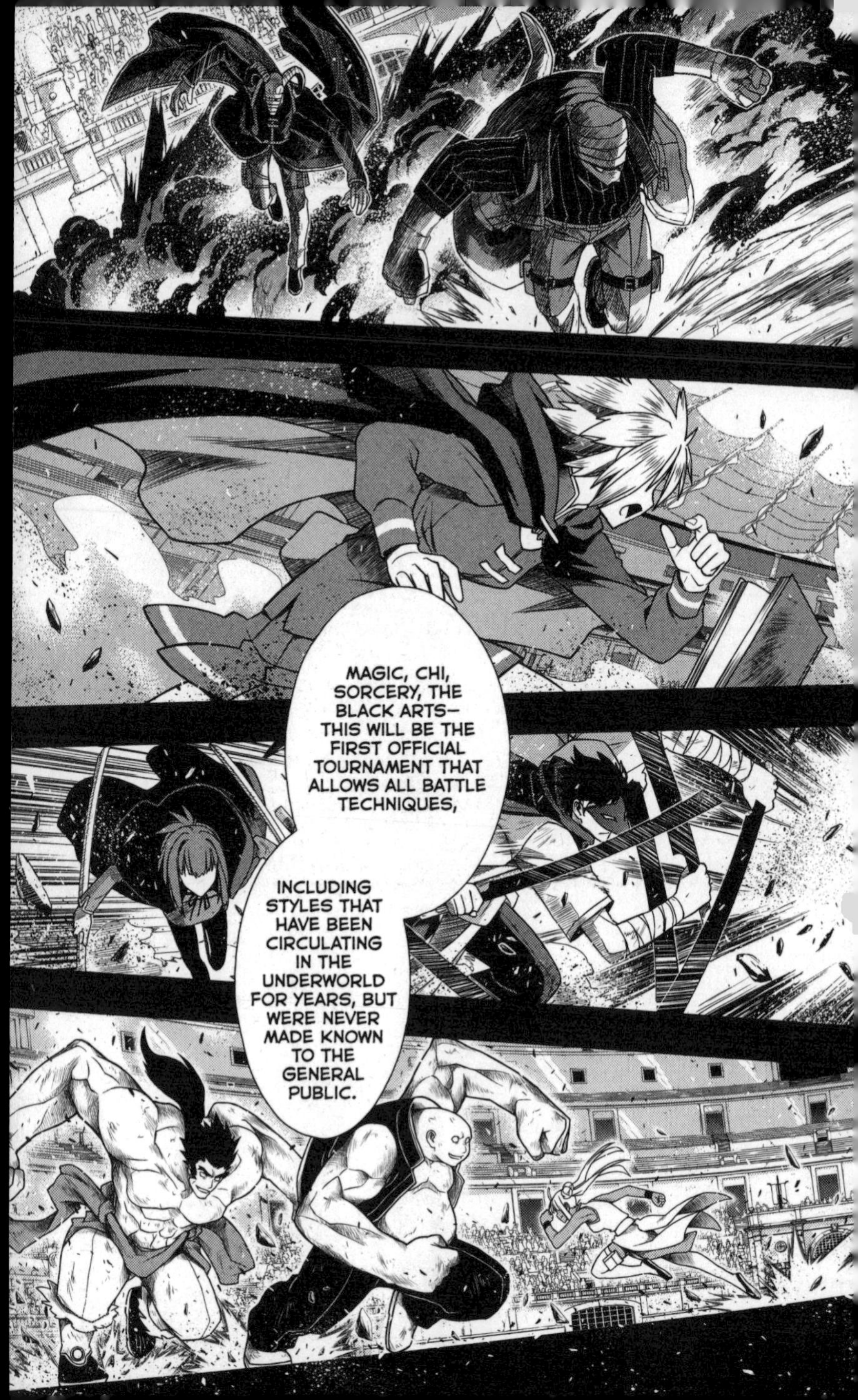
MAGIC, CHI, SORCERY, THE BLACK ARTS— THIS WILL BE THE FIRST OFFICIAL TOURNAMENT THAT ALLOWS ALL BATTLE TECHNIQUES,
INCLUDING STYLES THAT HAVE BEEN CIRCULATING IN THE UNDERWORLD FOR YEARS, BUT WERE NEVER MADE KNOWN TO THE GENERAL PUBLIC.

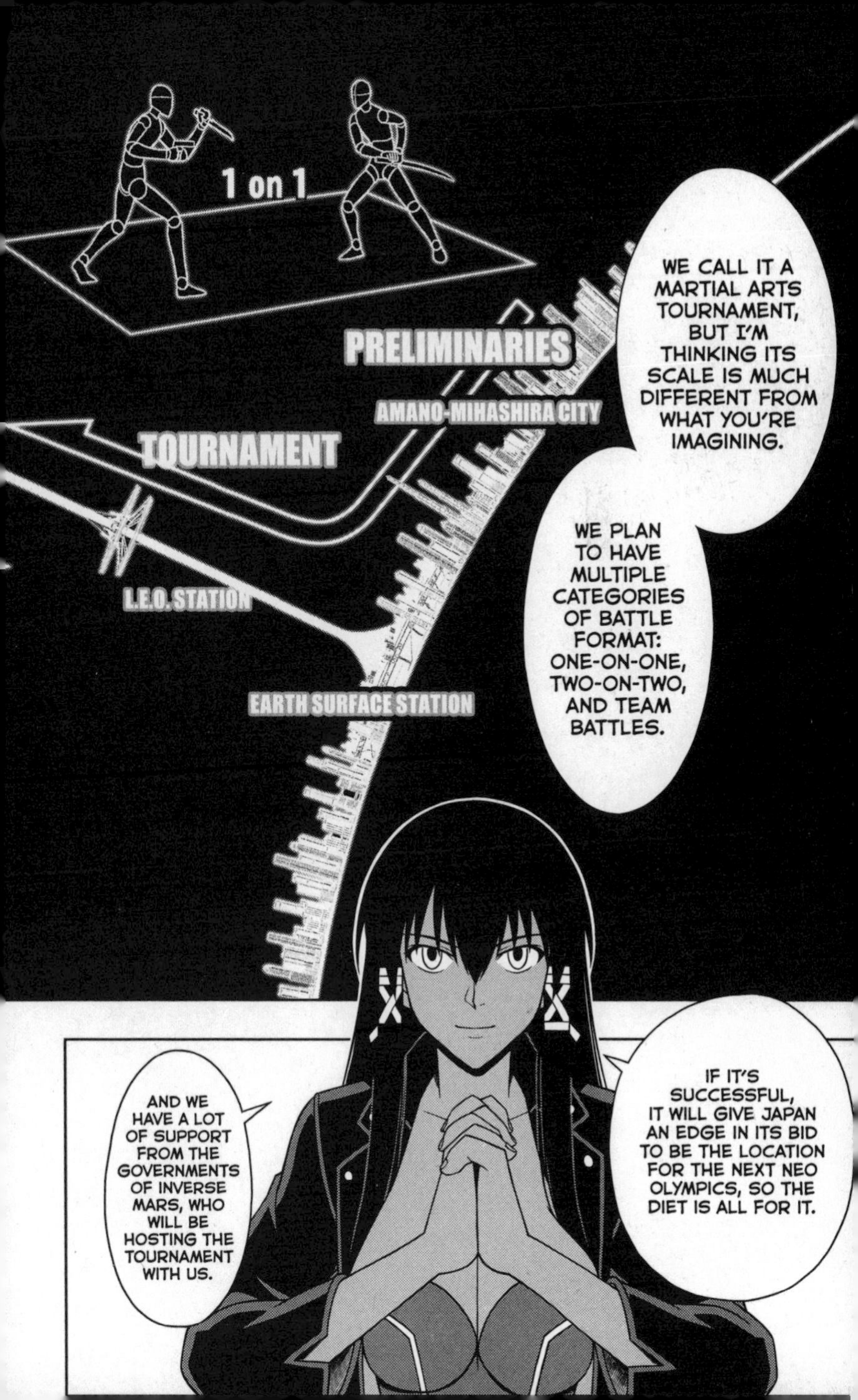
WE CALL IT A MARTIAL ARTS TOURNAMENT, BUT I'M THINKING ITS SCALE IS MUCH DIFFERENT FROM WHAT YOU'RE IMAGINING.
WE PLAN TO HAVE MULTIPLE CATEGORIES OF BATTLE FORMAT: ONE-ON-ONE, TWO-ON-TWO, AND TEAM BATTLES.
1 on 1
PRELIMINARIES
AMANO-MIHASHIRA CITY
TOURNAMENT
L.E.O. STATION
EARTH SURFACE STATION
IF IT'S SUCCESSFUL, IT WILL GIVE JAPAN AN EDGE IN ITS BID TO BE THE LOCATION FOR THE NEXT NEO OLYMPICS, SO THE DIET IS ALL FOR IT.
AND WE HAVE A LOT OF SUPPORT FROM THE GOVERNMENTS OF INVERSE MARS, WHO WILL BE HOSTING THE TOURNAMENT WITH US.

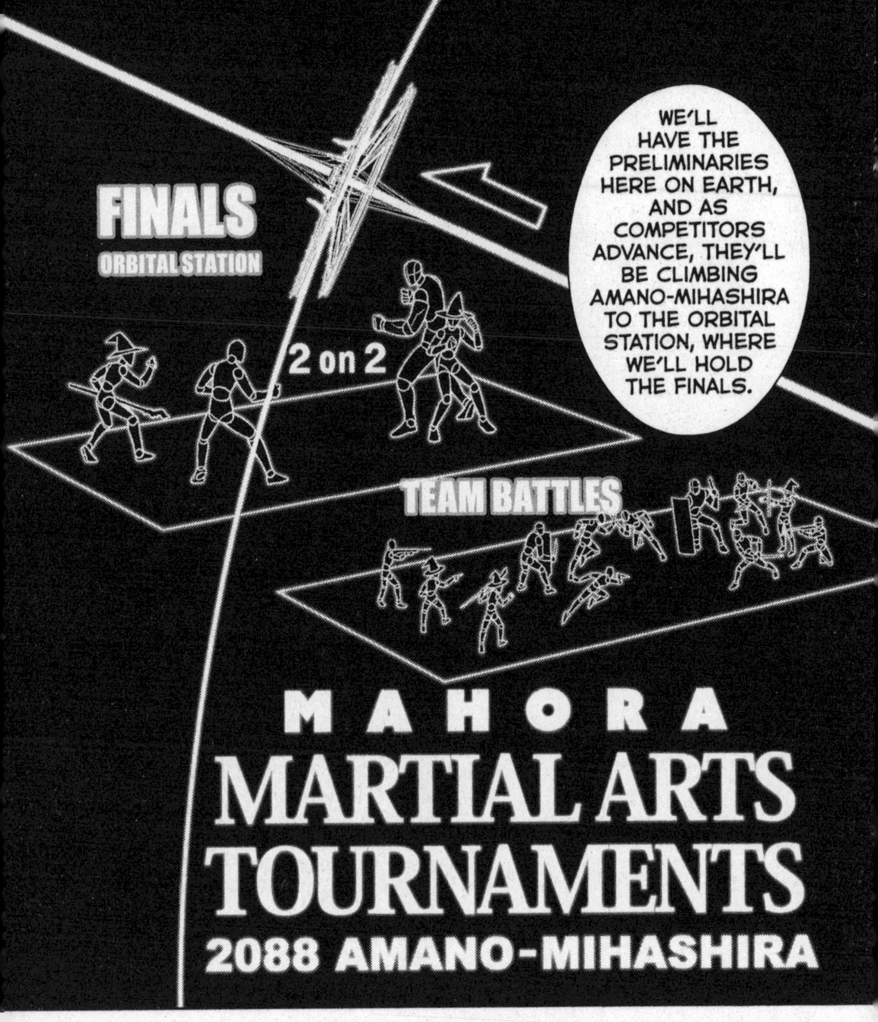
WE'LL HAVE THE PRELIMINARIES HERE ON EARTH, AND AS COMPETITORS ADVANCE, THEY'LL BE CLIMBING AMANO-MIHASHIRA TO THE ORBITAL STATION, WHERE WE'LL HOLD THE FINALS.
FINALS
ORBITAL STATION
2 on 2
TEAM BATTLES
MAHORA
MARTIAL ARTS
TOURNAMENTS
2088 AMANO-MIHASHIRA

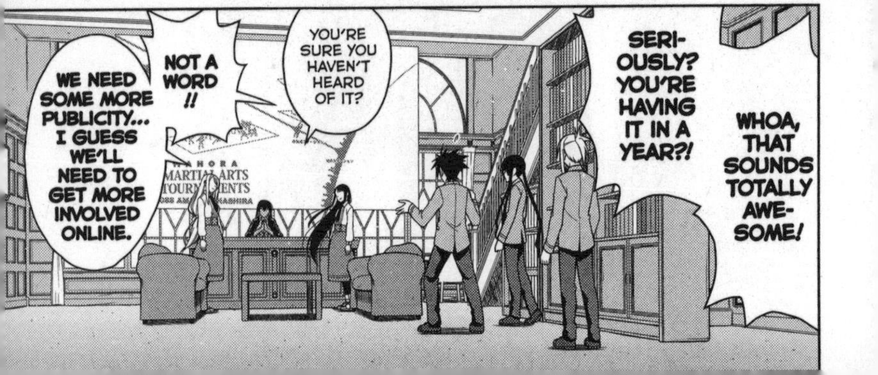
SERI-OUSLY? YOU'RE HAVING IT IN A YEAR?!
WHOA, THAT SOUNDS TOTALLY AWE-SOME!
YOU'RE SURE YOU HAVEN'T HEARD OF IT?
NOT A WORD!!
WE NEED SOME MORE PUBLICITY... I GUESS WE'LL NEED TO GET MORE INVOLVED ONLINE.

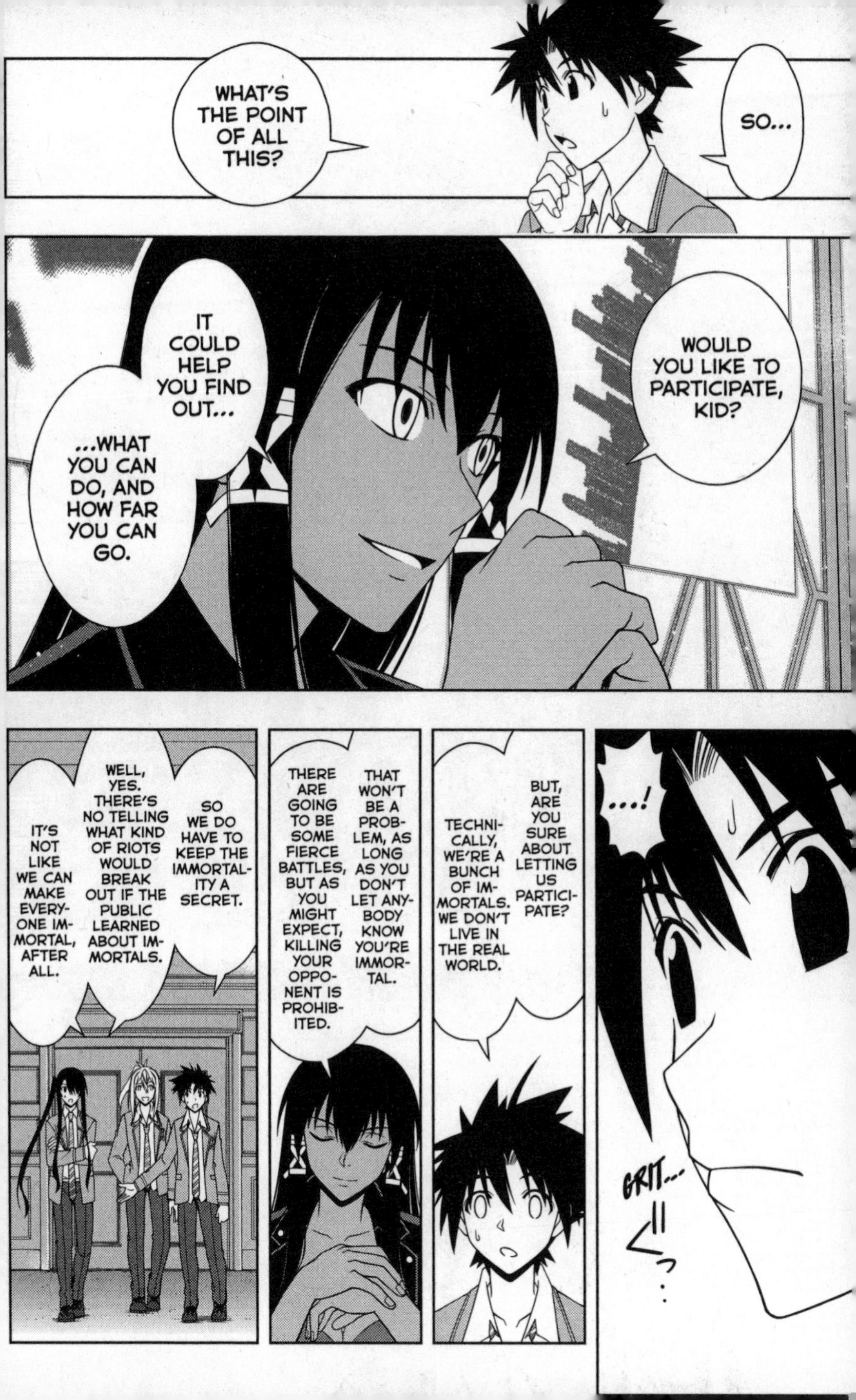
SO...
WHAT'S THE POINT OF ALL THIS?
WOULD YOU LIKE TO PARTICIPATE, KID?
IT COULD HELP YOU FIND OUT...
...WHAT YOU CAN DO, AND HOW FAR YOU CAN GO.
...!
GRIT...
BUT, ARE YOU SURE ABOUT LETTING US PARTICIPATE?
TECHNICALLY, WE'RE A BUNCH OF IMMORTALS. WE DON'T LIVE IN THE REAL WORLD.
THAT WON'T BE A PROBLEM, AS LONG AS YOU DON'T LET ANYBODY KNOW YOU'RE IMMORTAL.
THERE ARE GOING TO BE SOME FIERCE BATTLES, BUT AS YOU MIGHT EXPECT, KILLING YOUR OPPONENT IS PROHIBITED.
SO WE DO HAVE TO KEEP THE IMMORTALITY A SECRET.
WELL, YES. THERE'S NO TELLING WHAT KIND OF RIOTS WOULD BREAK OUT IF THE PUBLIC LEARNED ABOUT IMMORTALS.
IT'S NOT LIKE WE CAN MAKE EVERYONE IMMORTAL, AFTER ALL.

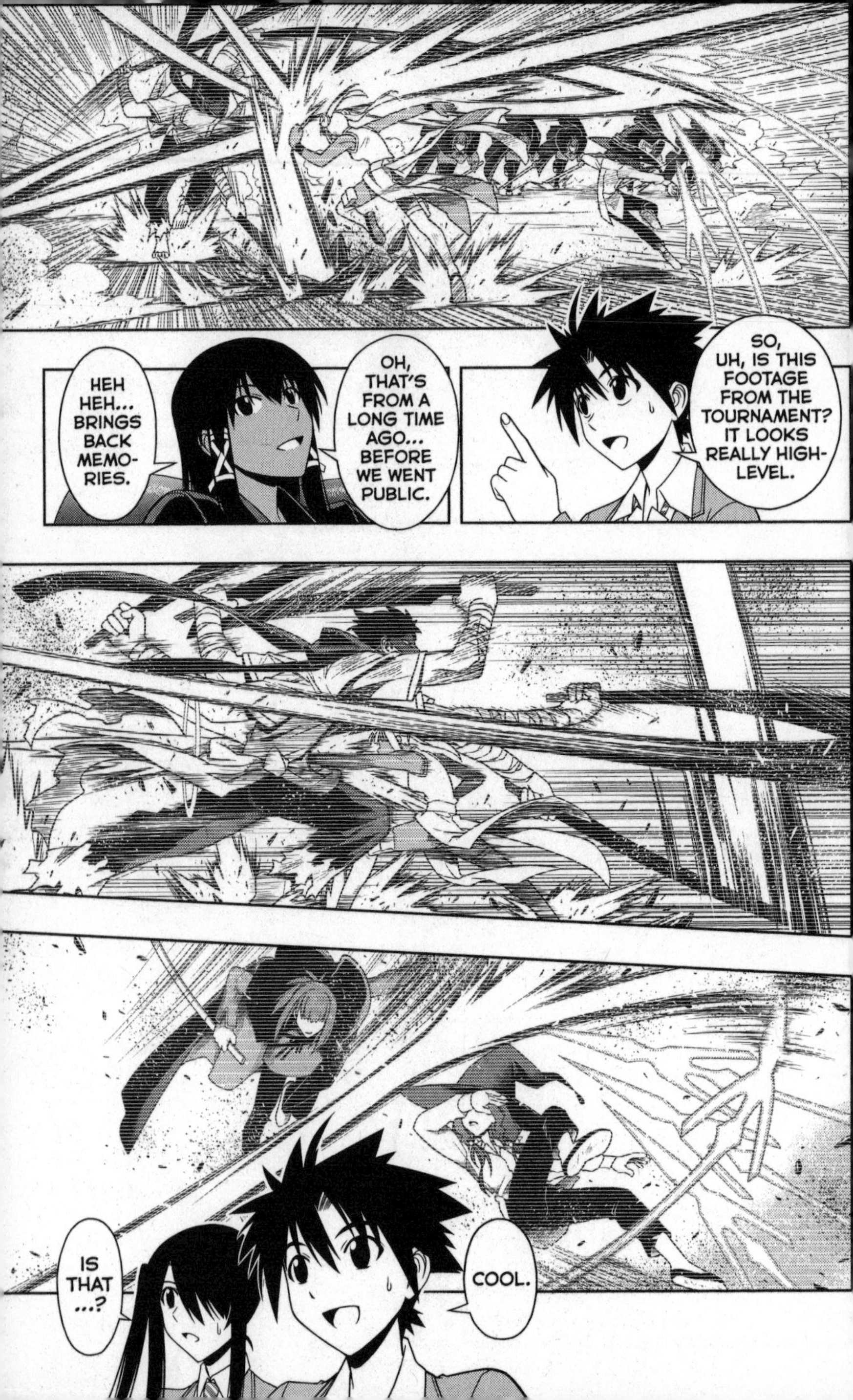
SO, UH, IS THIS FOOTAGE FROM THE TOURNAMENT? IT LOOKS REALLY HIGH-LEVEL.
OH, THAT'S FROM A LONG TIME AGO... BEFORE WE WENT PUBLIC.
HEH HEH... BRINGS BACK MEMO-RIES.
COOL.
IS THAT ...?

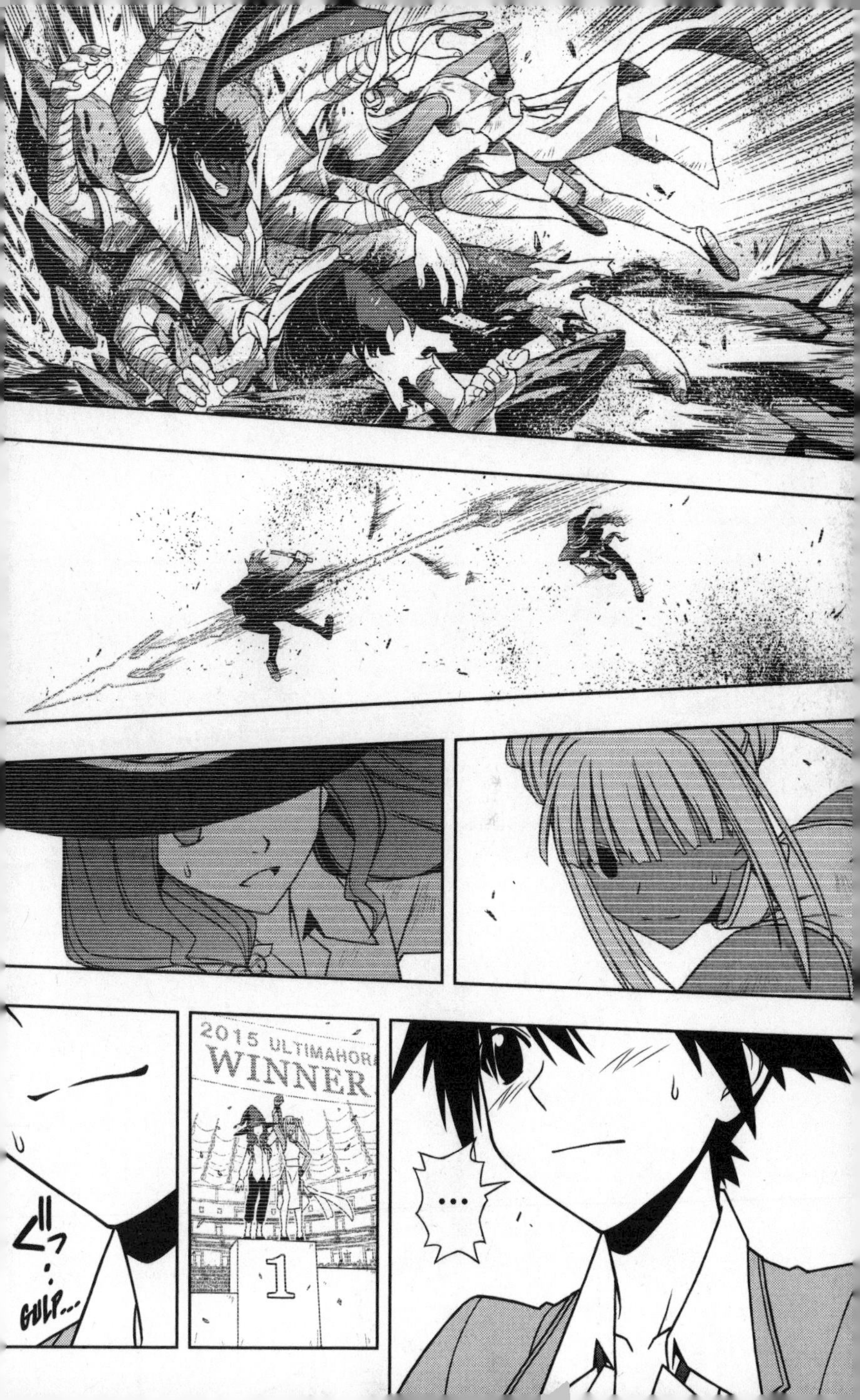
...
2015 ULTIMAHOR
WINNER
1
GULP...

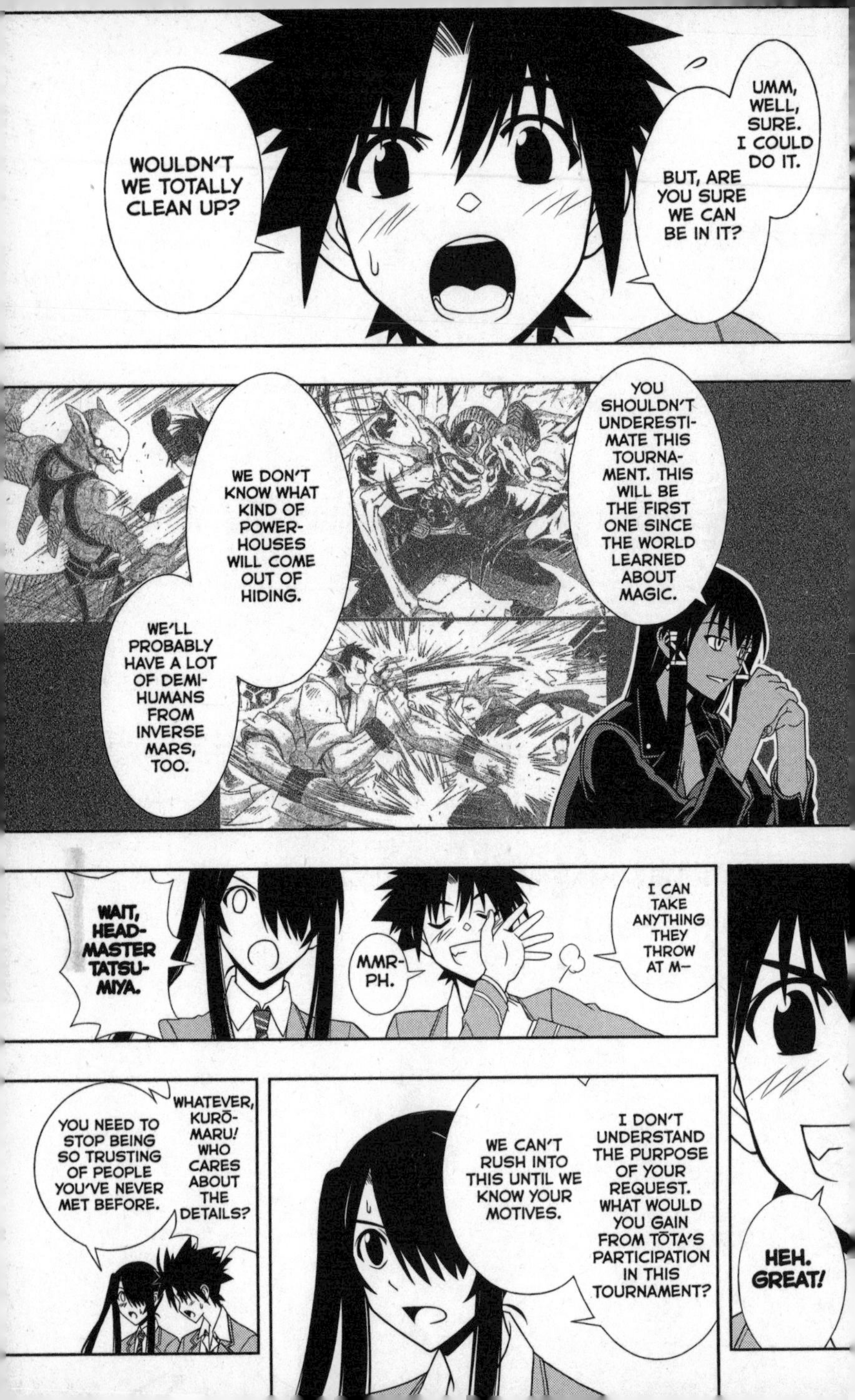

UMM, WELL, SURE. I COULD DO IT.
BUT, ARE YOU SURE WE CAN BE IN IT?
WOULDN'T WE TOTALLY CLEAN UP?
YOU SHOULDN'T UNDERESTIMATE THIS TOURNAMENT. THIS WILL BE THE FIRST ONE SINCE THE WORLD LEARNED ABOUT MAGIC.
WE DON'T KNOW WHAT KIND OF POWERHOUSES WILL COME OUT OF HIDING.
WE'LL PROBABLY HAVE A LOT OF DEMIHUMANS FROM INVERSE MARS, TOO.
HEH. GREAT!
I CAN TAKE ANYTHING THEY THROW AT M—
MMR-PH.
WAIT, HEADMASTER TATSUMIYA.
I DON'T UNDERSTAND THE PURPOSE OF YOUR REQUEST. WHAT WOULD YOU GAIN FROM TŌTA'S PARTICIPATION IN THIS TOURNAMENT?
WE CAN'T RUSH INTO THIS UNTIL WE KNOW YOUR MOTIVES.
WHATEVER, KURŌMARU! WHO CARES ABOUT THE DETAILS?
YOU NEED TO STOP BEING SO TRUSTING OF PEOPLE YOU'VE NEVER MET BEFORE.

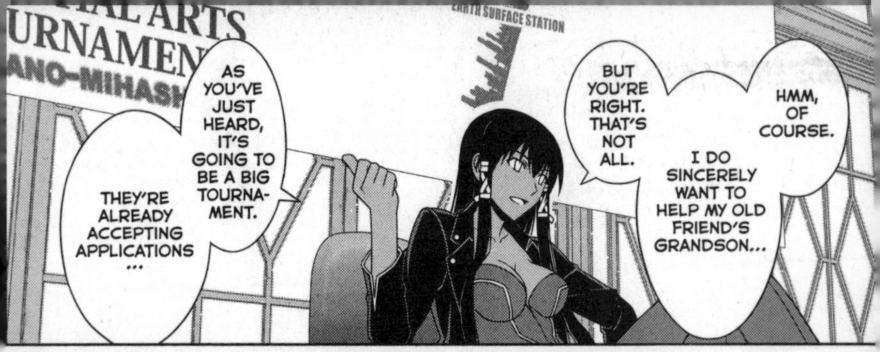
EARTH SURFACE STATION
HMM, OF COURSE.
I DO SINCERELY WANT TO HELP MY OLD FRIEND'S GRANDSON...
BUT YOU'RE RIGHT. THAT'S NOT ALL.
AS YOU'VE JUST HEARD, IT'S GOING TO BE A BIG TOURNAMENT.
THEY'RE ALREADY ACCEPTING APPLICATIONS...

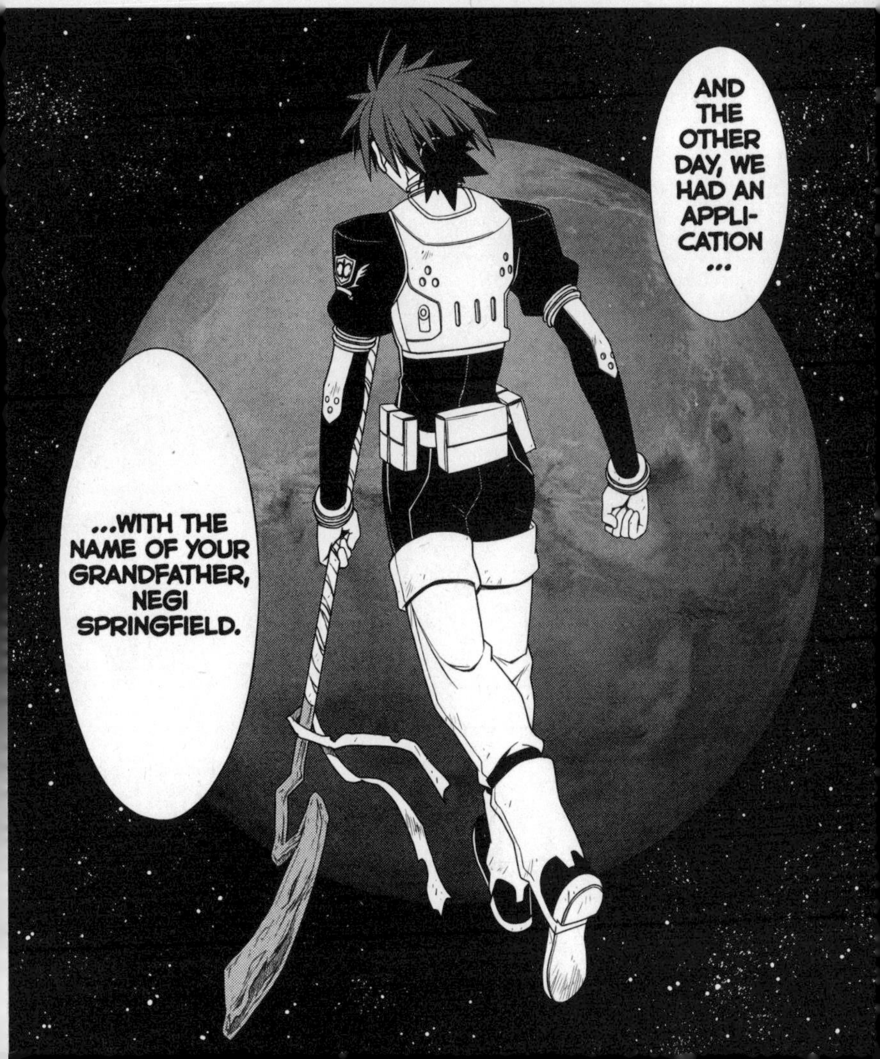
AND THE OTHER DAY, WE HAD AN APPLICATION...
...WITH THE NAME OF YOUR GRANDFATHER, NEGI SPRINGFIELD.

...HUH
?

...

WHAA-
AAAT
?!

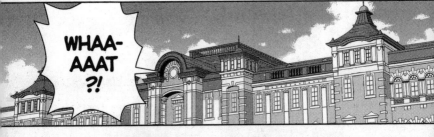

YOUR
GRAND-
FATHER'S
GOING TO
BE IN THE
TOURNAMENT
?

YOU
MEAN...YOUR
GRANDFATHER,
THE HERO...
THE MAGISTER
MAGI NEGI
SPRINGFIELD,
RIGHT?

BUT
ISN'T HE
SUPPOSED
TO BE
DEAD...NO,
I GUESS
NOT.

YEAH,
REMEMBER?
FATE SAID
HE'S ALIVE.

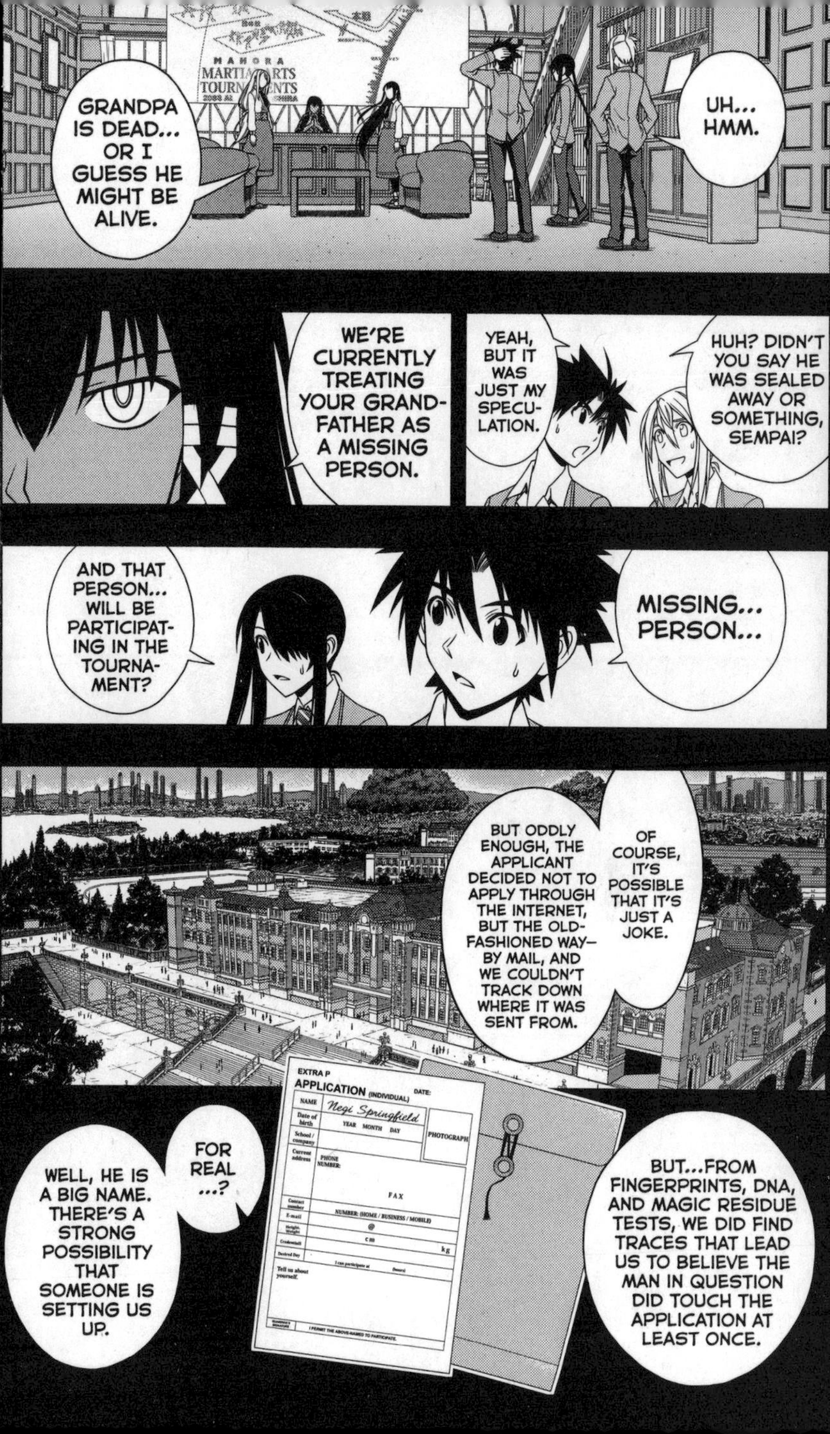
UH... HMM.
GRANDPA IS DEAD... OR I GUESS HE MIGHT BE ALIVE.
HUH? DIDN'T YOU SAY HE WAS SEALED AWAY OR SOMETHING, SEMPAI?
YEAH, BUT IT WAS JUST MY SPECULATION.
WE'RE CURRENTLY TREATING YOUR GRANDFATHER AS A MISSING PERSON.
MISSING... PERSON...
AND THAT PERSON... WILL BE PARTICIPATING IN THE TOURNAMENT?
OF COURSE, IT'S POSSIBLE THAT IT'S JUST A JOKE.
BUT ODDLY ENOUGH, THE APPLICANT DECIDED NOT TO APPLY THROUGH THE INTERNET, BUT THE OLD-FASHIONED WAY—BY MAIL, AND WE COULDN'T TRACK DOWN WHERE IT WAS SENT FROM.
BUT...FROM FINGERPRINTS, DNA, AND MAGIC RESIDUE TESTS, WE DID FIND TRACES THAT LEAD US TO BELIEVE THE MAN IN QUESTION DID TOUCH THE APPLICATION AT LEAST ONCE.
EXTRA P
APPLICATION (INDIVIDUAL)
DATE:
NAME
Negi Springfield
Date of birth
YEAR MONTH DAY
PHOTOGRAPH
School / company
Current address
PHONE NUMBER:
FAX
E-mail
Tell us about yourself.
I PERMIT THE ABOVE-NAMED TO PARTICIPATE.
FOR REAL ...?
WELL, HE IS A BIG NAME. THERE'S A STRONG POSSIBILITY THAT SOMEONE IS SETTING US UP.

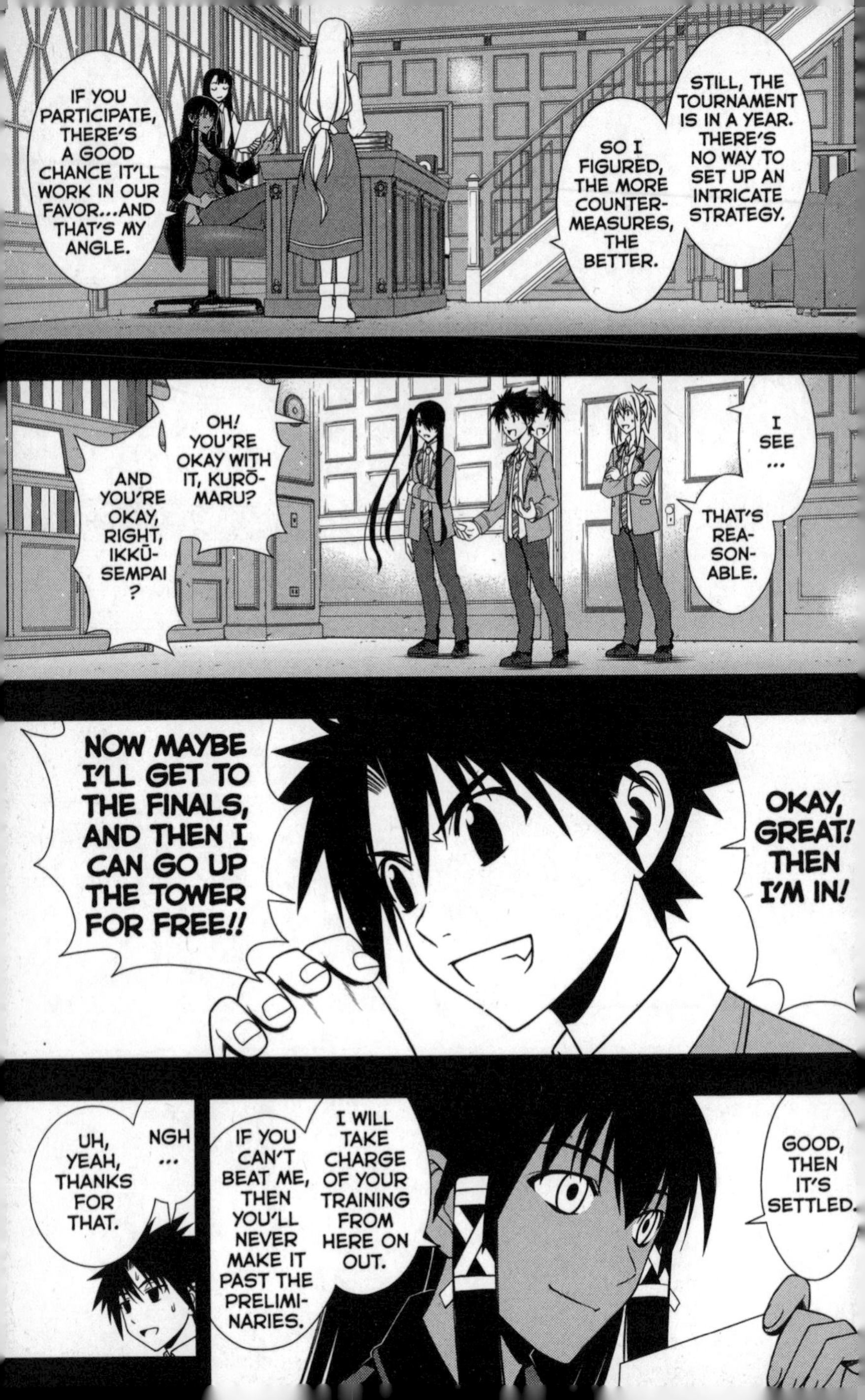

STILL, THE TOURNAMENT IS IN A YEAR. THERE'S NO WAY TO SET UP AN INTRICATE STRATEGY.
SO I FIGURED, THE MORE COUNTER-MEASURES, THE BETTER.
IF YOU PARTICIPATE, THERE'S A GOOD CHANCE IT'LL WORK IN OUR FAVOR...AND THAT'S MY ANGLE.
I SEE...
THAT'S REASONABLE.
OH! YOU'RE OKAY WITH IT, KURŌMARU?
AND YOU'RE OKAY, RIGHT, IKKŪ-SEMPAI?
OKAY, GREAT! THEN I'M IN!
NOW MAYBE I'LL GET TO THE FINALS, AND THEN I CAN GO UP THE TOWER FOR FREE!!
GOOD, THEN IT'S SETTLED.
I WILL TAKE CHARGE OF YOUR TRAINING FROM HERE ON OUT.
IF YOU CAN'T BEAT ME, THEN YOU'LL NEVER MAKE IT PAST THE PRELIMINARIES.
NGH...
UH, YEAH, THANKS FOR THAT.

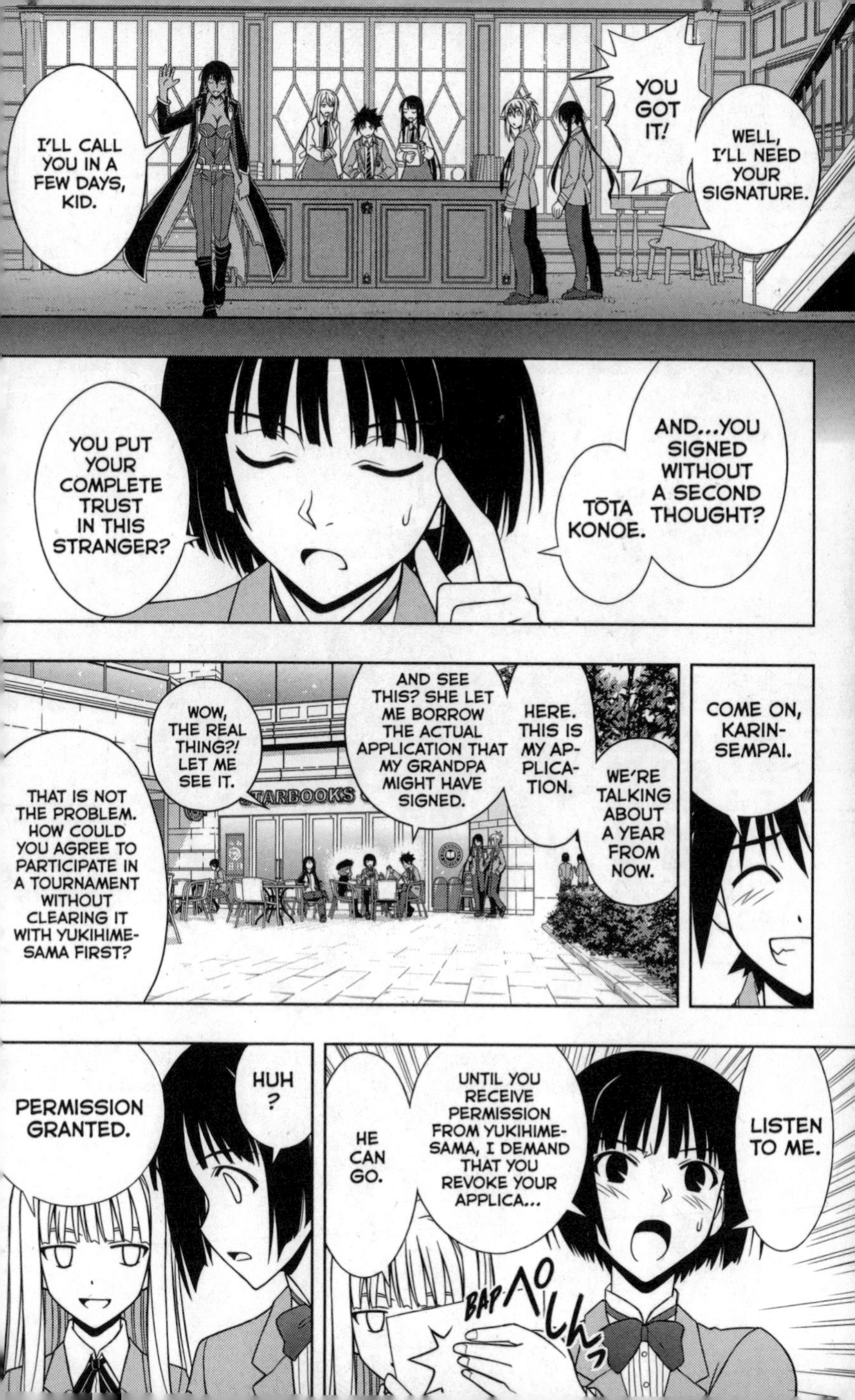
WELL, I'LL NEED YOUR SIGNATURE.
YOU GOT IT!
I'LL CALL YOU IN A FEW DAYS, KID.
AND...YOU SIGNED WITHOUT A SECOND THOUGHT?
TŌTA KONOE.
YOU PUT YOUR COMPLETE TRUST IN THIS STRANGER?
COME ON, KARIN-SEMPAI.
WE'RE TALKING ABOUT A YEAR FROM NOW.
HERE. THIS IS MY AP-PLICA-TION.
AND SEE THIS? SHE LET ME BORROW THE ACTUAL APPLICATION THAT MY GRANDPA MIGHT HAVE SIGNED.
WOW, THE REAL THING?! LET ME SEE IT.
STARBOOKS
THAT IS NOT THE PROBLEM. HOW COULD YOU AGREE TO PARTICIPATE IN A TOURNAMENT WITHOUT CLEARING IT WITH YUKIHIME-SAMA FIRST?
LISTEN TO ME.
UNTIL YOU RECEIVE PERMISSION FROM YUKIHIME-SAMA, I DEMAND THAT YOU REVOKE YOUR APPLICA...
HE CAN GO.
BAP
HUH?
PERMISSION GRANTED.

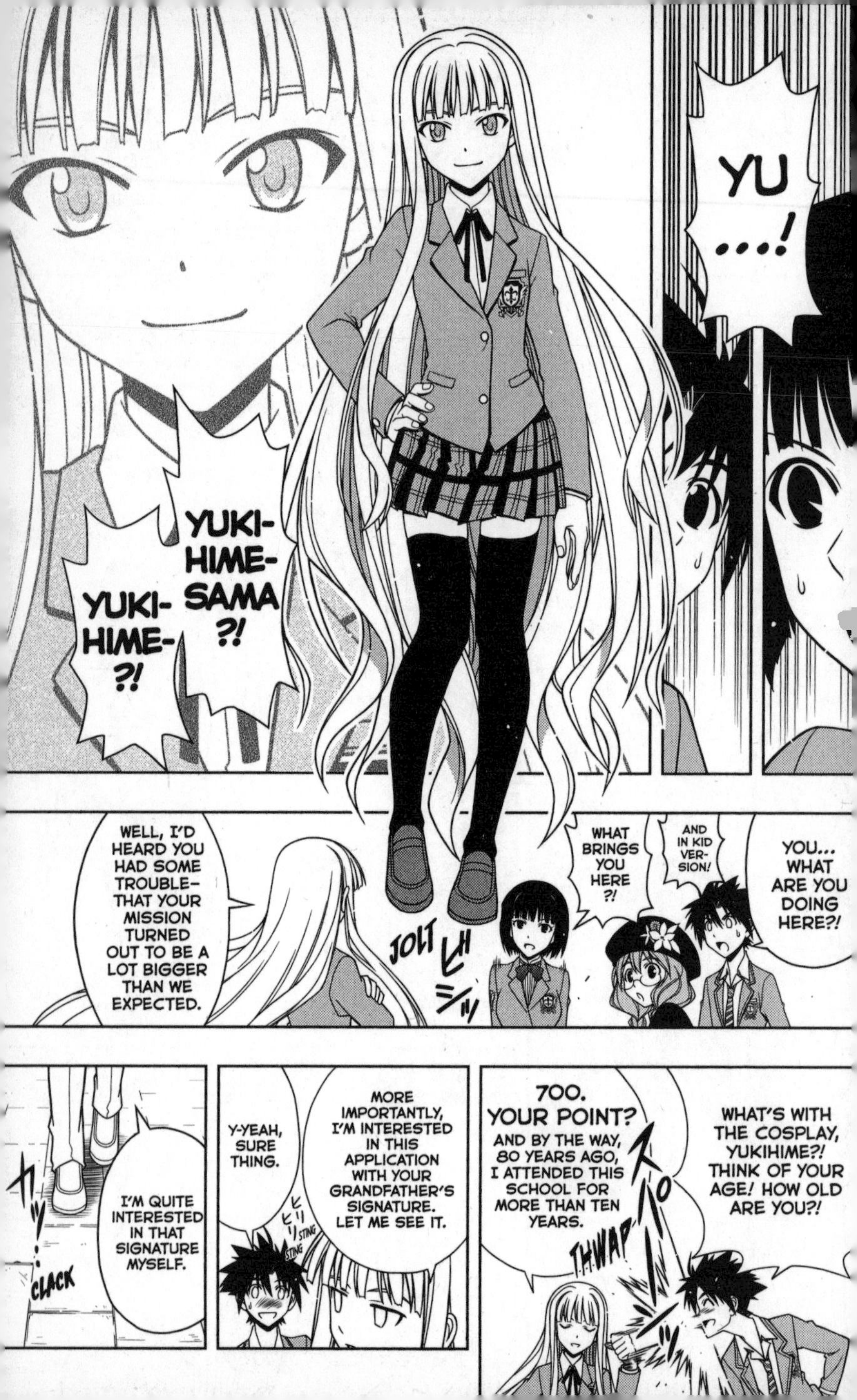
YU...!
YUKI-HIME-SAMA?!
YUKI-HIME-?!
YOU... WHAT ARE YOU DOING HERE?!
AND IN KID VER-SION!
WHAT BRINGS YOU HERE?!
JOLT
WELL, I'D HEARD YOU HAD SOME TROUBLE—THAT YOUR MISSION TURNED OUT TO BE A LOT BIGGER THAN WE EXPECTED.
WHAT'S WITH THE COSPLAY, YUKIHIME?! THINK OF YOUR AGE! HOW OLD ARE YOU?!
700. YOUR POINT?
AND BY THE WAY, 80 YEARS AGO, I ATTENDED THIS SCHOOL FOR MORE THAN TEN YEARS.
THWAP
MORE IMPORTANTLY, I'M INTERESTED IN THIS APPLICATION WITH YOUR GRANDFATHER'S SIGNATURE. LET ME SEE IT.
Y-YEAH, SURE THING.
STING STING
I'M QUITE INTERESTED IN THAT SIGNATURE MYSELF.
CLACK

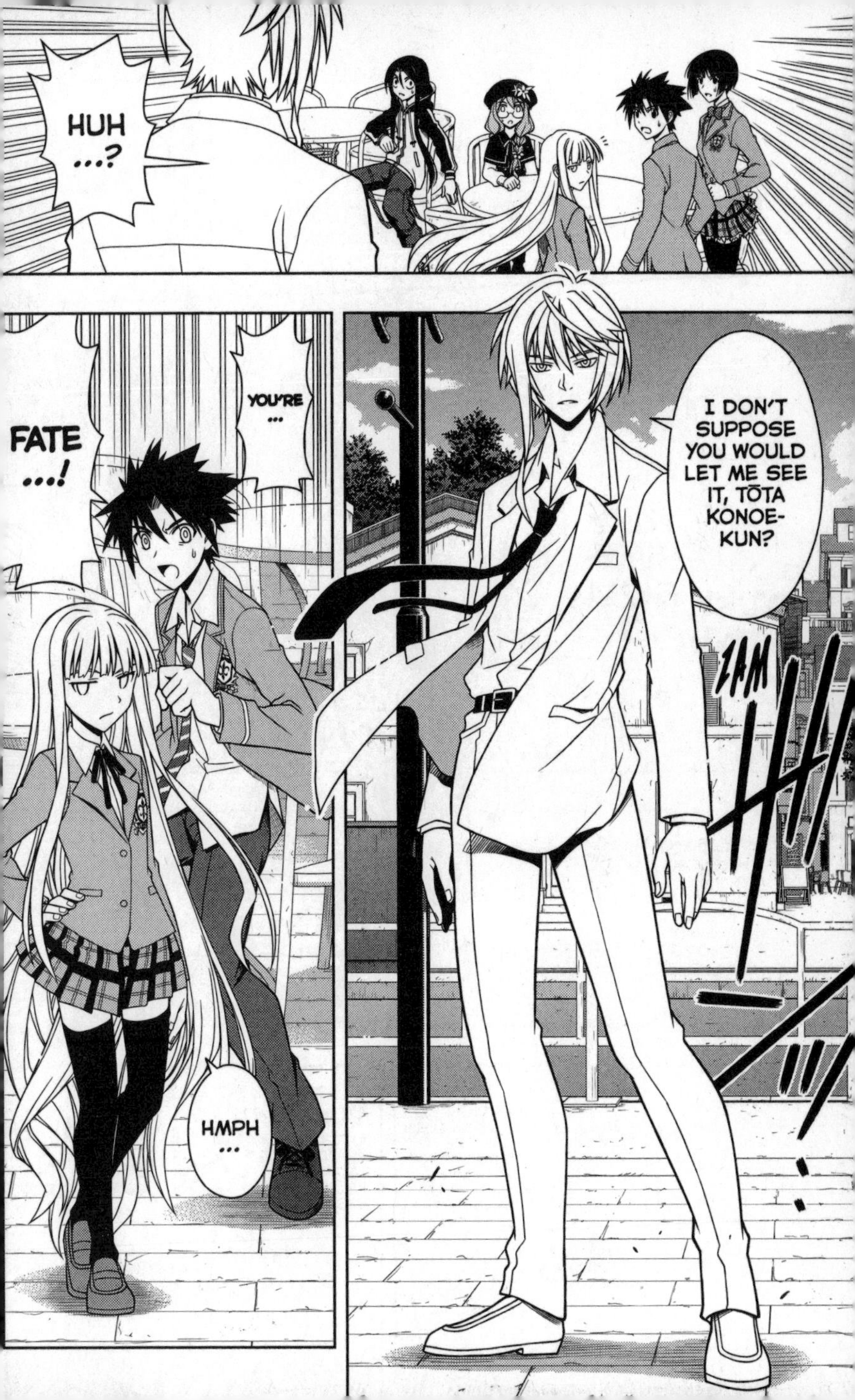
HUH ...?
I DON'T SUPPOSE YOU WOULD LET ME SEE IT, TŌTA KONOE-KUN?
ZAM
YOU'RE ...
FATE ...!
HMPH ...

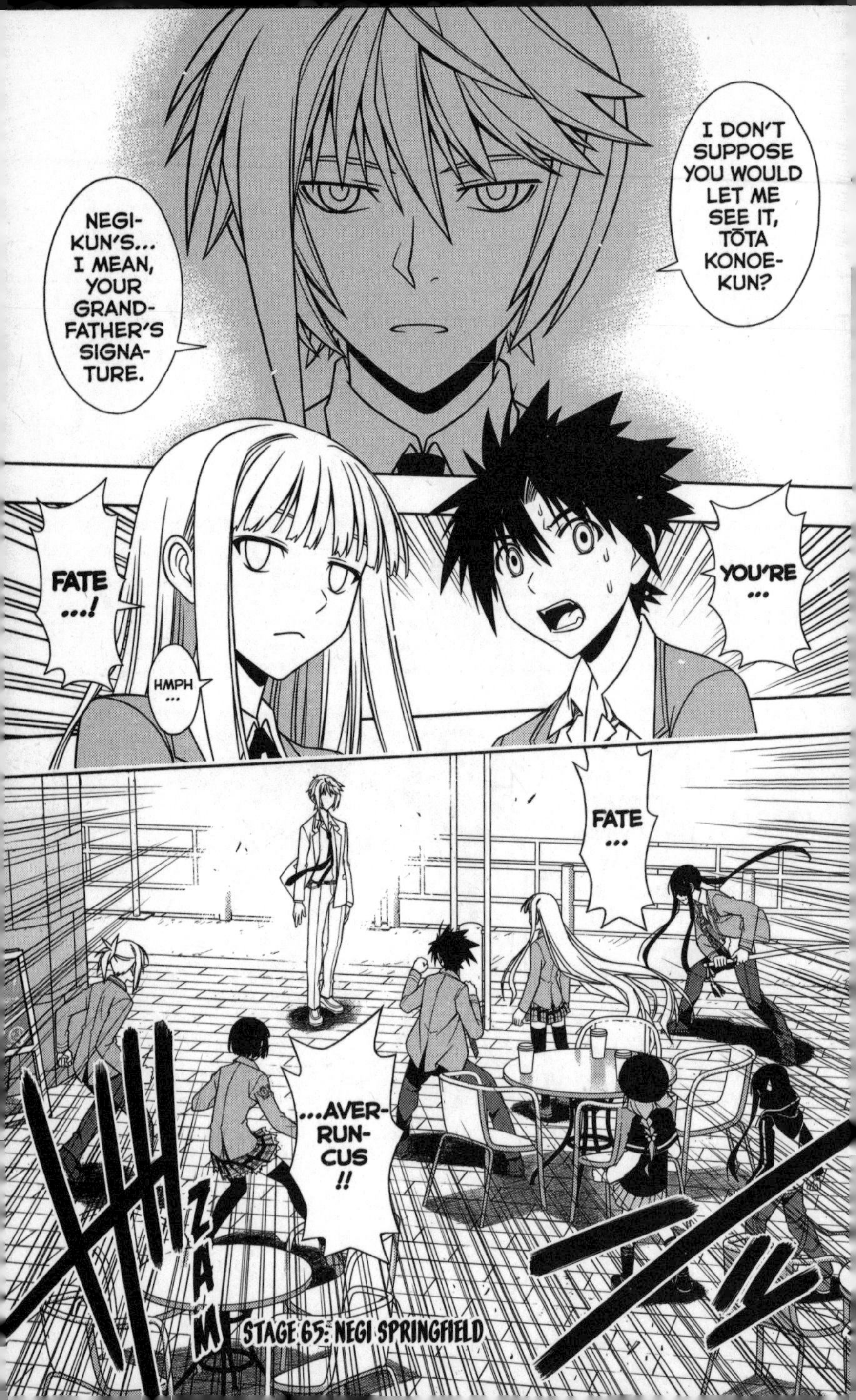
I DON'T SUPPOSE YOU WOULD LET ME SEE IT, TŌTA KONOE-KUN?
NEGI-KUN'S... I MEAN, YOUR GRANDFATHER'S SIGNATURE.
YOU'RE ...
FATE ...!
HMPH ...
FATE ...
...AVER-RUN-CUS !!
ZAM
STAGE 65: NEGI SPRINGFIELD

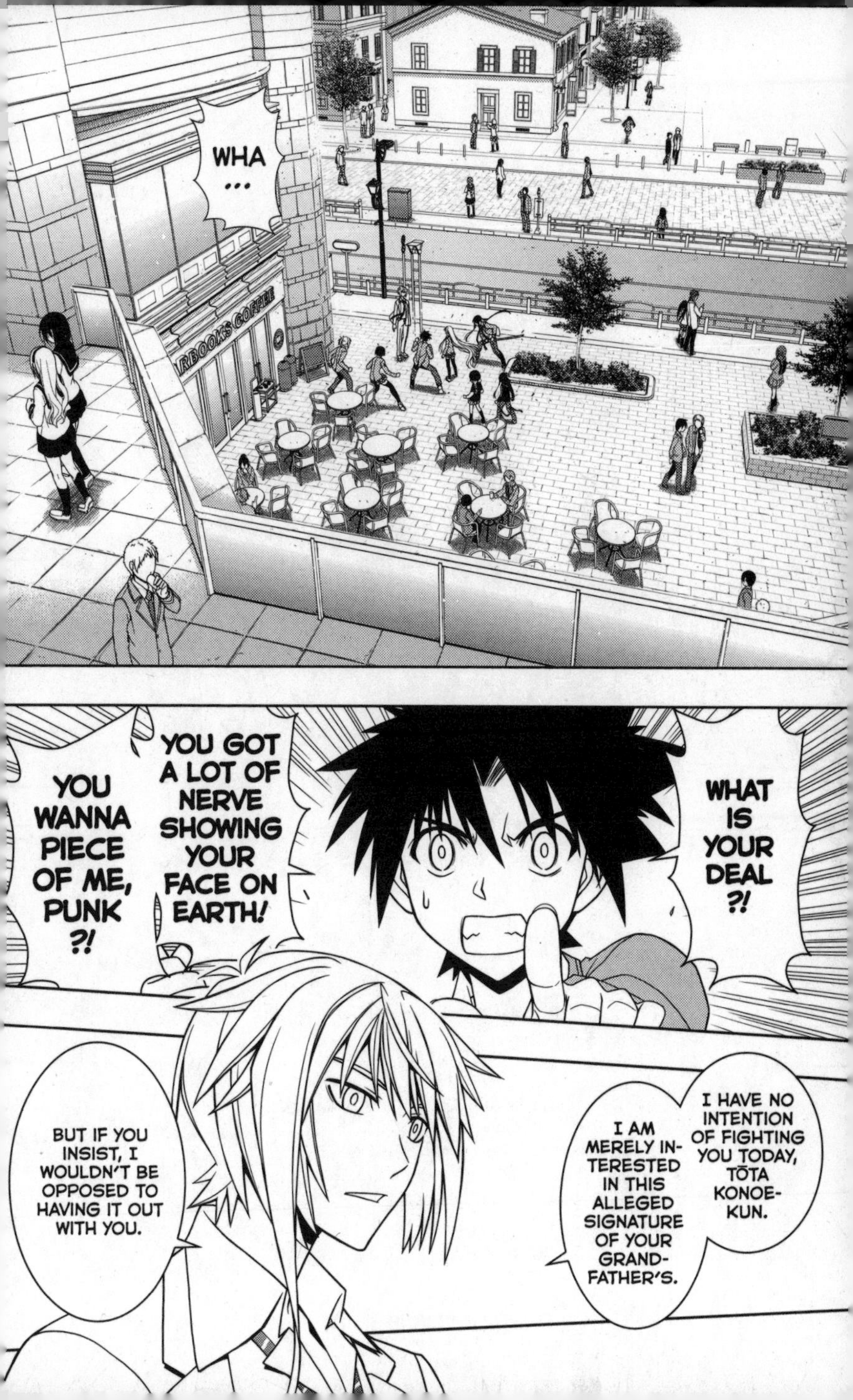
WHA...
RBOOKS COFFEE
WHAT IS YOUR DEAL?!
YOU GOT A LOT OF NERVE SHOWING YOUR FACE ON EARTH!
YOU WANNA PIECE OF ME, PUNK?!
I HAVE NO INTENTION OF FIGHTING YOU TODAY, TŌTA KONOE-KUN.
I AM MERELY INTERESTED IN THIS ALLEGED SIGNATURE OF YOUR GRANDFATHER'S.
BUT IF YOU INSIST, I WOULDN'T BE OPPOSED TO HAVING IT OUT WITH YOU.

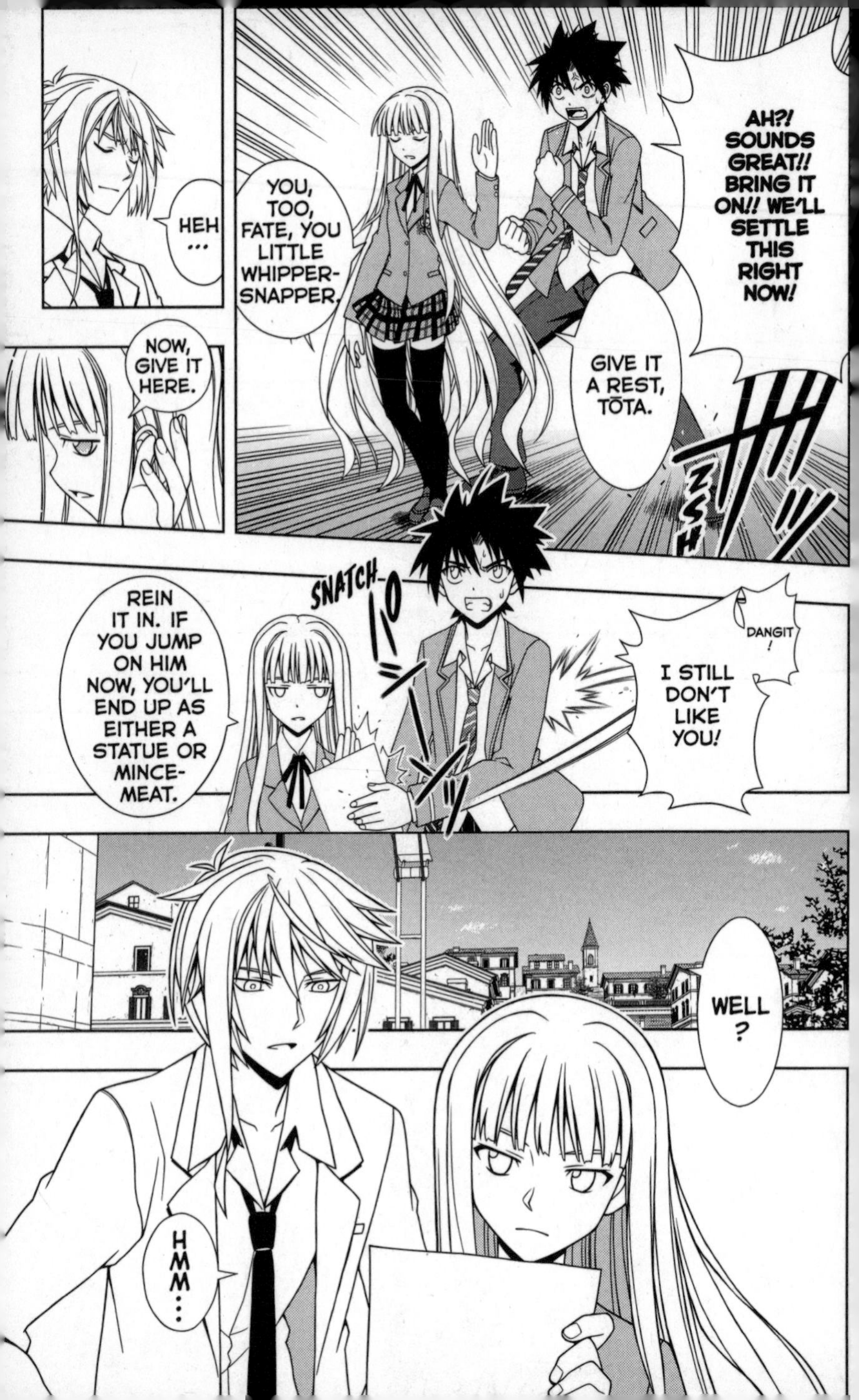
AH?! SOUNDS GREAT!! BRING IT ON!! WE'LL SETTLE THIS RIGHT NOW!
YOU, TOO, FATE, YOU LITTLE WHIPPER-SNAPPER.
GIVE IT A REST, TŌTA.
ZSH
HEH...
NOW, GIVE IT HERE.
DANGIT!
I STILL DON'T LIKE YOU!
SNATCH-
REIN IT IN. IF YOU JUMP ON HIM NOW, YOU'LL END UP AS EITHER A STATUE OR MINCE-MEAT.
WELL?
HMM...

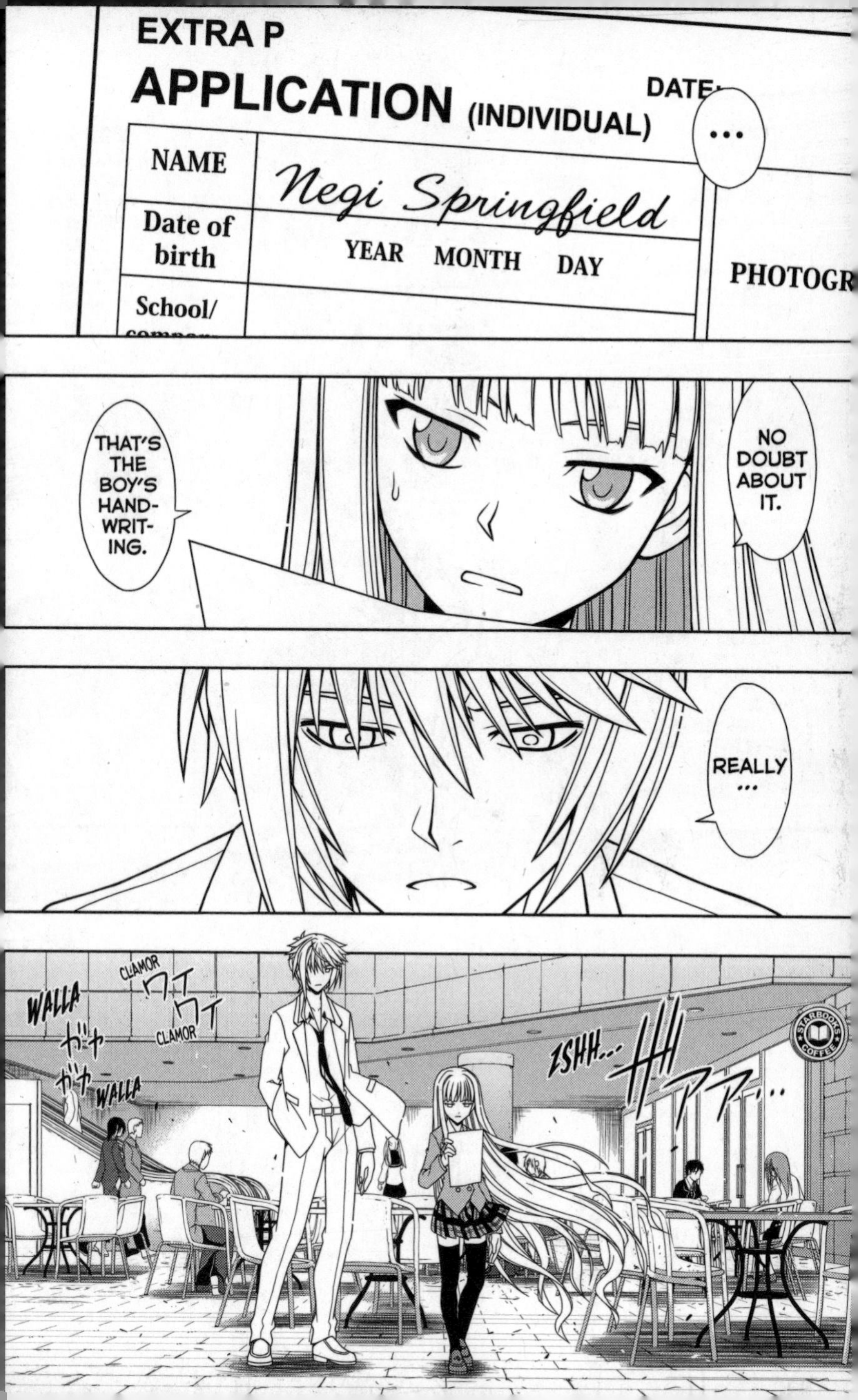
EXTRA P
APPLICATION (INDIVIDUAL)
DATE:
...
NAME
Negi Springfield
Date of birth
YEAR MONTH DAY
PHOTOGR
School/
NO DOUBT ABOUT IT.
THAT'S THE BOY'S HAND-WRIT-ING.
REALLY ...
ZSHH...
STARBOOKS COFFEE
CLAMOR
ワイワイ
CLAMOR
WALLA
ガヤガヤ
WALLA

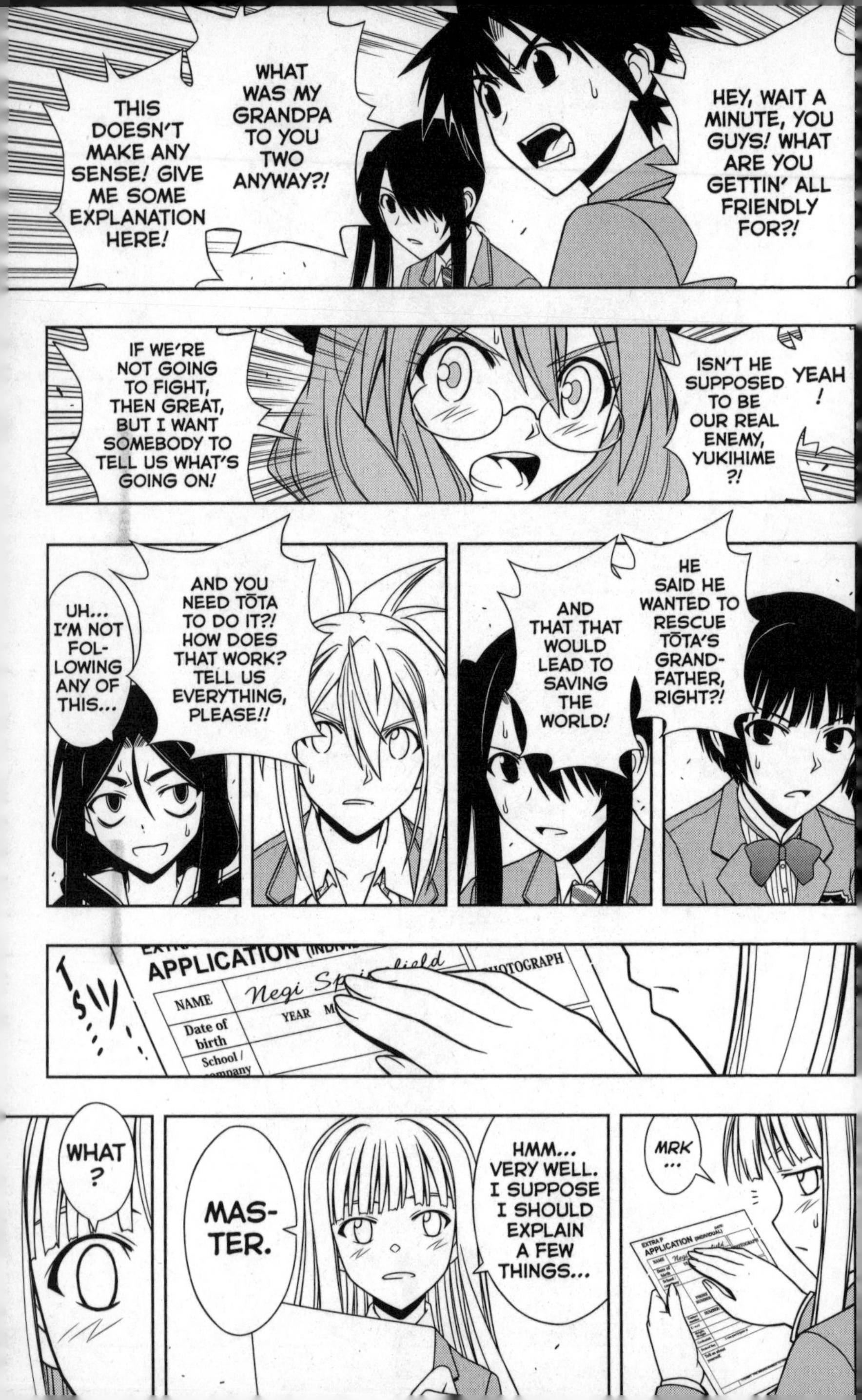
HEY, WAIT A MINUTE, YOU GUYS! WHAT ARE YOU GETTIN' ALL FRIENDLY FOR?!
WHAT WAS MY GRANDPA TO YOU TWO ANYWAY?!
THIS DOESN'T MAKE ANY SENSE! GIVE ME SOME EXPLANATION HERE!
ISN'T HE SUPPOSED TO BE OUR REAL ENEMY, YUKIHIME?!
YEAH!
IF WE'RE NOT GOING TO FIGHT, THEN GREAT, BUT I WANT SOMEBODY TO TELL US WHAT'S GOING ON!
HE SAID HE WANTED TO RESCUE TŌTA'S GRANDFATHER, RIGHT?!
AND THAT THAT WOULD LEAD TO SAVING THE WORLD!
AND YOU NEED TŌTA TO DO IT?! HOW DOES THAT WORK? TELL US EVERYTHING, PLEASE!!
UH... I'M NOT FOLLOWING ANY OF THIS...
APPLICATION
PHOTOGRAPH
NAME
Date of birth
YEAR
MRK...
HMM... VERY WELL. I SUPPOSE I SHOULD EXPLAIN A FEW THINGS...
MASTER.
WHAT?

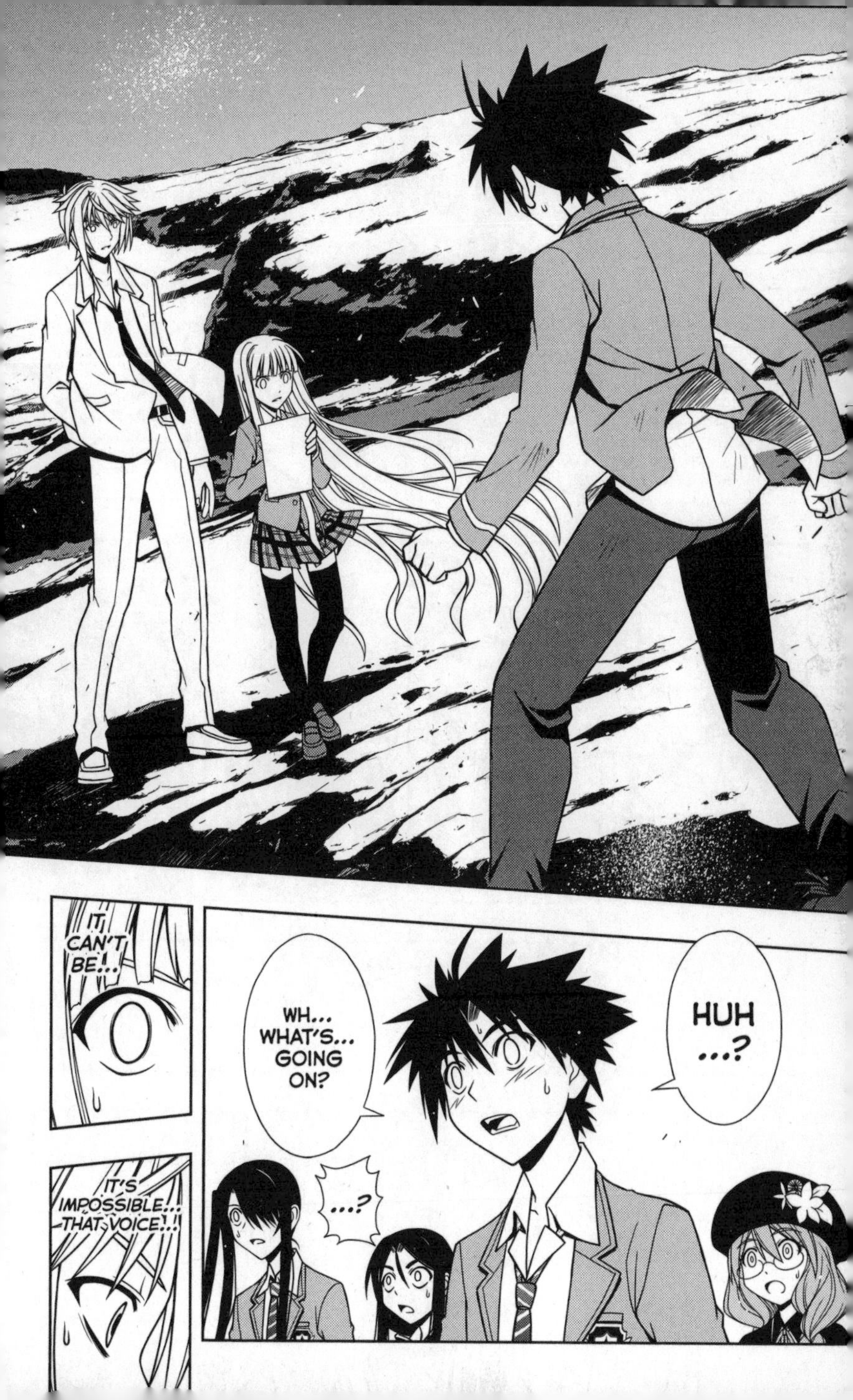
HUH ...?
WH... WHAT'S... GOING ON?
...?
IT CAN'T BE...
IT'S IMPOSSIBLE... THAT VOICE...

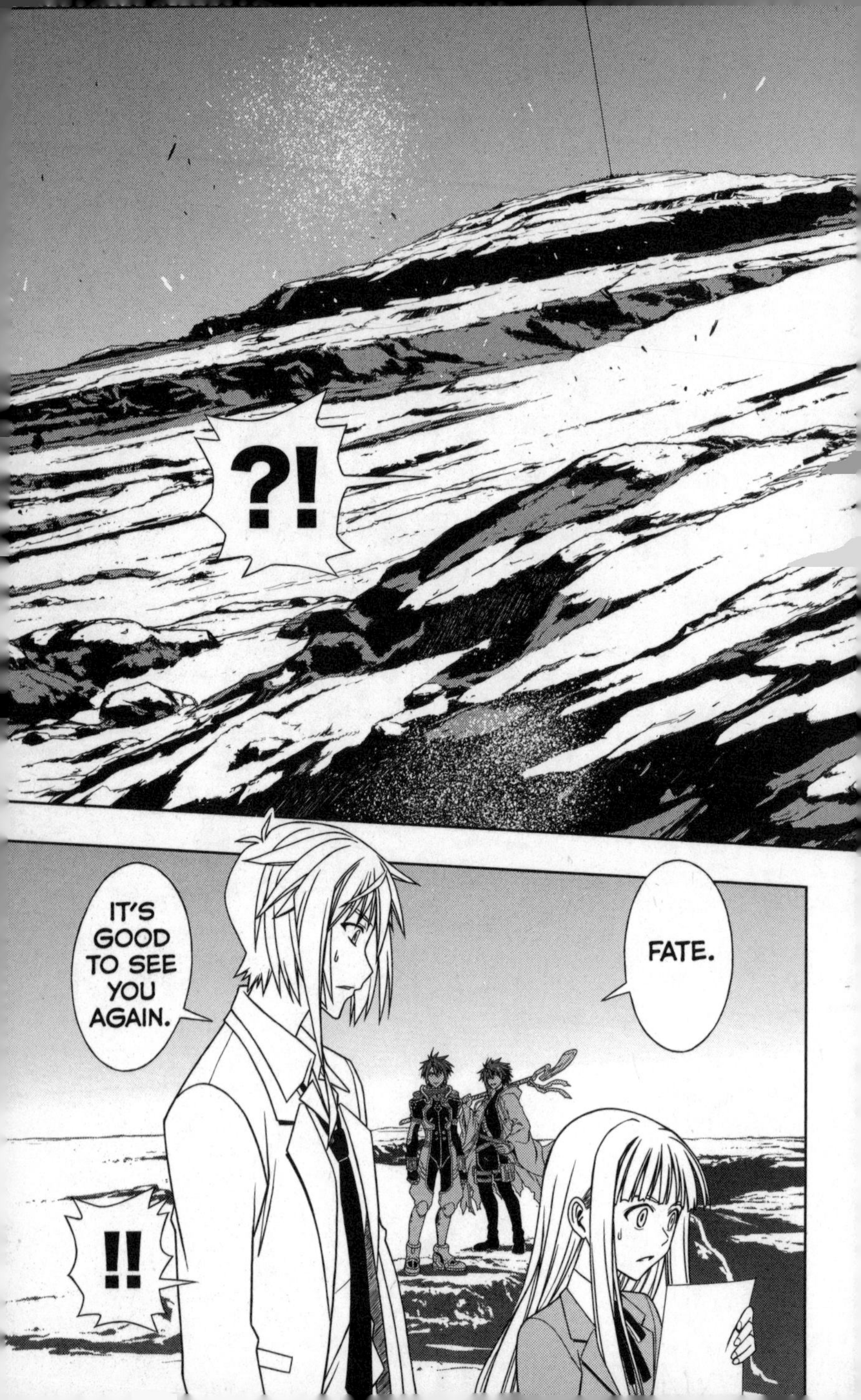
?!
FATE.
IT'S GOOD TO SEE YOU AGAIN.
!!

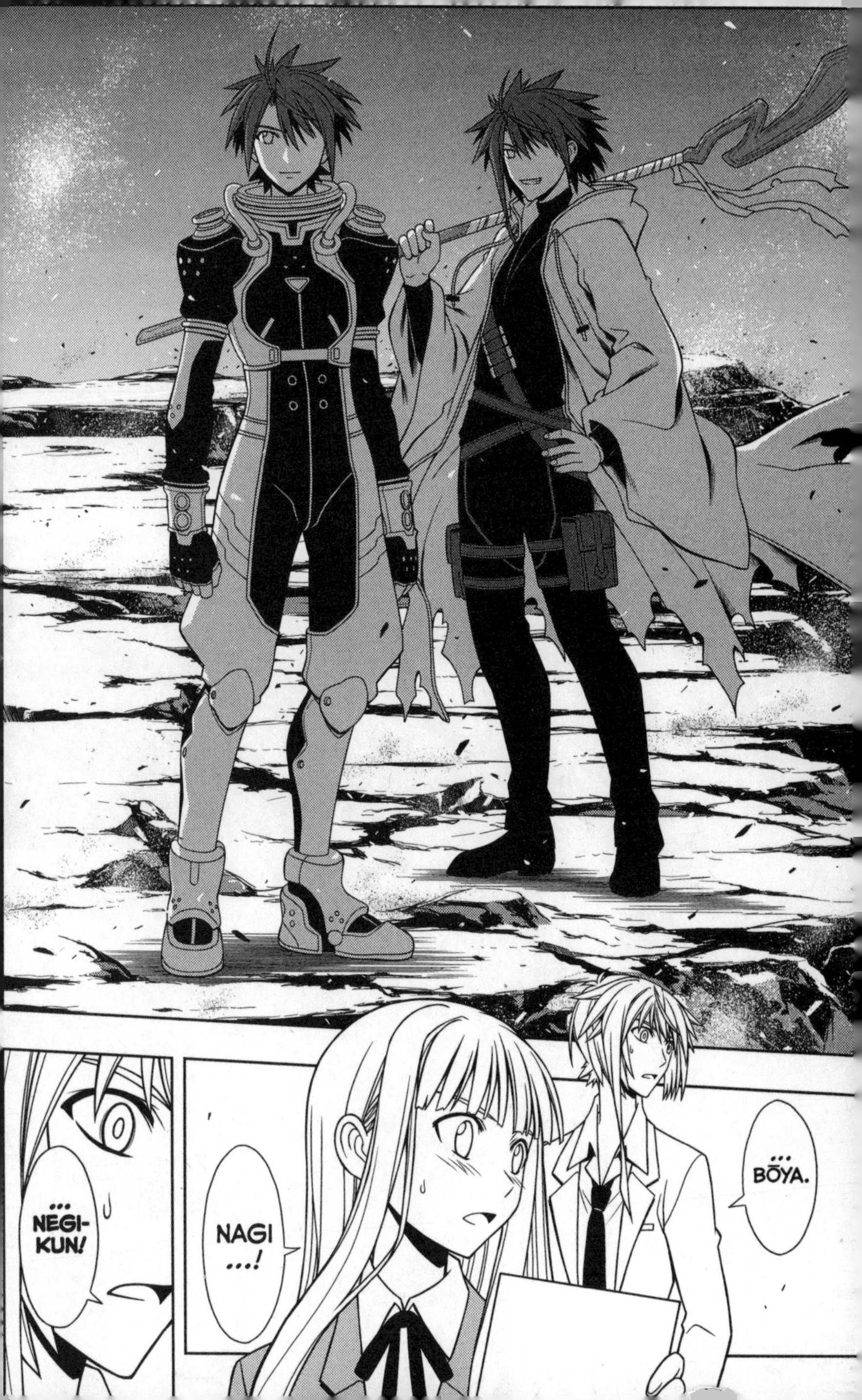
...BŌYA.
NAGI ...!
...NEGI-KUN!

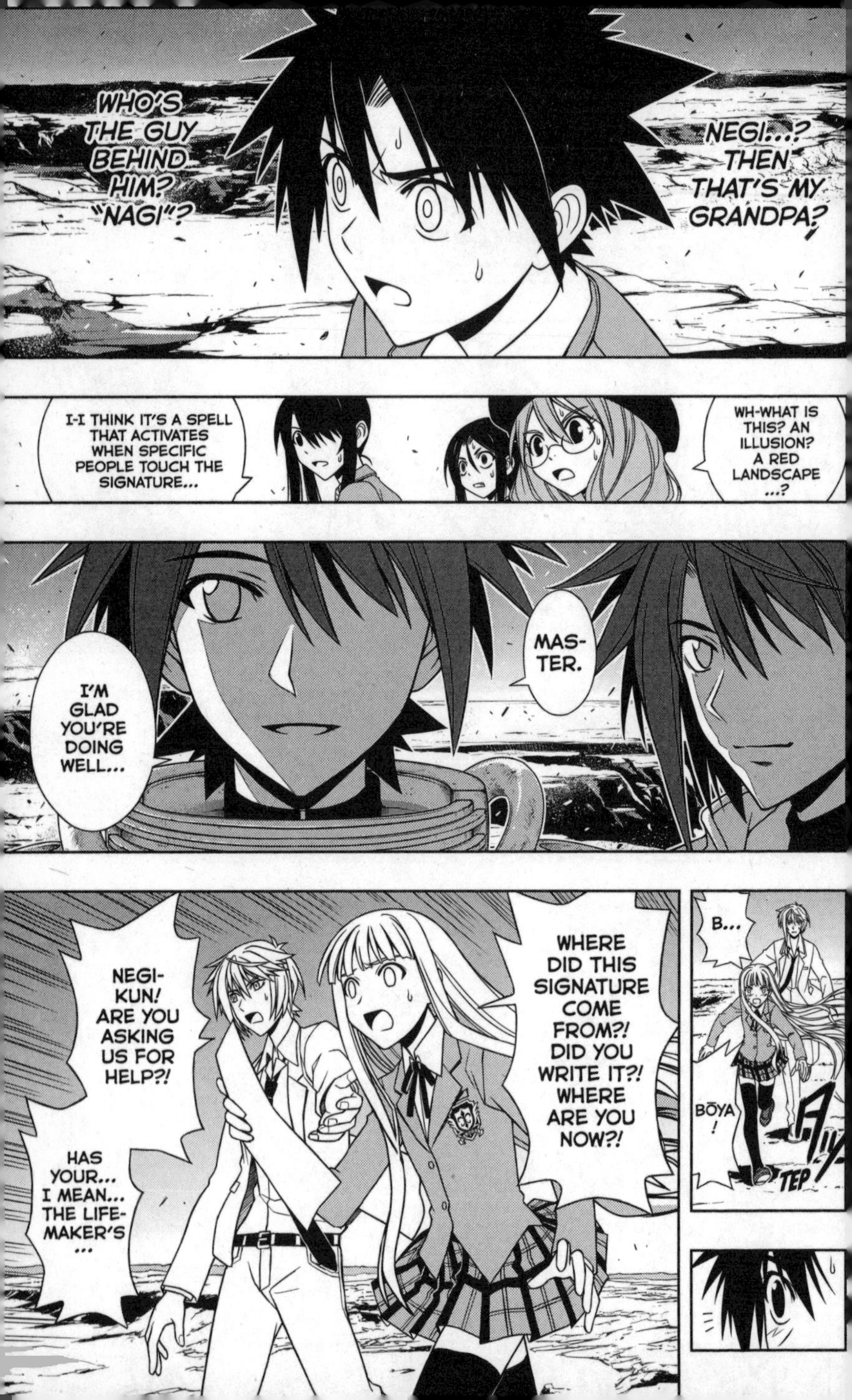
NEGI...? THEN THAT'S MY GRANDPA?
WHO'S THE GUY BEHIND HIM? "NAGI"?
WH-WHAT IS THIS? AN ILLUSION? A RED LANDSCAPE ...?
I-I THINK IT'S A SPELL THAT ACTIVATES WHEN SPECIFIC PEOPLE TOUCH THE SIGNATURE...
MASTER.
I'M GLAD YOU'RE DOING WELL...
B...
BŌYA!
TEP!
WHERE DID THIS SIGNATURE COME FROM?! DID YOU WRITE IT?! WHERE ARE YOU NOW?!
NEGI-KUN! ARE YOU ASKING US FOR HELP?!
HAS YOUR... I MEAN... THE LIFE-MAKER'S ...

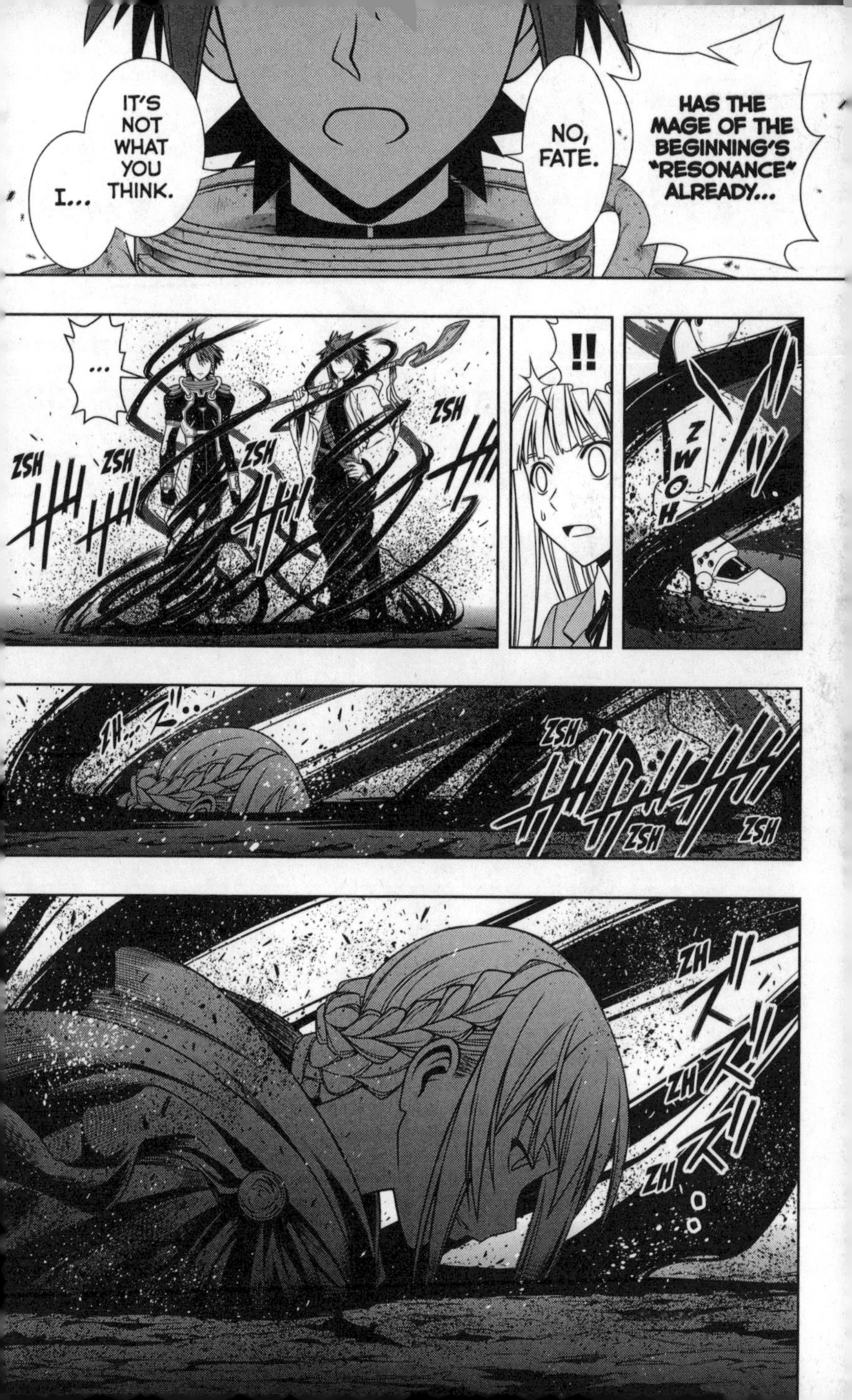
HAS THE MAGE OF THE BEGINNING'S "RESONANCE" ALREADY...
NO, FATE.
IT'S NOT WHAT YOU THINK.
I...
ZWOOH
!!
...
ZSH
ZSH
ZSH
ZSH
ZSH
ZSH
ZSH
ZH...
ZH
ZH
ZH

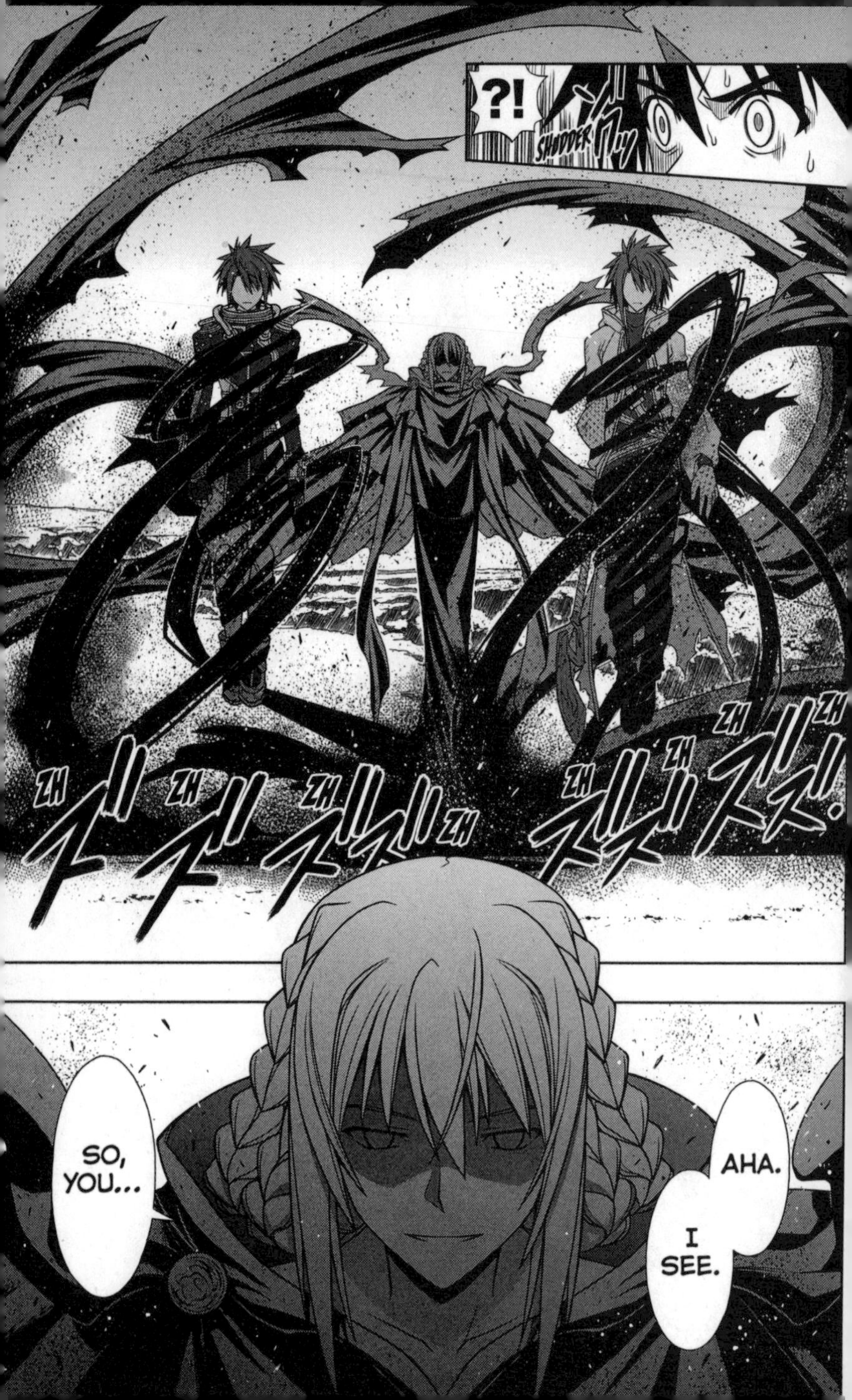

?!
SHUDDER
ZH
ZH
ZH
ZH
ZH
ZH
ZH
ZH
AHA.
I SEE.
SO, YOU...

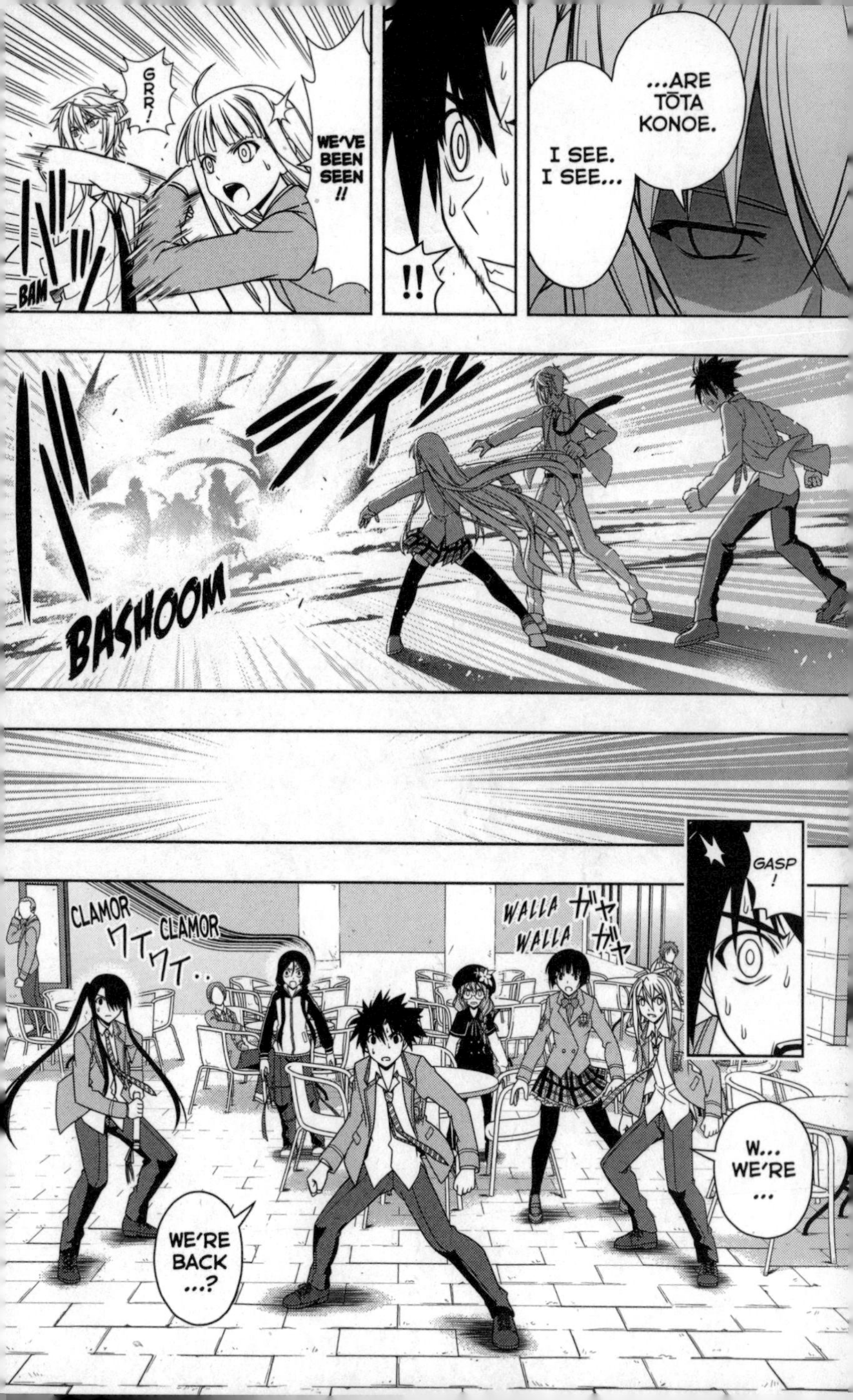
I SEE. I SEE...
...ARE TŌTA KONOE.
!!
WE'VE BEEN SEEN!!
GRR!
BAM
BASHOOM
GASP!
ガヤガヤ
WALLA WALLA
W... WE'RE...
CLAMOR ワイワイ.. CLAMOR
WE'RE BACK...?

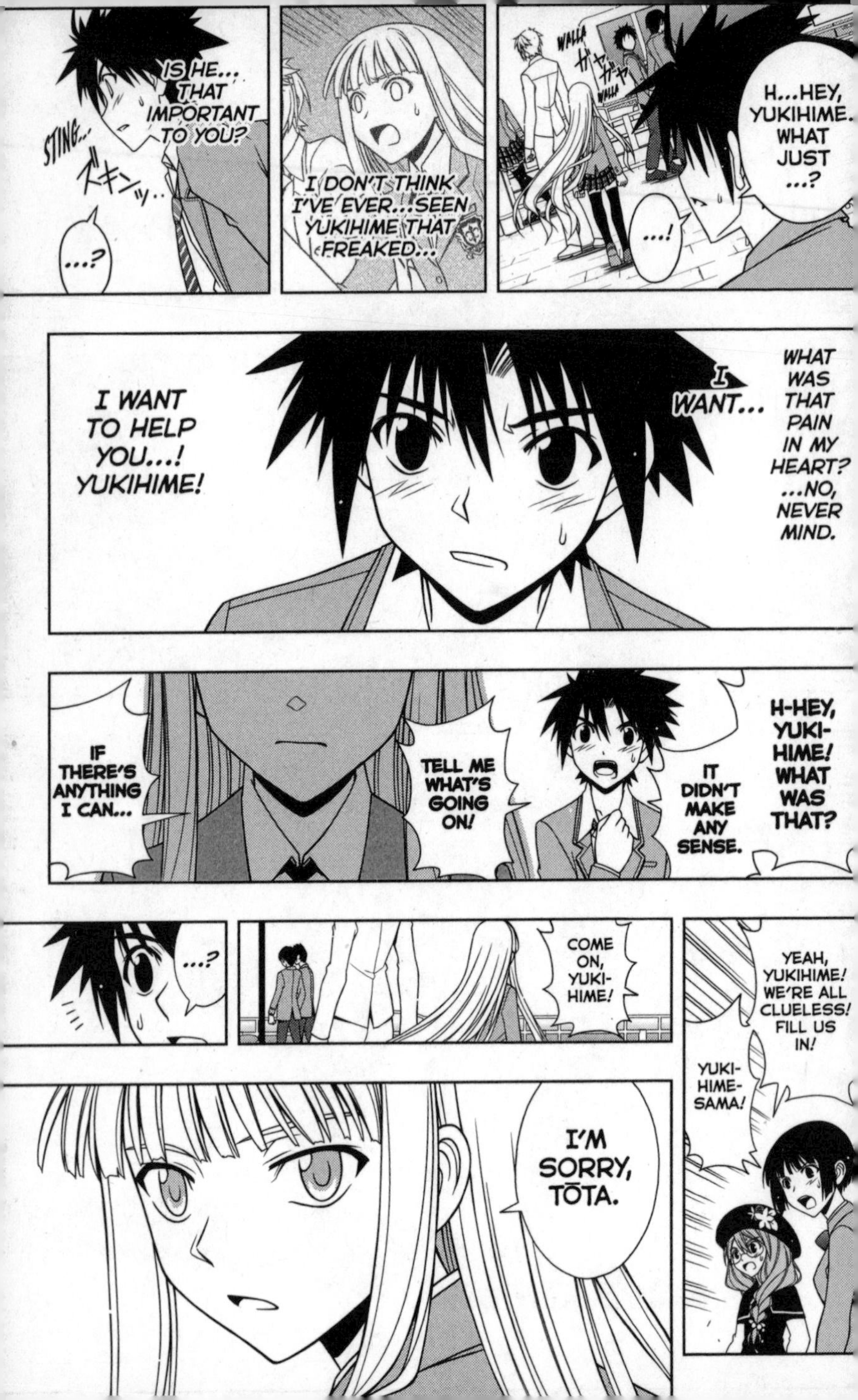

H...HEY, YUKIHIME. WHAT JUST ...?
WALLA ガヤガヤ WALLA
...!
I DON'T THINK I'VE EVER...SEEN YUKIHIME THAT FREAKED...
IS HE... THAT IMPORTANT TO YOU?
STING... ズキンッ...
...?
WHAT WAS THAT PAIN IN MY HEART? ...NO, NEVER MIND.
I WANT...
I WANT TO HELP YOU...! YUKIHIME!
H-HEY, YUKIHIME! WHAT WAS THAT?
IT DIDN'T MAKE ANY SENSE.
TELL ME WHAT'S GOING ON!
IF THERE'S ANYTHING I CAN...
YEAH, YUKIHIME! WE'RE ALL CLUELESS! FILL US IN!
YUKI-HIME-SAMA!
COME ON, YUKI-HIME!
...?
I'M SORRY, TŌTA.

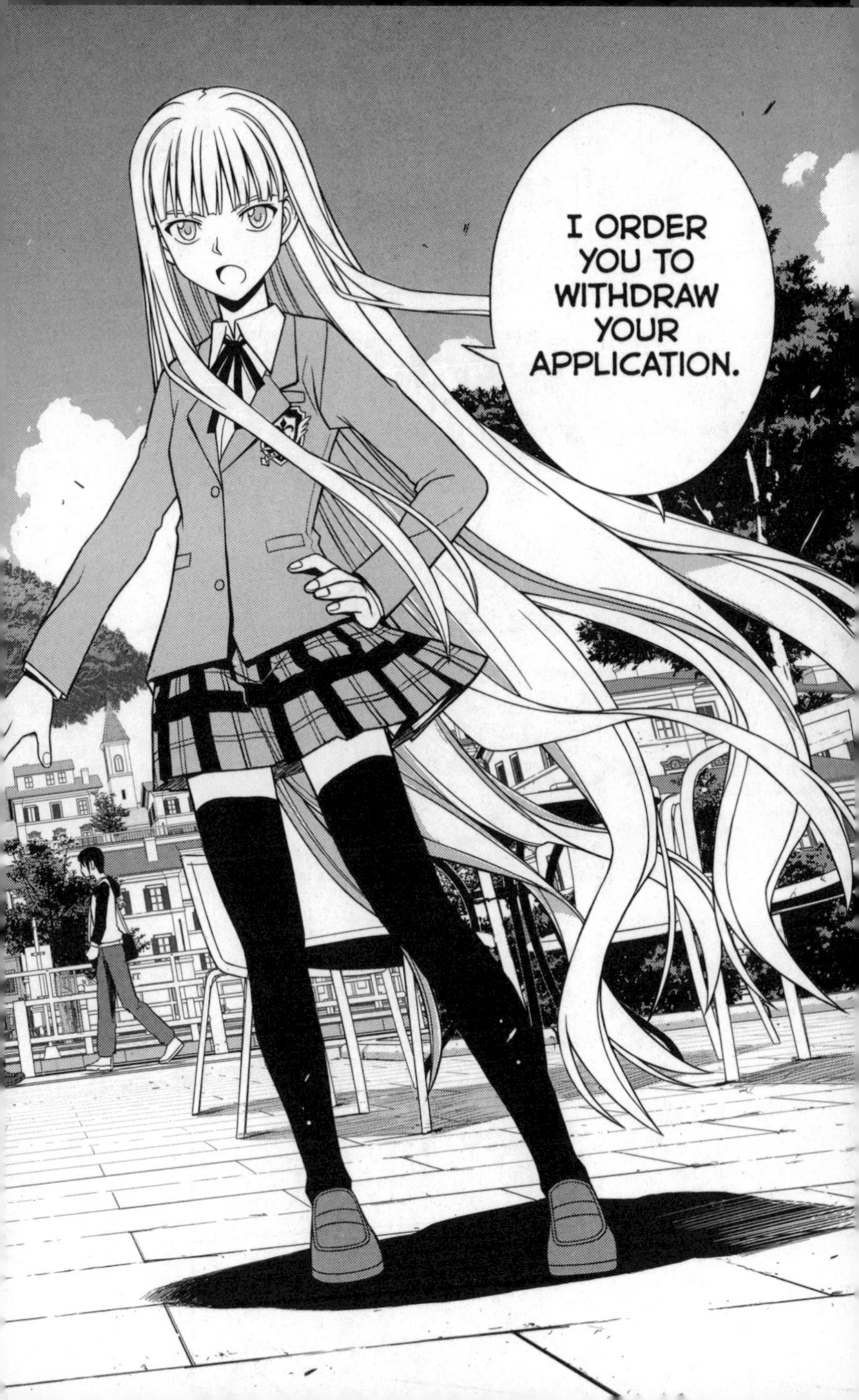
I ORDER YOU TO WITHDRAW YOUR APPLICATION.

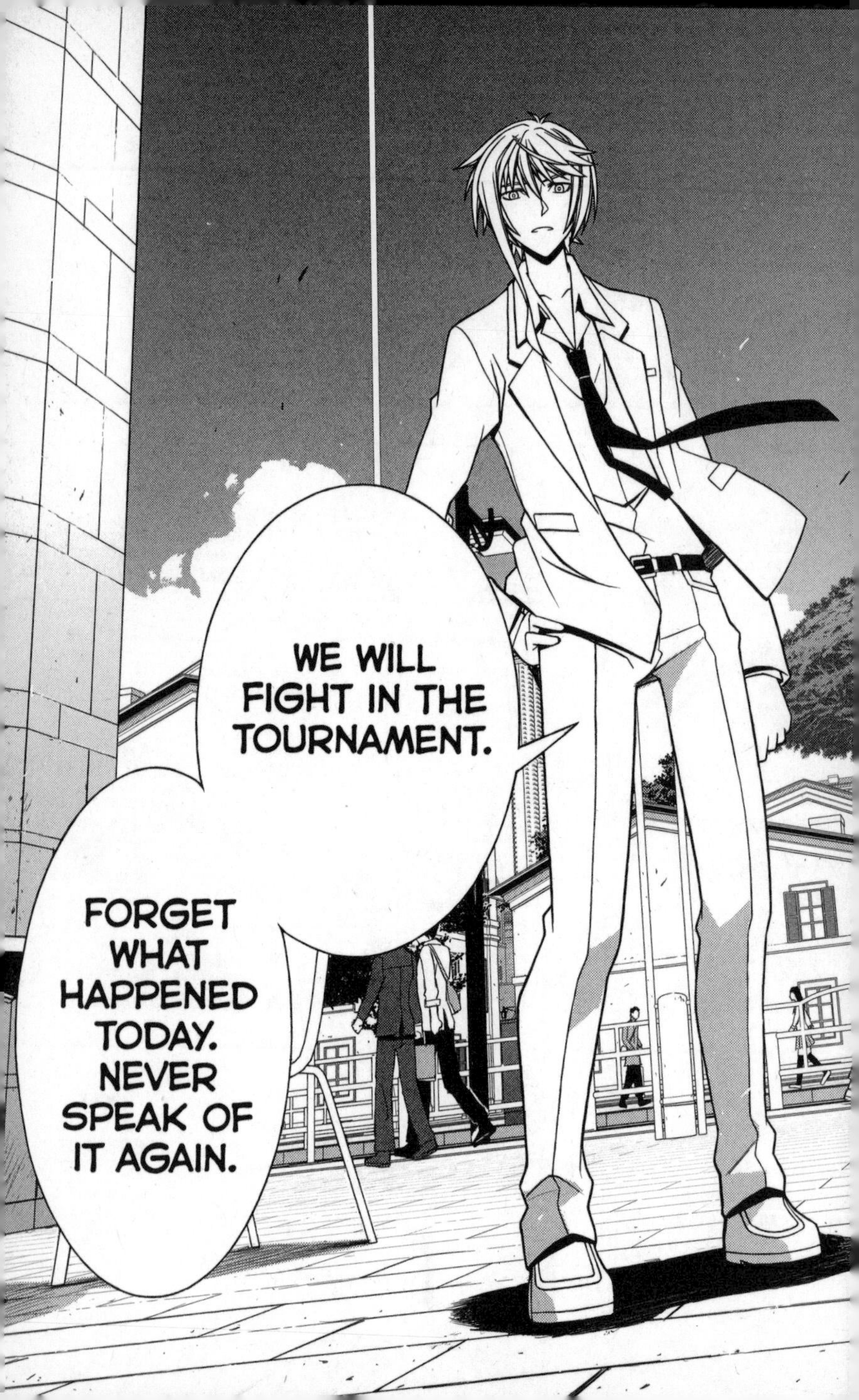
WE WILL FIGHT IN THE TOURNAMENT.
FORGET WHAT HAPPENED TODAY. NEVER SPEAK OF IT AGAIN.

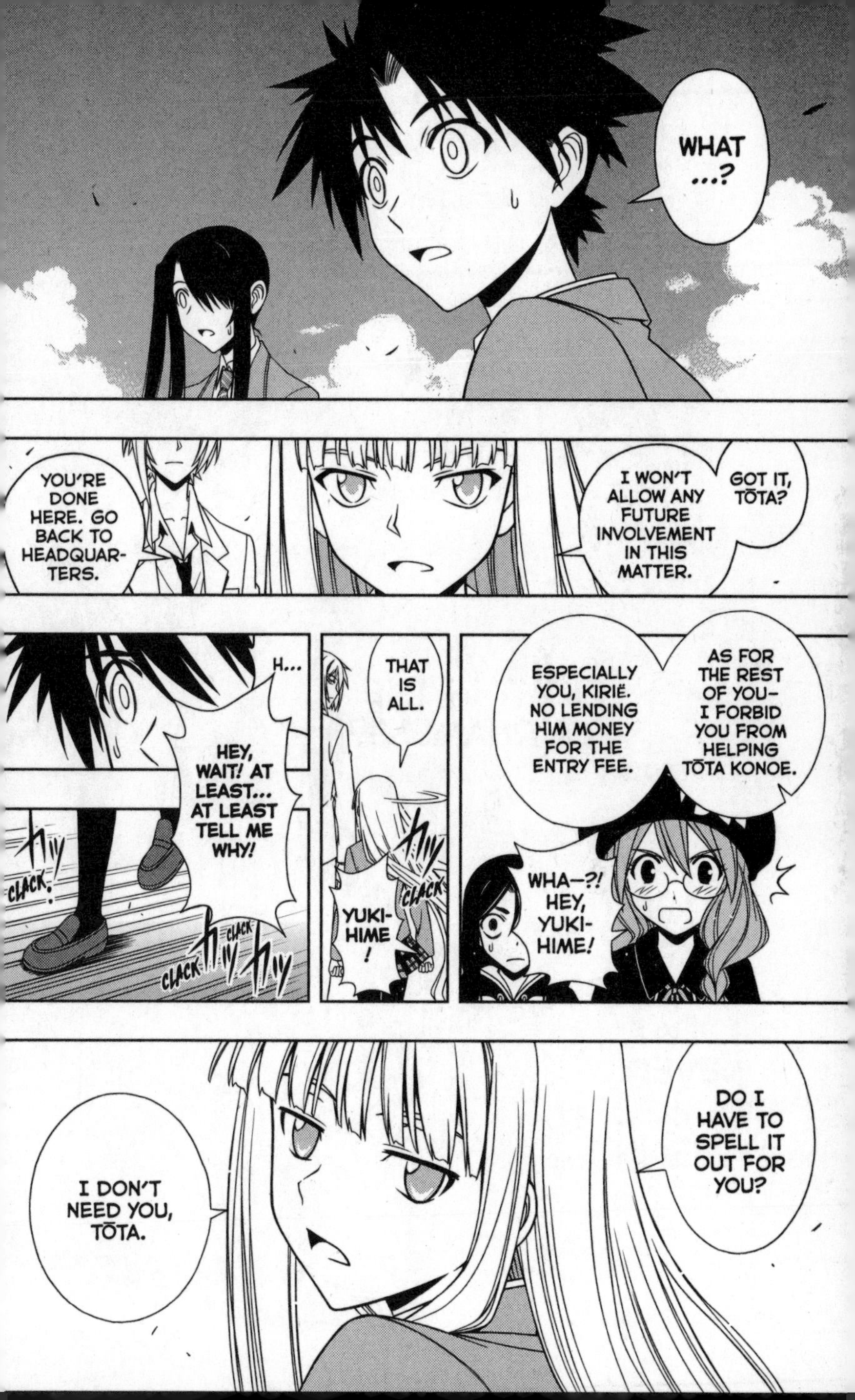
WHAT ...?
GOT IT, TŌTA?
I WON'T ALLOW ANY FUTURE INVOLVEMENT IN THIS MATTER.
YOU'RE DONE HERE. GO BACK TO HEADQUARTERS.
AS FOR THE REST OF YOU— I FORBID YOU FROM HELPING TŌTA KONOE.
ESPECIALLY YOU, KIRIË. NO LENDING HIM MONEY FOR THE ENTRY FEE.
WHA—?! HEY, YUKI-HIME!
THAT IS ALL.
CLACK
YUKI-HIME!
H...
HEY, WAIT! AT LEAST... AT LEAST TELL ME WHY!
CLACK
CLACK
CLACK
DO I HAVE TO SPELL IT OUT FOR YOU?
I DON'T NEED YOU, TŌTA.

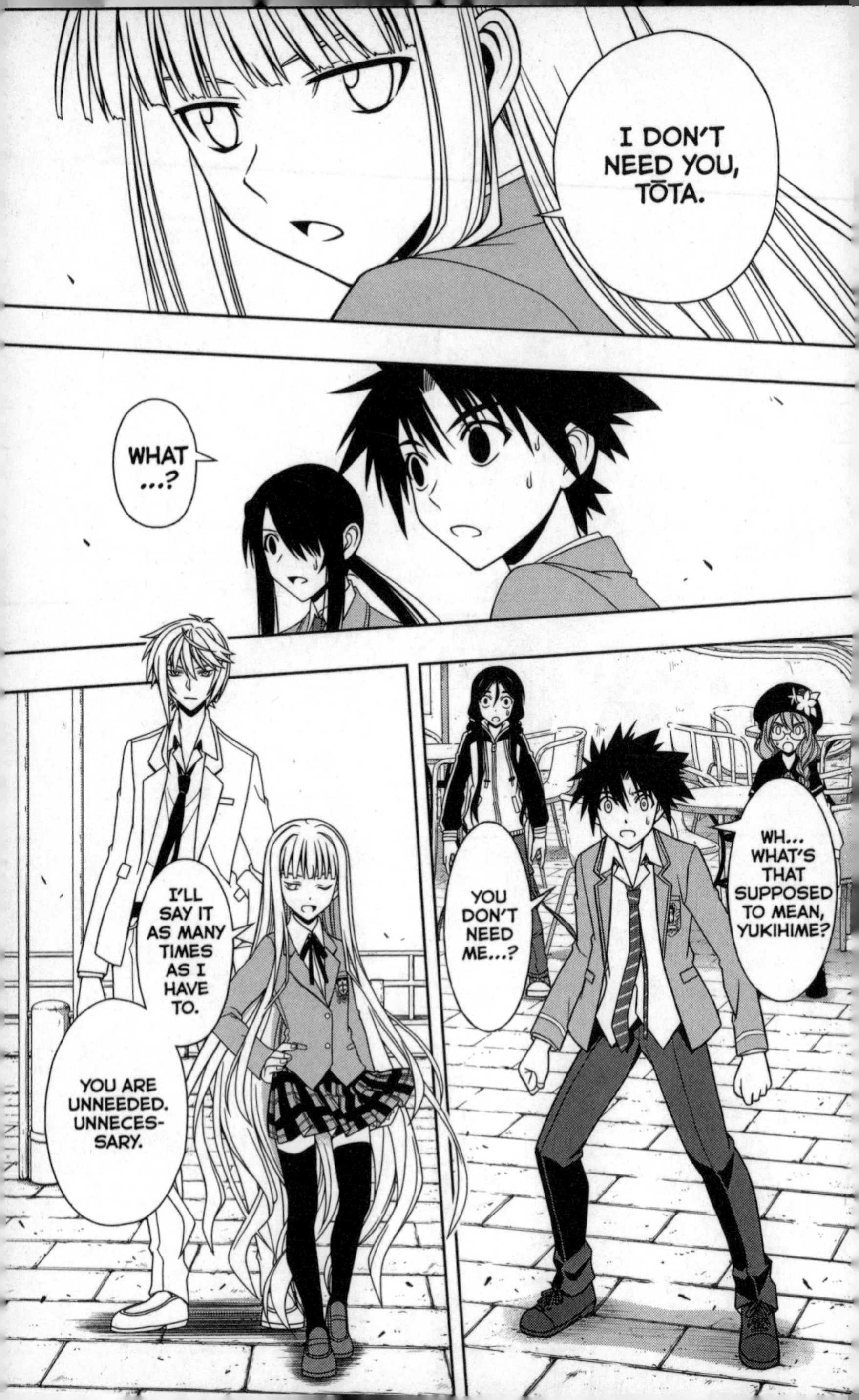
I DON'T NEED YOU, TŌTA.
WHAT ...?
WH... WHAT'S THAT SUPPOSED TO MEAN, YUKIHIME?
YOU DON'T NEED ME...?
I'LL SAY IT AS MANY TIMES AS I HAVE TO.
YOU ARE UNNEEDED. UNNECES-SARY.

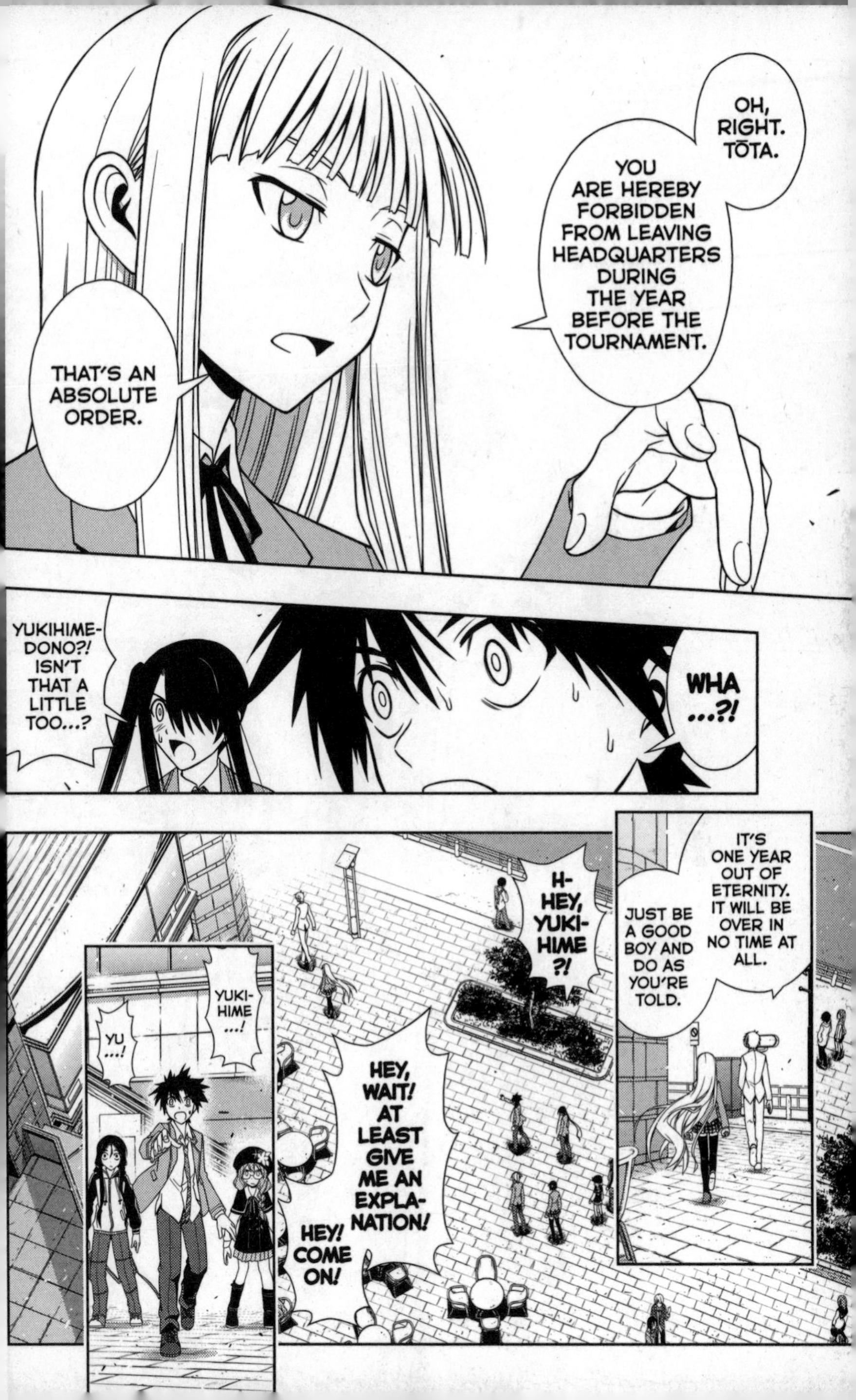
OH, RIGHT. TŌTA.
YOU ARE HEREBY FORBIDDEN FROM LEAVING HEADQUARTERS DURING THE YEAR BEFORE THE TOURNAMENT.
THAT'S AN ABSOLUTE ORDER.
WHA...?!
YUKIHIME-DONO?! ISN'T THAT A LITTLE TOO...?
IT'S ONE YEAR OUT OF ETERNITY. IT WILL BE OVER IN NO TIME AT ALL.
JUST BE A GOOD BOY AND DO AS YOU'RE TOLD.
H-HEY, YUKI-HIME?!
HEY, WAIT! AT LEAST GIVE ME AN EXPLA-NATION!
HEY! COME ON!
YUKI-HIME...!
YU...!

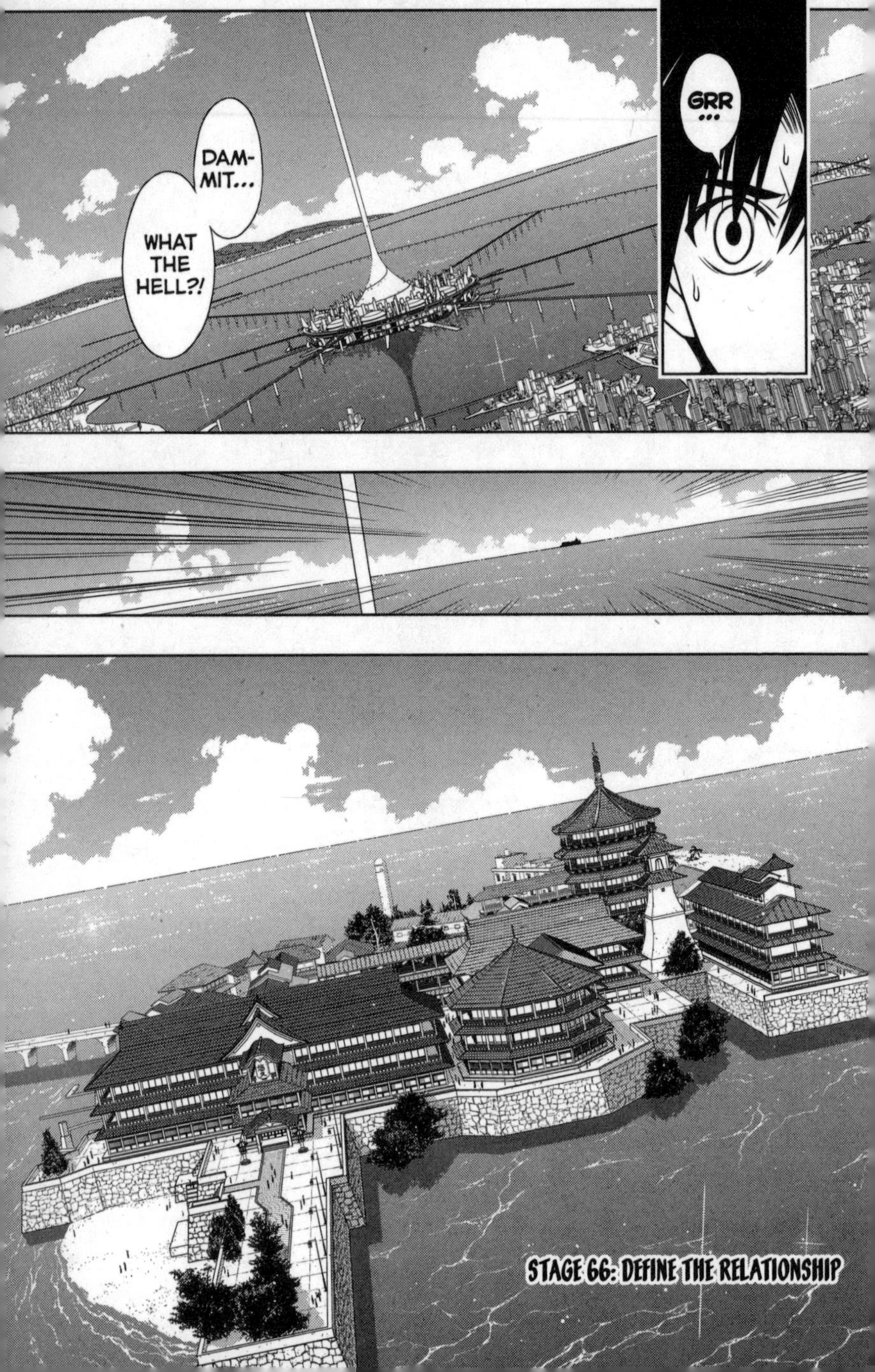
GRR...
DAMMIT...
WHAT THE HELL?!
STAGE 66: DEFINE THE RELATIONSHIP

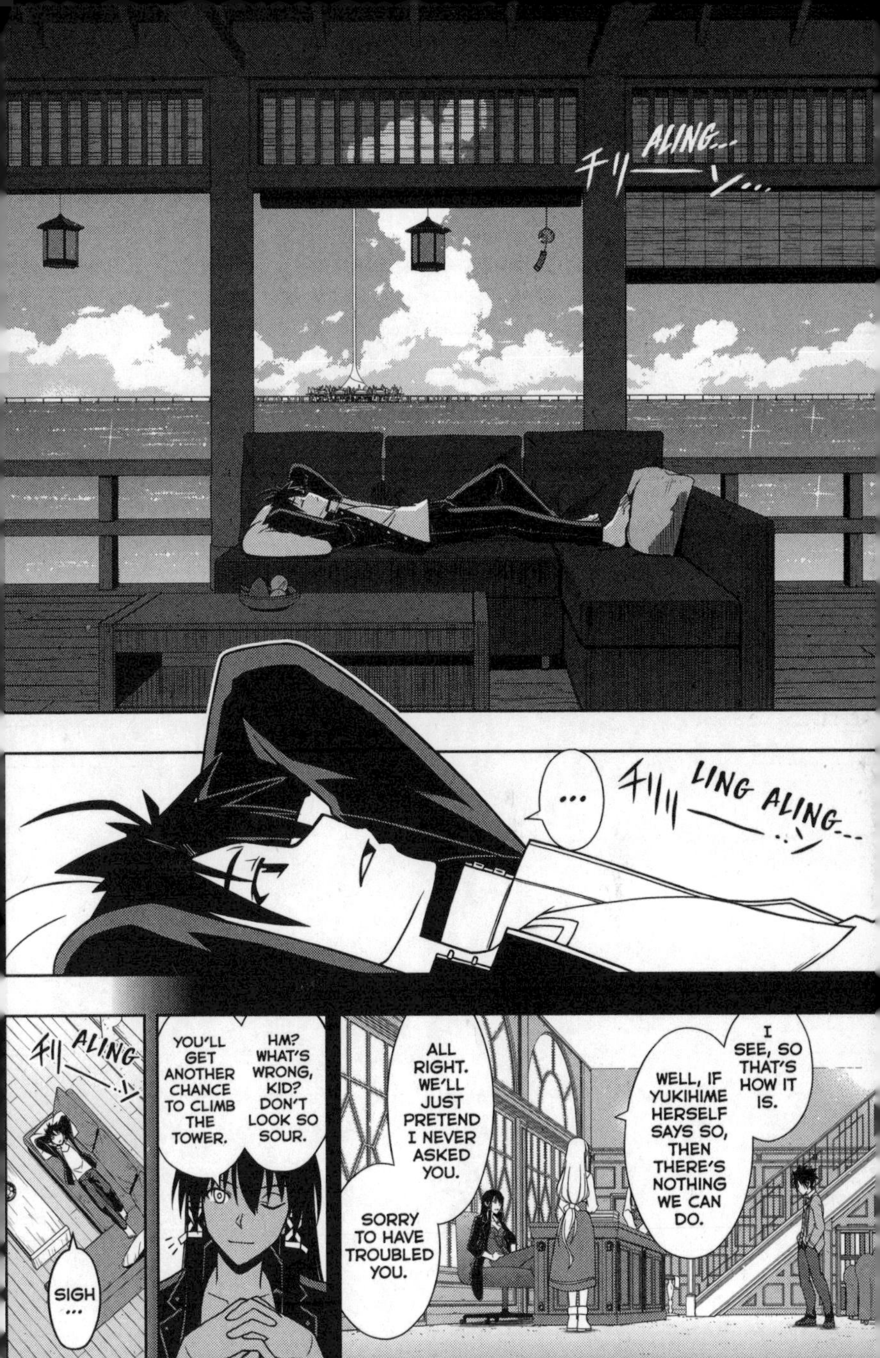
チリーーン…
ALING...
...
チリリーーン…
LING ALING...
I SEE, SO THAT'S HOW IT IS.
WELL, IF YUKIHIME HERSELF SAYS SO, THEN THERE'S NOTHING WE CAN DO.
ALL RIGHT. WE'LL JUST PRETEND I NEVER ASKED YOU.
SORRY TO HAVE TROUBLED YOU.
HM? WHAT'S WRONG, KID? DON'T LOOK SO SOUR.
YOU'LL GET ANOTHER CHANCE TO CLIMB THE TOWER.
チリーン…
ALING
SIGH...

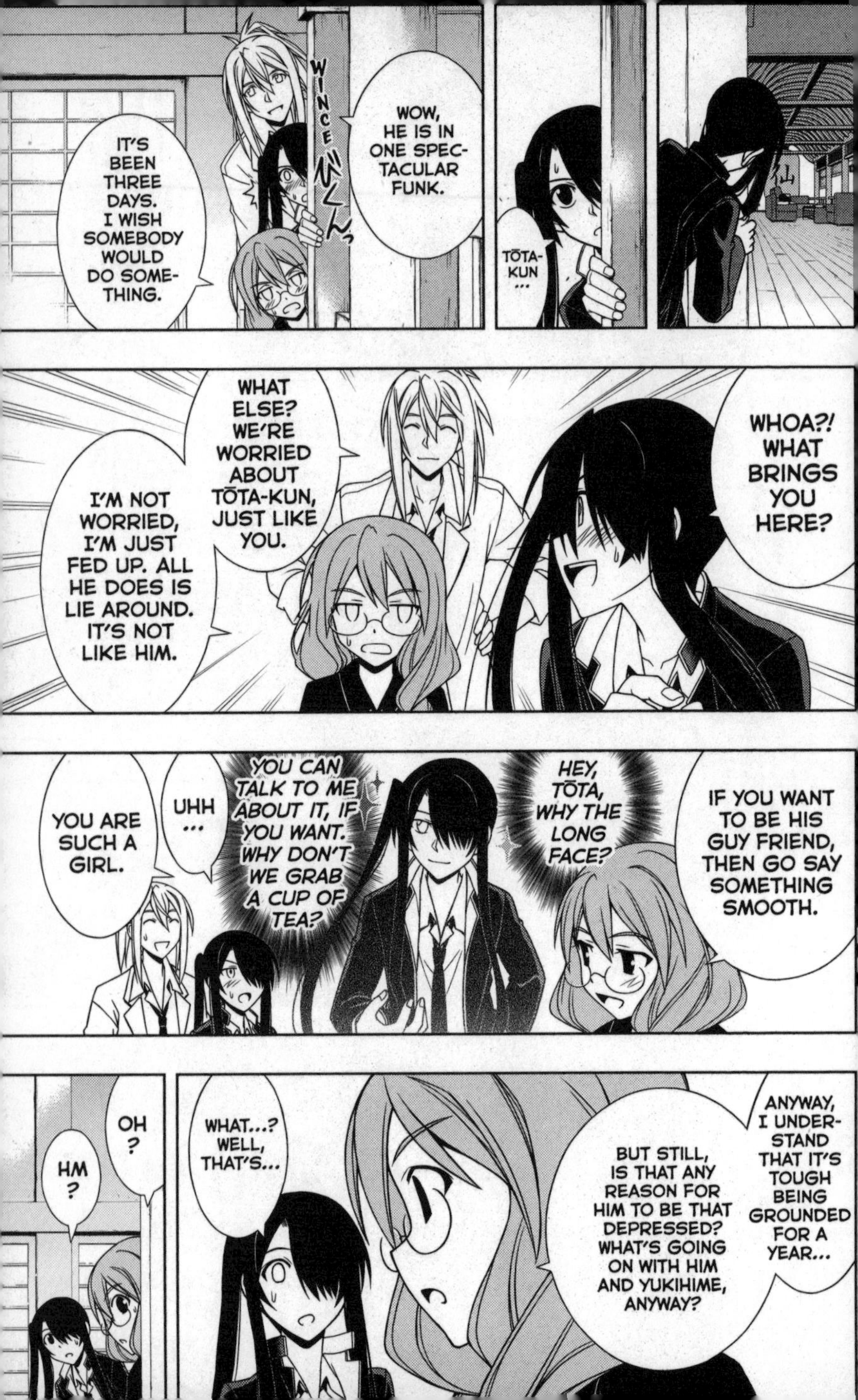
TŌTA-KUN...
WOW, HE IS IN ONE SPECTACULAR FUNK.
WINCE
IT'S BEEN THREE DAYS. I WISH SOMEBODY WOULD DO SOMETHING.
WHOA?! WHAT BRINGS YOU HERE?
WHAT ELSE? WE'RE WORRIED ABOUT TŌTA-KUN, JUST LIKE YOU.
I'M NOT WORRIED, I'M JUST FED UP. ALL HE DOES IS LIE AROUND. IT'S NOT LIKE HIM.
IF YOU WANT TO BE HIS GUY FRIEND, THEN GO SAY SOMETHING SMOOTH.
HEY, TŌTA, WHY THE LONG FACE?
YOU CAN TALK TO ME ABOUT IT, IF YOU WANT. WHY DON'T WE GRAB A CUP OF TEA?
UHH...
YOU ARE SUCH A GIRL.
ANYWAY, I UNDERSTAND THAT IT'S TOUGH BEING GROUNDED FOR A YEAR...
BUT STILL, IS THAT ANY REASON FOR HIM TO BE THAT DEPRESSED? WHAT'S GOING ON WITH HIM AND YUKIHIME, ANYWAY?
WHAT...? WELL, THAT'S...
OH?
HM?

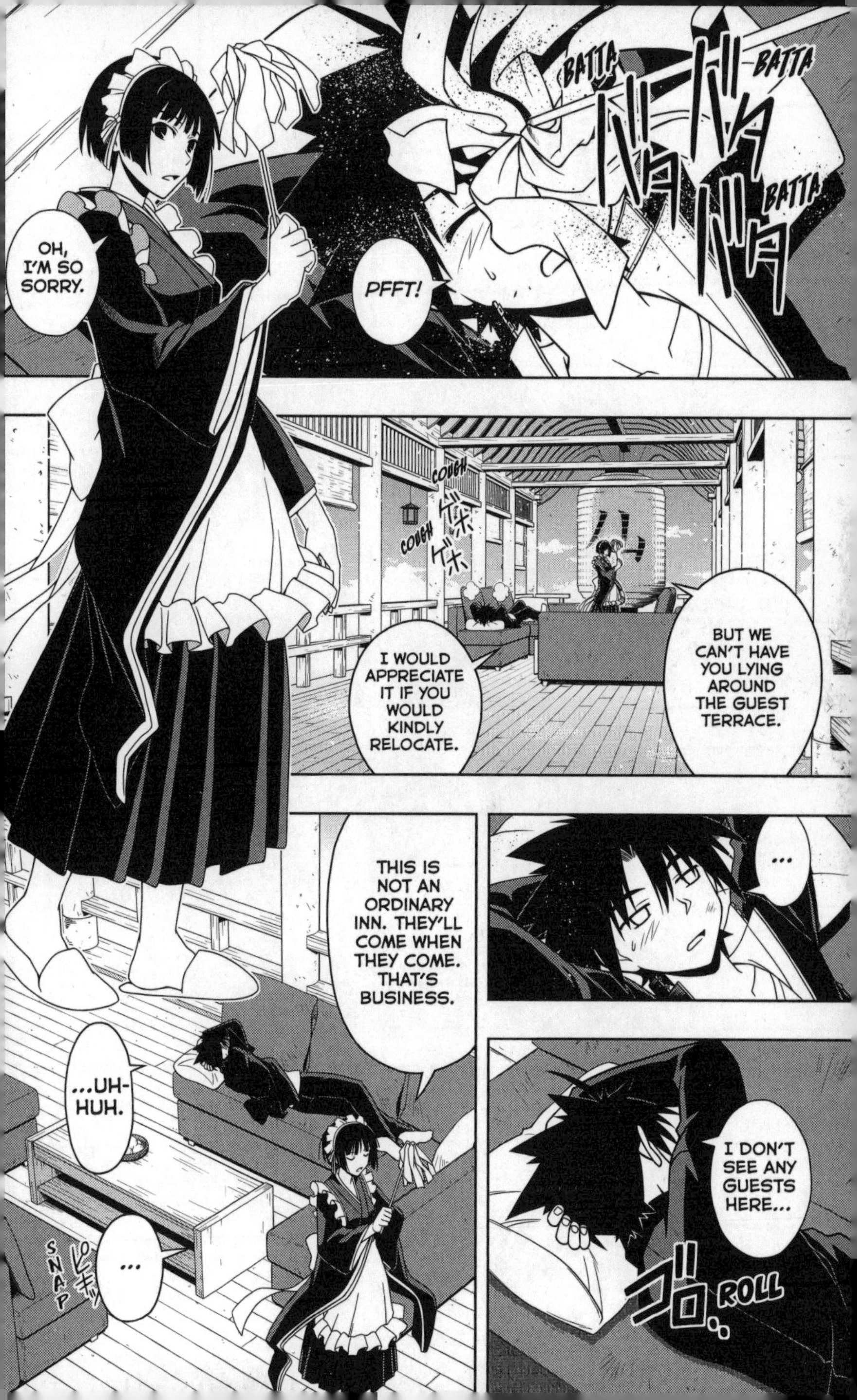
BATTA
バタバタ
BATTA
バタバタ
BATTA
PFFT!
OH, I'M SO SORRY.
BUT WE CAN'T HAVE YOU LYING AROUND THE GUEST TERRACE.
COUGH
ゲホ
COUGH
ゲホ
I WOULD APPRECIATE IT IF YOU WOULD KINDLY RELOCATE.
...
I DON'T SEE ANY GUESTS HERE...
ゴロ
ROLL
THIS IS NOT AN ORDINARY INN. THEY'LL COME WHEN THEY COME. THAT'S BUSINESS.
...UH-HUH.
...
ピキッ
SNAP

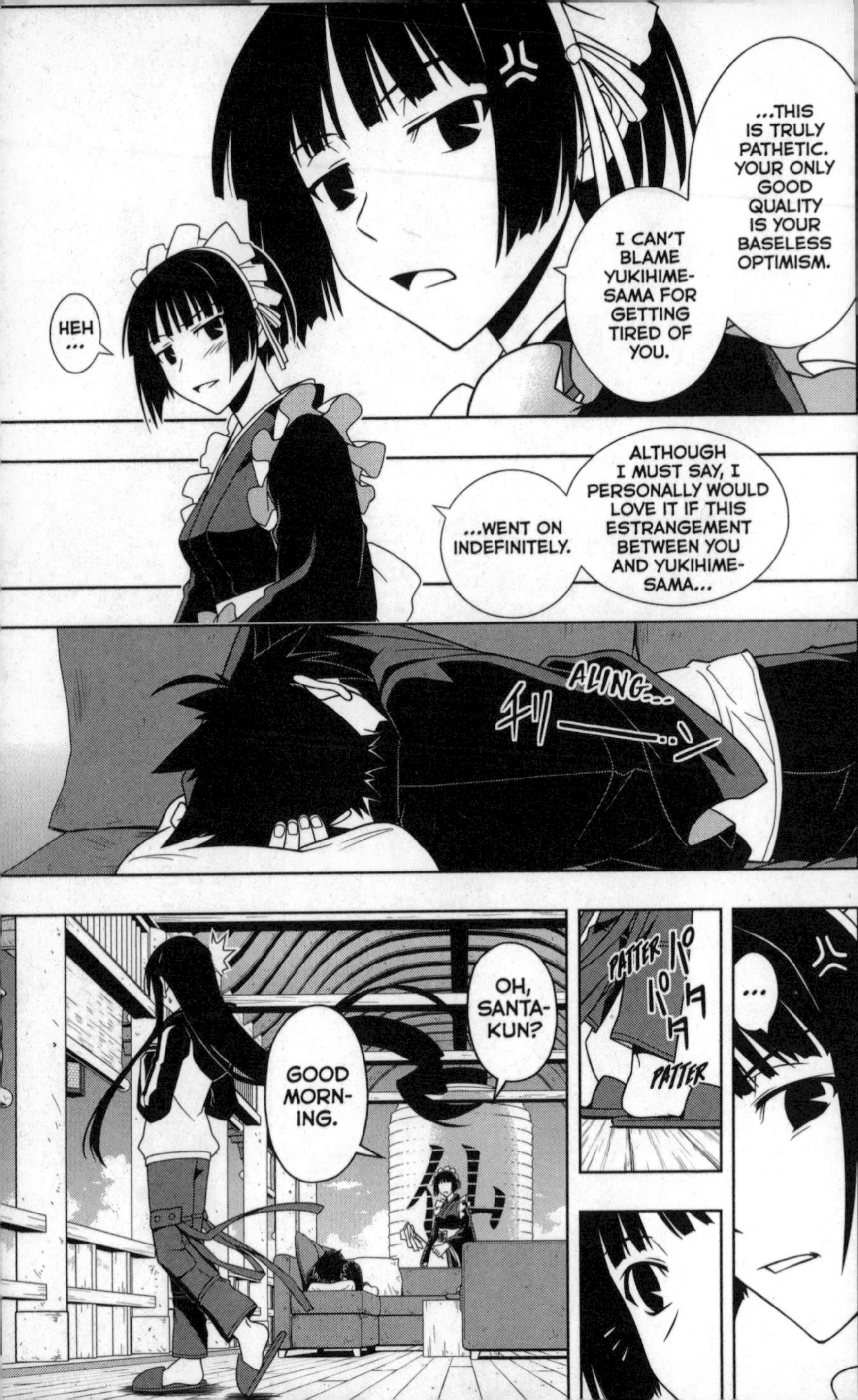
...THIS IS TRULY PATHETIC. YOUR ONLY GOOD QUALITY IS YOUR BASELESS OPTIMISM.
I CAN'T BLAME YUKIHIME-SAMA FOR GETTING TIRED OF YOU.
HEH...
ALTHOUGH I MUST SAY, I PERSONALLY WOULD LOVE IT IF THIS ESTRANGEMENT BETWEEN YOU AND YUKIHIME-SAMA...
...WENT ON INDEFINITELY.
ALING...
チリーン
...
PATTER
パタ
パタ
PATTER
OH, SANTA-KUN?
GOOD MORN-ING.

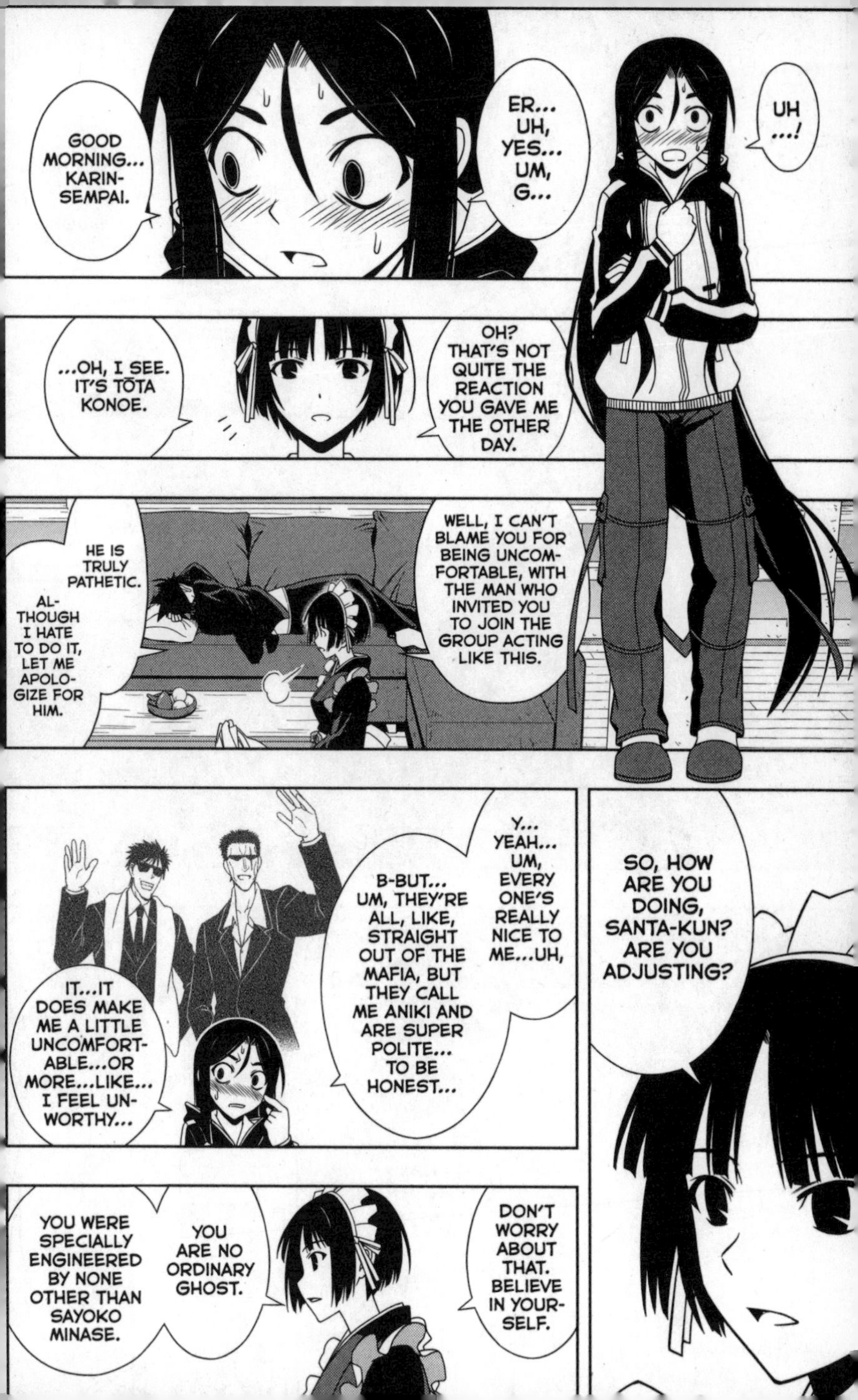
UH ...!
ER... UH, YES... UM, G...
GOOD MORNING... KARIN-SEMPAI.
OH? THAT'S NOT QUITE THE REACTION YOU GAVE ME THE OTHER DAY.
...OH, I SEE. IT'S TŌTA KONOE.
WELL, I CAN'T BLAME YOU FOR BEING UNCOM-FORTABLE, WITH THE MAN WHO INVITED YOU TO JOIN THE GROUP ACTING LIKE THIS.
HE IS TRULY PATHETIC.
AL-THOUGH I HATE TO DO IT, LET ME APOLO-GIZE FOR HIM.
SO, HOW ARE YOU DOING, SANTA-KUN? ARE YOU ADJUSTING?
Y... YEAH... UM, EVERY ONE'S REALLY NICE TO ME...UH,
B-BUT... UM, THEY'RE ALL, LIKE, STRAIGHT OUT OF THE MAFIA, BUT THEY CALL ME ANIKI AND ARE SUPER POLITE... TO BE HONEST...
IT...IT DOES MAKE ME A LITTLE UNCOMFORT-ABLE...OR MORE...LIKE... I FEEL UN-WORTHY...
DON'T WORRY ABOUT THAT. BELIEVE IN YOUR-SELF.
YOU ARE NO ORDINARY GHOST.
YOU WERE SPECIALLY ENGINEERED BY NONE OTHER THAN SAYOKO MINASE.

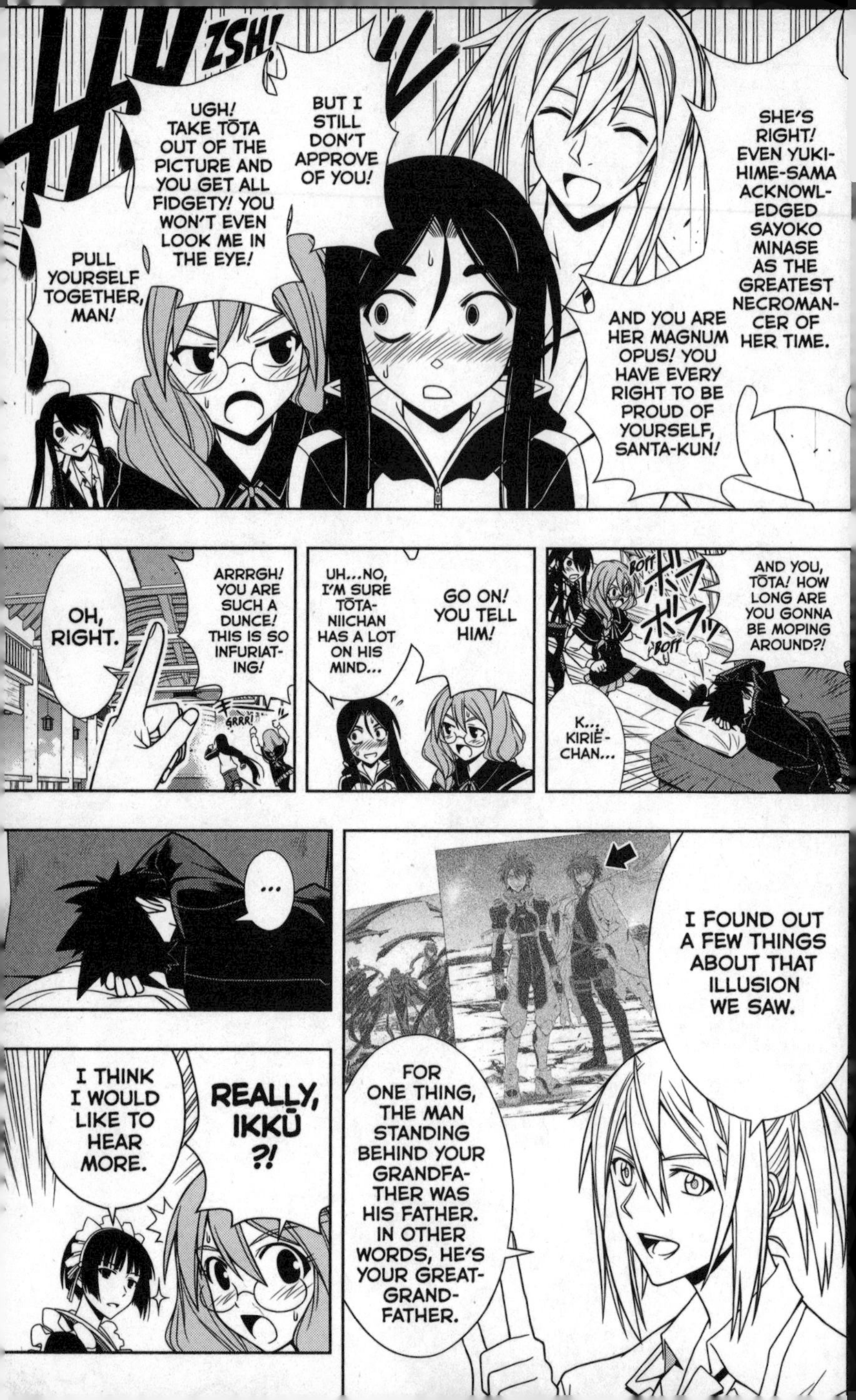
ZSH!
SHE'S RIGHT! EVEN YUKI-HIME-SAMA ACKNOWL-EDGED SAYOKO MINASE AS THE GREATEST NECROMAN-CER OF HER TIME.
AND YOU ARE HER MAGNUM OPUS! YOU HAVE EVERY RIGHT TO BE PROUD OF YOURSELF, SANTA-KUN!
BUT I STILL DON'T APPROVE OF YOU!
UGH! TAKE TŌTA OUT OF THE PICTURE AND YOU GET ALL FIDGETY! YOU WON'T EVEN LOOK ME IN THE EYE!
PULL YOURSELF TOGETHER, MAN!
AND YOU, TŌTA! HOW LONG ARE YOU GONNA BE MOPING AROUND?!
BOFF
BOFF
K... KIRIE-CHAN...
GO ON! YOU TELL HIM!
UH...NO, I'M SURE TŌTA-NIICHAN HAS A LOT ON HIS MIND...
ARRRGH! YOU ARE SUCH A DUNCE! THIS IS SO INFURIAT-ING!
OH, RIGHT.
GRRR!
I FOUND OUT A FEW THINGS ABOUT THAT ILLUSION WE SAW.
FOR ONE THING, THE MAN STANDING BEHIND YOUR GRANDFA-THER WAS HIS FATHER. IN OTHER WORDS, HE'S YOUR GREAT-GRAND-FATHER.
...
REALLY, IKKŪ?!
I THINK I WOULD LIKE TO HEAR MORE.

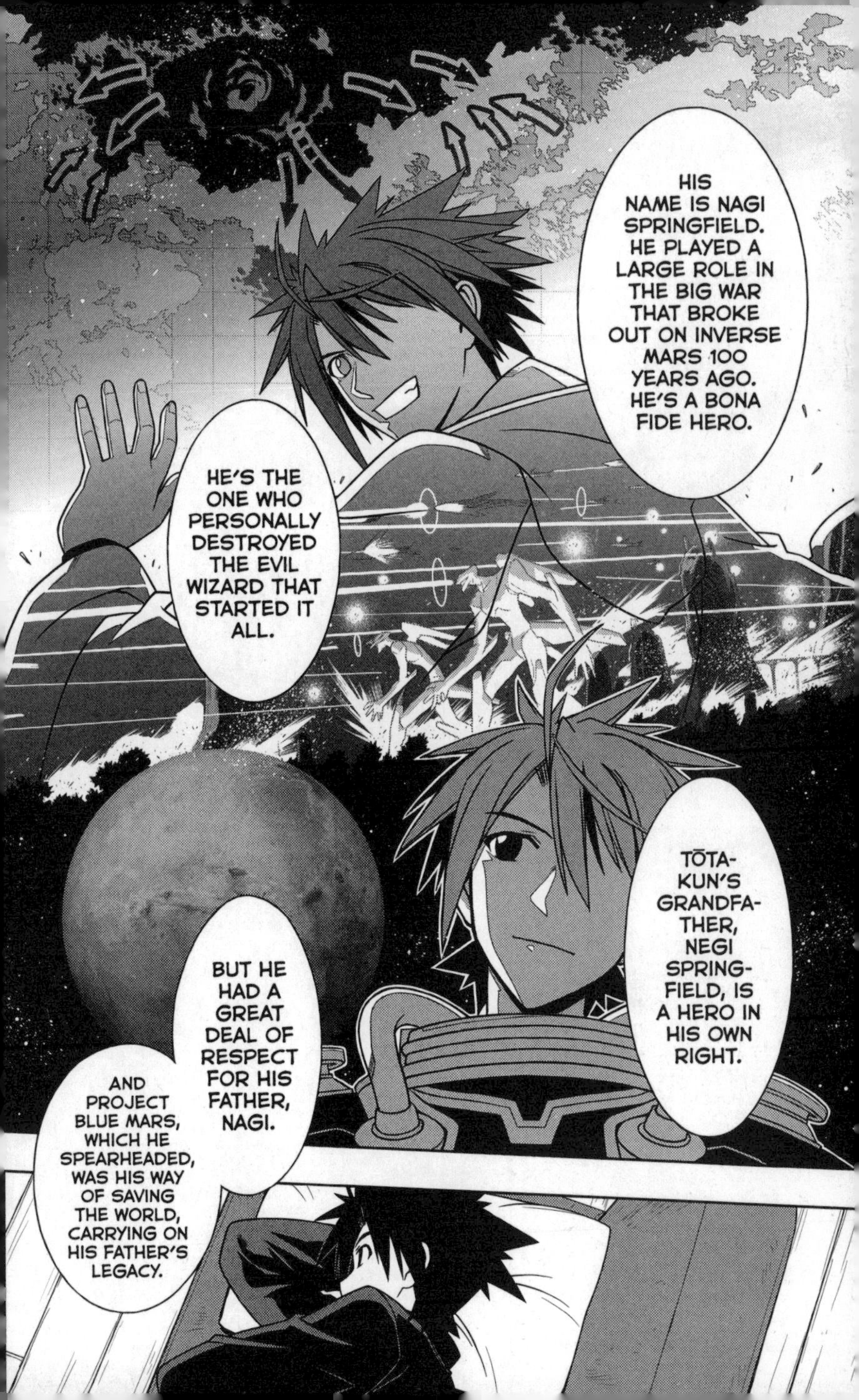
HIS NAME IS NAGI SPRINGFIELD. HE PLAYED A LARGE ROLE IN THE BIG WAR THAT BROKE OUT ON INVERSE MARS 100 YEARS AGO. HE'S A BONA FIDE HERO.
HE'S THE ONE WHO PERSONALLY DESTROYED THE EVIL WIZARD THAT STARTED IT ALL.
TŌTA-KUN'S GRANDFATHER, NEGI SPRINGFIELD, IS A HERO IN HIS OWN RIGHT.
BUT HE HAD A GREAT DEAL OF RESPECT FOR HIS FATHER, NAGI.
AND PROJECT BLUE MARS, WHICH HE SPEARHEADED, WAS HIS WAY OF SAVING THE WORLD, CARRYING ON HIS FATHER'S LEGACY.

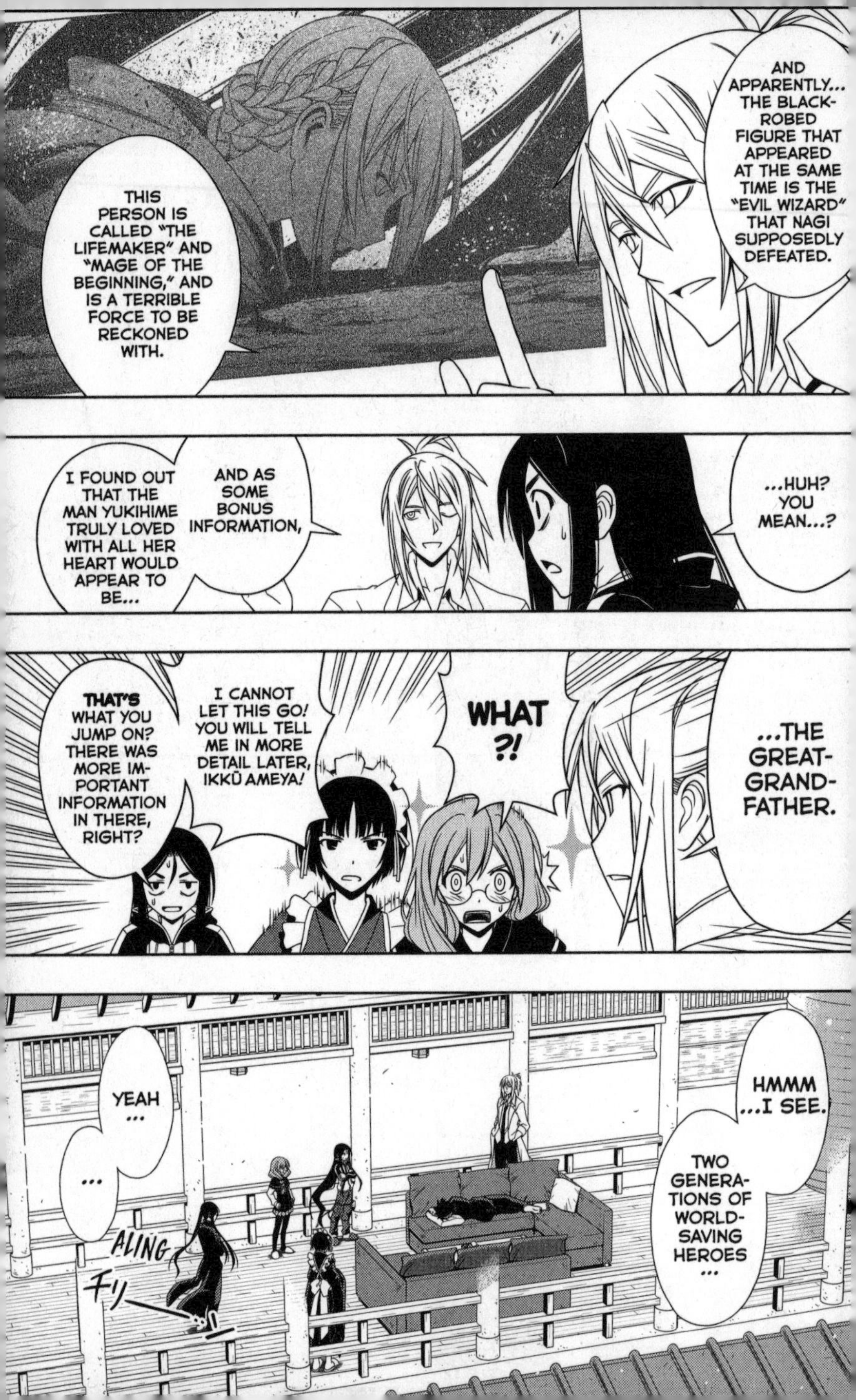
AND APPARENTLY... THE BLACK-ROBED FIGURE THAT APPEARED AT THE SAME TIME IS THE "EVIL WIZARD" THAT NAGI SUPPOSEDLY DEFEATED.
THIS PERSON IS CALLED "THE LIFEMAKER" AND "MAGE OF THE BEGINNING," AND IS A TERRIBLE FORCE TO BE RECKONED WITH.
...HUH? YOU MEAN...?
AND AS SOME BONUS INFORMATION,
I FOUND OUT THAT THE MAN YUKIHIME TRULY LOVED WITH ALL HER HEART WOULD APPEAR TO BE...
...THE GREAT-GRANDFATHER.
WHAT ?!
I CANNOT LET THIS GO! YOU WILL TELL ME IN MORE DETAIL LATER, IKKŪ AMEYA!
THAT'S WHAT YOU JUMP ON? THERE WAS MORE IM-PORTANT INFORMATION IN THERE, RIGHT?
HMMM ...I SEE.
TWO GENERA-TIONS OF WORLD-SAVING HEROES ...
YEAH ...
...
ALING
チリ

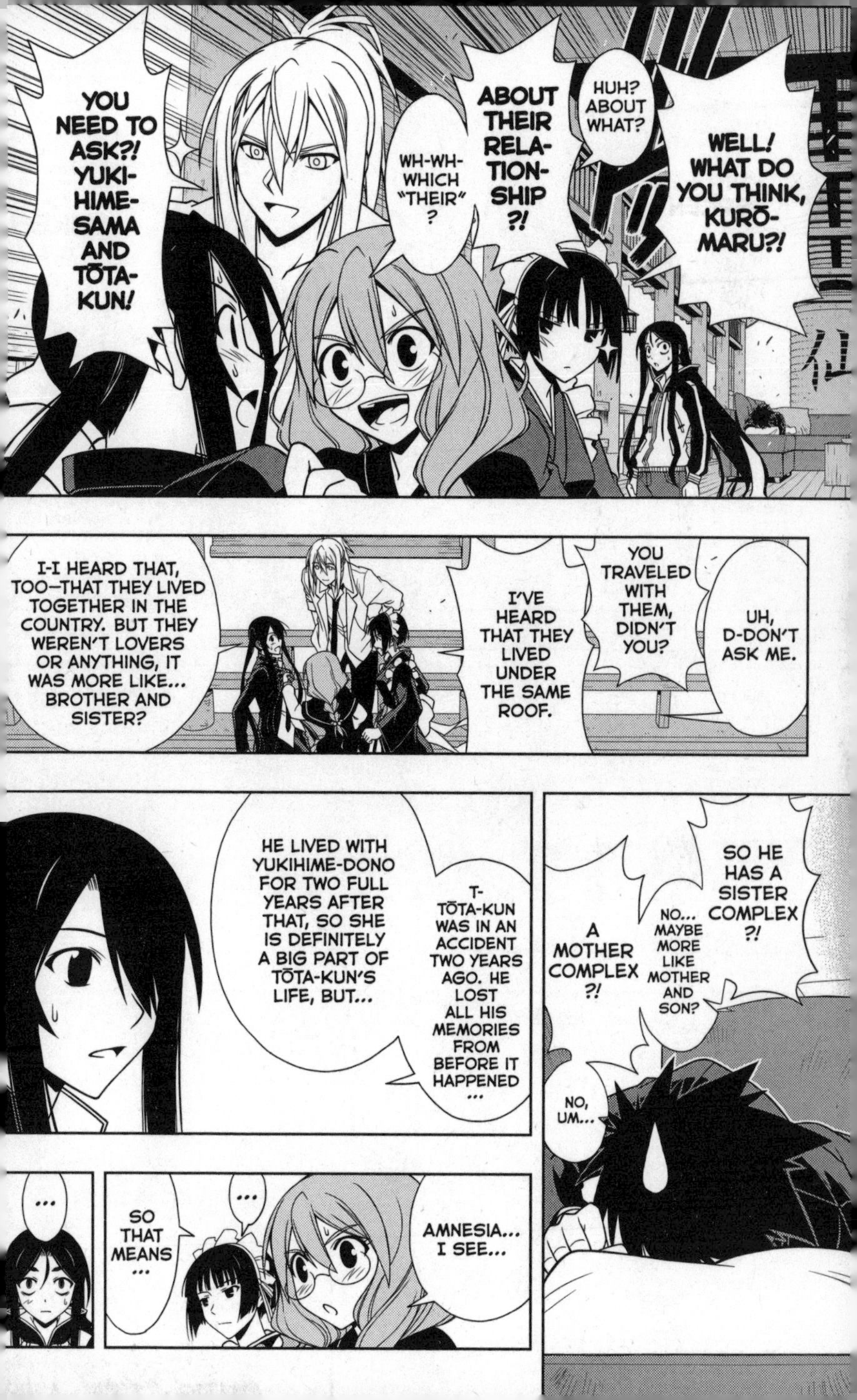

WELL! WHAT DO YOU THINK, KURŌ-MARU?!
HUH? ABOUT WHAT?
ABOUT THEIR RELA-TION-SHIP?!
WH-WH-WHICH "THEIR"?
YOU NEED TO ASK?! YUKI-HIME-SAMA AND TŌTA-KUN!
UH, D-DON'T ASK ME.
YOU TRAVELED WITH THEM, DIDN'T YOU?
I'VE HEARD THAT THEY LIVED UNDER THE SAME ROOF.
I-I HEARD THAT, TOO—THAT THEY LIVED TOGETHER IN THE COUNTRY. BUT THEY WEREN'T LOVERS OR ANYTHING, IT WAS MORE LIKE... BROTHER AND SISTER?
SO HE HAS A SISTER COMPLEX?!
NO... MAYBE MORE LIKE MOTHER AND SON?
A MOTHER COMPLEX?!
NO, UM...
T-TŌTA-KUN WAS IN AN ACCIDENT TWO YEARS AGO. HE LOST ALL HIS MEMORIES FROM BEFORE IT HAPPENED...
HE LIVED WITH YUKIHIME-DONO FOR TWO FULL YEARS AFTER THAT, SO SHE IS DEFINITELY A BIG PART OF TŌTA-KUN'S LIFE, BUT...
AMNESIA... I SEE...
...
SO THAT MEANS...
...

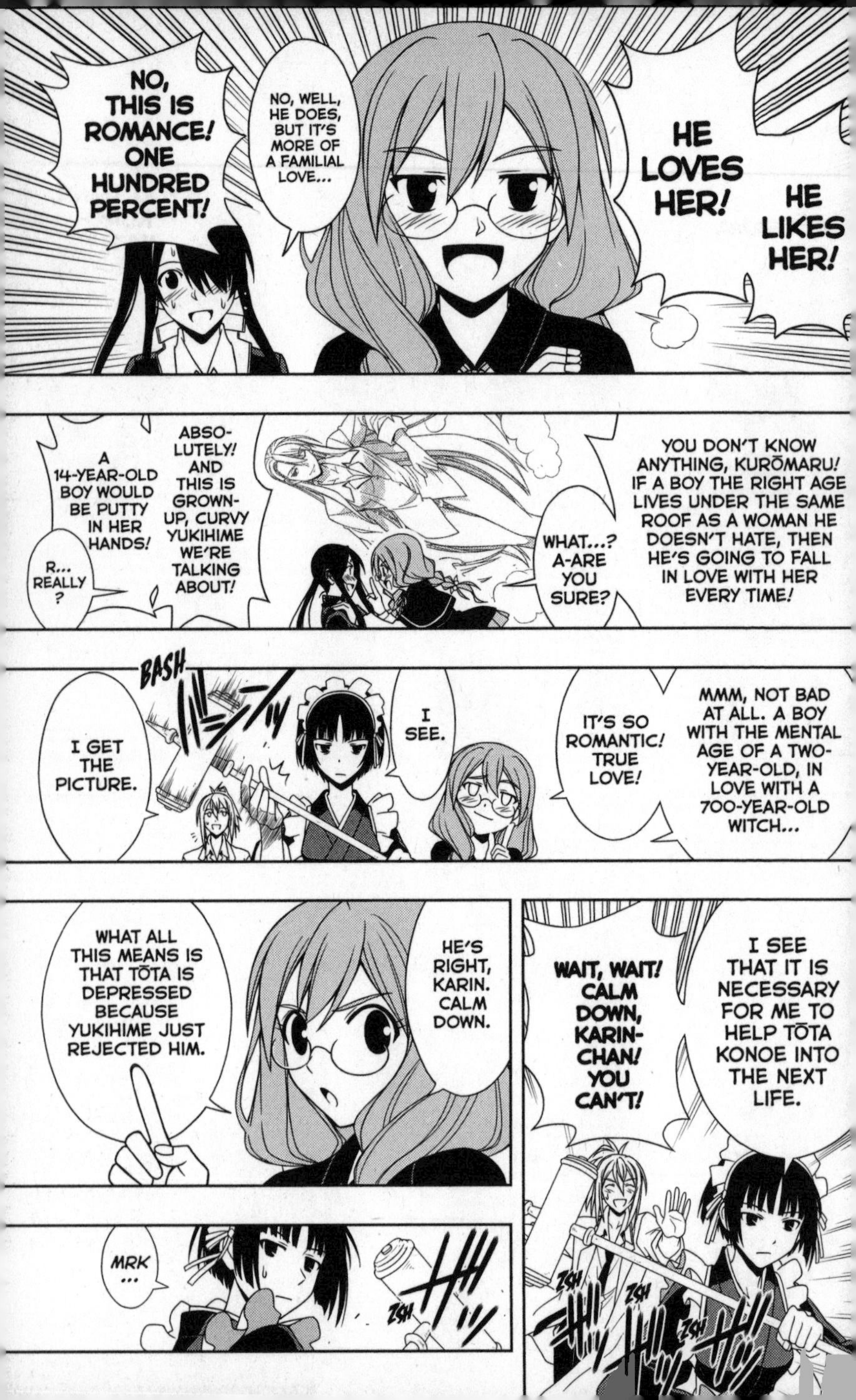
HE LIKES HER!
HE LOVES HER!
NO, WELL, HE DOES, BUT IT'S MORE OF A FAMILIAL LOVE...
NO, THIS IS ROMANCE! ONE HUNDRED PERCENT!
YOU DON'T KNOW ANYTHING, KURŌMARU! IF A BOY THE RIGHT AGE LIVES UNDER THE SAME ROOF AS A WOMAN HE DOESN'T HATE, THEN HE'S GOING TO FALL IN LOVE WITH HER EVERY TIME!
WHAT...? A-ARE YOU SURE?
ABSO-LUTELY! AND THIS IS GROWN-UP, CURVY YUKIHIME WE'RE TALKING ABOUT!
A 14-YEAR-OLD BOY WOULD BE PUTTY IN HER HANDS!
R... REALLY?
MMM, NOT BAD AT ALL. A BOY WITH THE MENTAL AGE OF A TWO-YEAR-OLD, IN LOVE WITH A 700-YEAR-OLD WITCH...
IT'S SO ROMANTIC! TRUE LOVE!
I SEE.
BASH
I GET THE PICTURE.
I SEE THAT IT IS NECESSARY FOR ME TO HELP TŌTA KONOE INTO THE NEXT LIFE.
WAIT, WAIT! CALM DOWN, KARIN-CHAN! YOU CAN'T!
ZSH
ZSH
ZSH
HE'S RIGHT, KARIN. CALM DOWN.
WHAT ALL THIS MEANS IS THAT TŌTA IS DEPRESSED BECAUSE YUKIHIME JUST REJECTED HIM.
MRK...
ZSH

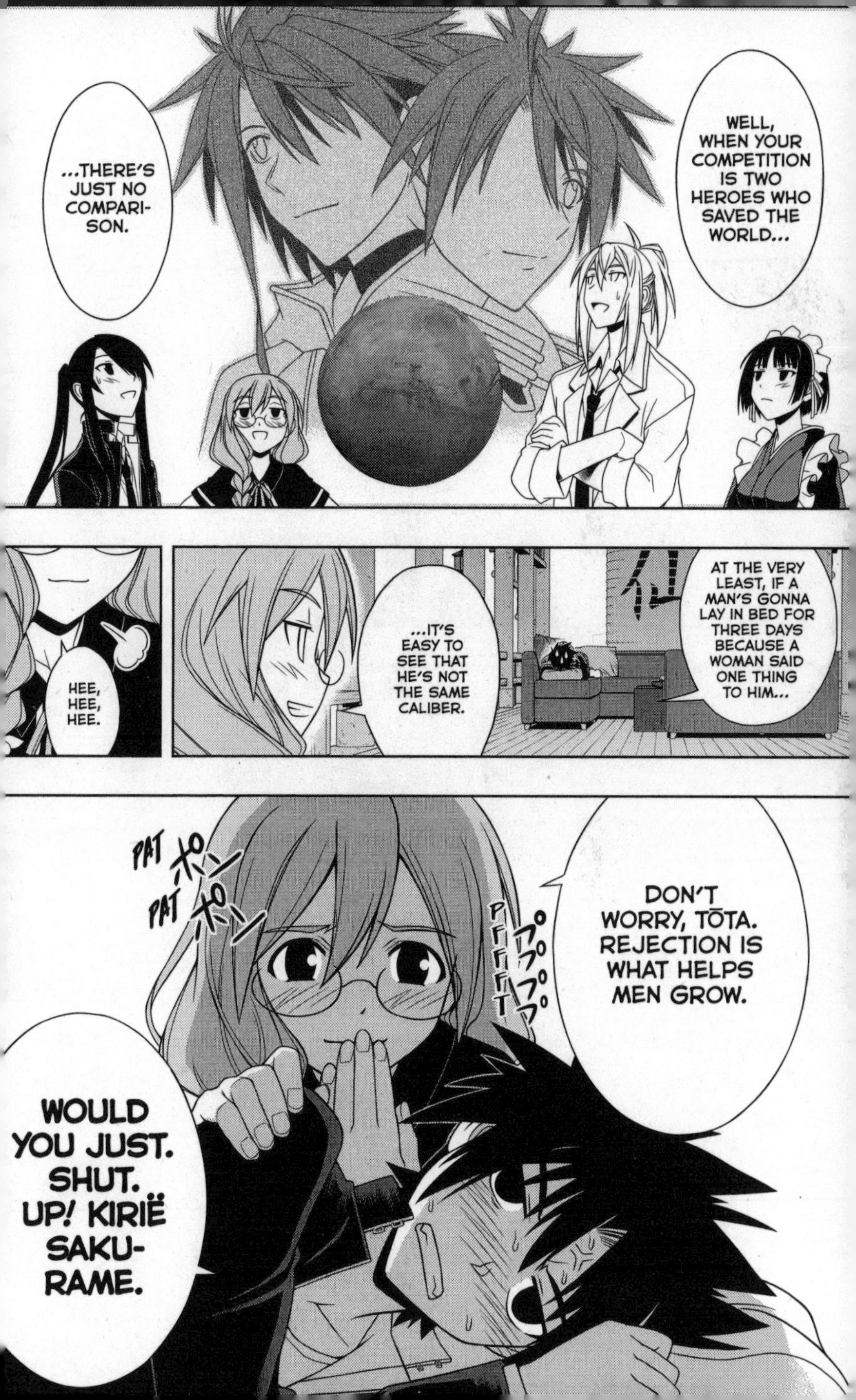
WELL, WHEN YOUR COMPETITION IS TWO HEROES WHO SAVED THE WORLD...
...THERE'S JUST NO COMPARISON.
AT THE VERY LEAST, IF A MAN'S GONNA LAY IN BED FOR THREE DAYS BECAUSE A WOMAN SAID ONE THING TO HIM...
...IT'S EASY TO SEE THAT HE'S NOT THE SAME CALIBER.
HEE, HEE, HEE.
DON'T WORRY, TŌTA. REJECTION IS WHAT HELPS MEN GROW.
PFFFT
PAT PAT
WOULD YOU JUST. SHUT. UP! KIRIË SAKURAME.

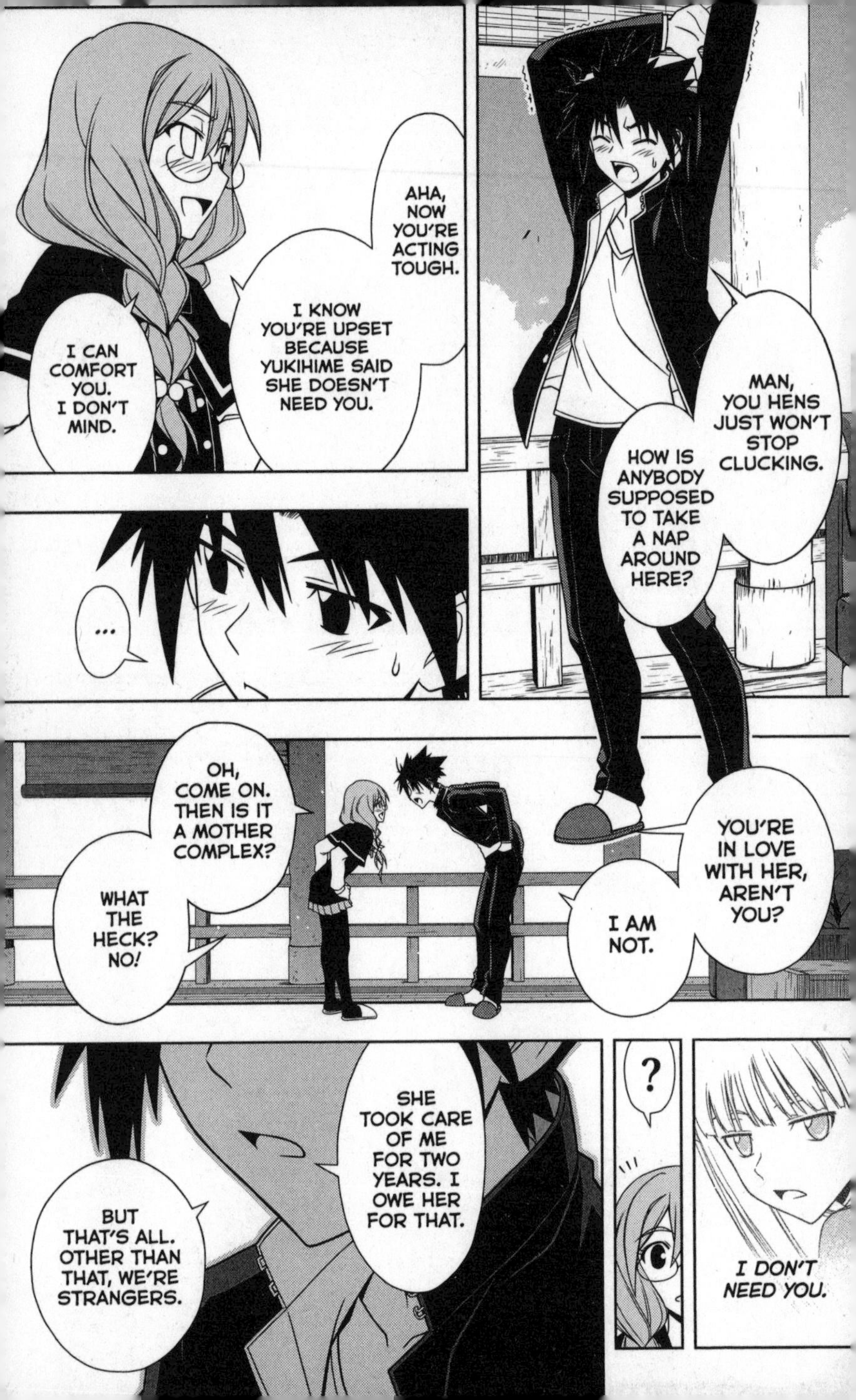
MAN, YOU HENS JUST WON'T STOP CLUCKING.
HOW IS ANYBODY SUPPOSED TO TAKE A NAP AROUND HERE?
AHA, NOW YOU'RE ACTING TOUGH.
I KNOW YOU'RE UPSET BECAUSE YUKIHIME SAID SHE DOESN'T NEED YOU.
I CAN COMFORT YOU. I DON'T MIND.
...
YOU'RE IN LOVE WITH HER, AREN'T YOU?
I AM NOT.
OH, COME ON. THEN IS IT A MOTHER COMPLEX?
WHAT THE HECK? NO!
I DON'T NEED YOU.
?
SHE TOOK CARE OF ME FOR TWO YEARS. I OWE HER FOR THAT.
BUT THAT'S ALL. OTHER THAN THAT, WE'RE STRANGERS.

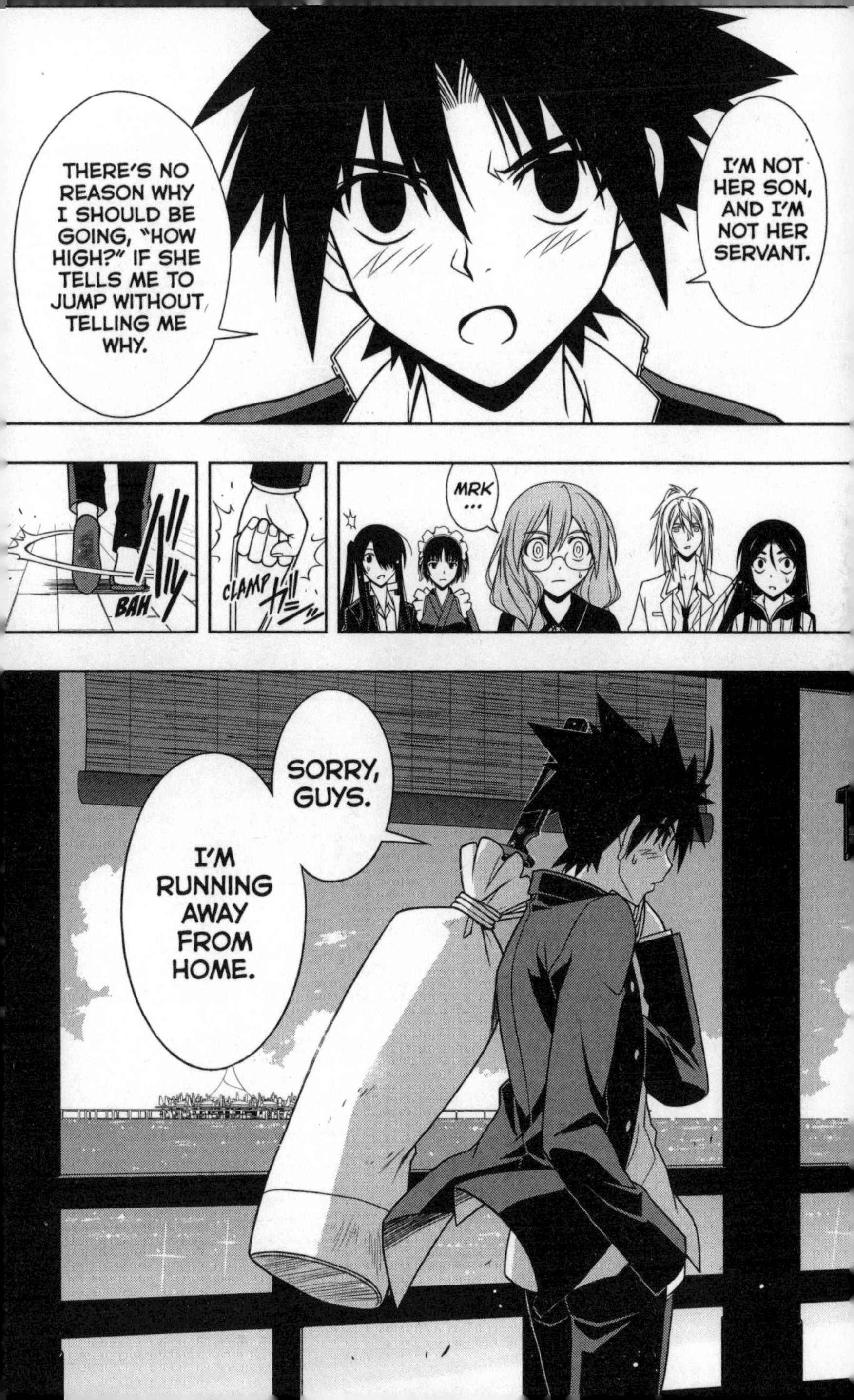
I'M NOT HER SON, AND I'M NOT HER SERVANT.
THERE'S NO REASON WHY I SHOULD BE GOING, "HOW HIGH?" IF SHE TELLS ME TO JUMP WITHOUT TELLING ME WHY.
MRK ...
CLAMP
BAH
SORRY, GUYS.
I'M RUNNING AWAY FROM HOME.

UQ HOLDER!

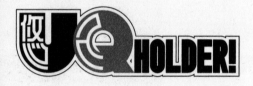

UQ HOLDER!

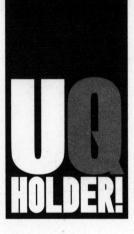

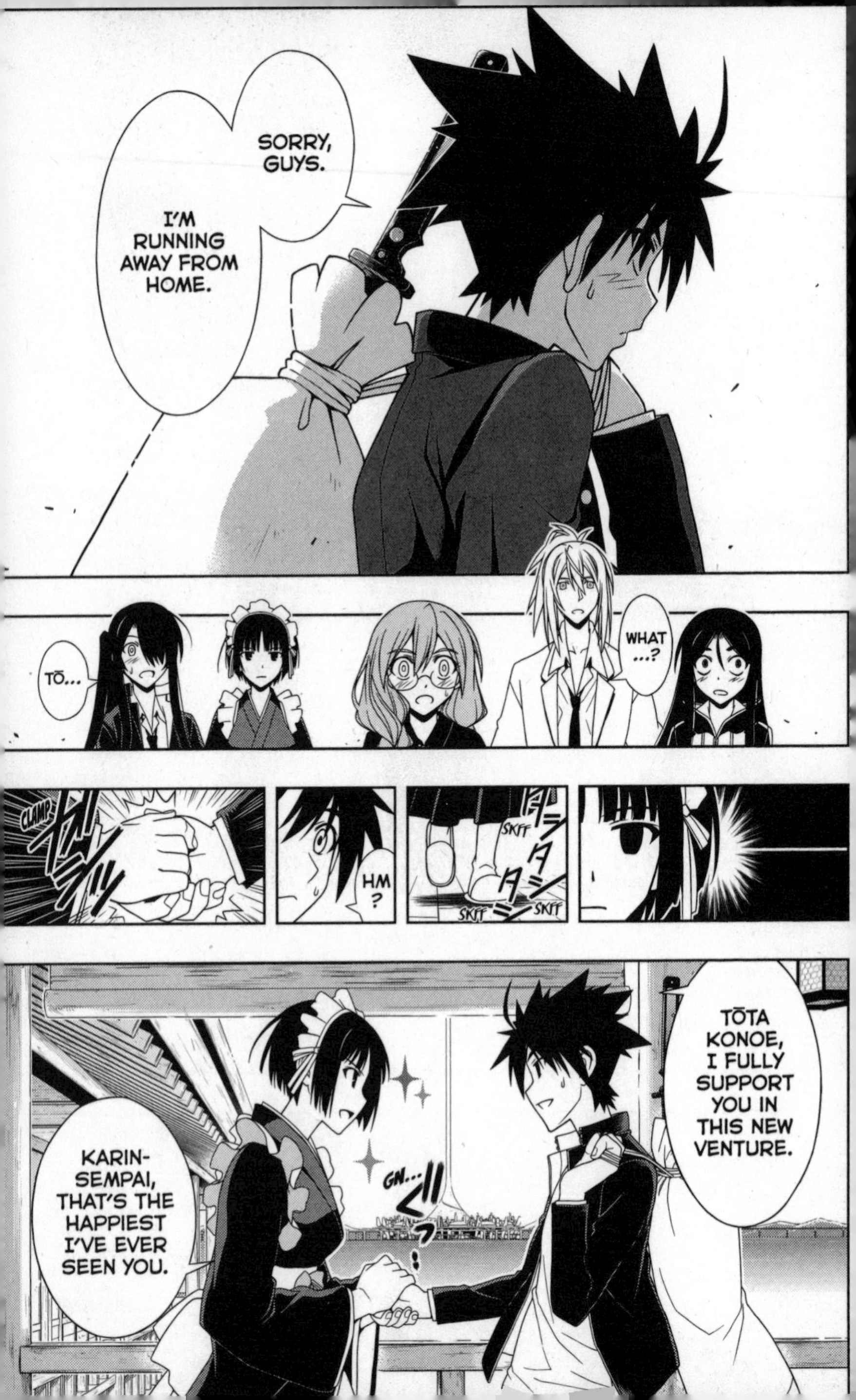
SORRY, GUYS.
I'M RUNNING AWAY FROM HOME.
WHAT ...?
TŌ...
SKFF
SKFF
SKFF
HM ?
CLAMP
TŌTA KONOE, I FULLY SUPPORT YOU IN THIS NEW VENTURE.
GN...!!
KARIN-SEMPAI, THAT'S THE HAPPIEST I'VE EVER SEEN YOU.

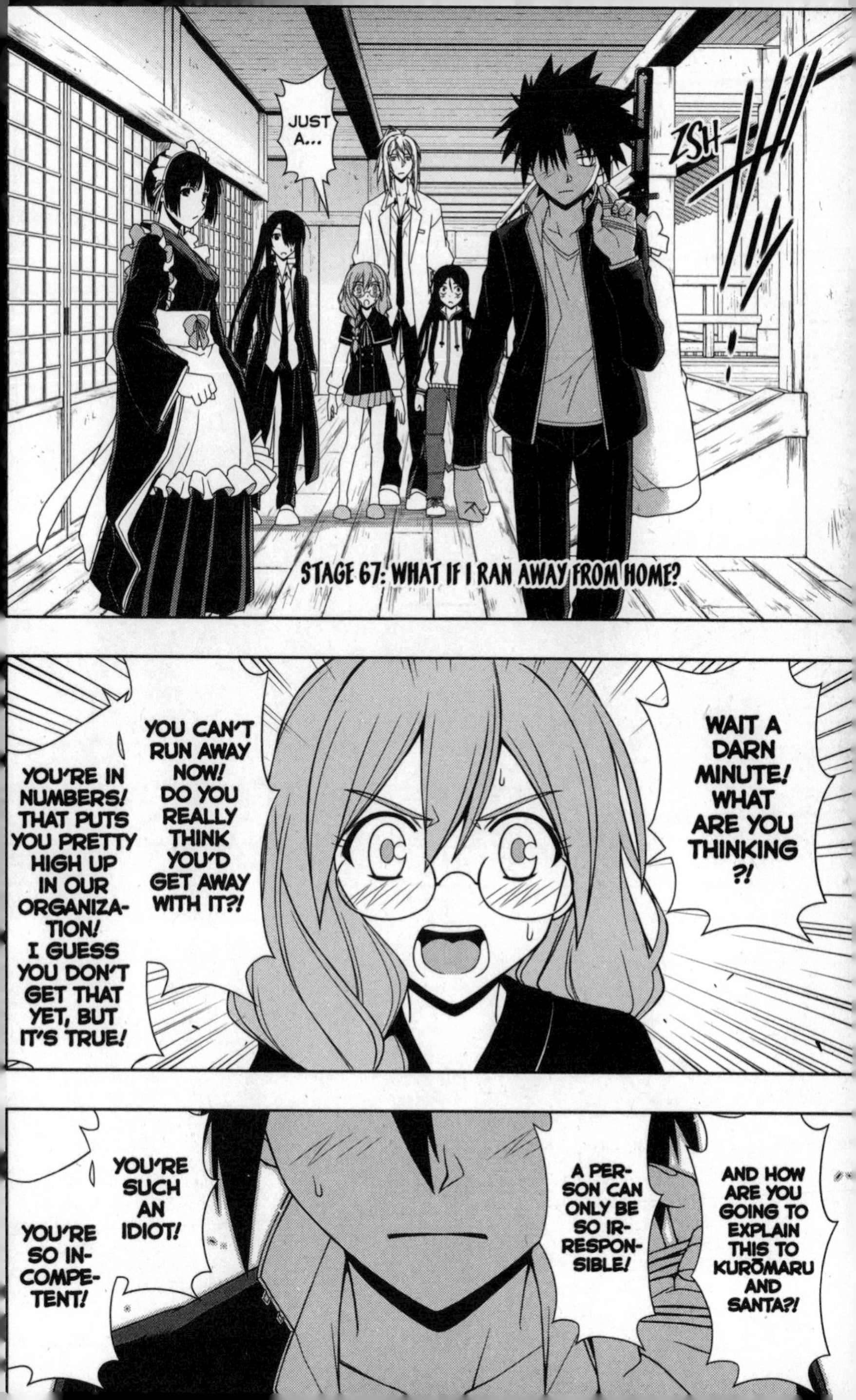
ZSH-!!!
JUST A...
STAGE 67: WHAT IF I RAN AWAY FROM HOME?
WAIT A DARN MINUTE! WHAT ARE YOU THINKING?!
YOU CAN'T RUN AWAY NOW! DO YOU REALLY THINK YOU'D GET AWAY WITH IT?!
YOU'RE IN NUMBERS! THAT PUTS YOU PRETTY HIGH UP IN OUR ORGANIZATION! I GUESS YOU DON'T GET THAT YET, BUT IT'S TRUE!
AND HOW ARE YOU GOING TO EXPLAIN THIS TO KURŌMARU AND SANTA?!
A PERSON CAN ONLY BE SO IRRESPONSIBLE!
YOU'RE SUCH AN IDIOT!
YOU'RE SO INCOMPETENT!

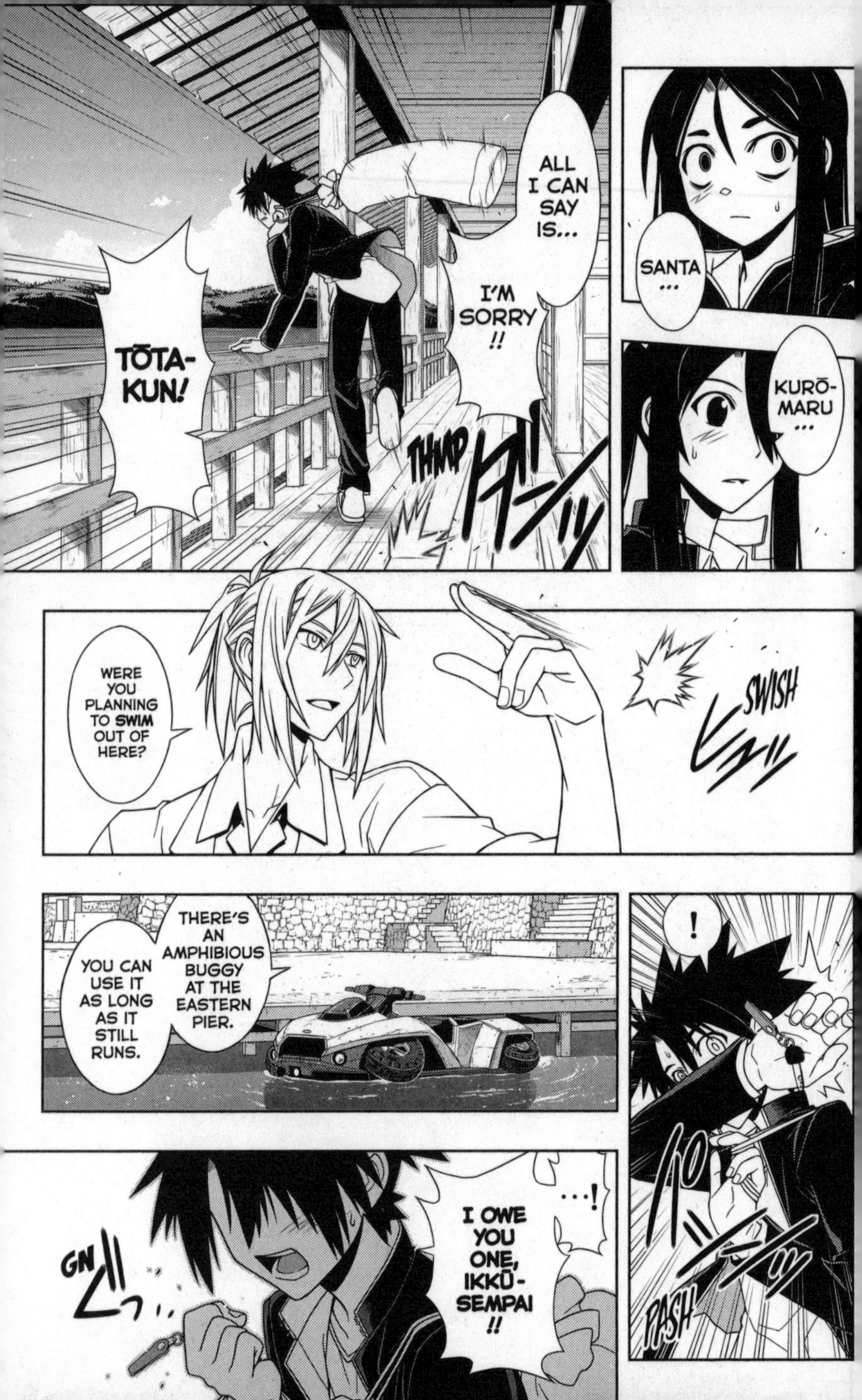
SANTA...
KURŌMARU...
ALL I CAN SAY IS...
I'M SORRY!!
THMP
TŌTA-KUN!
SWISH
WERE YOU PLANNING TO SWIM OUT OF HERE?
!
PASH
THERE'S AN AMPHIBIOUS BUGGY AT THE EASTERN PIER.
YOU CAN USE IT AS LONG AS IT STILL RUNS.
...!
I OWE YOU ONE, IKKŪ-SEMPAI!!
GN

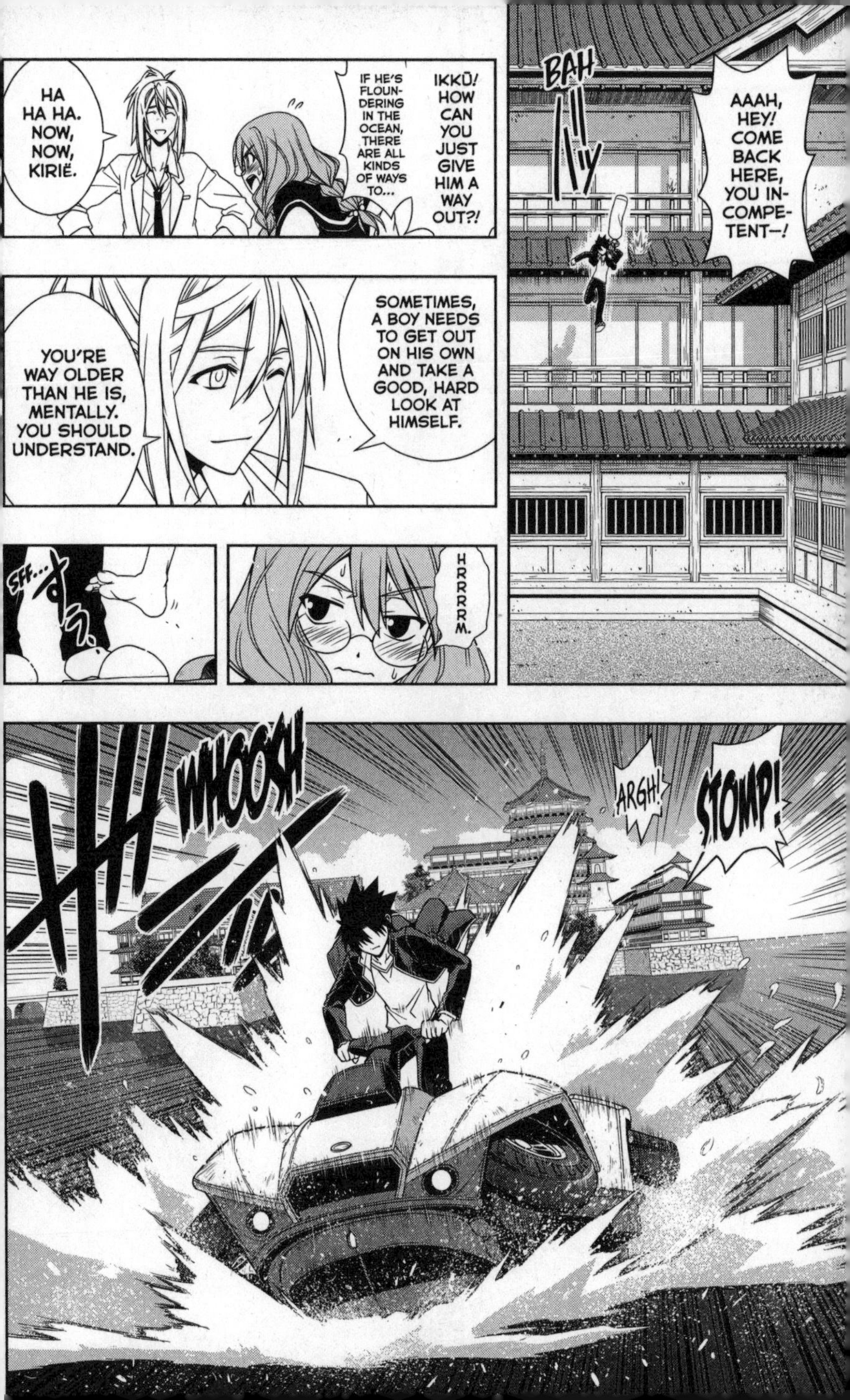
AAAH, HEY! COME BACK HERE, YOU INCOMPE-TENT–!
BAH
IKKŪ! HOW CAN YOU JUST GIVE HIM A WAY OUT?!
IF HE'S FLOUN-DERING IN THE OCEAN, THERE ARE ALL KINDS OF WAYS TO...
HA HA HA. NOW, NOW, KIRIË.
SOMETIMES, A BOY NEEDS TO GET OUT ON HIS OWN AND TAKE A GOOD, HARD LOOK AT HIMSELF.
YOU'RE WAY OLDER THAN HE IS, MENTALLY. YOU SHOULD UNDERSTAND.
HRRRRM.
SFF...
STOMP!
ARGH!
WHOOSH

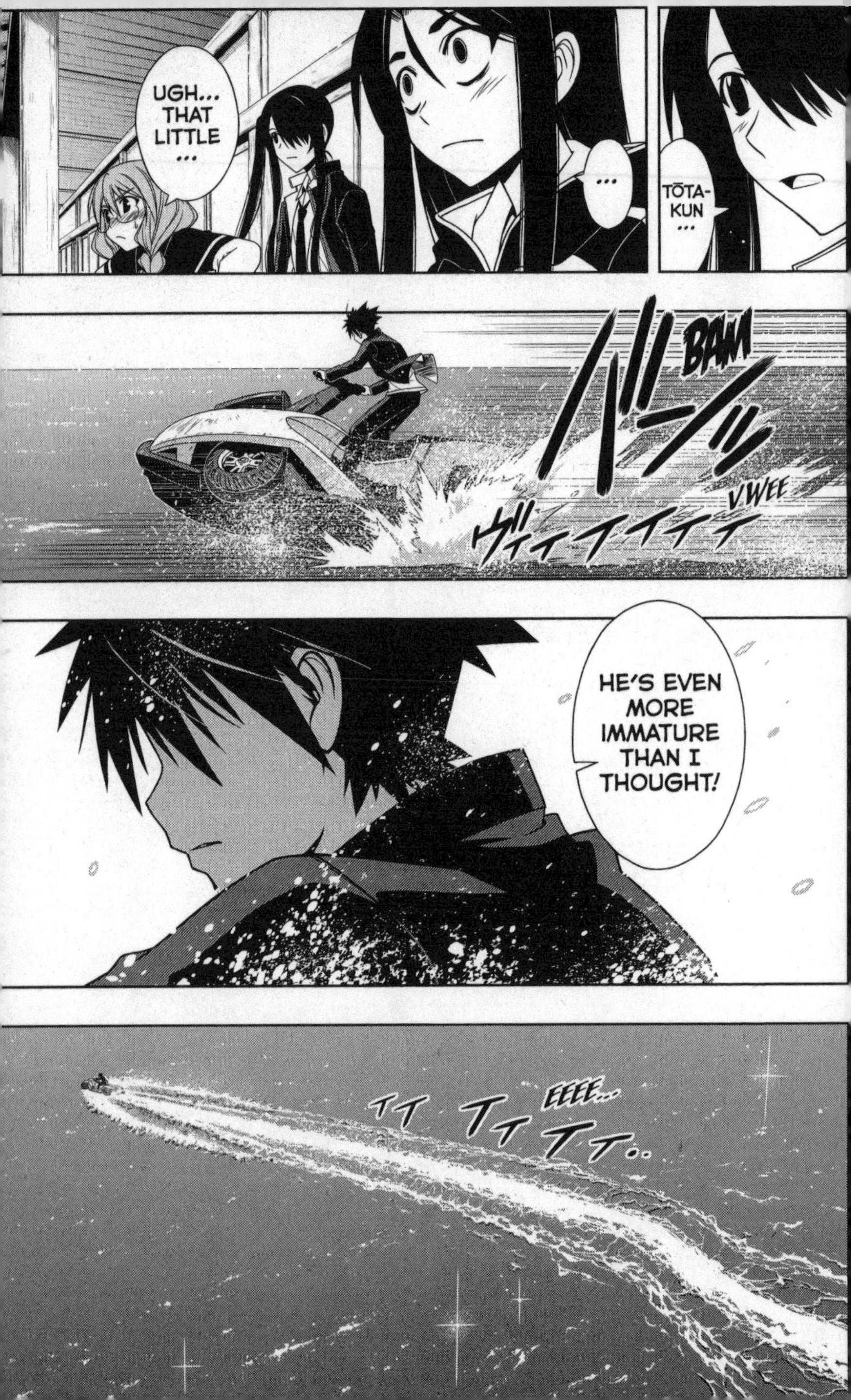
TŌTA-KUN ...
...
UGH... THAT LITTLE ...
BAM
V-WEE
HE'S EVEN MORE IMMATURE THAN I THOUGHT!
EEEE...

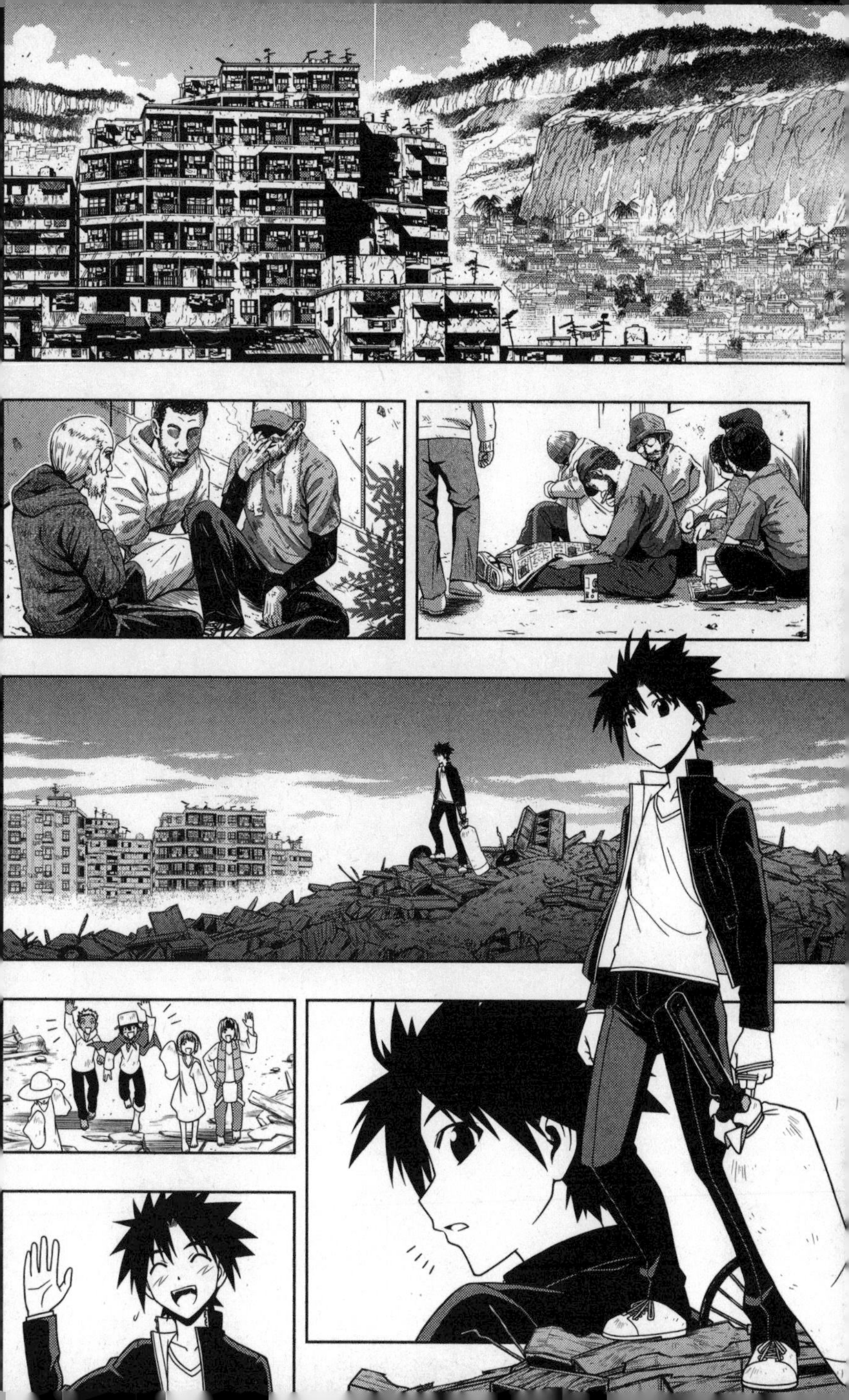

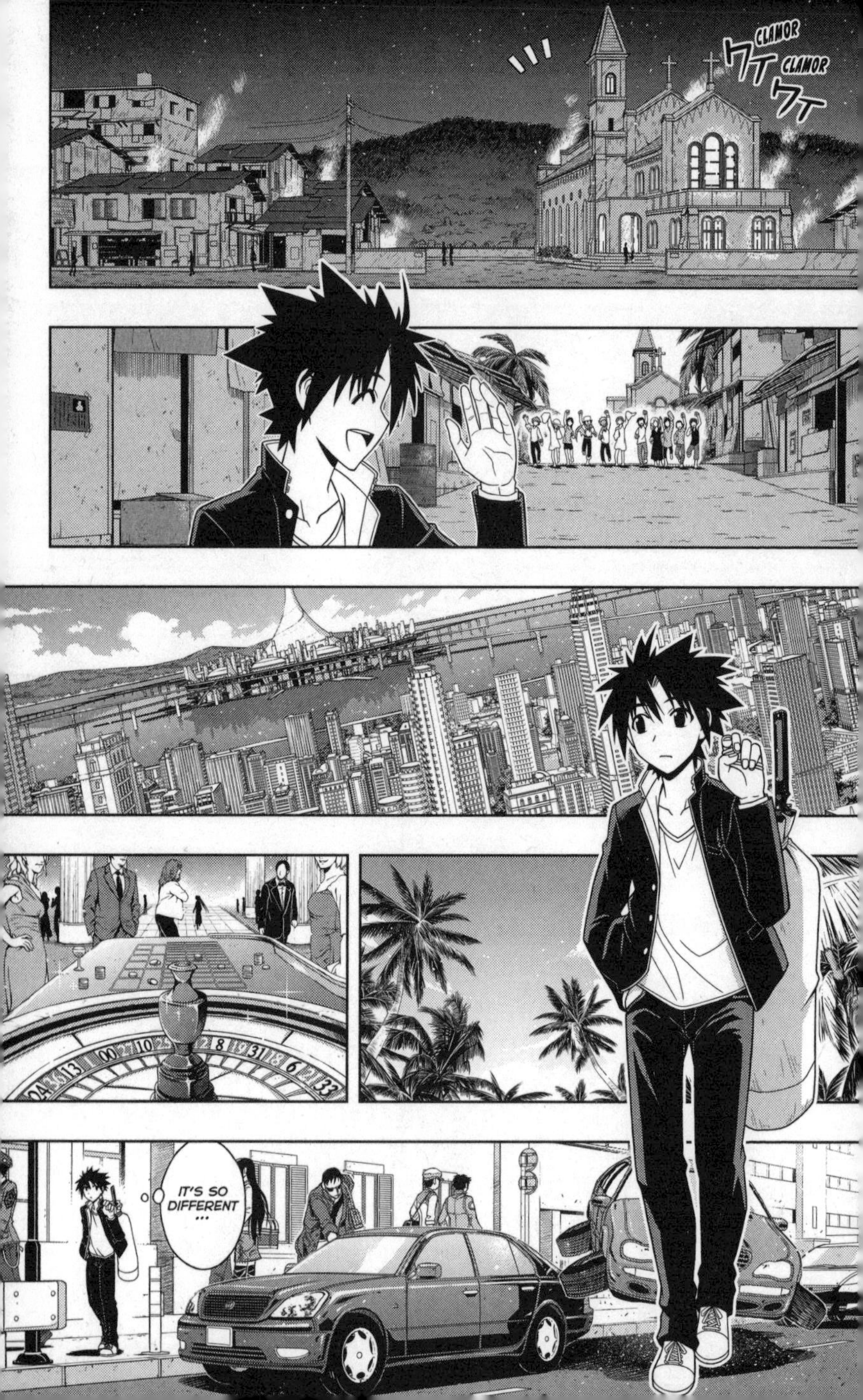
ワイ CLAMOR
ワイ CLAMOR
IT'S SO DIFFERENT ...

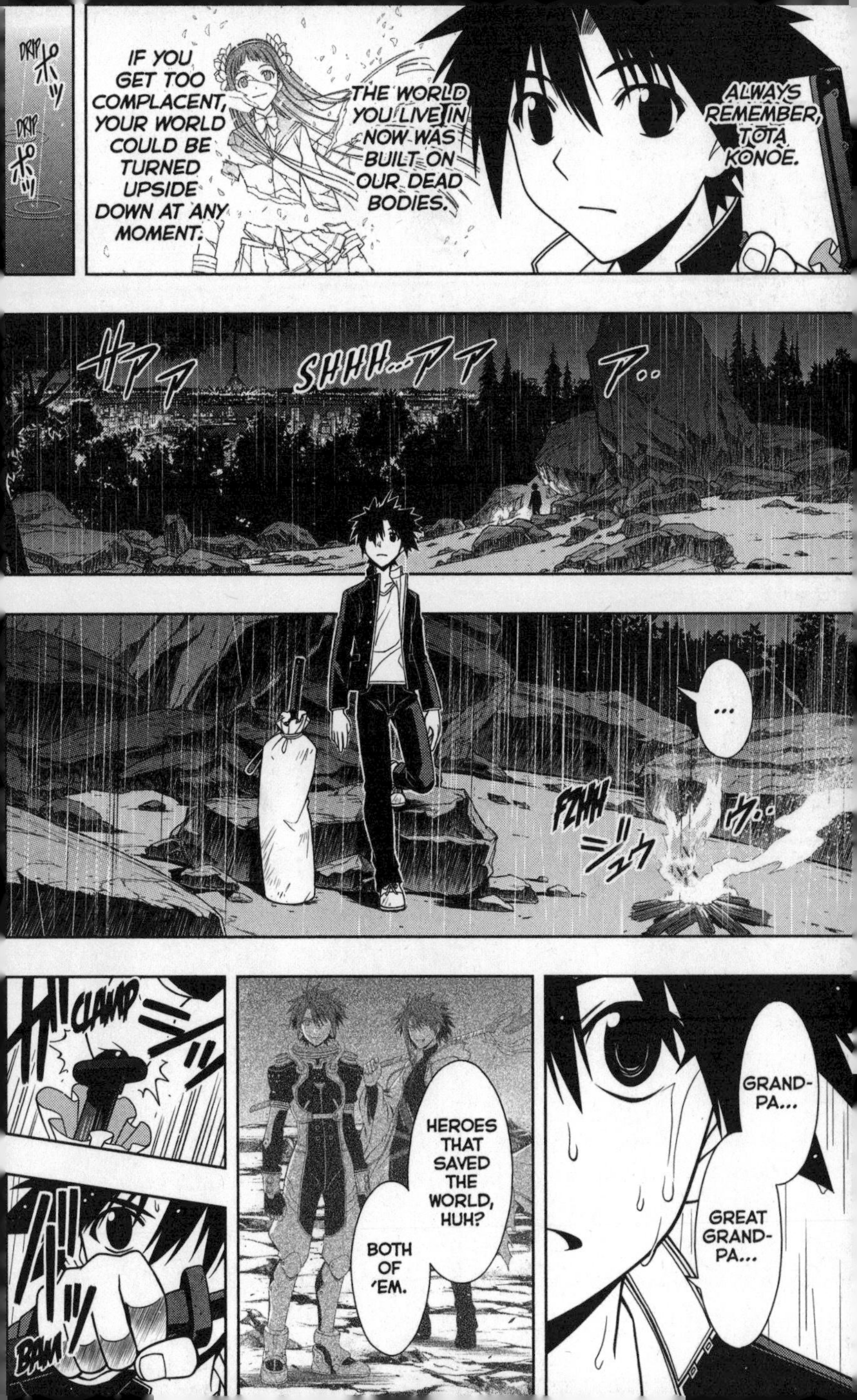
ALWAYS REMEMBER, TOTA KONOE.
THE WORLD YOU LIVE IN NOW WAS BUILT ON OUR DEAD BODIES.
IF YOU GET TOO COMPLACENT, YOUR WORLD COULD BE TURNED UPSIDE DOWN AT ANY MOMENT.
DRIP
DRIP
SHHH...
...
FZHH
GRAND-PA...
GREAT GRAND-PA...
HEROES THAT SAVED THE WORLD, HUH?
BOTH OF 'EM.
CLAMP
BAM

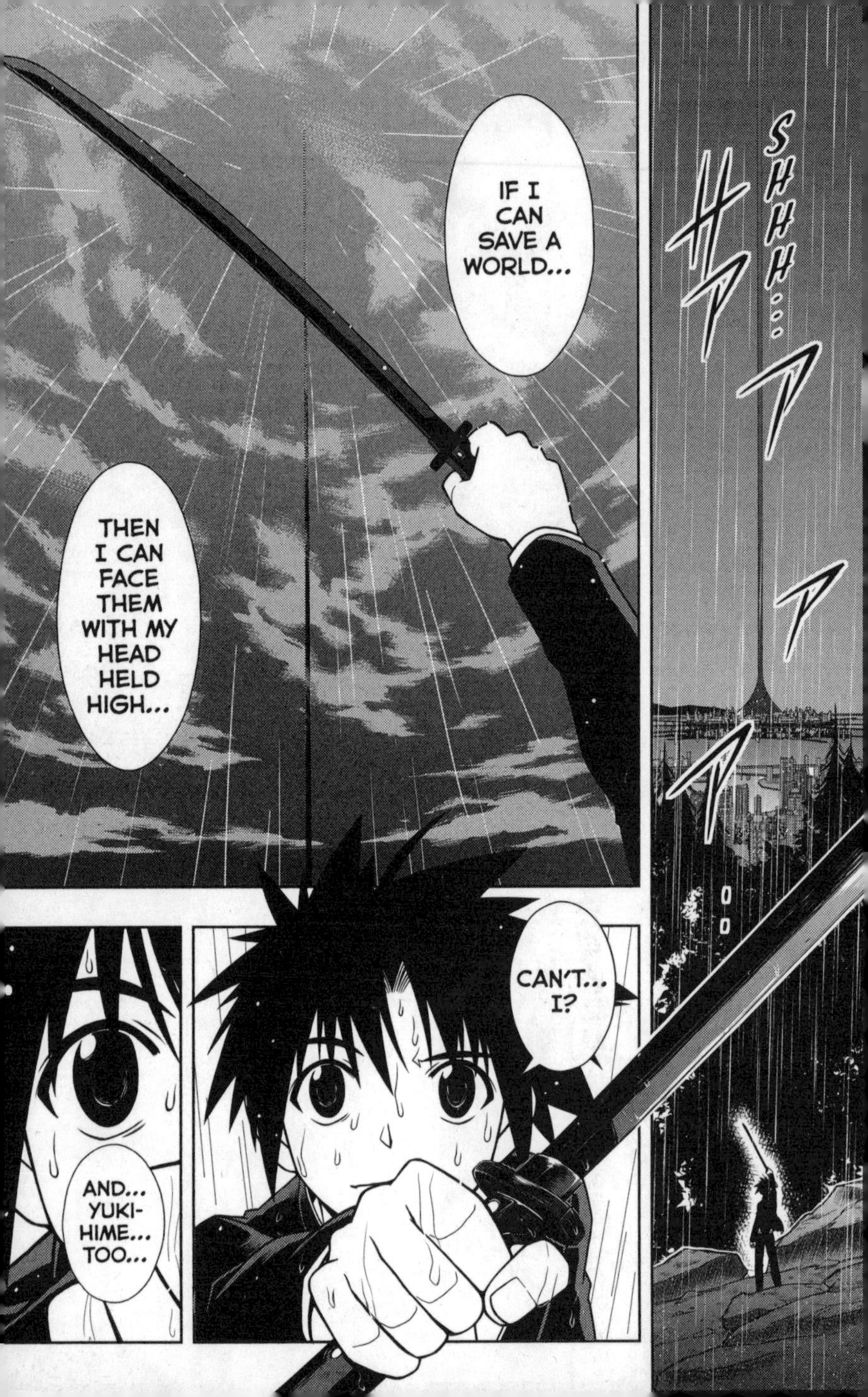
SHHHH...
IF I CAN SAVE A WORLD...
THEN I CAN FACE THEM WITH MY HEAD HELD HIGH...
CAN'T... I?
AND... YUKI-HIME... TOO...

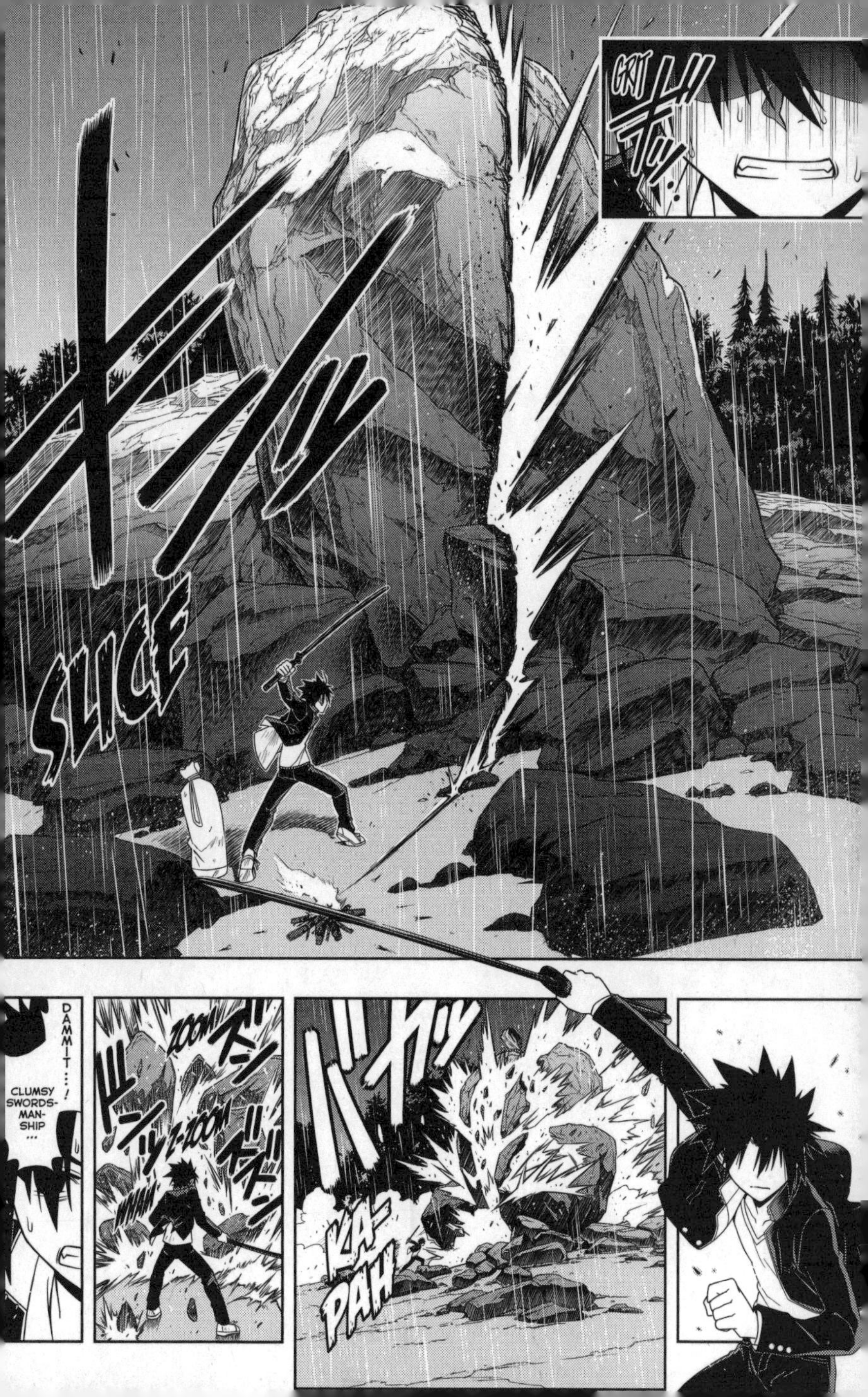
GRIT
SLICE
KA-PAH
ZOOM
Z-ZOOM
DAMMIT...!
CLUMSY SWORDS-MAN-SHIP...

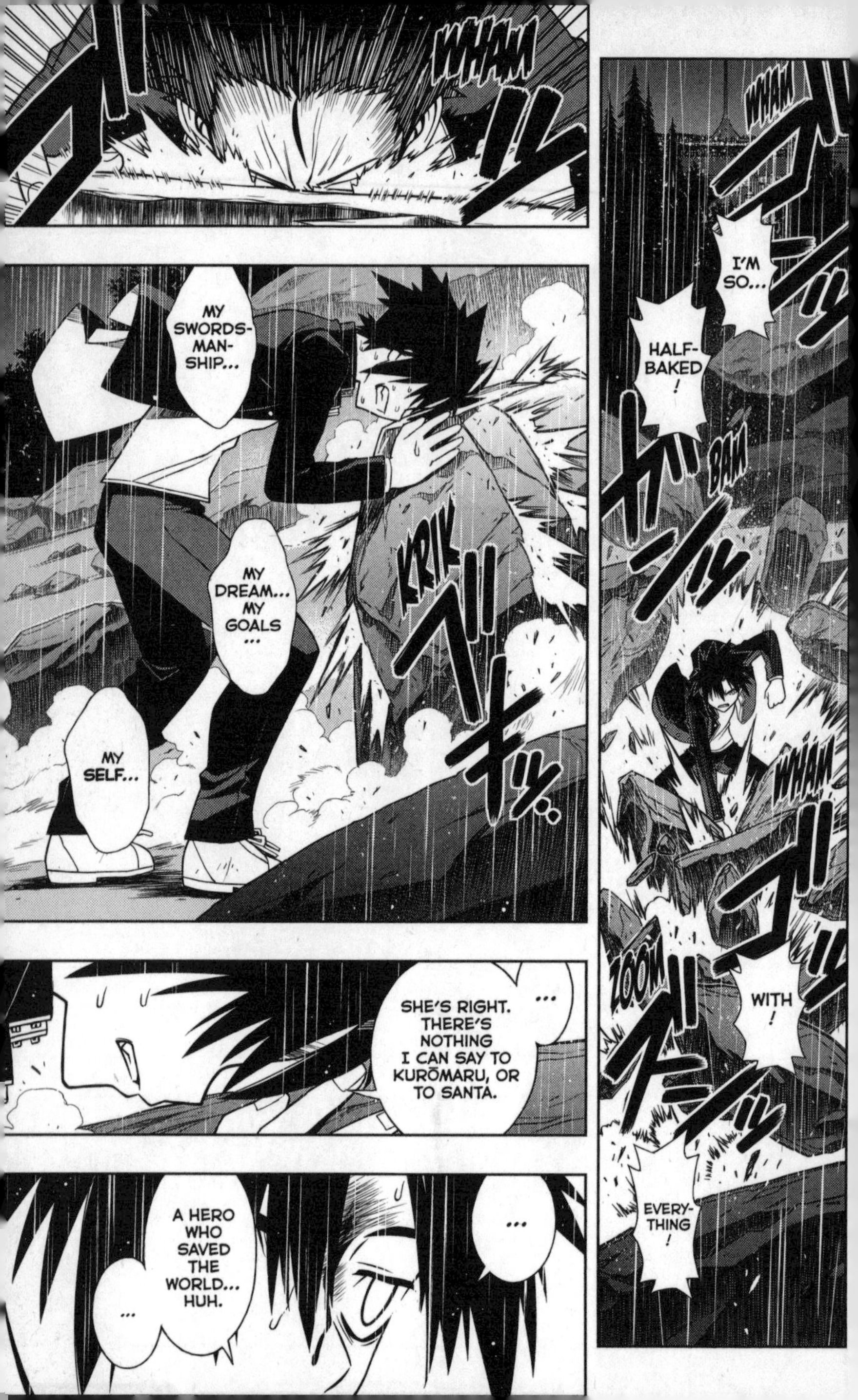
WHAM
I'M SO...
HALF-BAKED!
BAM
WHAM
WITH!
ZOOM
EVERYTHING!
WHAM
MY SWORDS-MAN-SHIP...
KRIK
MY DREAM... MY GOALS...
MY SELF...
...
SHE'S RIGHT. THERE'S NOTHING I CAN SAY TO KURŌMARU, OR TO SANTA.
...
A HERO WHO SAVED THE WORLD... HUH.
...

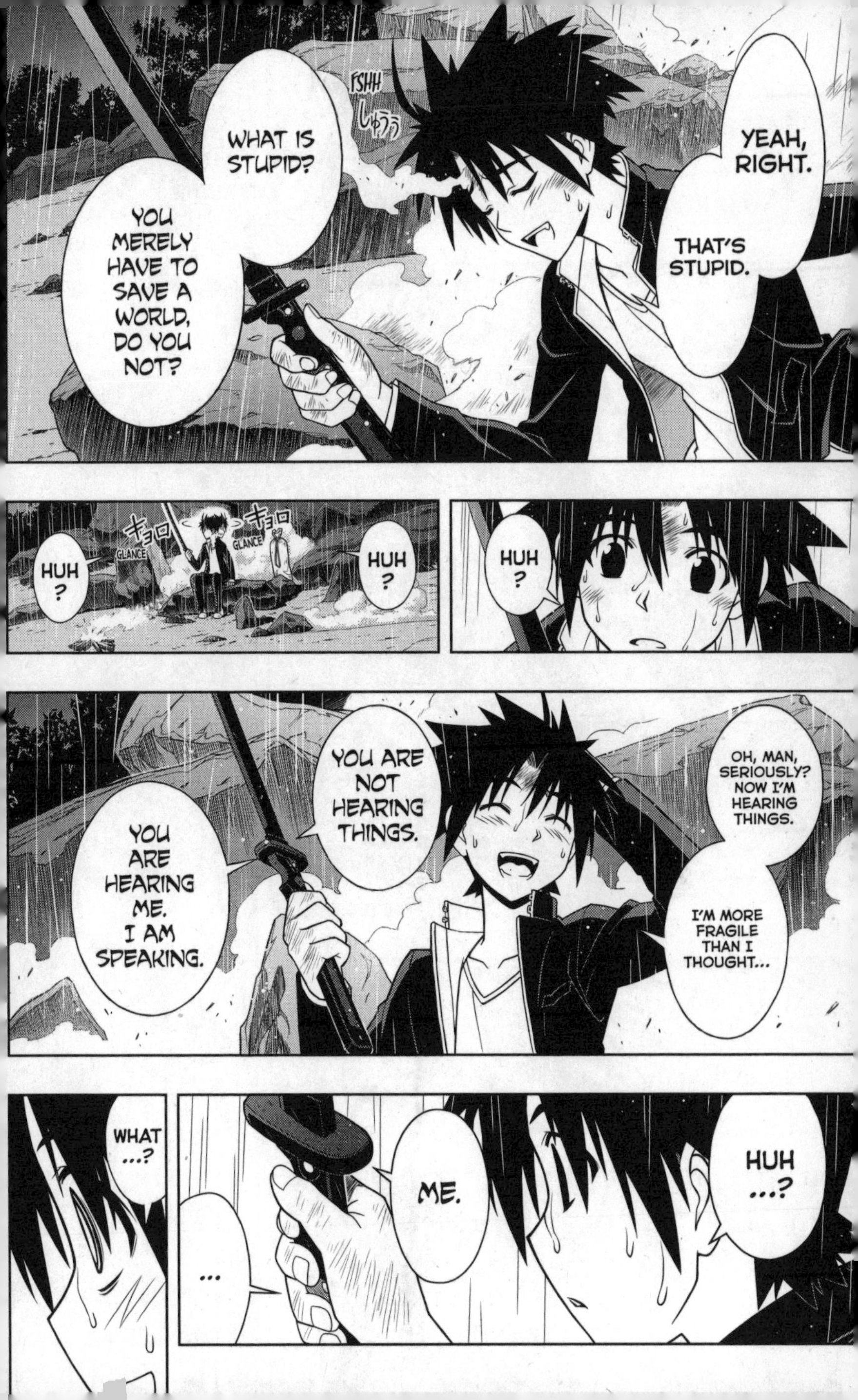
YEAH, RIGHT.
THAT'S STUPID.
FSHH
しゅうう
WHAT IS STUPID?
YOU MERELY HAVE TO SAVE A WORLD, DO YOU NOT?
HUH ?
HUH ?
キョロ
GLANCE
キョロ
GLANCE
HUH ?
OH, MAN, SERIOUSLY? NOW I'M HEARING THINGS.
I'M MORE FRAGILE THAN I THOUGHT...
YOU ARE NOT HEARING THINGS.
YOU ARE HEARING ME. I AM SPEAKING.
HUH ...?
ME.
...
WHAT ...?

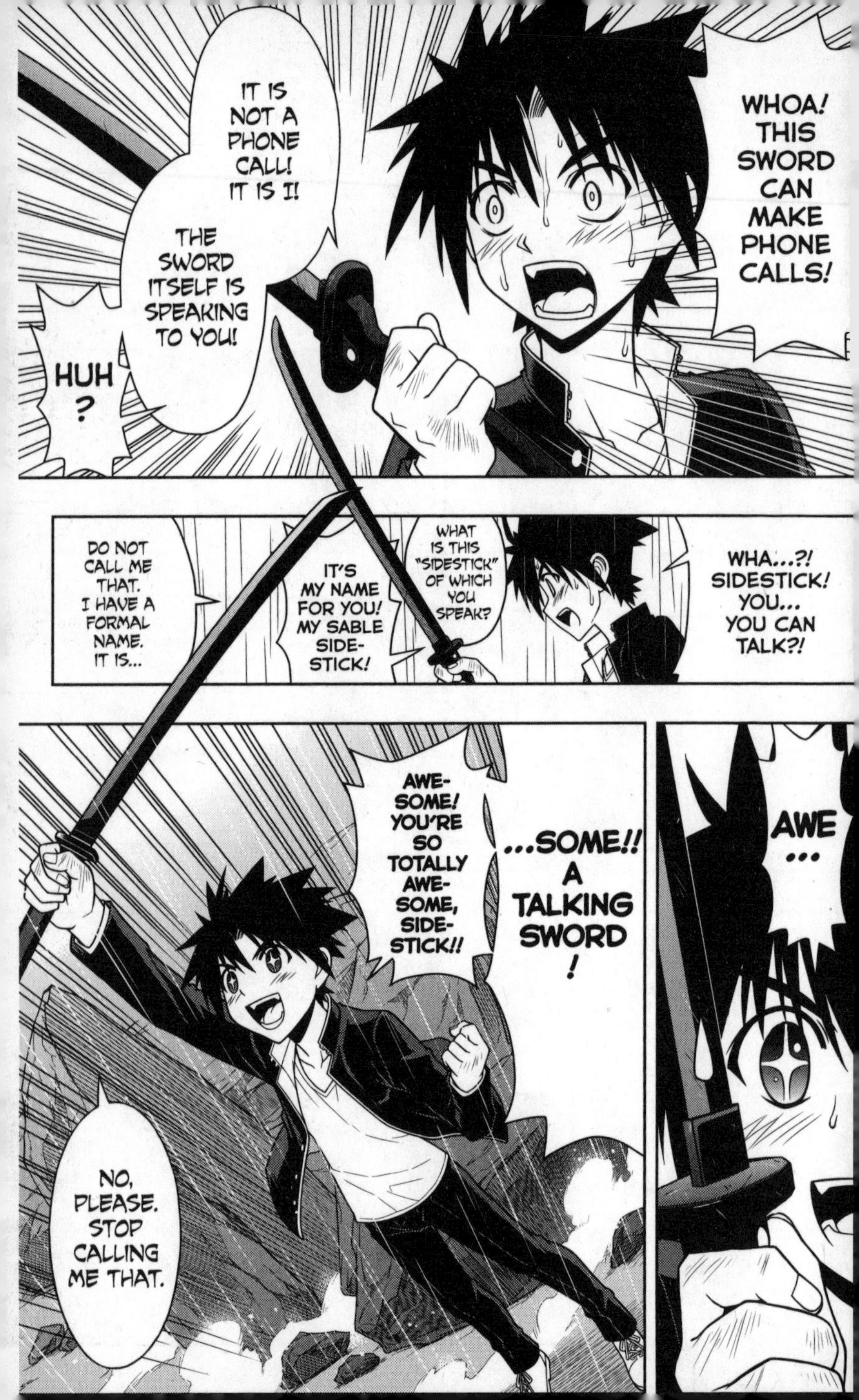
WHOA! THIS SWORD CAN MAKE PHONE CALLS!
IT IS NOT A PHONE CALL! IT IS I!
THE SWORD ITSELF IS SPEAKING TO YOU!
HUH?
WHA...?! SIDESTICK! YOU... YOU CAN TALK?!
WHAT IS THIS "SIDESTICK" OF WHICH YOU SPEAK?
IT'S MY NAME FOR YOU! MY SABLE SIDE-STICK!
DO NOT CALL ME THAT. I HAVE A FORMAL NAME. IT IS...
AWE...
...SOME!! A TALKING SWORD!
AWE-SOME! YOU'RE SO TOTALLY AWE-SOME, SIDE-STICK!!
NO, PLEASE. STOP CALLING ME THAT.

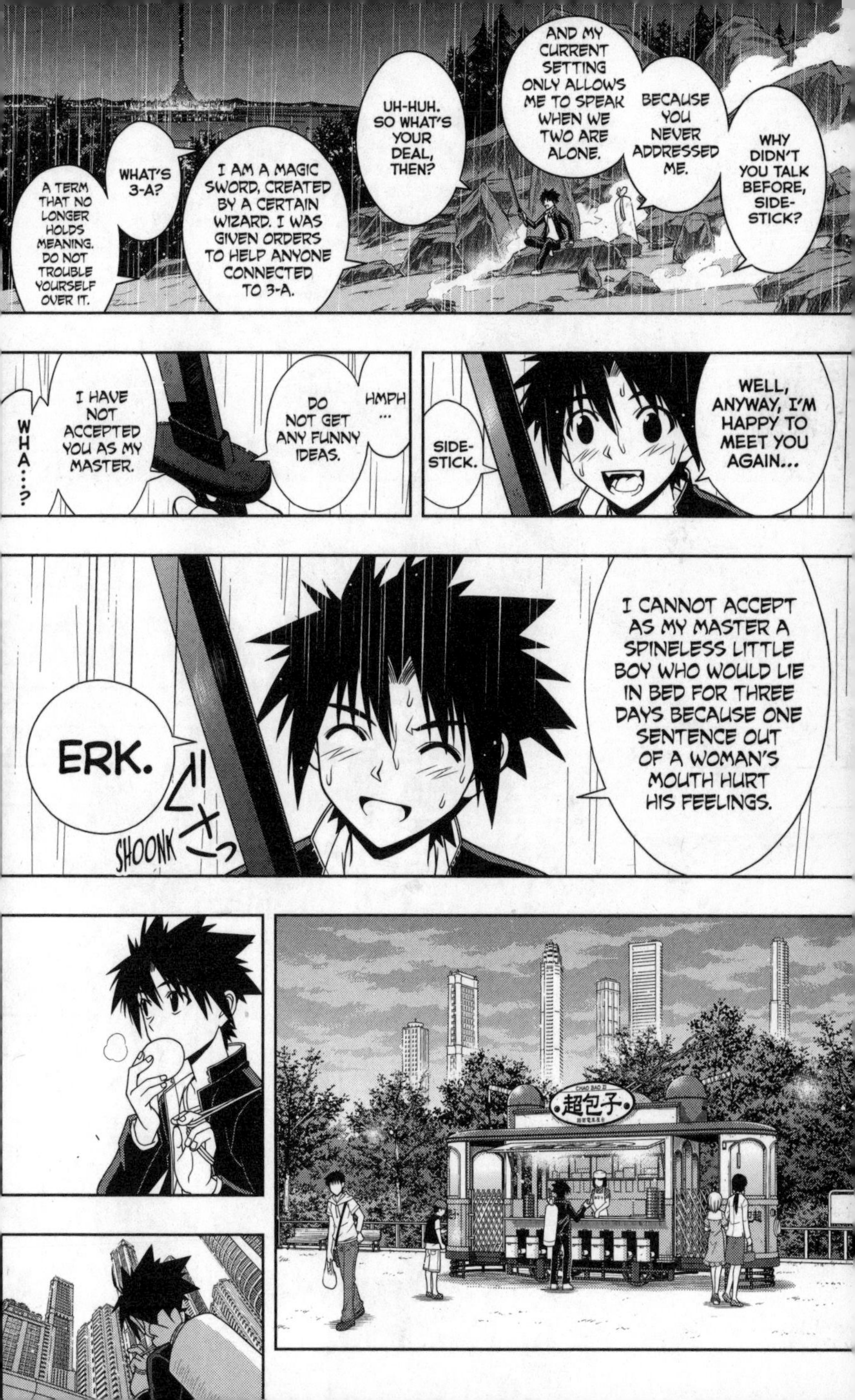
WHY DIDN'T YOU TALK BEFORE, SIDE-STICK?
BECAUSE YOU NEVER ADDRESSED ME.
AND MY CURRENT SETTING ONLY ALLOWS ME TO SPEAK WHEN WE TWO ARE ALONE.
UH-HUH. SO WHAT'S YOUR DEAL, THEN?
I AM A MAGIC SWORD, CREATED BY A CERTAIN WIZARD. I WAS GIVEN ORDERS TO HELP ANYONE CONNECTED TO 3-A.
WHAT'S 3-A?
A TERM THAT NO LONGER HOLDS MEANING. DO NOT TROUBLE YOURSELF OVER IT.
WELL, ANYWAY, I'M HAPPY TO MEET YOU AGAIN...
SIDE-STICK.
HMPH...
DO NOT GET ANY FUNNY IDEAS.
I HAVE NOT ACCEPTED YOU AS MY MASTER.
WHA...?
I CANNOT ACCEPT AS MY MASTER A SPINELESS LITTLE BOY WHO WOULD LIE IN BED FOR THREE DAYS BECAUSE ONE SENTENCE OUT OF A WOMAN'S MOUTH HURT HIS FEELINGS.
ERK.
SHOONK
CHAO BAO ZI
超包子

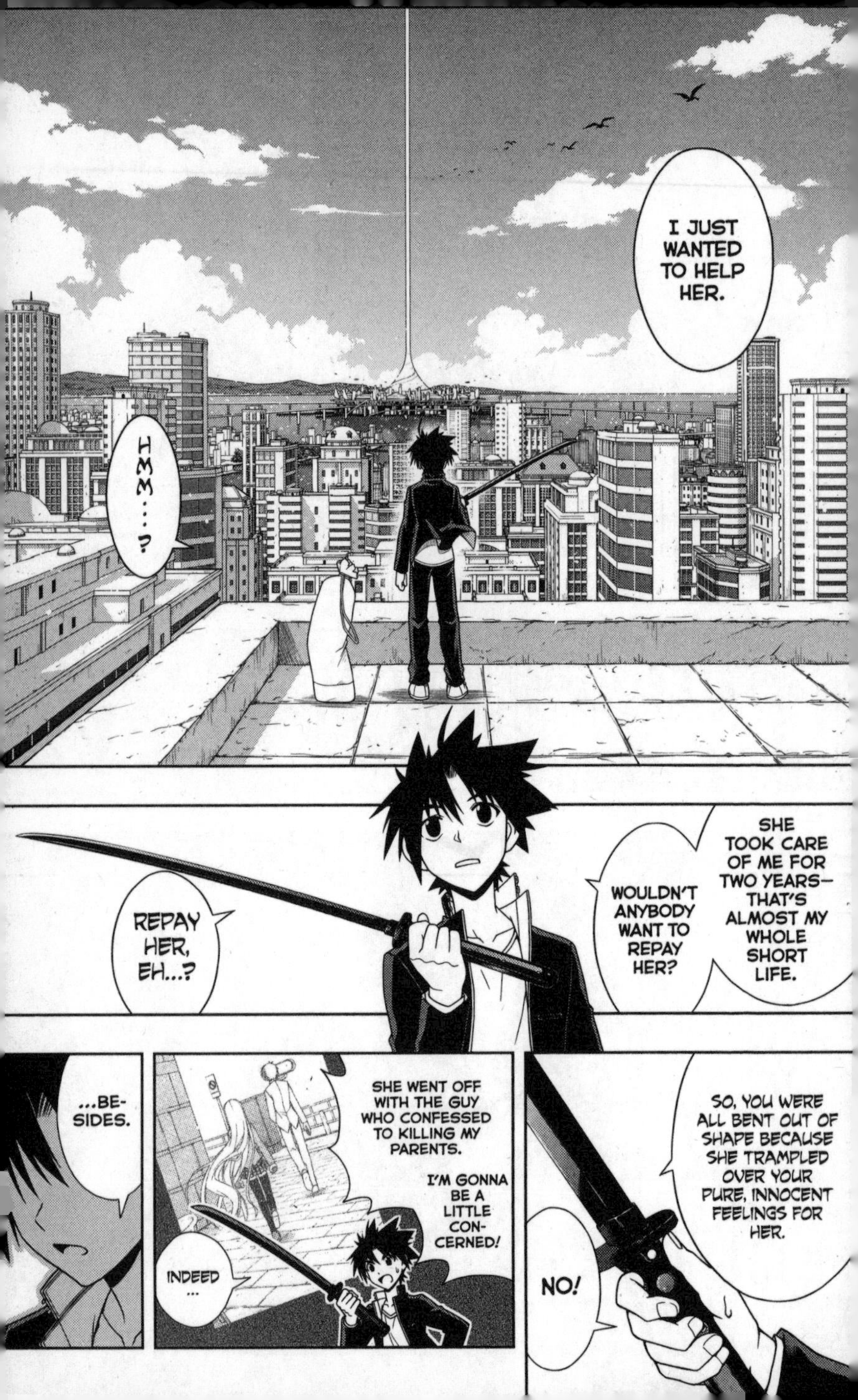
I JUST WANTED TO HELP HER.
HMM...?
SHE TOOK CARE OF ME FOR TWO YEARS—THAT'S ALMOST MY WHOLE SHORT LIFE.
WOULDN'T ANYBODY WANT TO REPAY HER?
REPAY HER, EH...?
SO, YOU WERE ALL BENT OUT OF SHAPE BECAUSE SHE TRAMPLED OVER YOUR PURE, INNOCENT FEELINGS FOR HER.
NO!
SHE WENT OFF WITH THE GUY WHO CONFESSED TO KILLING MY PARENTS.
I'M GONNA BE A LITTLE CONCERNED!
INDEED...
...BESIDES.

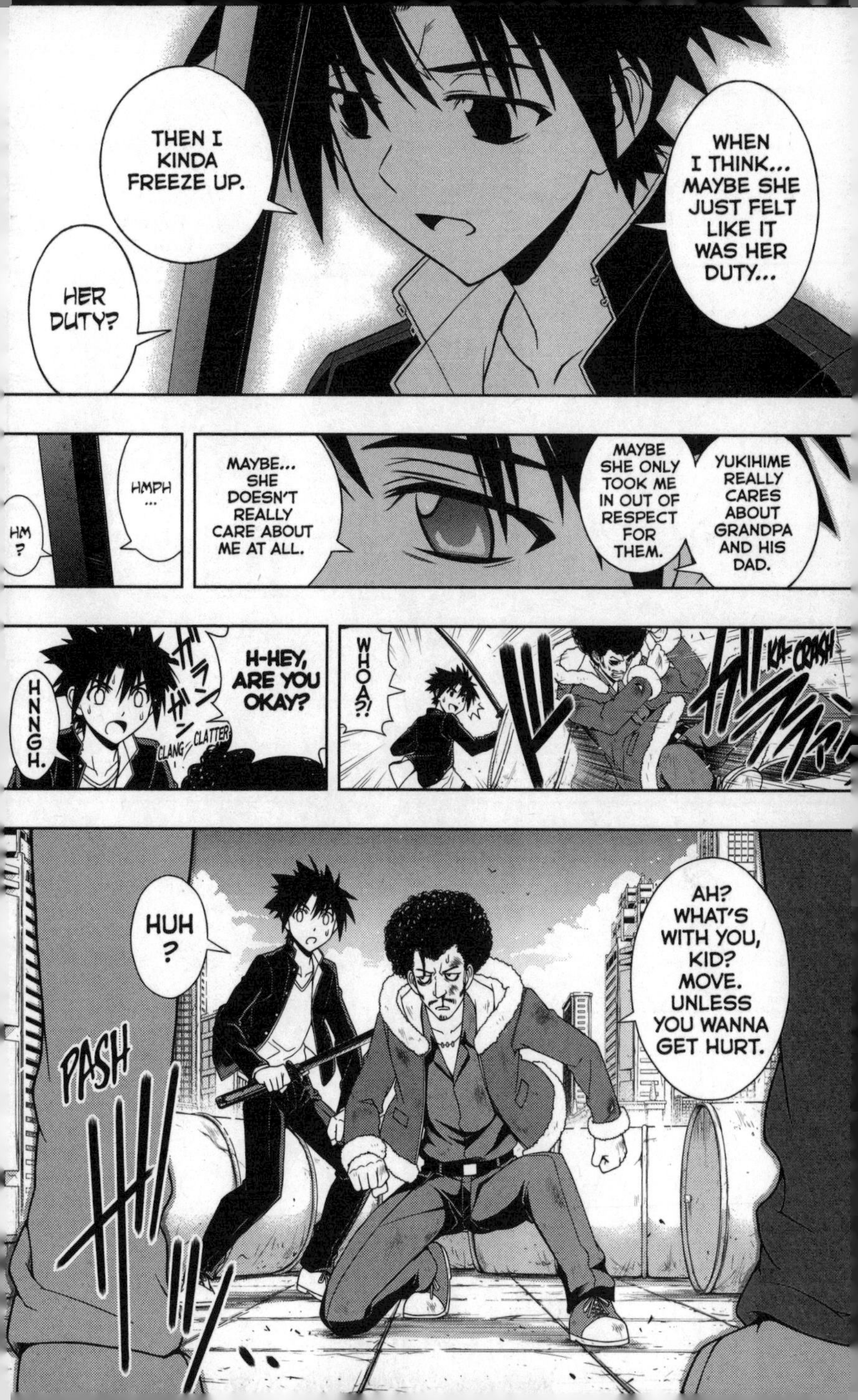
WHEN I THINK... MAYBE SHE JUST FELT LIKE IT WAS HER DUTY...
THEN I KINDA FREEZE UP.
HER DUTY?
YUKIHIME REALLY CARES ABOUT GRANDPA AND HIS DAD.
MAYBE SHE ONLY TOOK ME IN OUT OF RESPECT FOR THEM.
MAYBE... SHE DOESN'T REALLY CARE ABOUT ME AT ALL.
HMPH...
HM?
KA-CRASH
WHOA?!
H-HEY, ARE YOU OKAY?
CLATTER
CLANG
HNNGH.
AH? WHAT'S WITH YOU, KID? MOVE. UNLESS YOU WANNA GET HURT.
HUH?
PASH

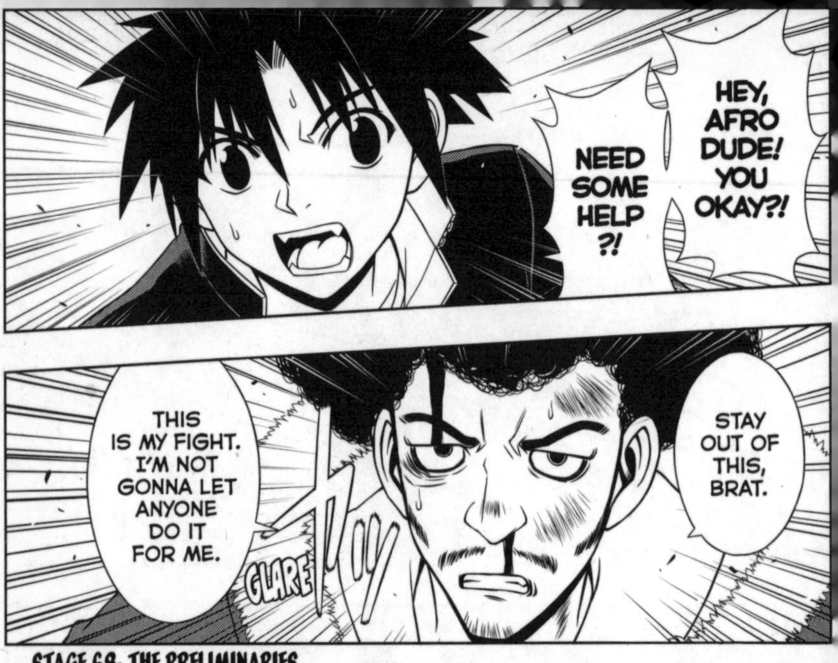
HEY, AFRO DUDE! YOU OKAY?!
NEED SOME HELP ?!
STAY OUT OF THIS, BRAT.
GLARE
THIS IS MY FIGHT. I'M NOT GONNA LET ANYONE DO IT FOR ME.

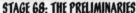

STAGE 68: THE PRELIMINARIES

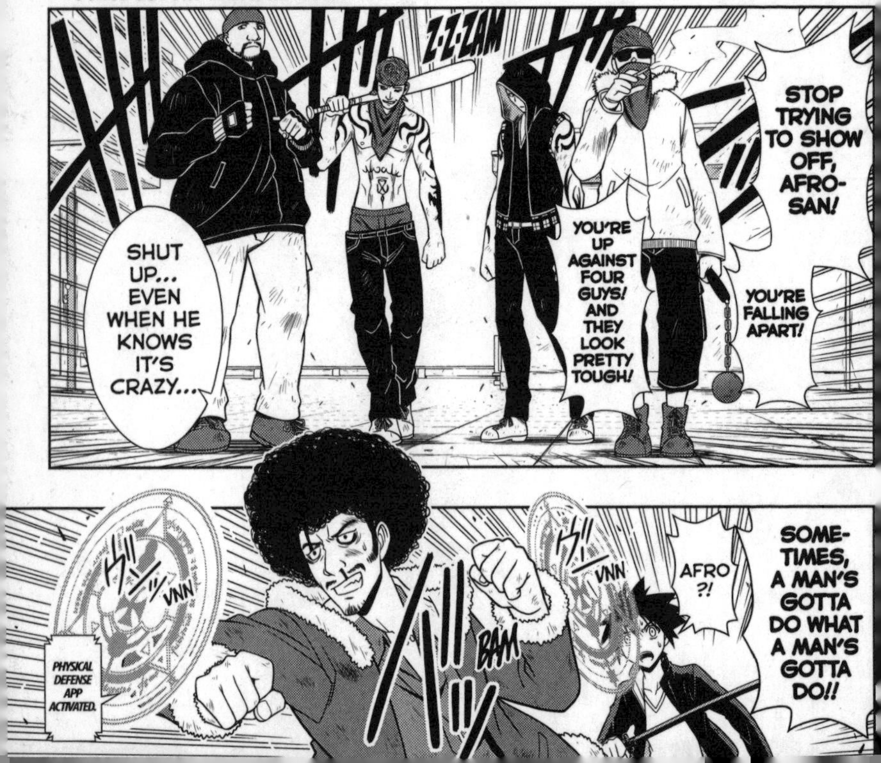
Z-Z-ZAM
STOP TRYING TO SHOW OFF, AFRO-SAN!
YOU'RE FALLING APART!
YOU'RE UP AGAINST FOUR GUYS! AND THEY LOOK PRETTY TOUGH!
SHUT UP... EVEN WHEN HE KNOWS IT'S CRAZY...
SOME-TIMES, A MAN'S GOTTA DO WHAT A MAN'S GOTTA DO!!
AFRO ?!
VNN
BAM
VNN
PHYSICAL DEFENSE APP ACTIVATED.

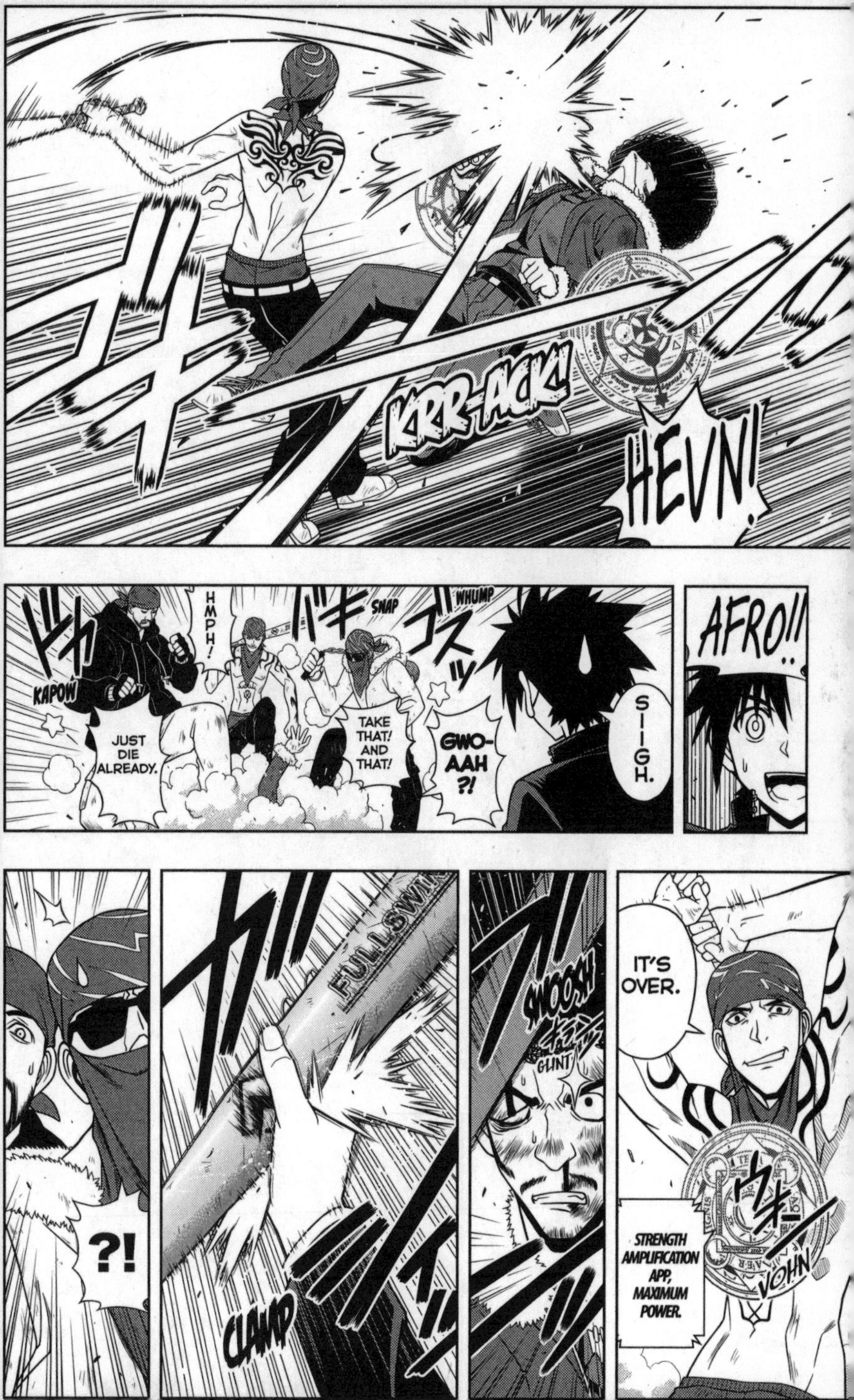
KRR-ACK!
HEVN!
AFRO!!..
S-I-I-G-H.
GWO-AAH?!
WHUMP
TAKE THAT! AND THAT!
SNAP
HMPH!
KAPOW
JUST DIE ALREADY.
IT'S OVER.
STRENGTH AMPLIFICATION APP, MAXIMUM POWER.
VOHN
SWOOSH
GLINT
CLAMP
?!

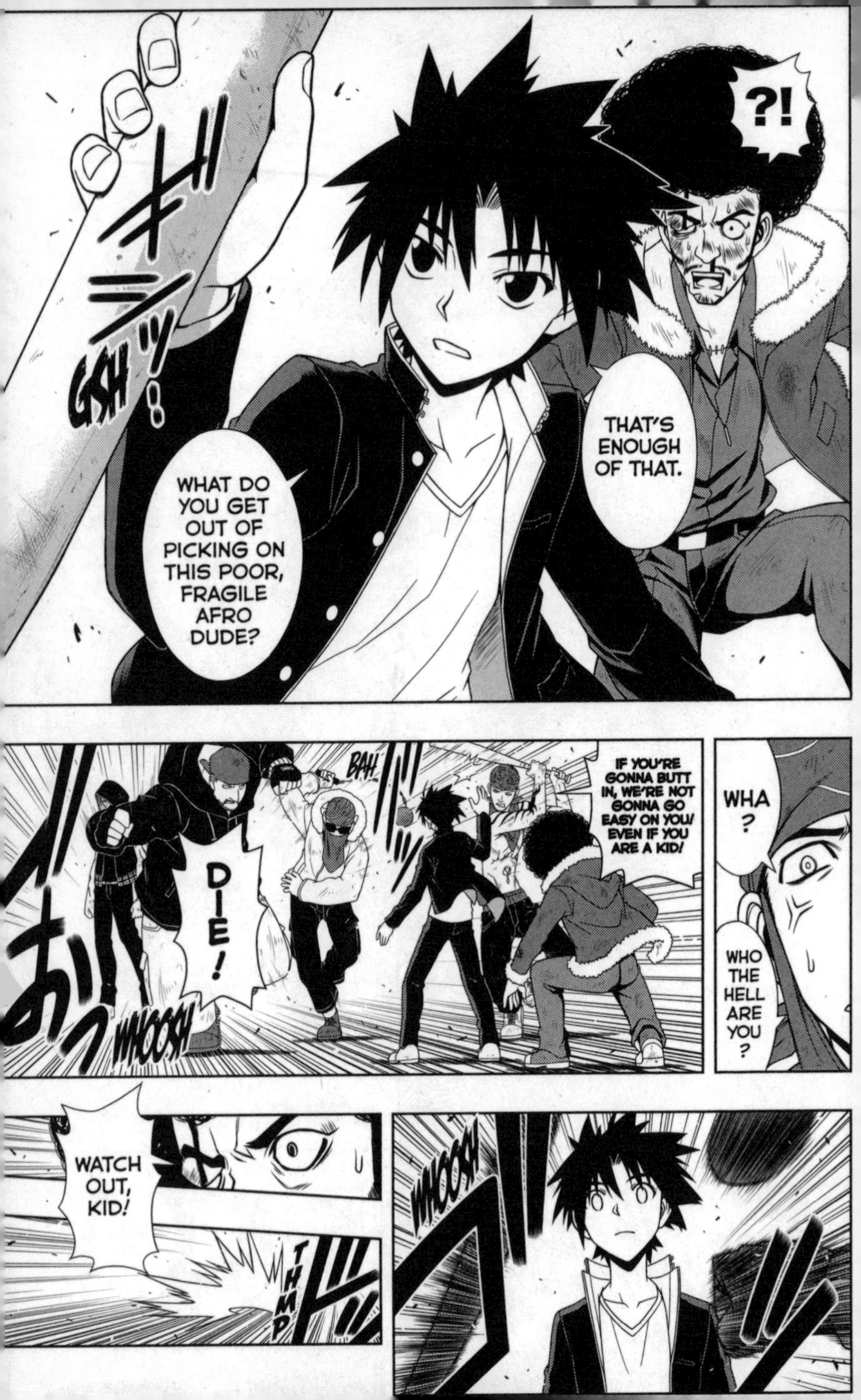
?!
THAT'S ENOUGH OF THAT.
WHAT DO YOU GET OUT OF PICKING ON THIS POOR, FRAGILE AFRO DUDE?
GSH
WHA?
WHO THE HELL ARE YOU?
IF YOU'RE GONNA BUTT IN, WE'RE NOT GONNA GO EASY ON YOU! EVEN IF YOU ARE A KID!
BAH
DIE!
WHOOSH
WHOOSH
WATCH OUT, KID!
THUMP

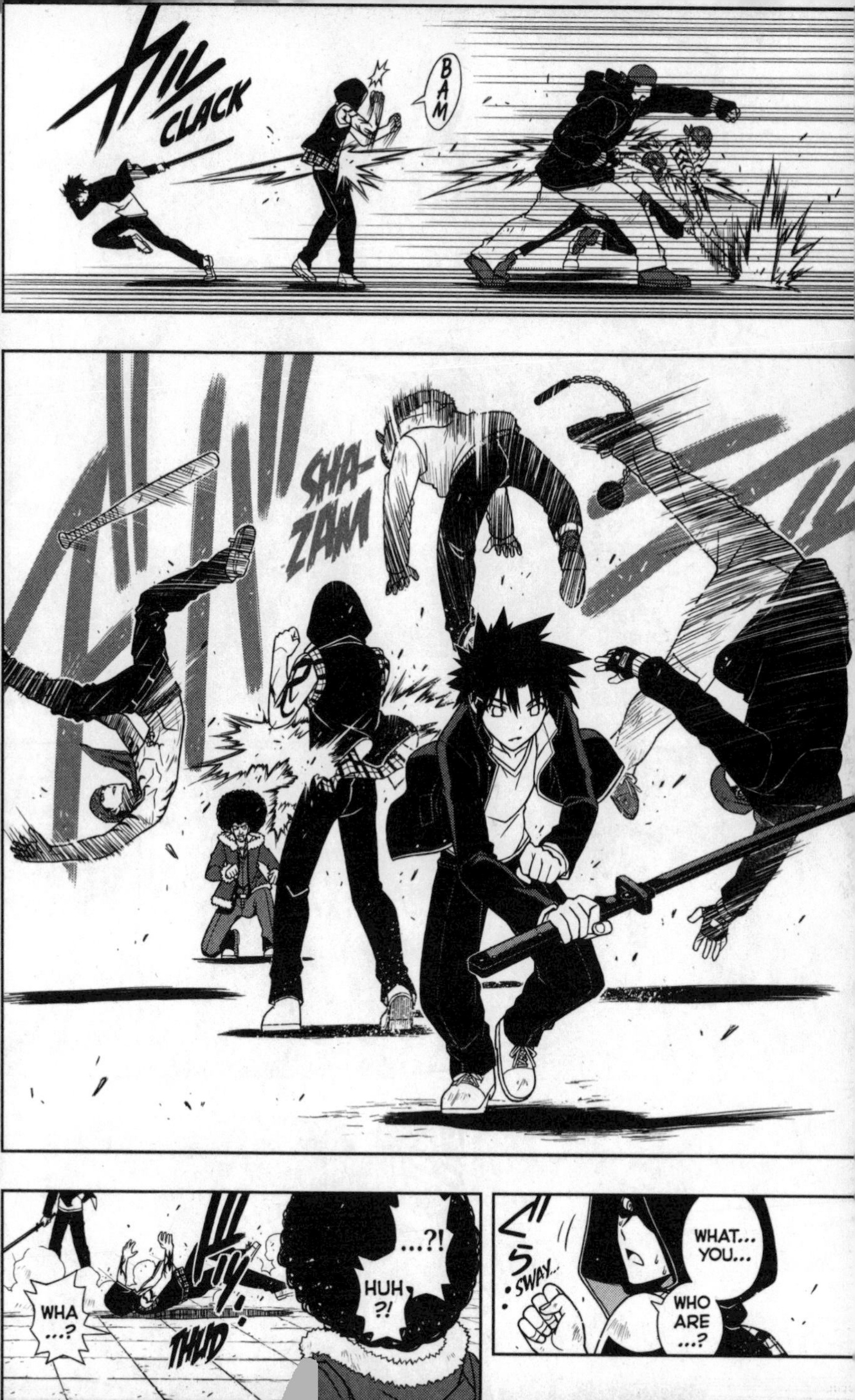
BAM
CLACK
SHA-ZAM
WHAT... YOU...
SWAY...
WHO ARE ...?
...?!
HUH ?!
WHA ...?
THUD

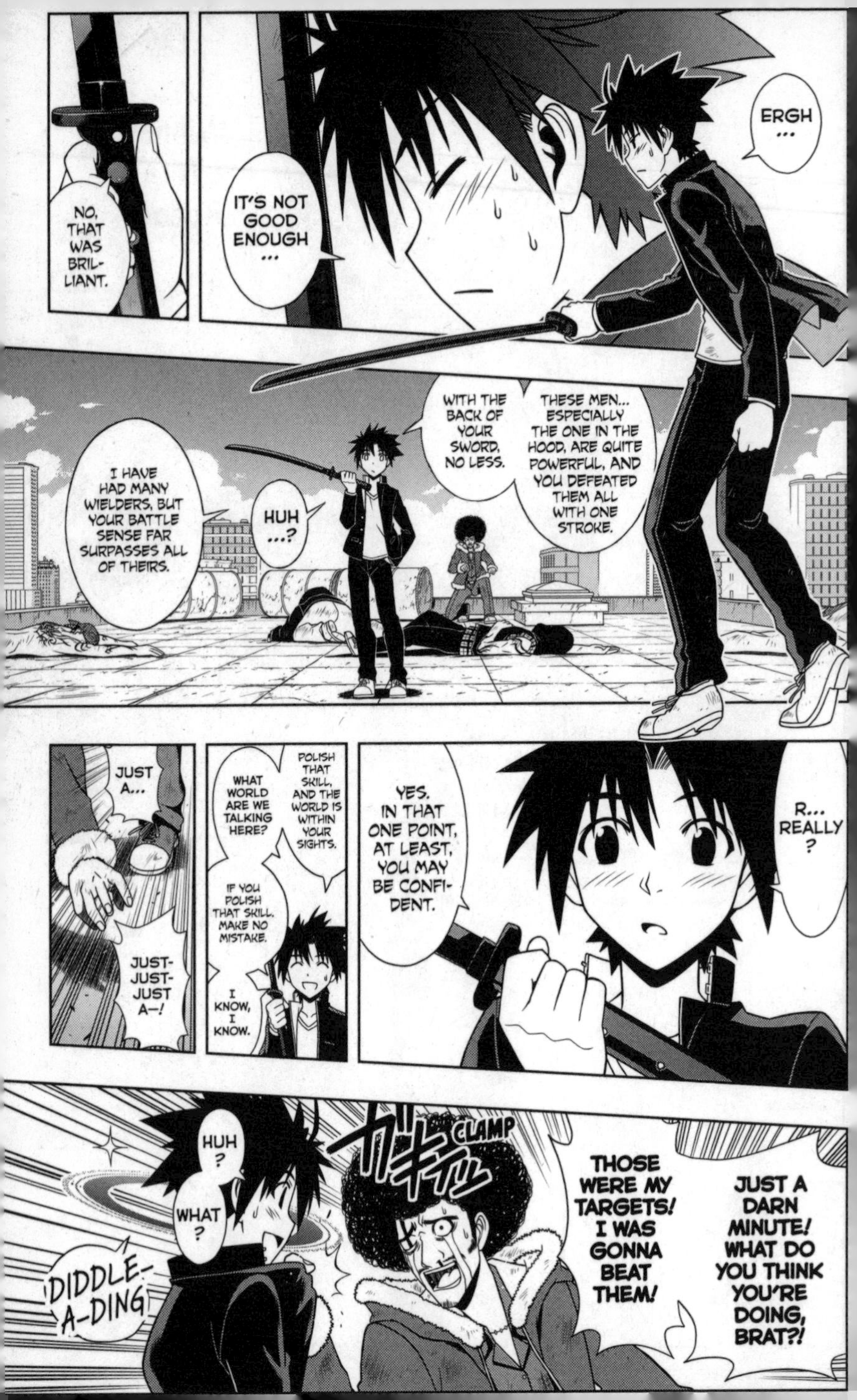
ERGH...
IT'S NOT GOOD ENOUGH...
NO, THAT WAS BRIL-LIANT.
THESE MEN... ESPECIALLY THE ONE IN THE HOOD, ARE QUITE POWERFUL, AND YOU DEFEATED THEM ALL WITH ONE STROKE.
WITH THE BACK OF YOUR SWORD, NO LESS.
HUH...?
I HAVE HAD MANY WIELDERS, BUT YOUR BATTLE SENSE FAR SURPASSES ALL OF THEIRS.
R... REALLY?
YES. IN THAT ONE POINT, AT LEAST, YOU MAY BE CONFI-DENT.
POLISH THAT SKILL, AND THE WORLD IS WITHIN YOUR SIGHTS.
WHAT WORLD ARE WE TALKING HERE?
IF YOU POLISH THAT SKILL. MAKE NO MISTAKE.
I KNOW, I KNOW.
JUST A...
JUST-JUST-JUST A—!
JUST A DARN MINUTE! WHAT DO YOU THINK YOU'RE DOING, BRAT?!
THOSE WERE MY TARGETS! I WAS GONNA BEAT THEM!
CLAMP
HUH?
WHAT?
DIDDLE-A-DING

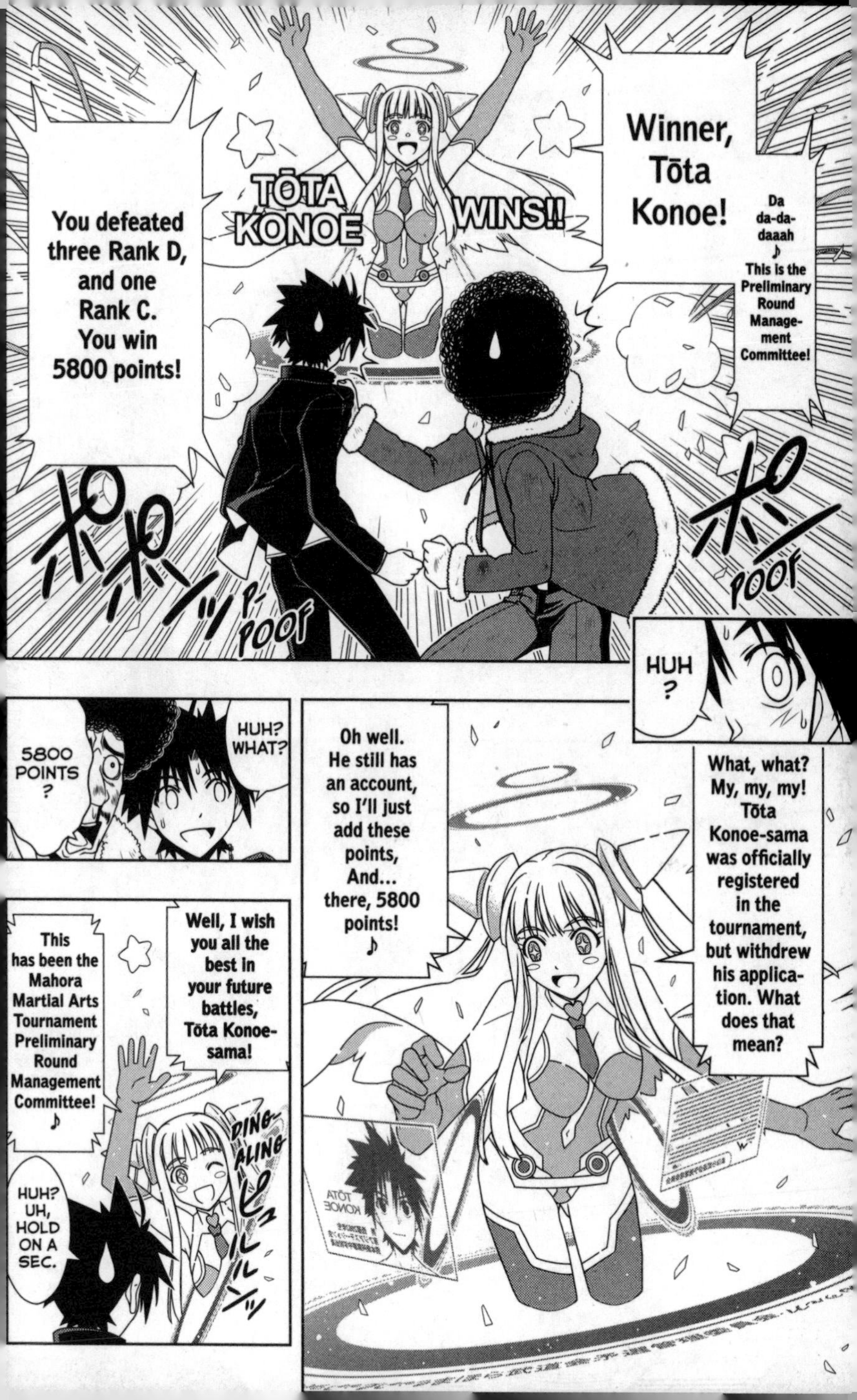

Winner, Tōta Konoe!
Da da-da-daaah ♪ This is the Preliminary Round Management Committee!
TŌTA KONOE WINS!!
You defeated three Rank D, and one Rank C. You win 5800 points!
POOF
P-POOF
HUH?
What, what? My, my, my! Tōta Konoe-sama was officially registered in the tournament, but withdrew his application. What does that mean?
Oh well. He still has an account, so I'll just add these points, And... there, 5800 points! ♪
TŌTA KONOE
HUH? WHAT?
5800 POINTS?
Well, I wish you all the best in your future battles, Tōta Konoe-sama!
This has been the Mahora Martial Arts Tournament Preliminary Round Management Committee! ♪
DING-ALING
HUH? UH, HOLD ON A SEC.

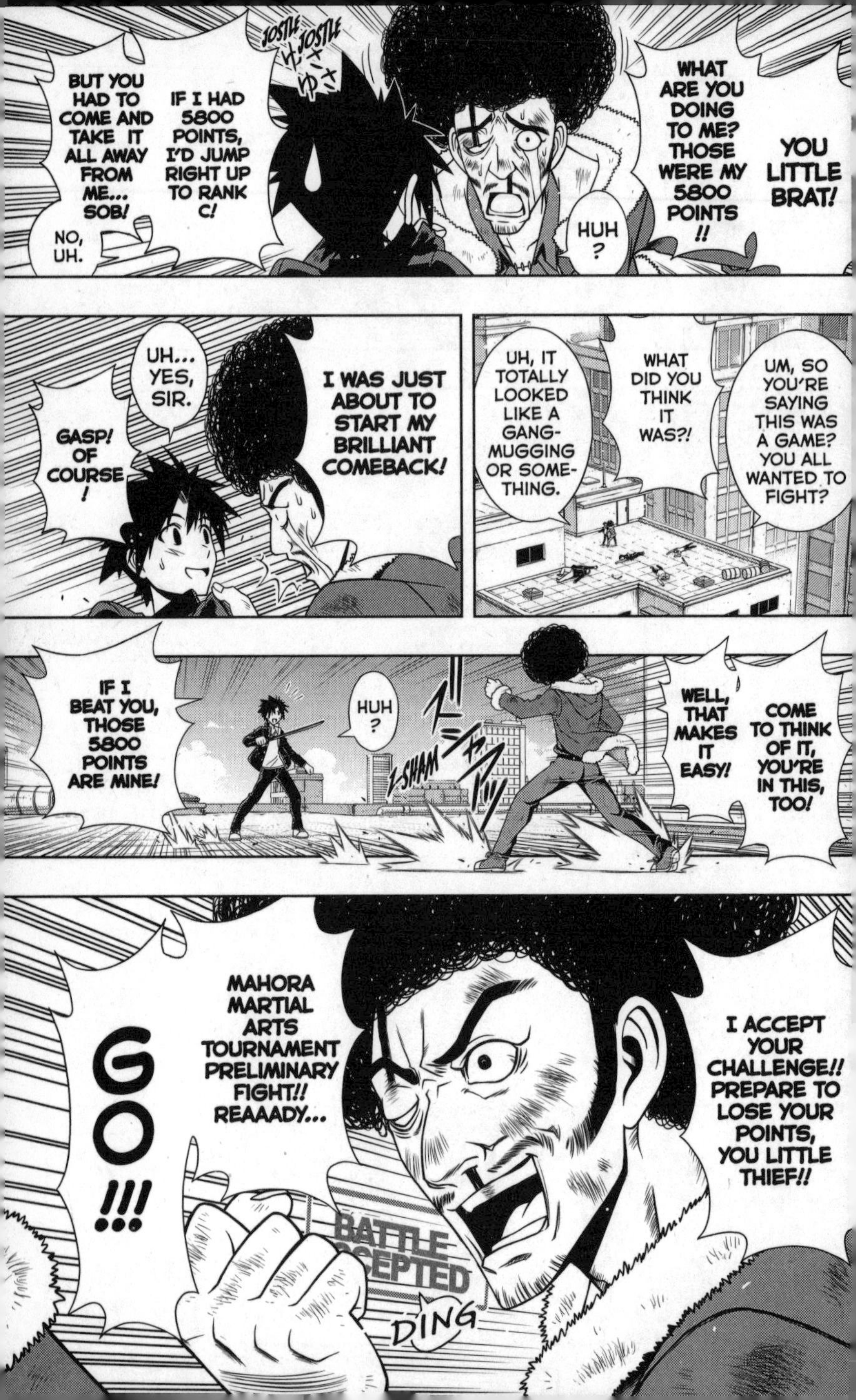
YOU LITTLE BRAT!
WHAT ARE YOU DOING TO ME? THOSE WERE MY 5800 POINTS!!
HUH?
JOSTLE JOSTLE
IF I HAD 5800 POINTS, I'D JUMP RIGHT UP TO RANK C!
BUT YOU HAD TO COME AND TAKE IT ALL AWAY FROM ME... SOB!
NO, UH.
UM, SO YOU'RE SAYING THIS WAS A GAME? YOU ALL WANTED TO FIGHT?
WHAT DID YOU THINK IT WAS?!
UH, IT TOTALLY LOOKED LIKE A GANG-MUGGING OR SOMETHING.
I WAS JUST ABOUT TO START MY BRILLIANT COMEBACK!
UH... YES, SIR.
GASP! OF COURSE!
COME TO THINK OF IT, YOU'RE IN THIS, TOO!
WELL, THAT MAKES IT EASY!
SHAM
HUH?
IF I BEAT YOU, THOSE 5800 POINTS ARE MINE!
I ACCEPT YOUR CHALLENGE!! PREPARE TO LOSE YOUR POINTS, YOU LITTLE THIEF!!
MAHORA MARTIAL ARTS TOURNAMENT PRELIMINARY FIGHT!! REAAADY...
GO!!!
BATTLE
CEPTED
DING

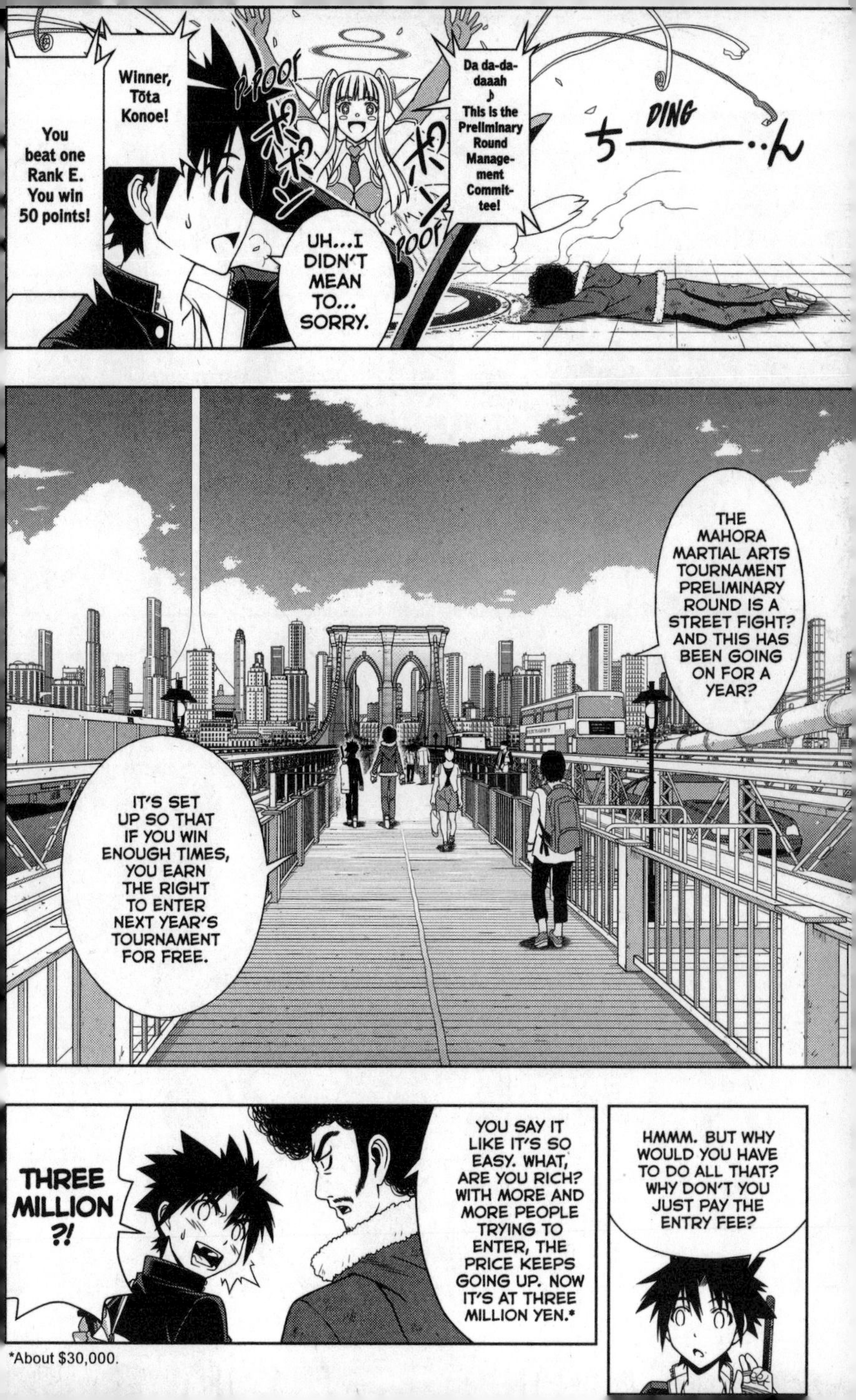
DING
ち——…ん
Da da-da-daaah ♪ This is the Preliminary Round Management Committee!
P-POOF
POOF
Winner, Tōta Konoe!
You beat one Rank E. You win 50 points!
UH...I DIDN'T MEAN TO... SORRY.
THE MAHORA MARTIAL ARTS TOURNAMENT PRELIMINARY ROUND IS A STREET FIGHT? AND THIS HAS BEEN GOING ON FOR A YEAR?
IT'S SET UP SO THAT IF YOU WIN ENOUGH TIMES, YOU EARN THE RIGHT TO ENTER NEXT YEAR'S TOURNAMENT FOR FREE.
HMMM. BUT WHY WOULD YOU HAVE TO DO ALL THAT? WHY DON'T YOU JUST PAY THE ENTRY FEE?
YOU SAY IT LIKE IT'S SO EASY. WHAT, ARE YOU RICH? WITH MORE AND MORE PEOPLE TRYING TO ENTER, THE PRICE KEEPS GOING UP. NOW IT'S AT THREE MILLION YEN.*
THREE MILLION ?!

*About $30,000.

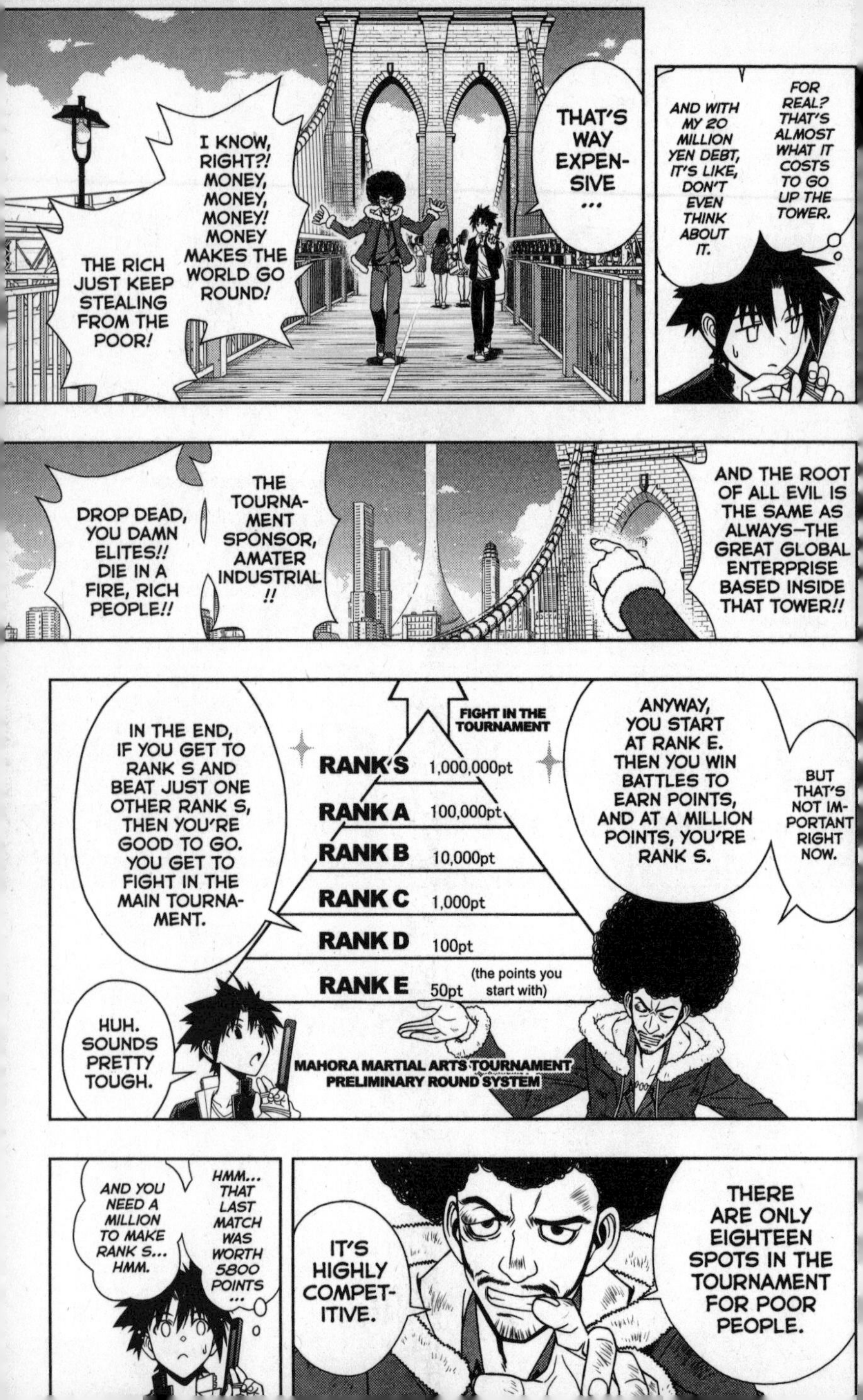
FOR REAL? THAT'S ALMOST WHAT IT COSTS TO GO UP THE TOWER.
AND WITH MY 20 MILLION YEN DEBT, IT'S LIKE, DON'T EVEN THINK ABOUT IT.
THAT'S WAY EXPEN-SIVE...
I KNOW, RIGHT?! MONEY, MONEY, MONEY! MONEY MAKES THE WORLD GO ROUND!
THE RICH JUST KEEP STEALING FROM THE POOR!
AND THE ROOT OF ALL EVIL IS THE SAME AS ALWAYS—THE GREAT GLOBAL ENTERPRISE BASED INSIDE THAT TOWER!!
THE TOURNA-MENT SPONSOR, AMATER INDUSTRIAL!!
DROP DEAD, YOU DAMN ELITES!! DIE IN A FIRE, RICH PEOPLE!!
ANYWAY, YOU START AT RANK E. THEN YOU WIN BATTLES TO EARN POINTS, AND AT A MILLION POINTS, YOU'RE RANK S.
BUT THAT'S NOT IM-PORTANT RIGHT NOW.
FIGHT IN THE TOURNAMENT
RANK S 1,000,000pt
RANK A 100,000pt
RANK B 10,000pt
RANK C 1,000pt
RANK D 100pt
RANK E 50pt (the points you start with)
MAHORA MARTIAL ARTS TOURNAMENT PRELIMINARY ROUND SYSTEM
IN THE END, IF YOU GET TO RANK S AND BEAT JUST ONE OTHER RANK S, THEN YOU'RE GOOD TO GO. YOU GET TO FIGHT IN THE MAIN TOURNA-MENT.
HUH. SOUNDS PRETTY TOUGH.
THERE ARE ONLY EIGHTEEN SPOTS IN THE TOURNAMENT FOR POOR PEOPLE.
IT'S HIGHLY COMPET-ITIVE.
HMM... THAT LAST MATCH WAS WORTH 5800 POINTS...
AND YOU NEED A MILLION TO MAKE RANK S... HMM.

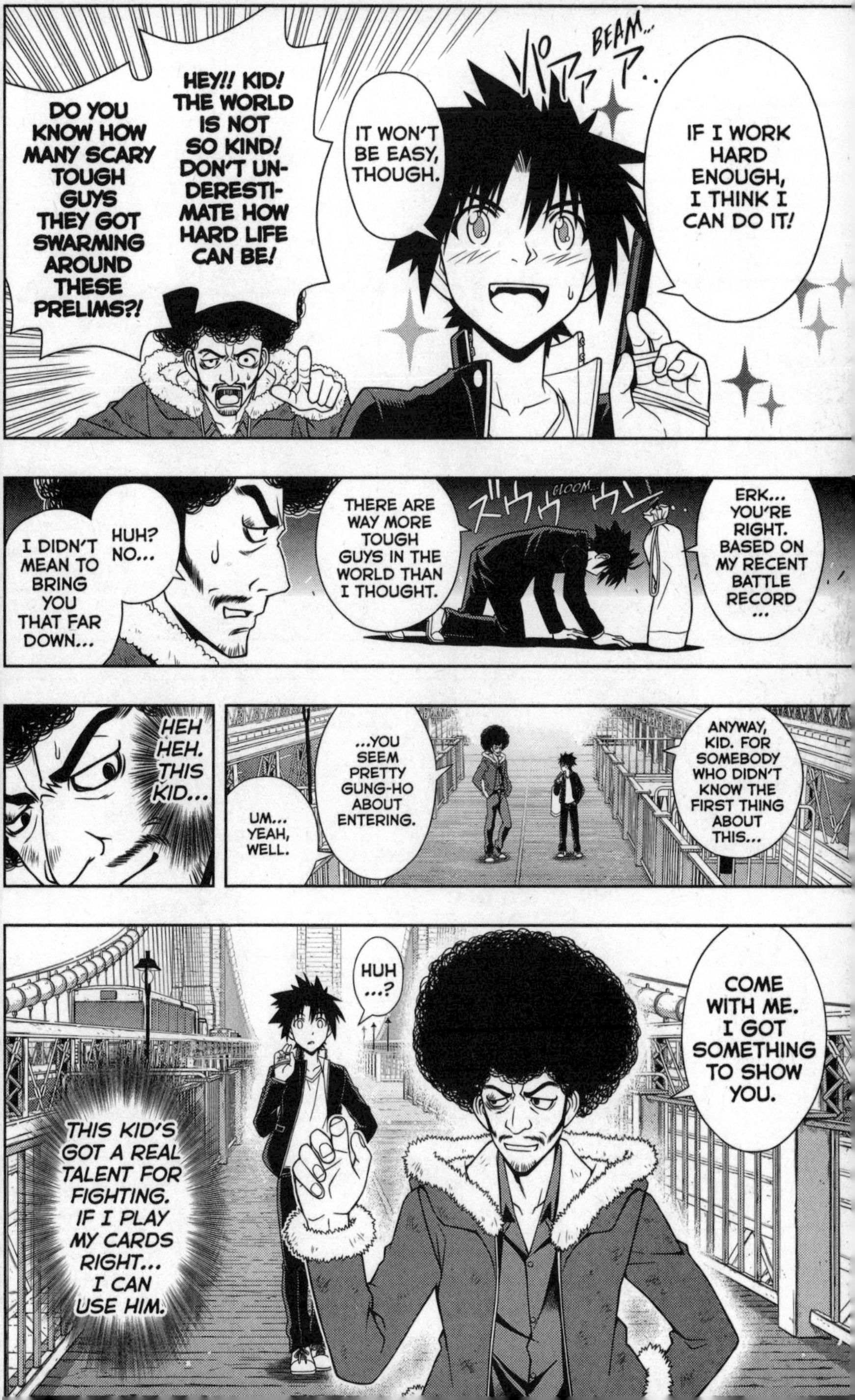

パァァア...
BEAM...
IF I WORK HARD ENOUGH, I THINK I CAN DO IT!
IT WON'T BE EASY, THOUGH.
HEY!! KID! THE WORLD IS NOT SO KIND! DON'T UN-DERESTI-MATE HOW HARD LIFE CAN BE!
DO YOU KNOW HOW MANY SCARY TOUGH GUYS THEY GOT SWARMING AROUND THESE PRELIMS?!
ERK... YOU'RE RIGHT. BASED ON MY RECENT BATTLE RECORD...
ズゥゥゥン
GLOOM...
THERE ARE WAY MORE TOUGH GUYS IN THE WORLD THAN I THOUGHT.
HUH? NO...
I DIDN'T MEAN TO BRING YOU THAT FAR DOWN...
ANYWAY, KID. FOR SOMEBODY WHO DIDN'T KNOW THE FIRST THING ABOUT THIS...
...YOU SEEM PRETTY GUNG-HO ABOUT ENTERING.
UM... YEAH, WELL.
HEH HEH. THIS KID...
COME WITH ME. I GOT SOMETHING TO SHOW YOU.
HUH...?
THIS KID'S GOT A REAL TALENT FOR FIGHTING. IF I PLAY MY CARDS RIGHT... I CAN USE HIM.

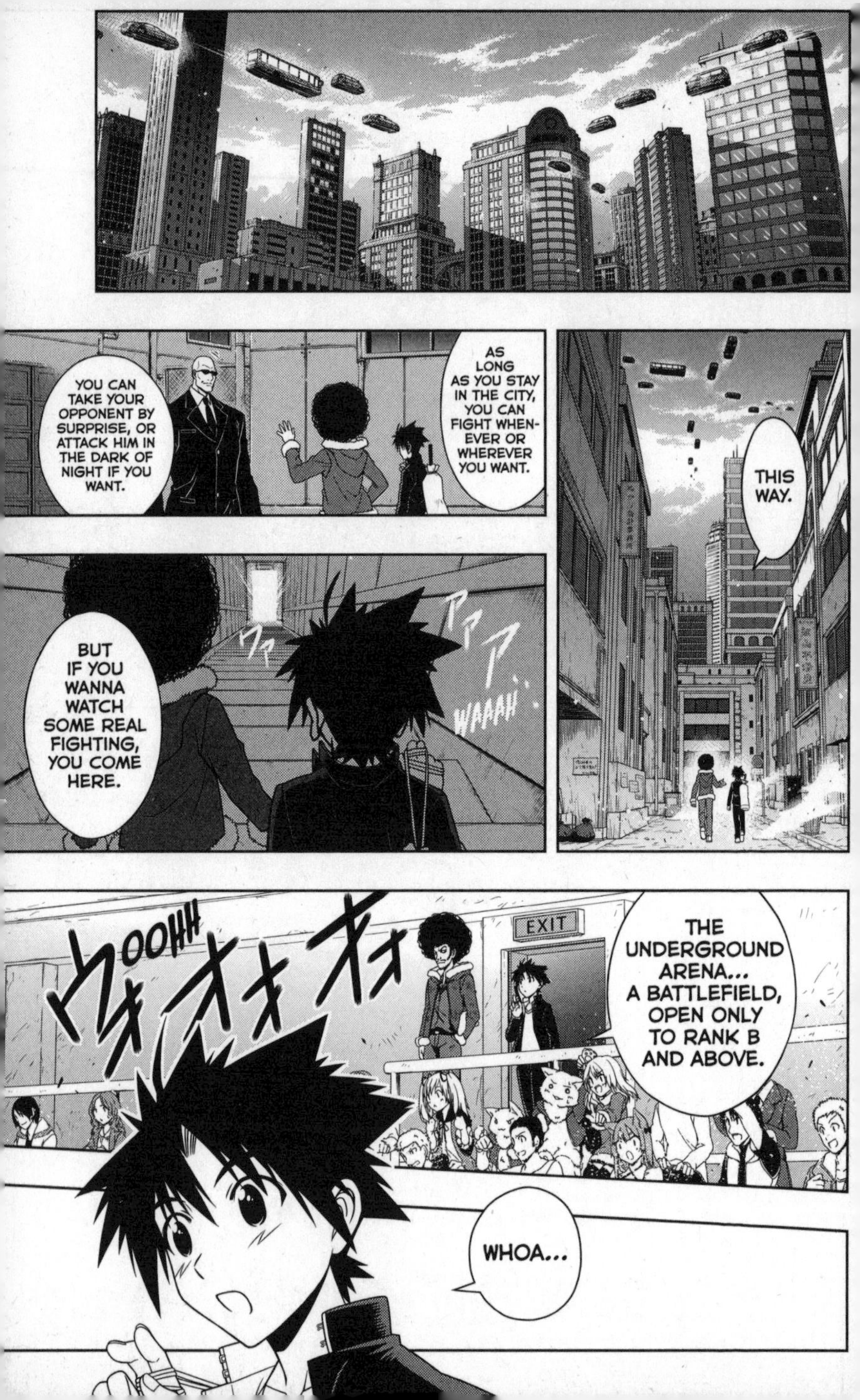
THIS WAY.
AS LONG AS YOU STAY IN THE CITY, YOU CAN FIGHT WHEN-EVER OR WHEREVER YOU WANT.
YOU CAN TAKE YOUR OPPONENT BY SURPRISE, OR ATTACK HIM IN THE DARK OF NIGHT IF YOU WANT.
WAAAH
BUT IF YOU WANNA WATCH SOME REAL FIGHTING, YOU COME HERE.
EXIT
THE UNDERGROUND ARENA... A BATTLEFIELD, OPEN ONLY TO RANK B AND ABOVE.
OOHHH
WHOA...

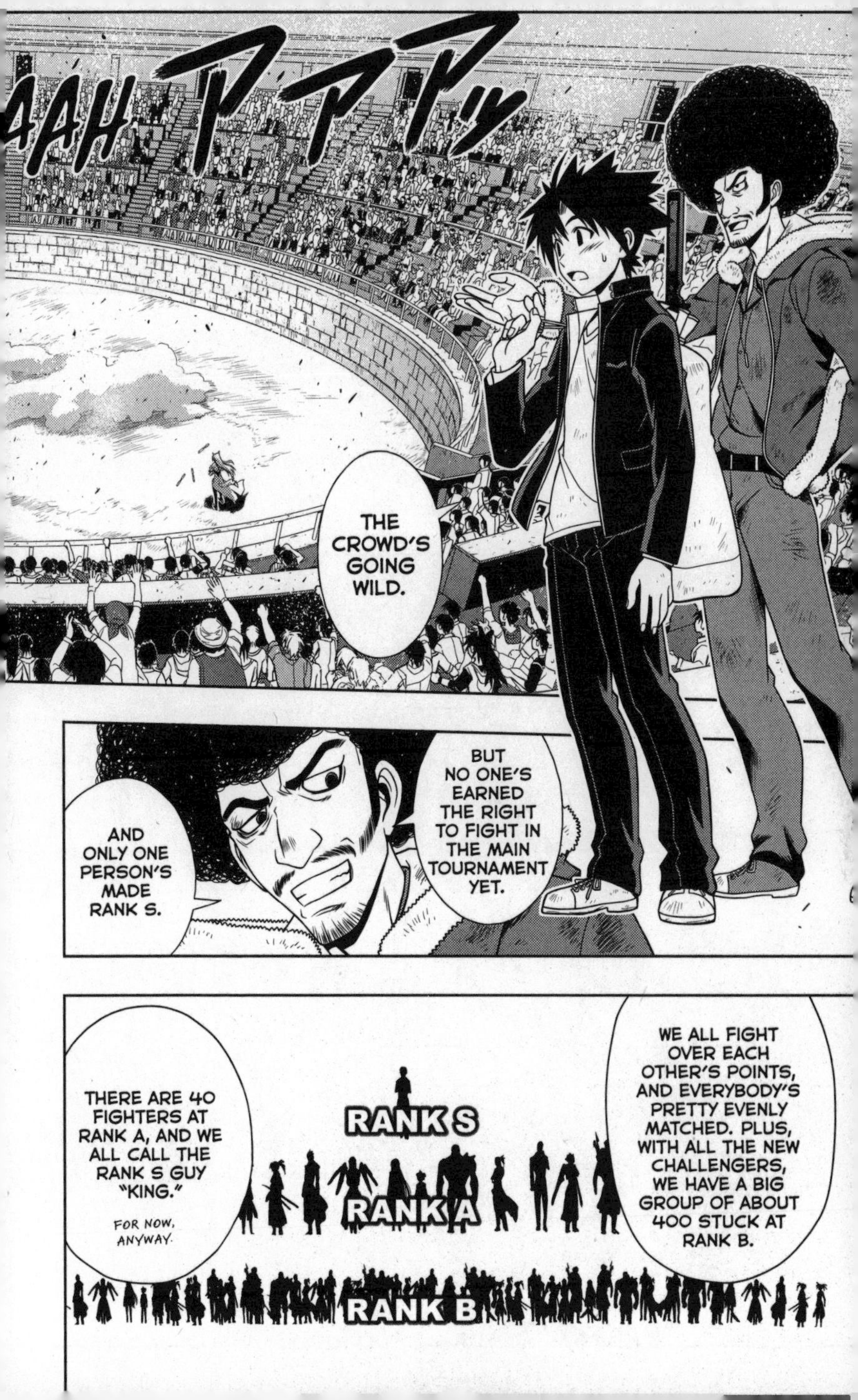
AH アアアッ
THE CROWD'S GOING WILD.
BUT NO ONE'S EARNED THE RIGHT TO FIGHT IN THE MAIN TOURNAMENT YET.
AND ONLY ONE PERSON'S MADE RANK S.
WE ALL FIGHT OVER EACH OTHER'S POINTS, AND EVERYBODY'S PRETTY EVENLY MATCHED. PLUS, WITH ALL THE NEW CHALLENGERS, WE HAVE A BIG GROUP OF ABOUT 400 STUCK AT RANK B.
RANK S
RANK A
RANK B
THERE ARE 40 FIGHTERS AT RANK A, AND WE ALL CALL THE RANK S GUY "KING."
FOR NOW, ANYWAY.

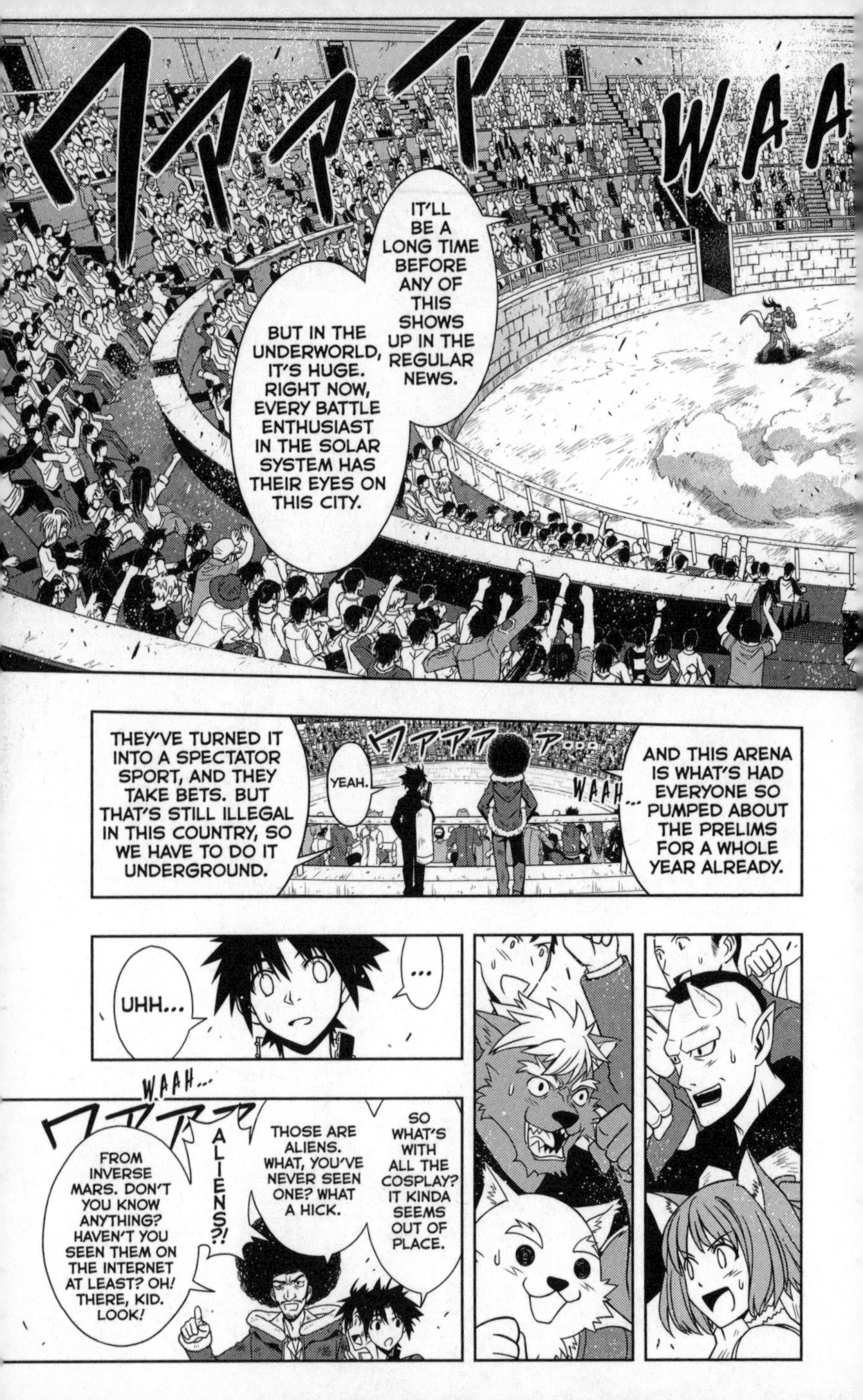
WAA
IT'LL BE A LONG TIME BEFORE ANY OF THIS SHOWS UP IN THE REGULAR NEWS.
BUT IN THE UNDERWORLD, IT'S HUGE. RIGHT NOW, EVERY BATTLE ENTHUSIAST IN THE SOLAR SYSTEM HAS THEIR EYES ON THIS CITY.
AND THIS ARENA IS WHAT'S HAD EVERYONE SO PUMPED ABOUT THE PRELIMS FOR A WHOLE YEAR ALREADY.
WAAH...
YEAH.
THEY'VE TURNED IT INTO A SPECTATOR SPORT, AND THEY TAKE BETS. BUT THAT'S STILL ILLEGAL IN THIS COUNTRY, SO WE HAVE TO DO IT UNDERGROUND.
...
UHH...
SO WHAT'S WITH ALL THE COSPLAY? IT KINDA SEEMS OUT OF PLACE.
THOSE ARE ALIENS. WHAT, YOU'VE NEVER SEEN ONE? WHAT A HICK.
ALIENS?!
FROM INVERSE MARS. DON'T YOU KNOW ANYTHING? HAVEN'T YOU SEEN THEM ON THE INTERNET AT LEAST? OH! THERE, KID. LOOK!
WAAH...

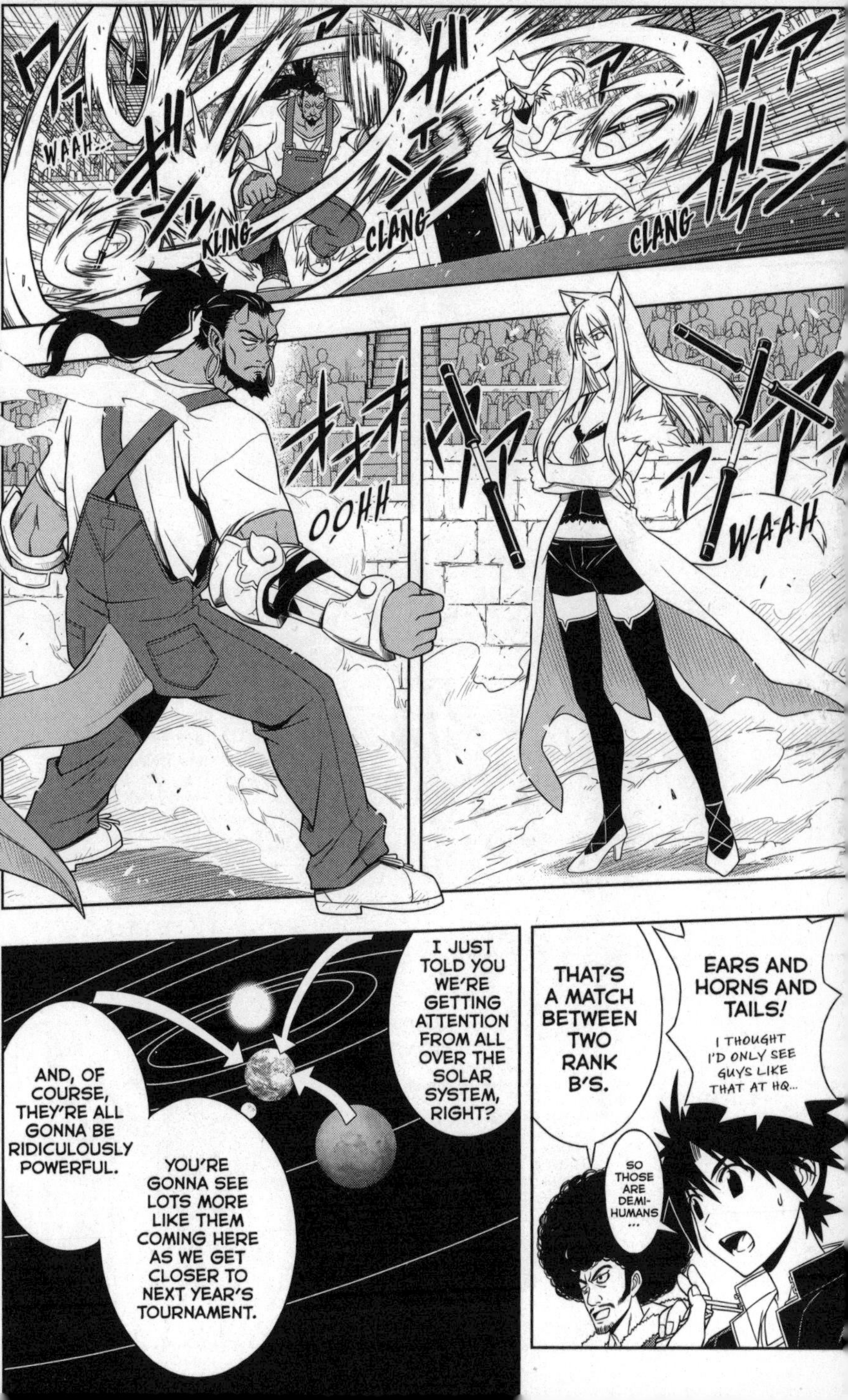
CLANG
CLANG
KLING
WAAH...
WAAH
OOHH
EARS AND HORNS AND TAILS!
I THOUGHT I'D ONLY SEE GUYS LIKE THAT AT HQ...
THAT'S A MATCH BETWEEN TWO RANK B'S.
SO THOSE ARE DEMI-HUMANS...
I JUST TOLD YOU WE'RE GETTING ATTENTION FROM ALL OVER THE SOLAR SYSTEM, RIGHT?
AND, OF COURSE, THEY'RE ALL GONNA BE RIDICULOUSLY POWERFUL.
YOU'RE GONNA SEE LOTS MORE LIKE THEM COMING HERE AS WE GET CLOSER TO NEXT YEAR'S TOURNAMENT.

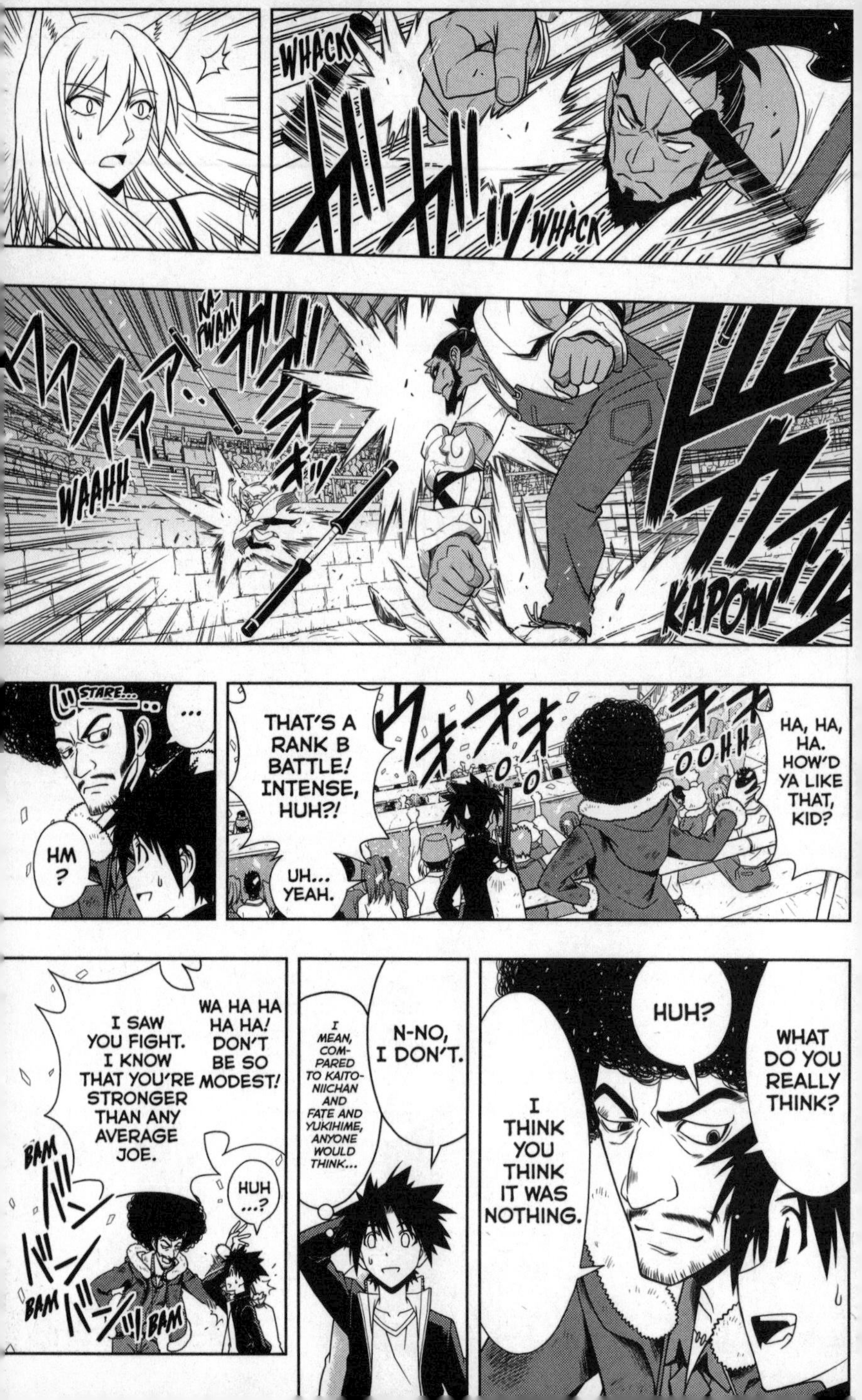
WHACK
WHACK
NA-FWAM
KAPOW
WAAHH
HA, HA, HA. HOW'D YA LIKE THAT, KID?
OOHH
THAT'S A RANK B BATTLE! INTENSE, HUH?!
UH... YEAH.
STARE...
...
HM ?
WHAT DO YOU REALLY THINK?
HUH?
I THINK YOU THINK IT WAS NOTHING.
N-NO, I DON'T.
I MEAN, COMPARED TO KAITO-NIICHAN AND FATE AND YUKIHIME, ANYONE WOULD THINK...
WA HA HA HA HA! DON'T BE SO MODEST!
I SAW YOU FIGHT. I KNOW THAT YOU'RE STRONGER THAN ANY AVERAGE JOE.
HUH ...?
BAM
BAM
BAM

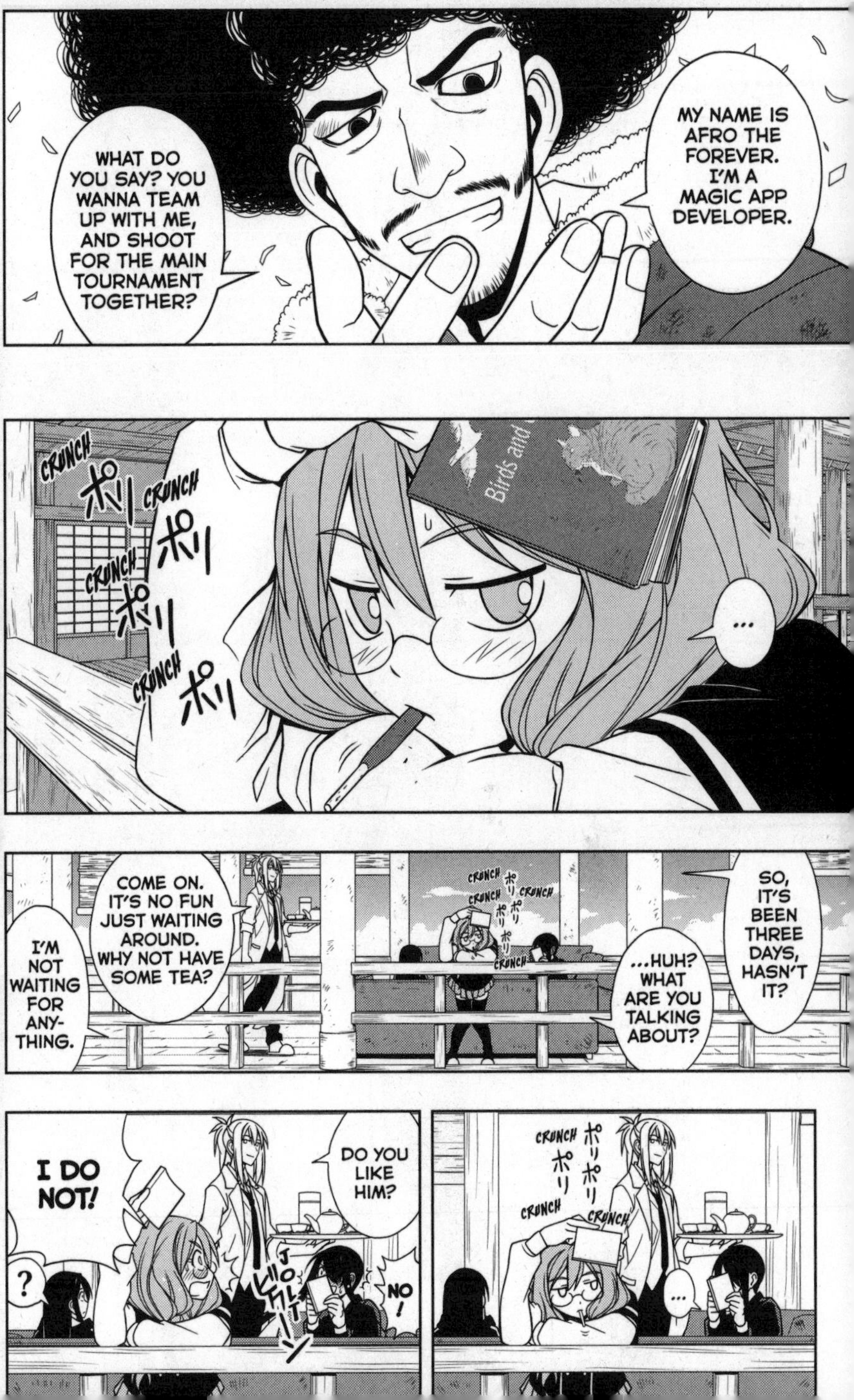
MY NAME IS AFRO THE FOREVER. I'M A MAGIC APP DEVELOPER.
WHAT DO YOU SAY? YOU WANNA TEAM UP WITH ME, AND SHOOT FOR THE MAIN TOURNAMENT TOGETHER?
...
CRUNCH ポリ
CRUNCH ポリ
CRUNCH ポリ
CRUNCH ポリ
SO, IT'S BEEN THREE DAYS, HASN'T IT?
...HUH? WHAT ARE YOU TALKING ABOUT?
CRUNCH ポリ CRUNCH ポリ CRUNCH ポリ CRUNCH ポリ
COME ON. IT'S NO FUN JUST WAITING AROUND. WHY NOT HAVE SOME TEA?
I'M NOT WAITING FOR ANYTHING.
CRUNCH ポリポリ CRUNCH ポリ CRUNCH
...
DO YOU LIKE HIM?
NO!
JOLT ビクーン
I DO NOT!
?

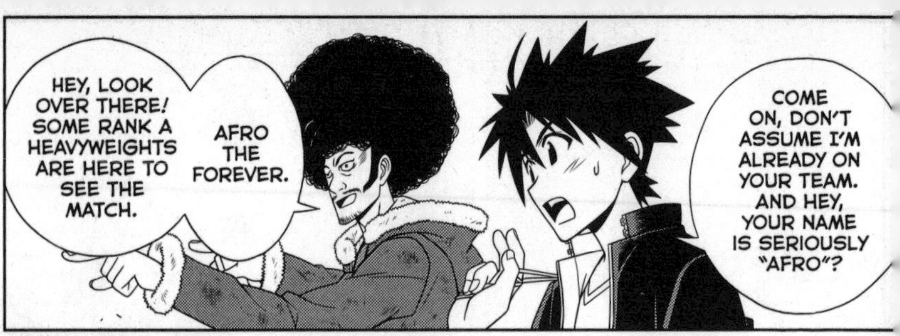
COME ON, DON'T ASSUME I'M ALREADY ON YOUR TEAM. AND HEY, YOUR NAME IS SERIOUSLY "AFRO"?
AFRO THE FOREVER.
HEY, LOOK OVER THERE! SOME RANK A HEAVYWEIGHTS ARE HERE TO SEE THE MATCH.

STAGE 69: USING APPS

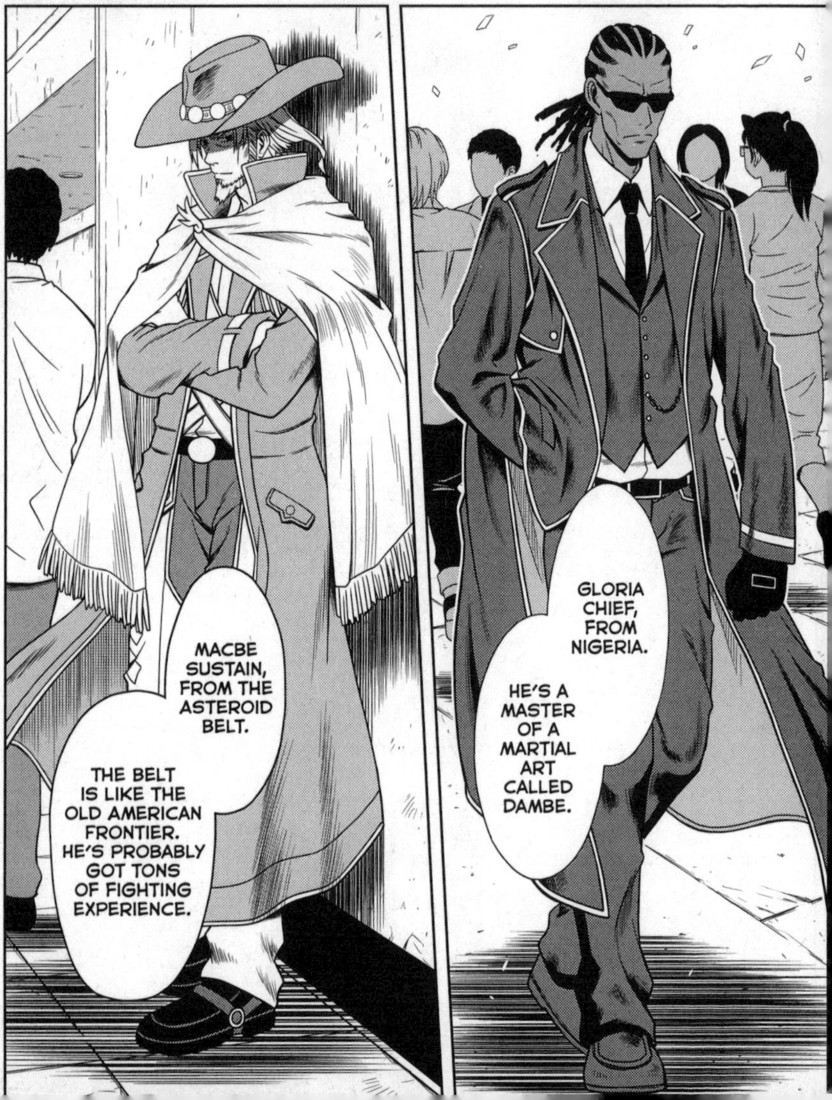
GLORIA CHIEF, FROM NIGERIA.
HE'S A MASTER OF A MARTIAL ART CALLED DAMBE.
MACBE SUSTAIN, FROM THE ASTEROID BELT.
THE BELT IS LIKE THE OLD AMERICAN FRONTIER. HE'S PROBABLY GOT TONS OF FIGHTING EXPERIENCE.

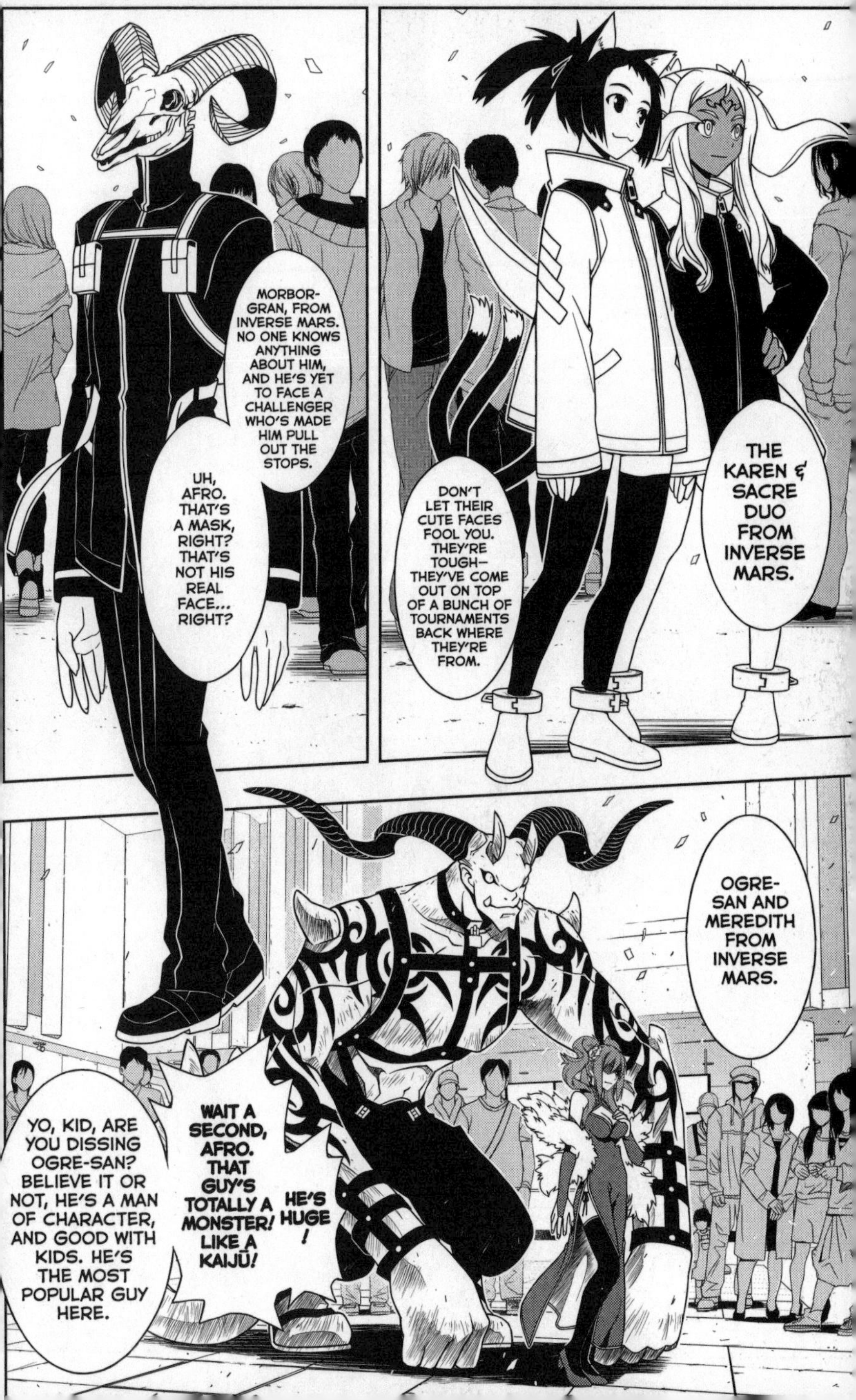
THE KAREN & SACRE DUO FROM INVERSE MARS.
DON'T LET THEIR CUTE FACES FOOL YOU. THEY'RE TOUGH—THEY'VE COME OUT ON TOP OF A BUNCH OF TOURNAMENTS BACK WHERE THEY'RE FROM.
MORBORGRAN, FROM INVERSE MARS. NO ONE KNOWS ANYTHING ABOUT HIM, AND HE'S YET TO FACE A CHALLENGER WHO'S MADE HIM PULL OUT THE STOPS.
UH, AFRO. THAT'S A MASK, RIGHT? THAT'S NOT HIS REAL FACE... RIGHT?
OGRE-SAN AND MEREDITH FROM INVERSE MARS.
HE'S HUGE!
WAIT A SECOND, AFRO. THAT GUY'S TOTALLY A MONSTER! LIKE A KAIJŪ!
YO, KID, ARE YOU DISSING OGRE-SAN? BELIEVE IT OR NOT, HE'S A MAN OF CHARACTER, AND GOOD WITH KIDS. HE'S THE MOST POPULAR GUY HERE.

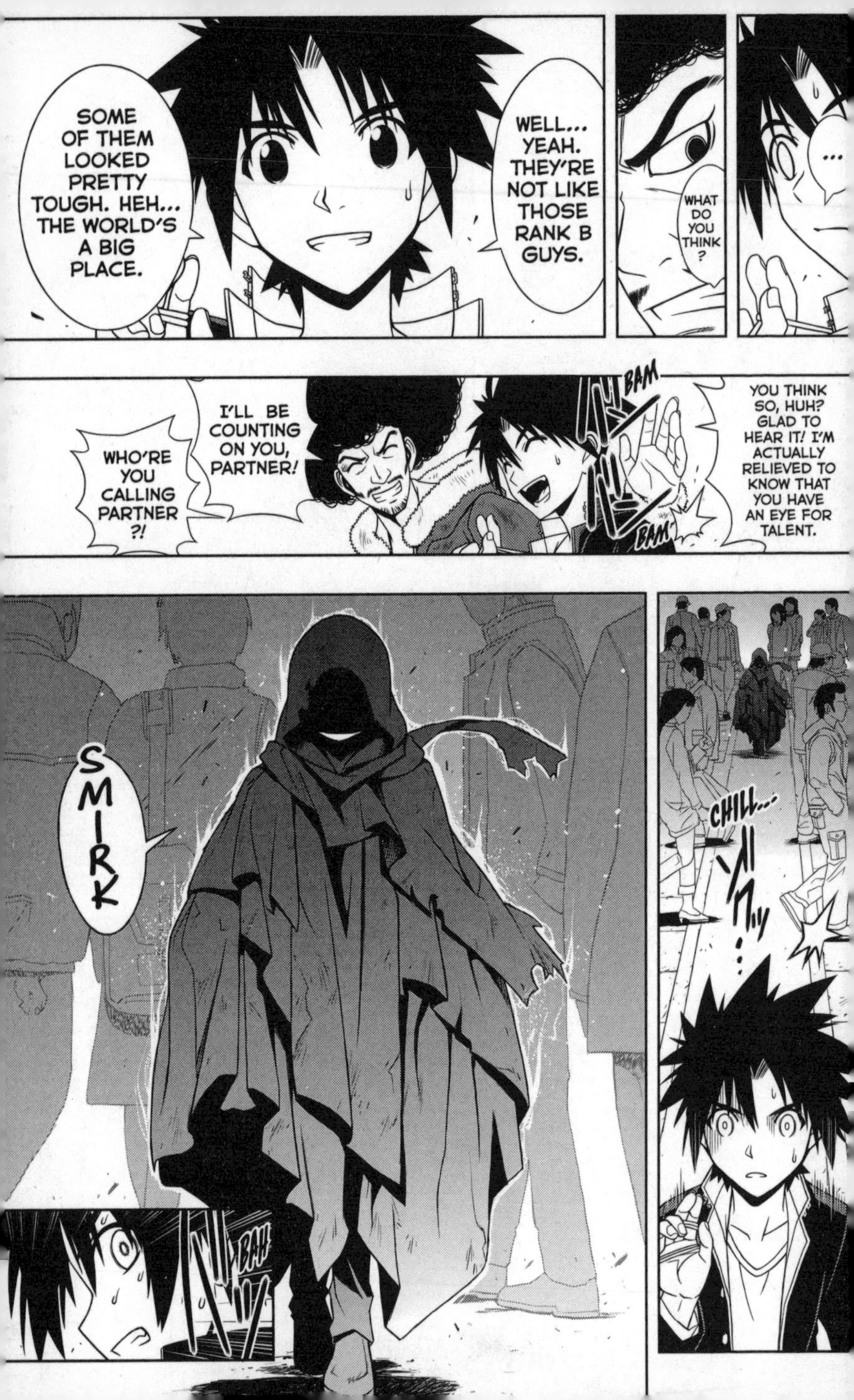
...
WHAT DO YOU THINK?
WELL... YEAH. THEY'RE NOT LIKE THOSE RANK B GUYS.
SOME OF THEM LOOKED PRETTY TOUGH. HEH... THE WORLD'S A BIG PLACE.
YOU THINK SO, HUH? GLAD TO HEAR IT! I'M ACTUALLY RELIEVED TO KNOW THAT YOU HAVE AN EYE FOR TALENT.
BAM
BAM
I'LL BE COUNTING ON YOU, PARTNER!
WHO'RE YOU CALLING PARTNER?!
CHILL...
SMIRK
BAH

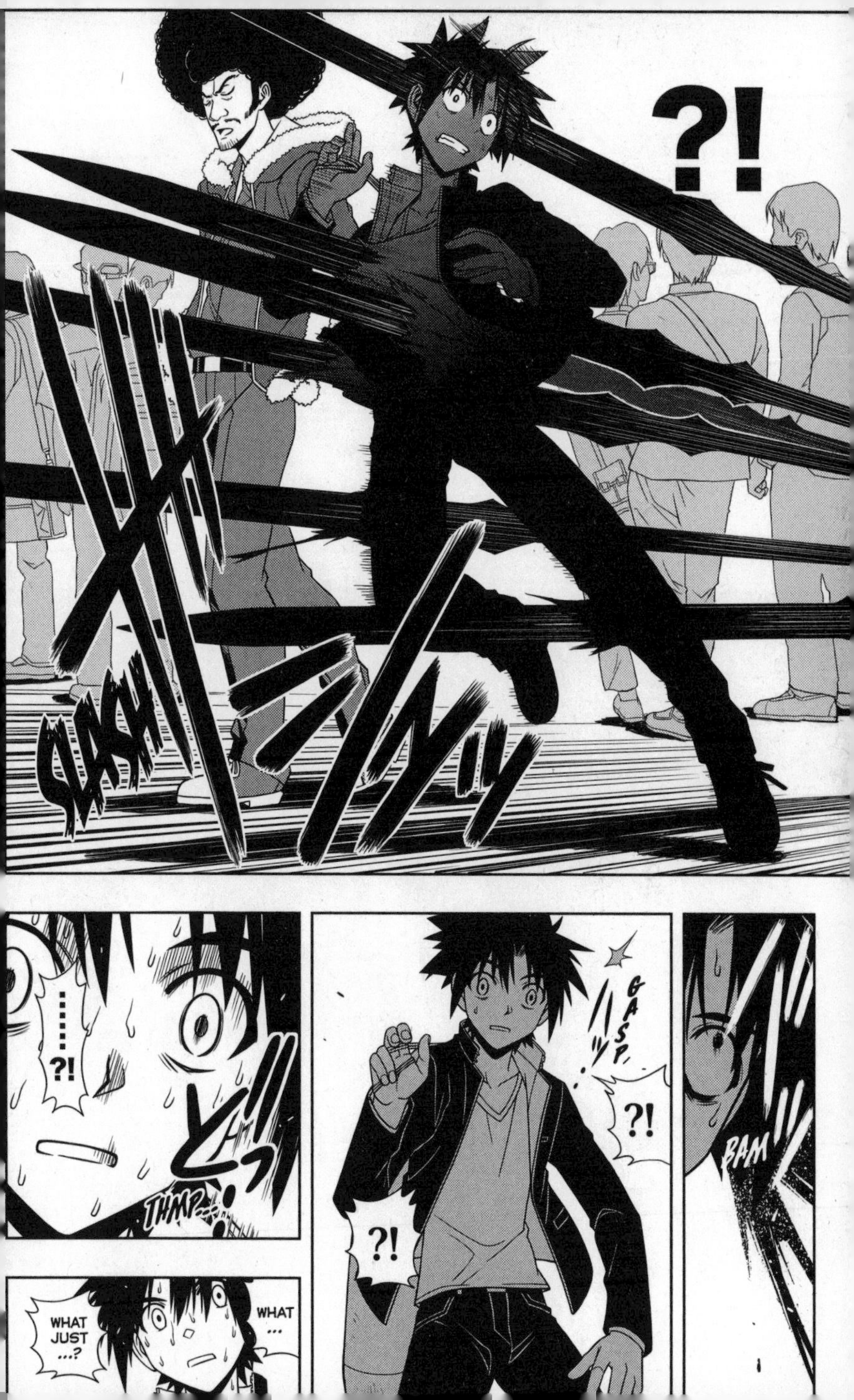
?!
SLASH
BAM
GASP
?!
?!
......
?!
THMP...
WHAT
...
WHAT
JUST
...?

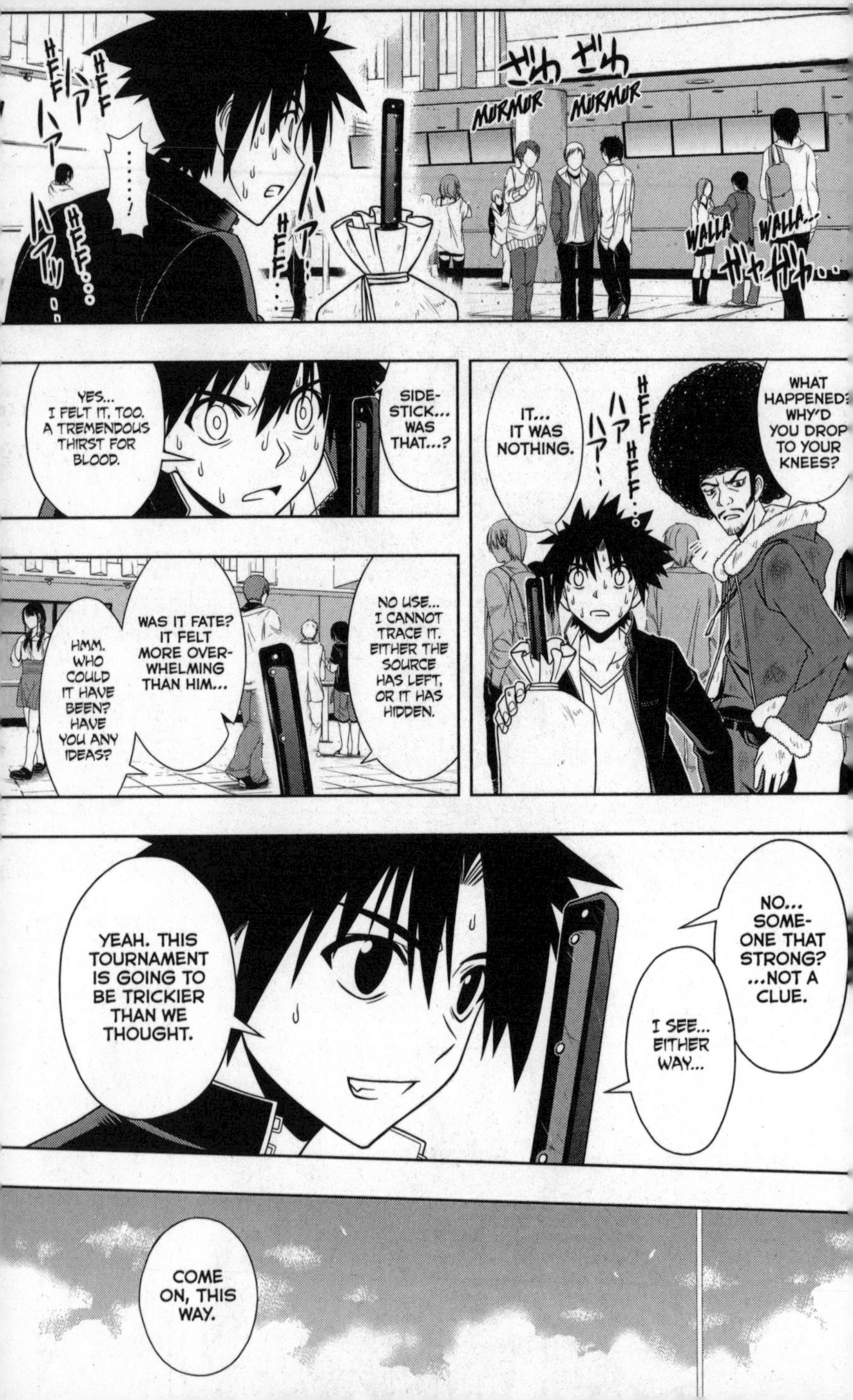
ざわざわ
MURMUR MURMUR
WALLA WALLA...
ガヤガヤ...
HFF ハア... HFF...
......!
HFF ハァ HFF
ハアッ HFF...
WHAT HAPPENED? WHY'D YOU DROP TO YOUR KNEES?
HFF ハァ ハァ... HFF...
IT... IT WAS NOTHING.
SIDE-STICK... WAS THAT...?
YES... I FELT IT, TOO. A TREMENDOUS THIRST FOR BLOOD.
NO USE... I CANNOT TRACE IT. EITHER THE SOURCE HAS LEFT, OR IT HAS HIDDEN.
WAS IT FATE? IT FELT MORE OVER-WHELMING THAN HIM...
HMM. WHO COULD IT HAVE BEEN? HAVE YOU ANY IDEAS?
NO... SOME-ONE THAT STRONG? ...NOT A CLUE.
I SEE... EITHER WAY...
YEAH. THIS TOURNAMENT IS GOING TO BE TRICKIER THAN WE THOUGHT.
COME ON, THIS WAY.

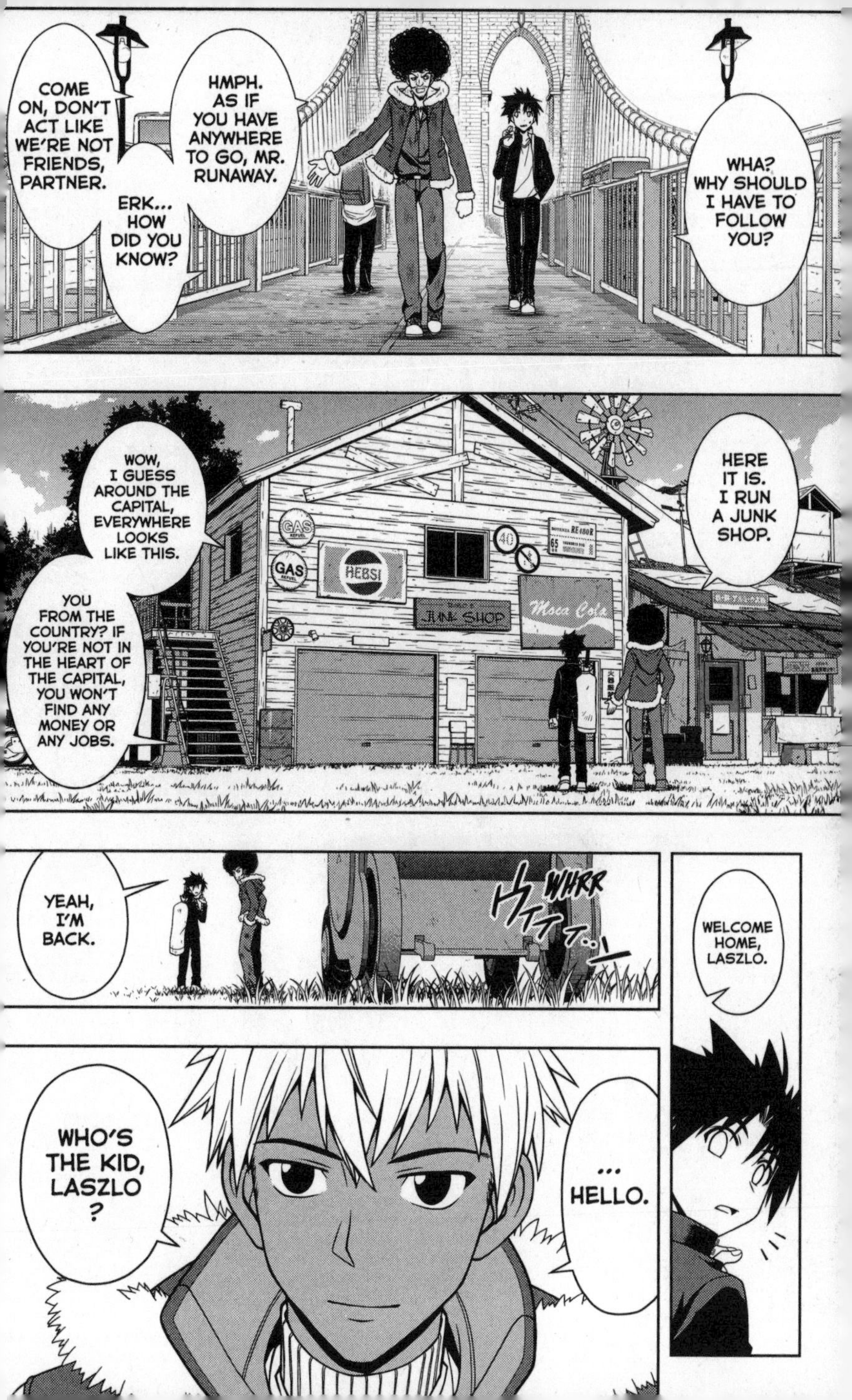
WHA? WHY SHOULD I HAVE TO FOLLOW YOU?
HMPH. AS IF YOU HAVE ANYWHERE TO GO, MR. RUNAWAY.
COME ON, DON'T ACT LIKE WE'RE NOT FRIENDS, PARTNER.
ERK... HOW DID YOU KNOW?
HERE IT IS. I RUN A JUNK SHOP.
WOW, I GUESS AROUND THE CAPITAL, EVERYWHERE LOOKS LIKE THIS.
YOU FROM THE COUNTRY? IF YOU'RE NOT IN THE HEART OF THE CAPITAL, YOU WON'T FIND ANY MONEY OR ANY JOBS.
GAS
GAS
HEBSI
40
JUNK SHOP
Moca Cola
WELCOME HOME, LASZLO.
YEAH, I'M BACK.
WHRR
WHO'S THE KID, LASZLO?
...HELLO.

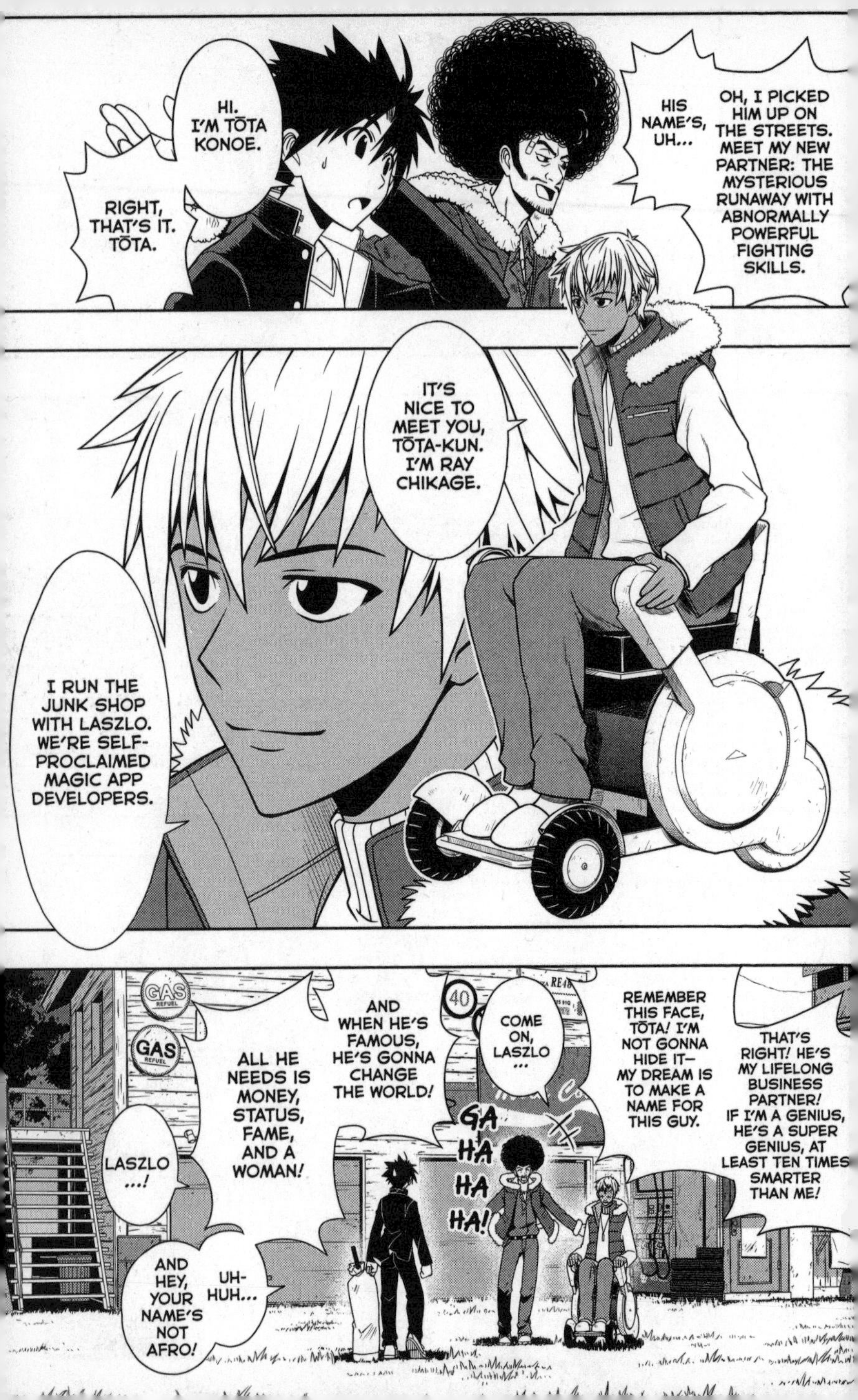
OH, I PICKED HIM UP ON THE STREETS. MEET MY NEW PARTNER: THE MYSTERIOUS RUNAWAY WITH ABNORMALLY POWERFUL FIGHTING SKILLS.
HIS NAME'S, UH...
HI. I'M TŌTA KONOE.
RIGHT, THAT'S IT. TŌTA.
IT'S NICE TO MEET YOU, TŌTA-KUN. I'M RAY CHIKAGE.
I RUN THE JUNK SHOP WITH LASZLO. WE'RE SELF-PROCLAIMED MAGIC APP DEVELOPERS.
THAT'S RIGHT! HE'S MY LIFELONG BUSINESS PARTNER! IF I'M A GENIUS, HE'S A SUPER GENIUS, AT LEAST TEN TIMES SMARTER THAN ME!
REMEMBER THIS FACE, TŌTA! I'M NOT GONNA HIDE IT— MY DREAM IS TO MAKE A NAME FOR THIS GUY.
COME ON, LASZLO...
GA HA HA HA!
AND WHEN HE'S FAMOUS, HE'S GONNA CHANGE THE WORLD!
ALL HE NEEDS IS MONEY, STATUS, FAME, AND A WOMAN!
LASZLO...!
UH-HUH...
AND HEY, YOUR NAME'S NOT AFRO!
GAS REFUEL
GAS REFUEL
40

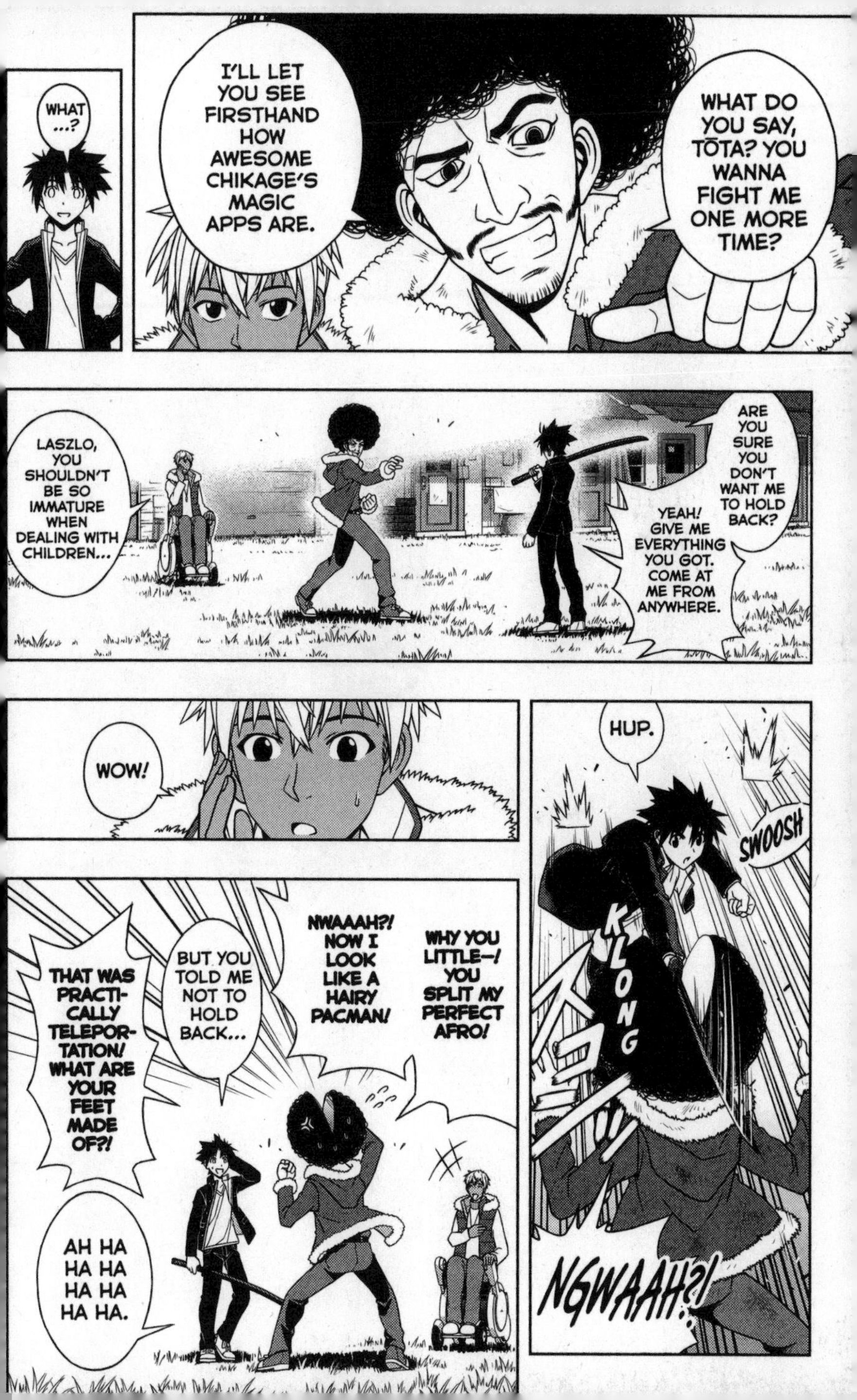
WHAT DO YOU SAY, TŌTA? YOU WANNA FIGHT ME ONE MORE TIME?
I'LL LET YOU SEE FIRSTHAND HOW AWESOME CHIKAGE'S MAGIC APPS ARE.
WHAT ...?
ARE YOU SURE YOU DON'T WANT ME TO HOLD BACK?
YEAH! GIVE ME EVERYTHING YOU GOT. COME AT ME FROM ANYWHERE.
LASZLO, YOU SHOULDN'T BE SO IMMATURE WHEN DEALING WITH CHILDREN...
HUP.
SWOOSH
KLONG
NGWAAH?!
WOW!
WHY YOU LITTLE--! YOU SPLIT MY PERFECT AFRO!
NWAAAH?! NOW I LOOK LIKE A HAIRY PACMAN!
BUT YOU TOLD ME NOT TO HOLD BACK...
THAT WAS PRACTICALLY TELEPORTATION! WHAT ARE YOUR FEET MADE OF?!
AH HA HA HA HA HA HA HA.

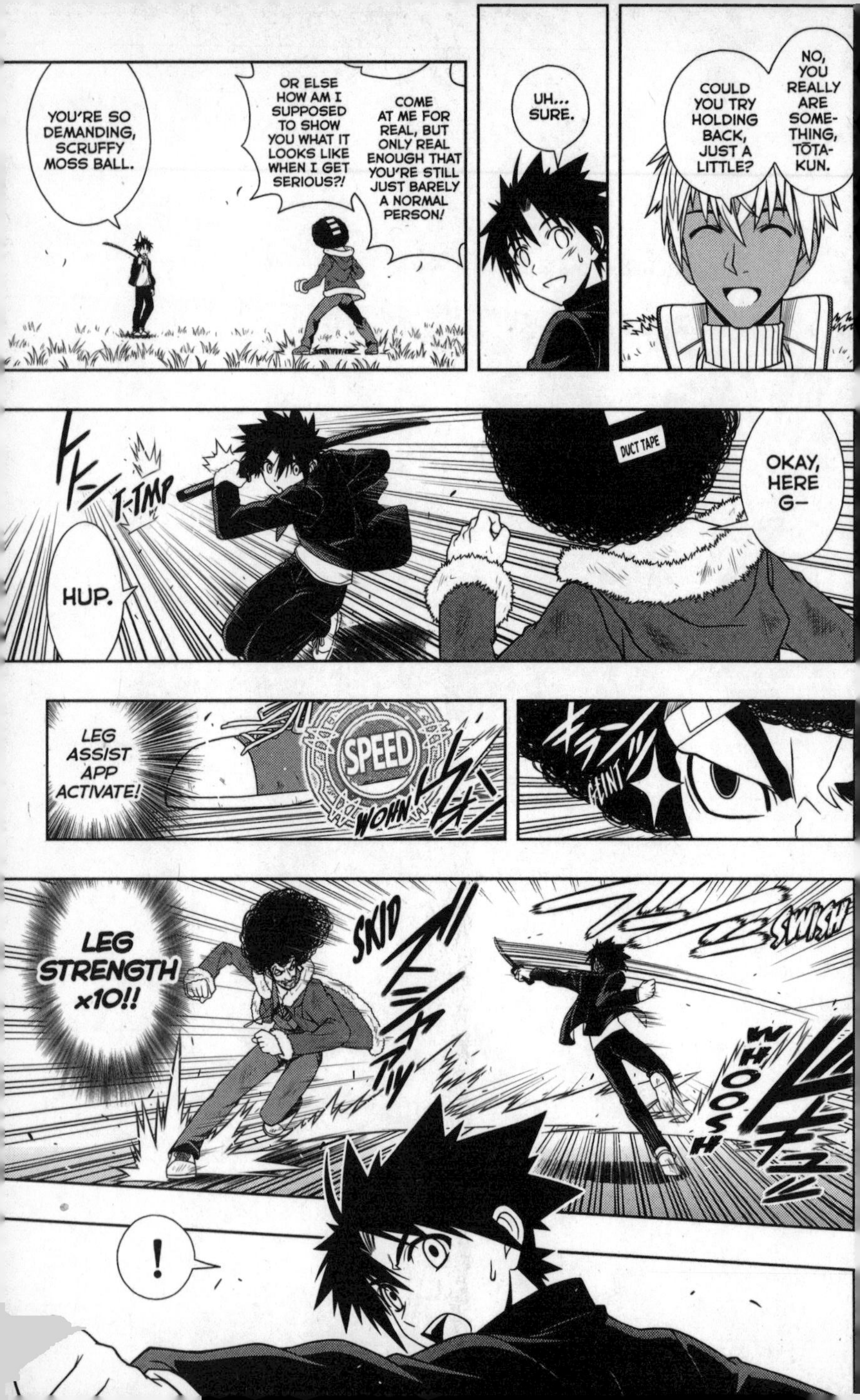
NO, YOU REALLY ARE SOMETHING, TŌTA-KUN.
COULD YOU TRY HOLDING BACK, JUST A LITTLE?
UH... SURE.
COME AT ME FOR REAL, BUT ONLY REAL ENOUGH THAT YOU'RE STILL JUST BARELY A NORMAL PERSON!
OR ELSE HOW AM I SUPPOSED TO SHOW YOU WHAT IT LOOKS LIKE WHEN I GET SERIOUS?!
YOU'RE SO DEMANDING, SCRUFFY MOSS BALL.
OKAY, HERE G—
DUCT TAPE
T-TMP
HUP.
GLINT
SPEED
WOHN
LEG ASSIST APP ACTIVATE!
SWISH
WHOOSH
SKID
LEG STRENGTH x10!!
!

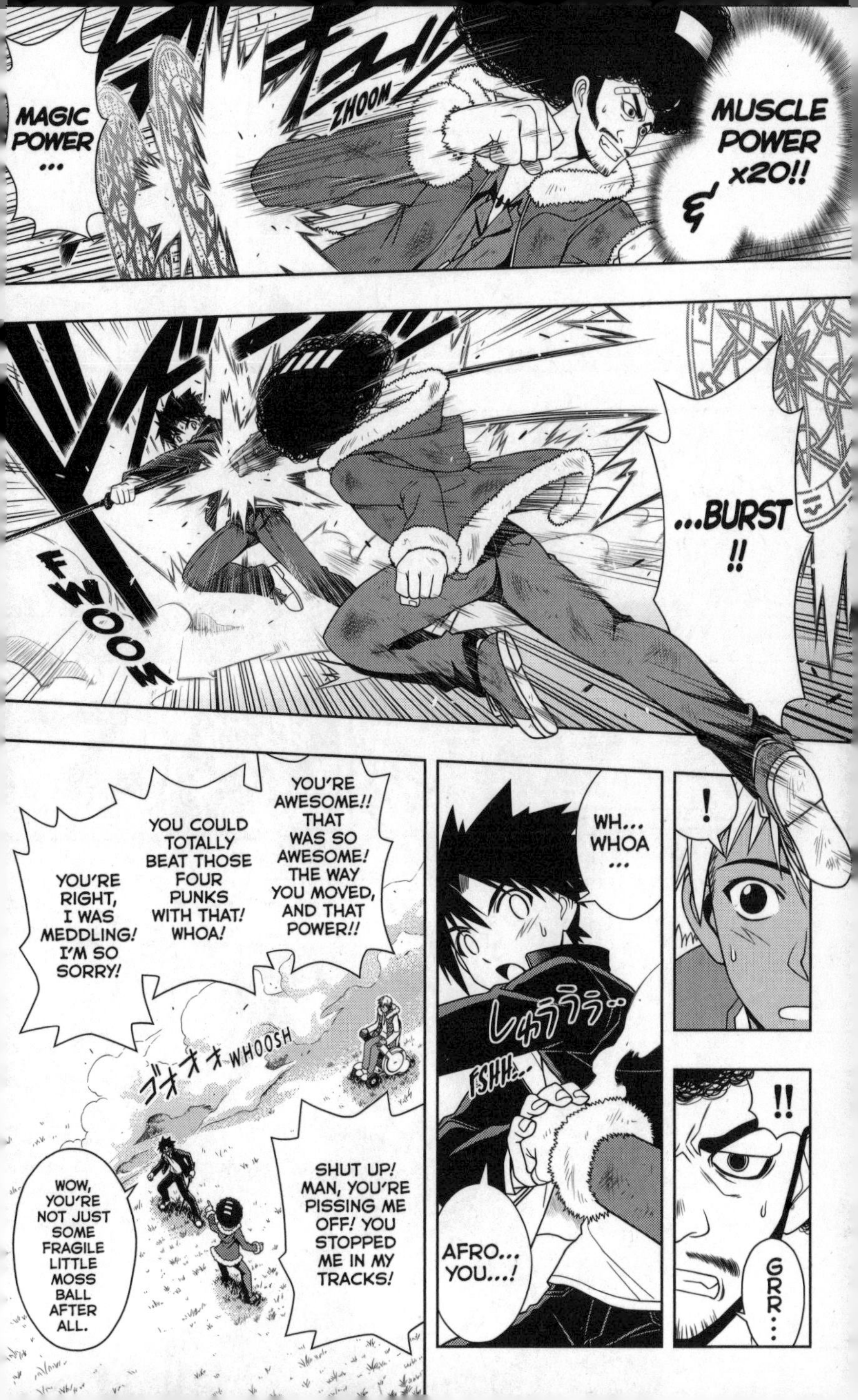
MUSCLE POWER x20!!
&
ZHOOM
MAGIC POWER ...
...BURST!!
FWOOM
!
!!
GRR...
WH... WHOA...
FSHH...
AFRO... YOU...!
YOU'RE AWESOME!! THAT WAS SO AWESOME! THE WAY YOU MOVED, AND THAT POWER!!
YOU COULD TOTALLY BEAT THOSE FOUR PUNKS WITH THAT! WHOA!
YOU'RE RIGHT, I WAS MEDDLING! I'M SO SORRY!
WHOOSH
SHUT UP! MAN, YOU'RE PISSING ME OFF! YOU STOPPED ME IN MY TRACKS!
WOW, YOU'RE NOT JUST SOME FRAGILE LITTLE MOSS BALL AFTER ALL.

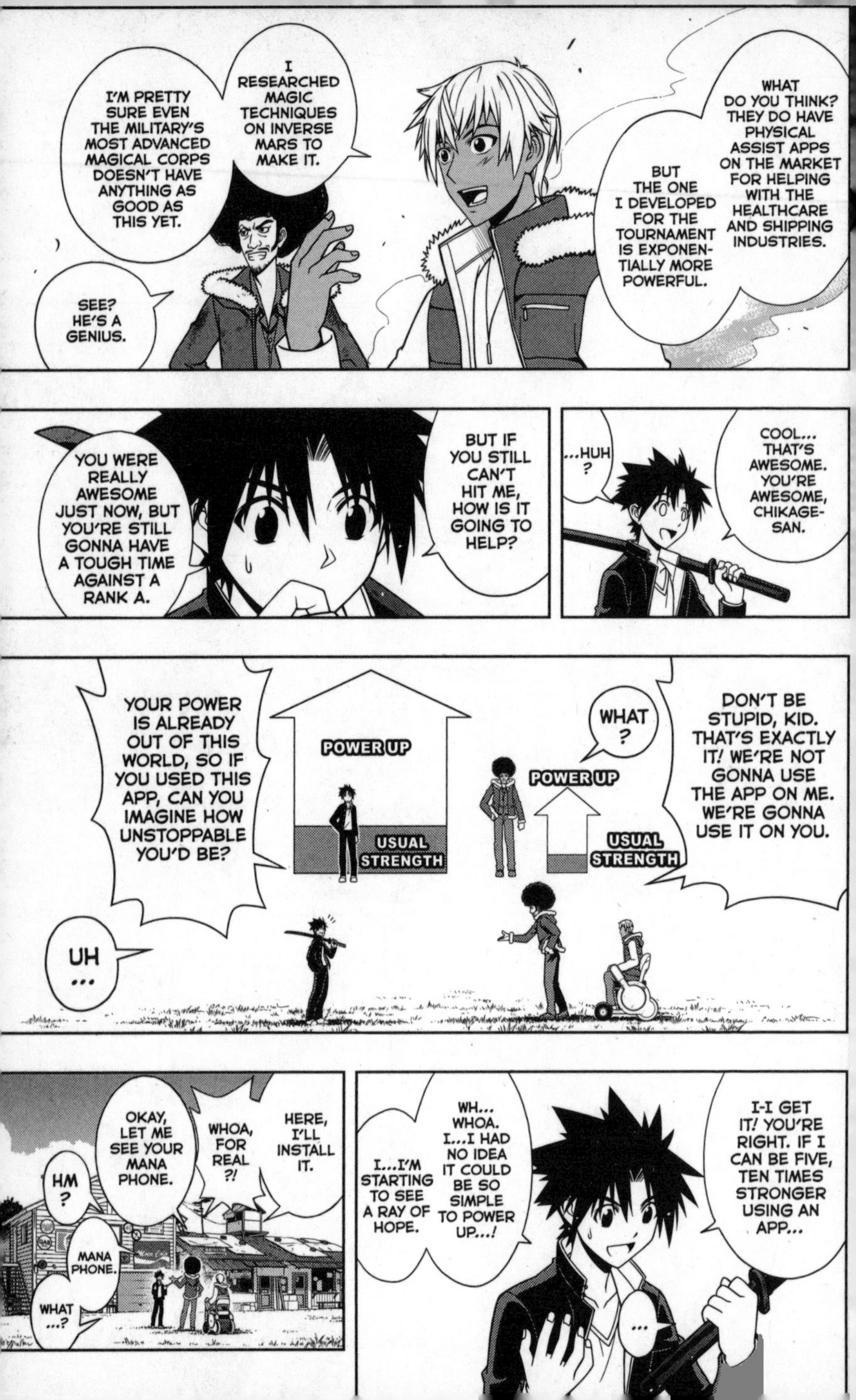
WHAT DO YOU THINK? THEY DO HAVE PHYSICAL ASSIST APPS ON THE MARKET FOR HELPING WITH THE HEALTHCARE AND SHIPPING INDUSTRIES.
BUT THE ONE I DEVELOPED FOR THE TOURNAMENT IS EXPONEN-TIALLY MORE POWERFUL.
I RESEARCHED MAGIC TECHNIQUES ON INVERSE MARS TO MAKE IT.
I'M PRETTY SURE EVEN THE MILITARY'S MOST ADVANCED MAGICAL CORPS DOESN'T HAVE ANYTHING AS GOOD AS THIS YET.
SEE? HE'S A GENIUS.
COOL... THAT'S AWESOME. YOU'RE AWESOME, CHIKAGE-SAN.
...HUH?
BUT IF YOU STILL CAN'T HIT ME, HOW IS IT GOING TO HELP?
YOU WERE REALLY AWESOME JUST NOW, BUT YOU'RE STILL GONNA HAVE A TOUGH TIME AGAINST A RANK A.
DON'T BE STUPID, KID. THAT'S EXACTLY IT! WE'RE NOT GONNA USE THE APP ON ME. WE'RE GONNA USE IT ON YOU.
WHAT?
POWER UP
USUAL STRENGTH
POWER UP
USUAL STRENGTH
YOUR POWER IS ALREADY OUT OF THIS WORLD, SO IF YOU USED THIS APP, CAN YOU IMAGINE HOW UNSTOPPABLE YOU'D BE?
UH...
I-I GET IT! YOU'RE RIGHT. IF I CAN BE FIVE, TEN TIMES STRONGER USING AN APP...
WH... WHOA. I...I HAD NO IDEA IT COULD BE SO SIMPLE TO POWER UP...!
I...I'M STARTING TO SEE A RAY OF HOPE.
...
HERE, I'LL INSTALL IT.
WHOA, FOR REAL?!
OKAY, LET ME SEE YOUR MANA PHONE.
HM?
MANA PHONE.
WHAT...?

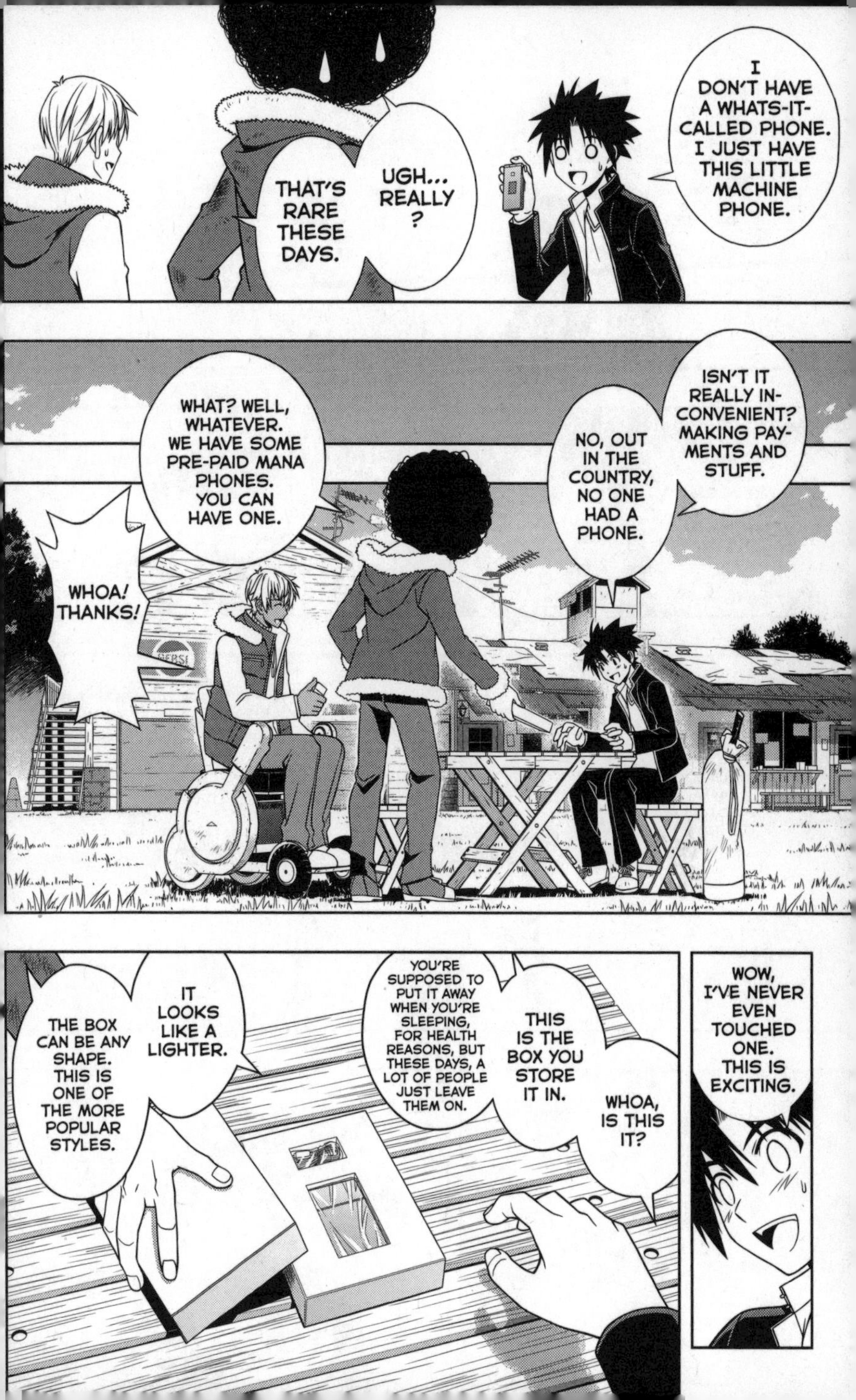
I DON'T HAVE A WHATS-IT-CALLED PHONE. I JUST HAVE THIS LITTLE MACHINE PHONE.
UGH... REALLY?
THAT'S RARE THESE DAYS.
ISN'T IT REALLY IN-CONVENIENT? MAKING PAY-MENTS AND STUFF.
NO, OUT IN THE COUNTRY, NO ONE HAD A PHONE.
WHAT? WELL, WHATEVER. WE HAVE SOME PRE-PAID MANA PHONES. YOU CAN HAVE ONE.
WHOA! THANKS!
WOW, I'VE NEVER EVEN TOUCHED ONE. THIS IS EXCITING.
WHOA, IS THIS IT?
THIS IS THE BOX YOU STORE IT IN.
YOU'RE SUPPOSED TO PUT IT AWAY WHEN YOU'RE SLEEPING, FOR HEALTH REASONS, BUT THESE DAYS, A LOT OF PEOPLE JUST LEAVE THEM ON.
IT LOOKS LIKE A LIGHTER.
THE BOX CAN BE ANY SHAPE. THIS IS ONE OF THE MORE POPULAR STYLES.

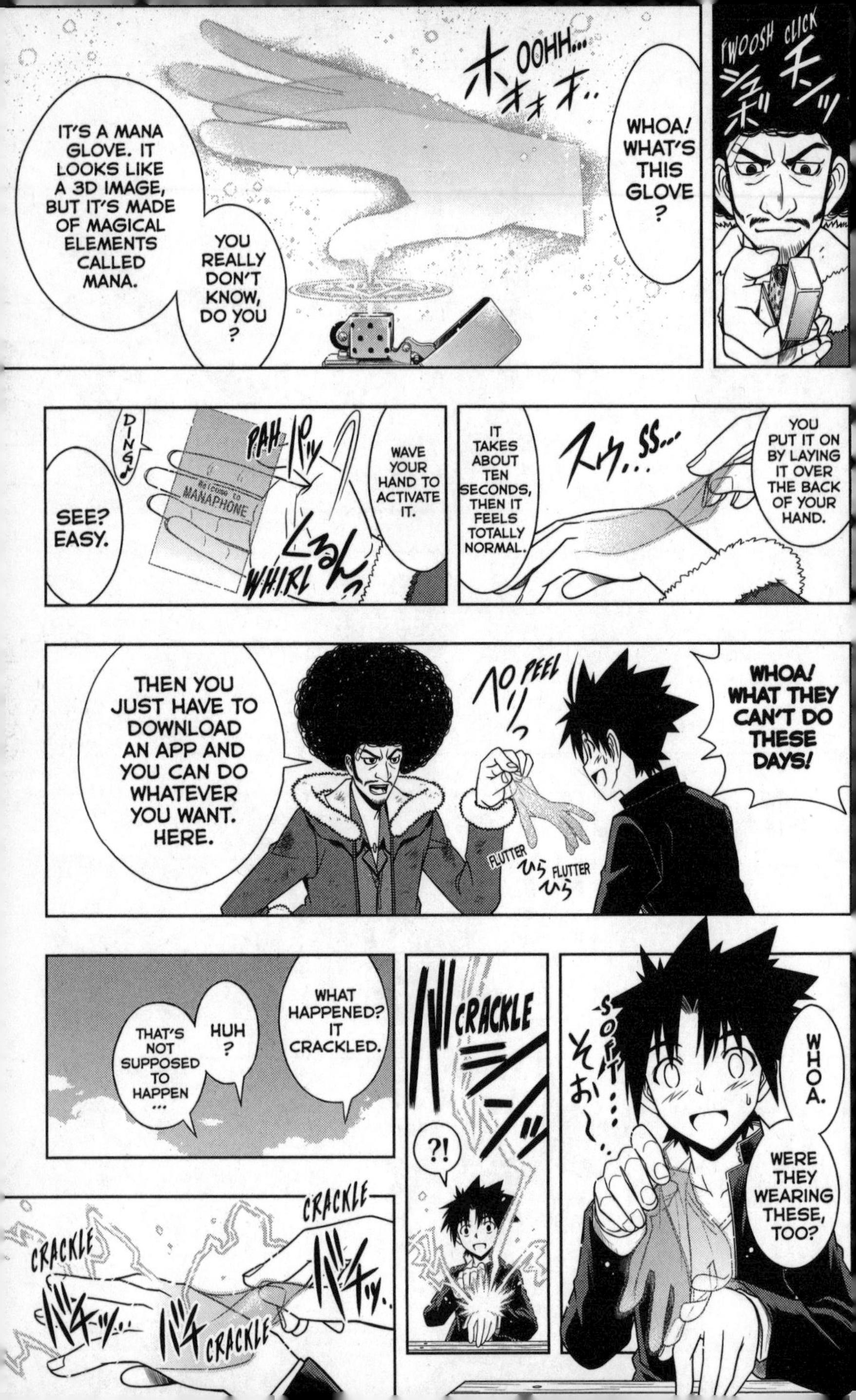

FWOOSH CLICK
シュボ チンッ
WHOA! WHAT'S THIS GLOVE?
OOHH...
ホオォォ..
YOU REALLY DON'T KNOW, DO YOU?
IT'S A MANA GLOVE. IT LOOKS LIKE A 3D IMAGE, BUT IT'S MADE OF MAGICAL ELEMENTS CALLED MANA.
YOU PUT IT ON BY LAYING IT OVER THE BACK OF YOUR HAND.
SS...
スゥ...
IT TAKES ABOUT TEN SECONDS, THEN IT FEELS TOTALLY NORMAL.
WAVE YOUR HAND TO ACTIVATE IT.
PAH
パッ
WHIRL
くるんっ
Welcome to MANAPHONE
DING♪
SEE? EASY.
WHOA! WHAT THEY CAN'T DO THESE DAYS!
PEEL
ペリッ
THEN YOU JUST HAVE TO DOWNLOAD AN APP AND YOU CAN DO WHATEVER YOU WANT. HERE.
FLUTTER
ひら
FLUTTER
ひら
WHOA. WERE THEY WEARING THESE, TOO?
SOFT...
そお〜...
CRACKLE
バリッ
?!
WHAT HAPPENED? IT CRACKLED.
HUH?
THAT'S NOT SUPPOSED TO HAPPEN...
CRACKLE
CRACKLE
CRACKLE
バチッ
バチッ
バチッ

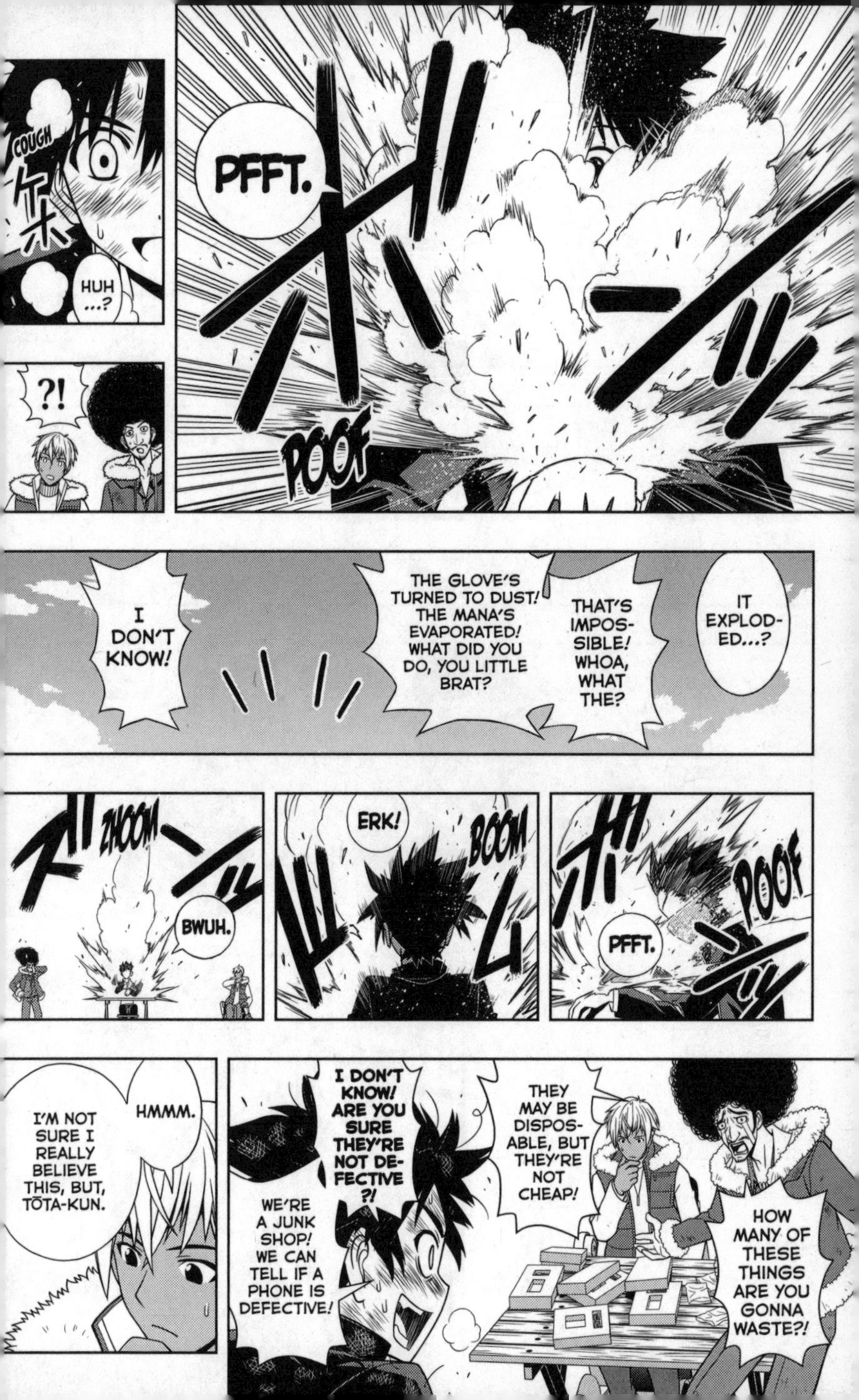

PFFT.
POOF
COUGH
HUH ...?
?!
IT EXPLODED...?
THAT'S IMPOSSIBLE! WHOA, WHAT THE?
THE GLOVE'S TURNED TO DUST! THE MANA'S EVAPORATED! WHAT DID YOU DO, YOU LITTLE BRAT?
I DON'T KNOW!
POOF
PFFT.
ERK!
BOOM
ZHOOM
BWUH.
HOW MANY OF THESE THINGS ARE YOU GONNA WASTE?!
THEY MAY BE DISPOSABLE, BUT THEY'RE NOT CHEAP!
I DON'T KNOW! ARE YOU SURE THEY'RE NOT DEFECTIVE?!
WE'RE A JUNK SHOP! WE CAN TELL IF A PHONE IS DEFECTIVE!
HMMM.
I'M NOT SURE I REALLY BELIEVE THIS, BUT, TŌTA-KUN.

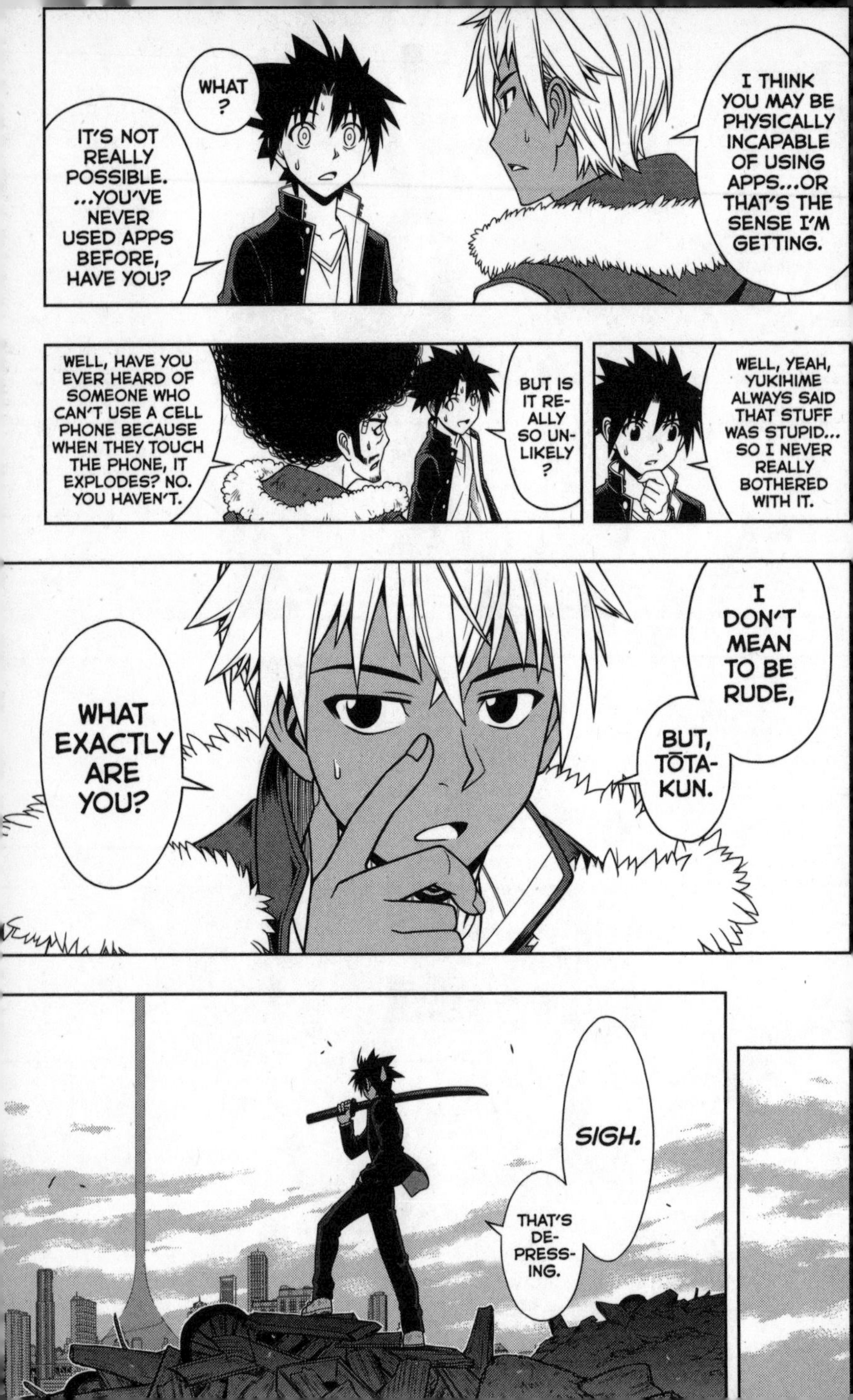
I THINK YOU MAY BE PHYSICALLY INCAPABLE OF USING APPS...OR THAT'S THE SENSE I'M GETTING.
WHAT?
IT'S NOT REALLY POSSIBLE. ...YOU'VE NEVER USED APPS BEFORE, HAVE YOU?
WELL, YEAH, YUKIHIME ALWAYS SAID THAT STUFF WAS STUPID... SO I NEVER REALLY BOTHERED WITH IT.
BUT IS IT REALLY SO UNLIKELY?
WELL, HAVE YOU EVER HEARD OF SOMEONE WHO CAN'T USE A CELL PHONE BECAUSE WHEN THEY TOUCH THE PHONE, IT EXPLODES? NO. YOU HAVEN'T.
I DON'T MEAN TO BE RUDE,
BUT, TŌTA-KUN.
WHAT EXACTLY ARE YOU?
SIGH.
THAT'S DEPRESSING.

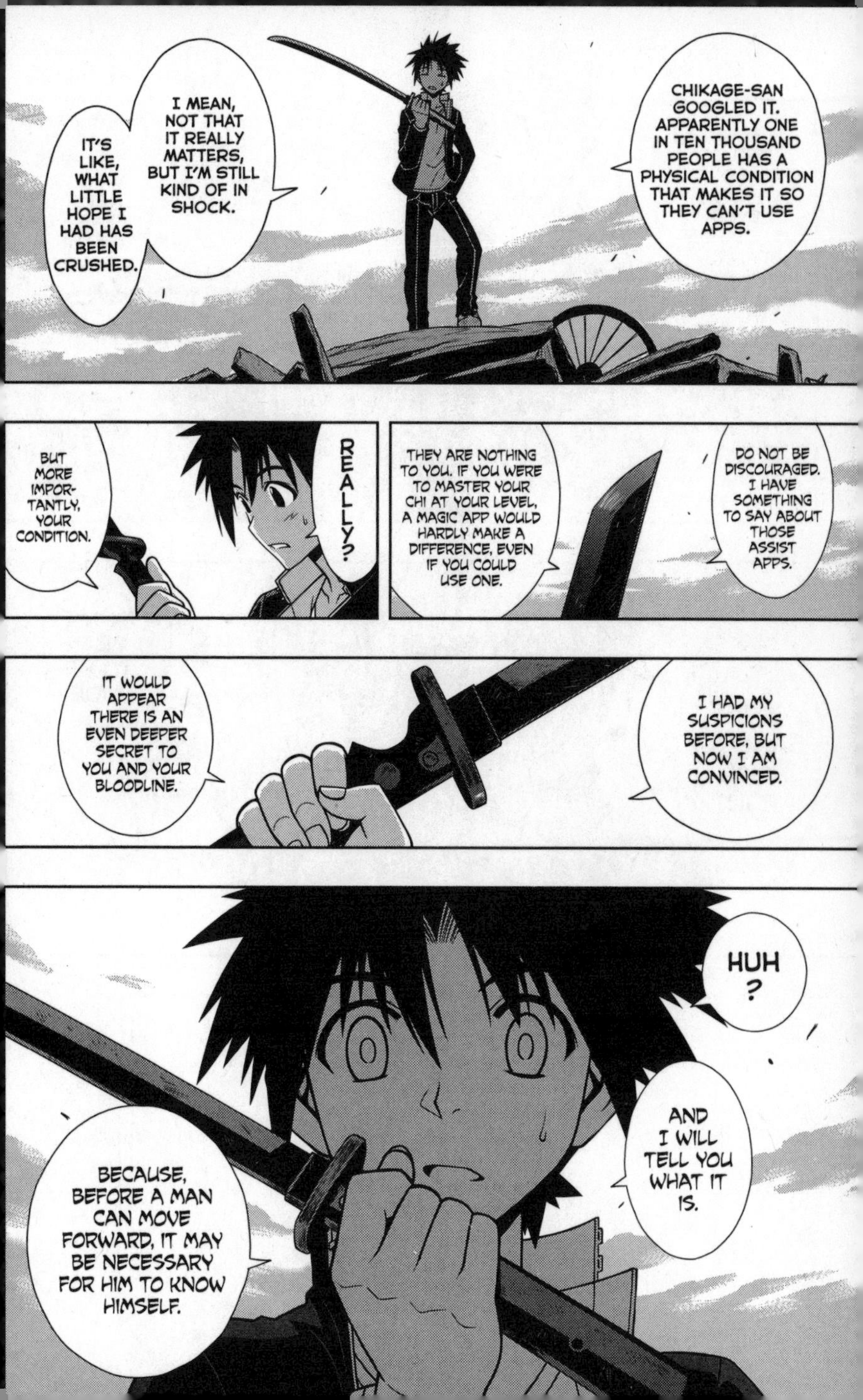
CHIKAGE-SAN GOOGLED IT. APPARENTLY ONE IN TEN THOUSAND PEOPLE HAS A PHYSICAL CONDITION THAT MAKES IT SO THEY CAN'T USE APPS.
I MEAN, NOT THAT IT REALLY MATTERS, BUT I'M STILL KIND OF IN SHOCK.
IT'S LIKE, WHAT LITTLE HOPE I HAD HAS BEEN CRUSHED.
DO NOT BE DISCOURAGED. I HAVE SOMETHING TO SAY ABOUT THOSE ASSIST APPS.
THEY ARE NOTHING TO YOU. IF YOU WERE TO MASTER YOUR CHI AT YOUR LEVEL, A MAGIC APP WOULD HARDLY MAKE A DIFFERENCE, EVEN IF YOU COULD USE ONE.
REALLY?
BUT MORE IMPOR-TANTLY, YOUR CONDITION.
I HAD MY SUSPICIONS BEFORE, BUT NOW I AM CONVINCED.
IT WOULD APPEAR THERE IS AN EVEN DEEPER SECRET TO YOU AND YOUR BLOODLINE.
HUH?
AND I WILL TELL YOU WHAT IT IS.
BECAUSE, BEFORE A MAN CAN MOVE FORWARD, IT MAY BE NECESSARY FOR HIM TO KNOW HIMSELF.

UQ HOLDER!

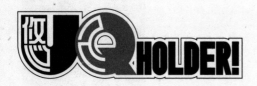

UQ HOLDER!

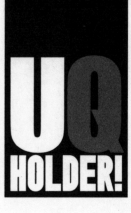

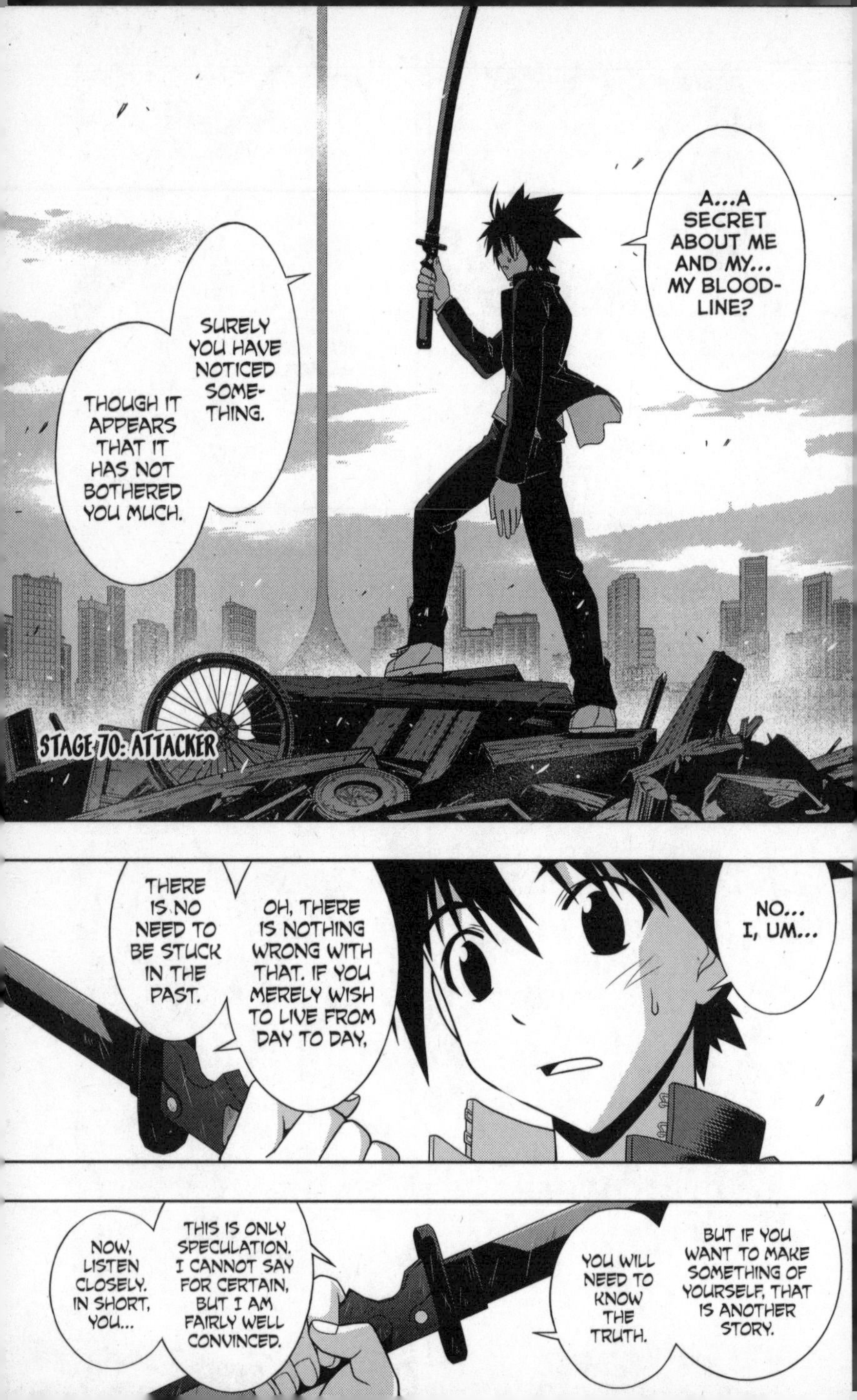
A...A SECRET ABOUT ME AND MY... MY BLOODLINE?
SURELY YOU HAVE NOTICED SOMETHING.
THOUGH IT APPEARS THAT IT HAS NOT BOTHERED YOU MUCH.
STAGE 70: ATTACKER
NO... I, UM...
OH, THERE IS NOTHING WRONG WITH THAT. IF YOU MERELY WISH TO LIVE FROM DAY TO DAY,
THERE IS NO NEED TO BE STUCK IN THE PAST.
BUT IF YOU WANT TO MAKE SOMETHING OF YOURSELF, THAT IS ANOTHER STORY.
YOU WILL NEED TO KNOW THE TRUTH.
THIS IS ONLY SPECULATION. I CANNOT SAY FOR CERTAIN, BUT I AM FAIRLY WELL CONVINCED.
NOW, LISTEN CLOSELY. IN SHORT, YOU...

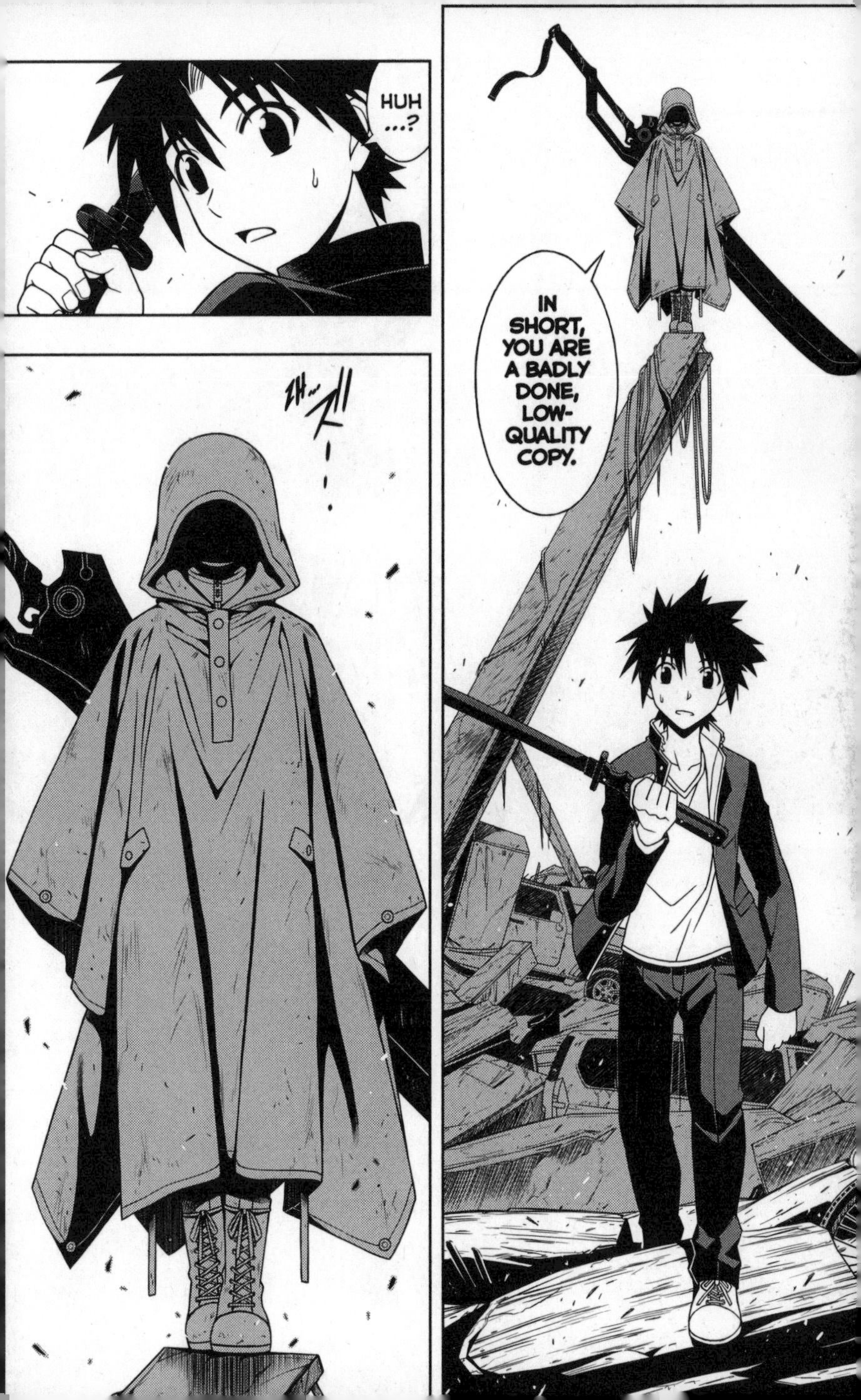
IN SHORT, YOU ARE A BADLY DONE, LOW-QUALITY COPY.
HUH ...?
ZH...

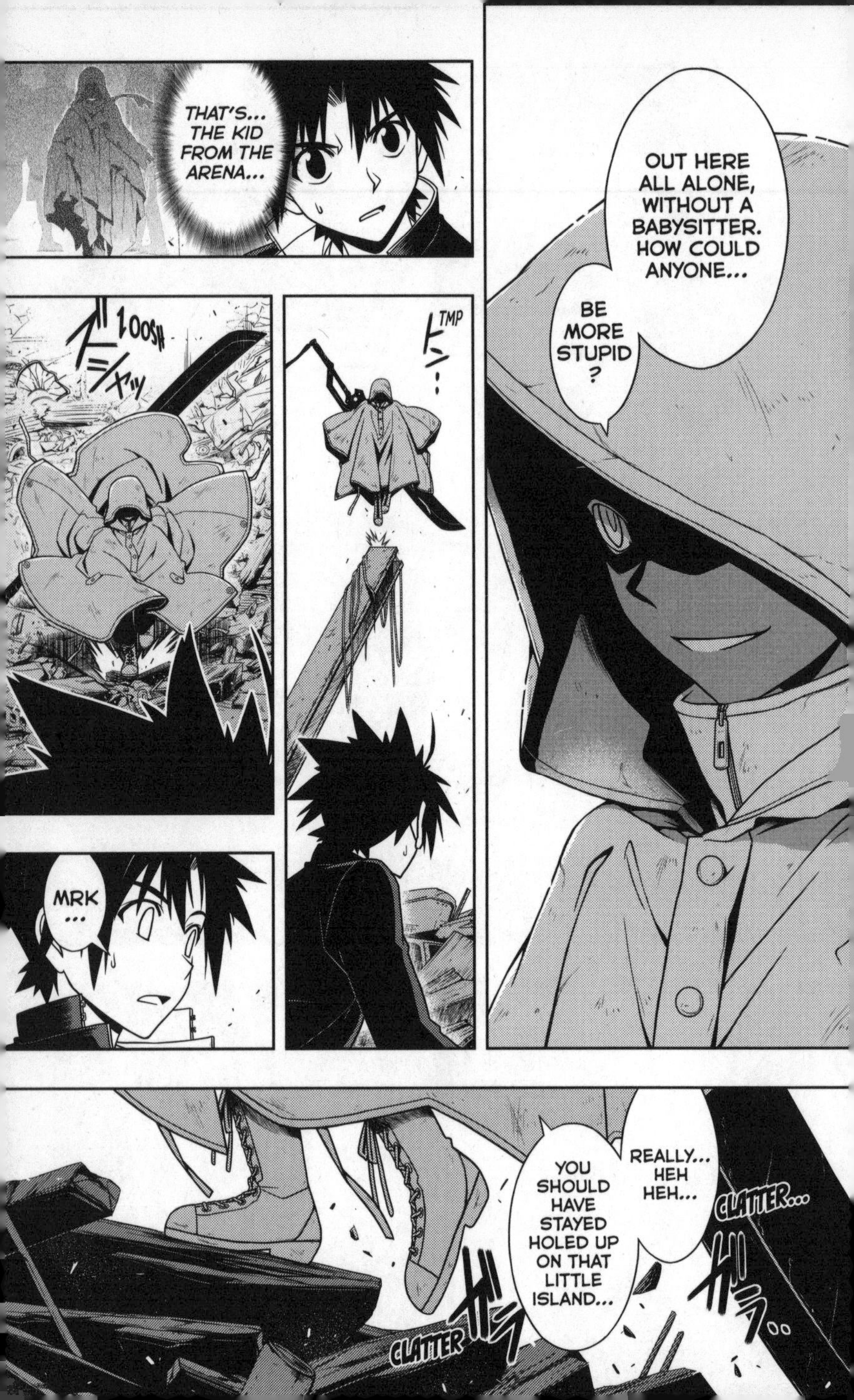

OUT HERE ALL ALONE, WITHOUT A BABYSITTER. HOW COULD ANYONE...
BE MORE STUPID?
THAT'S... THE KID FROM THE ARENA...
TMP
WOOSH
MRK...
REALLY... HEH HEH...
YOU SHOULD HAVE STAYED HOLED UP ON THAT LITTLE ISLAND...
CLATTER...
CLATTER

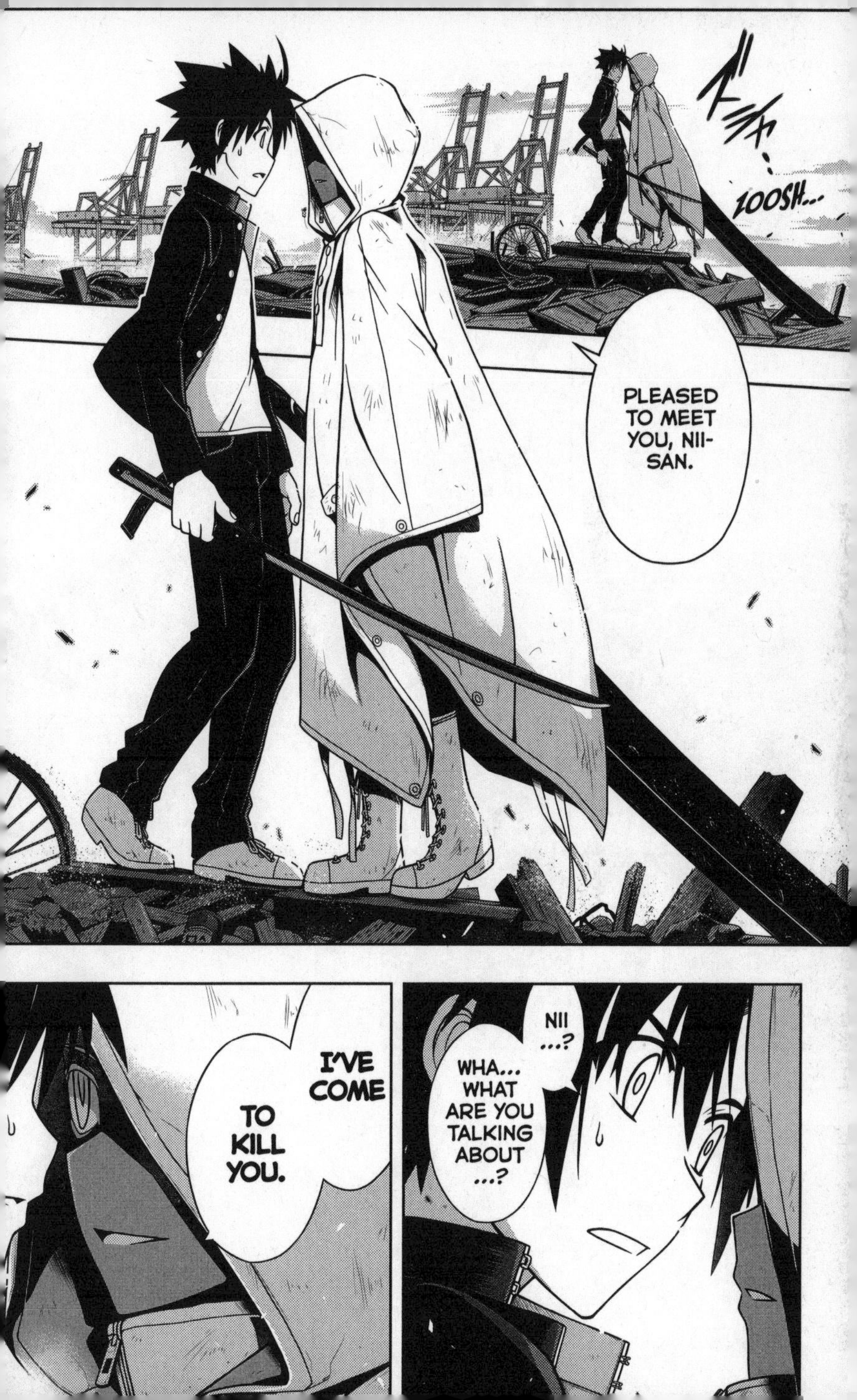
ZOOSH...
PLEASED TO MEET YOU, NII-SAN.
NII ...?
WHA... WHAT ARE YOU TALKING ABOUT ...?
I'VE COME
TO KILL YOU.

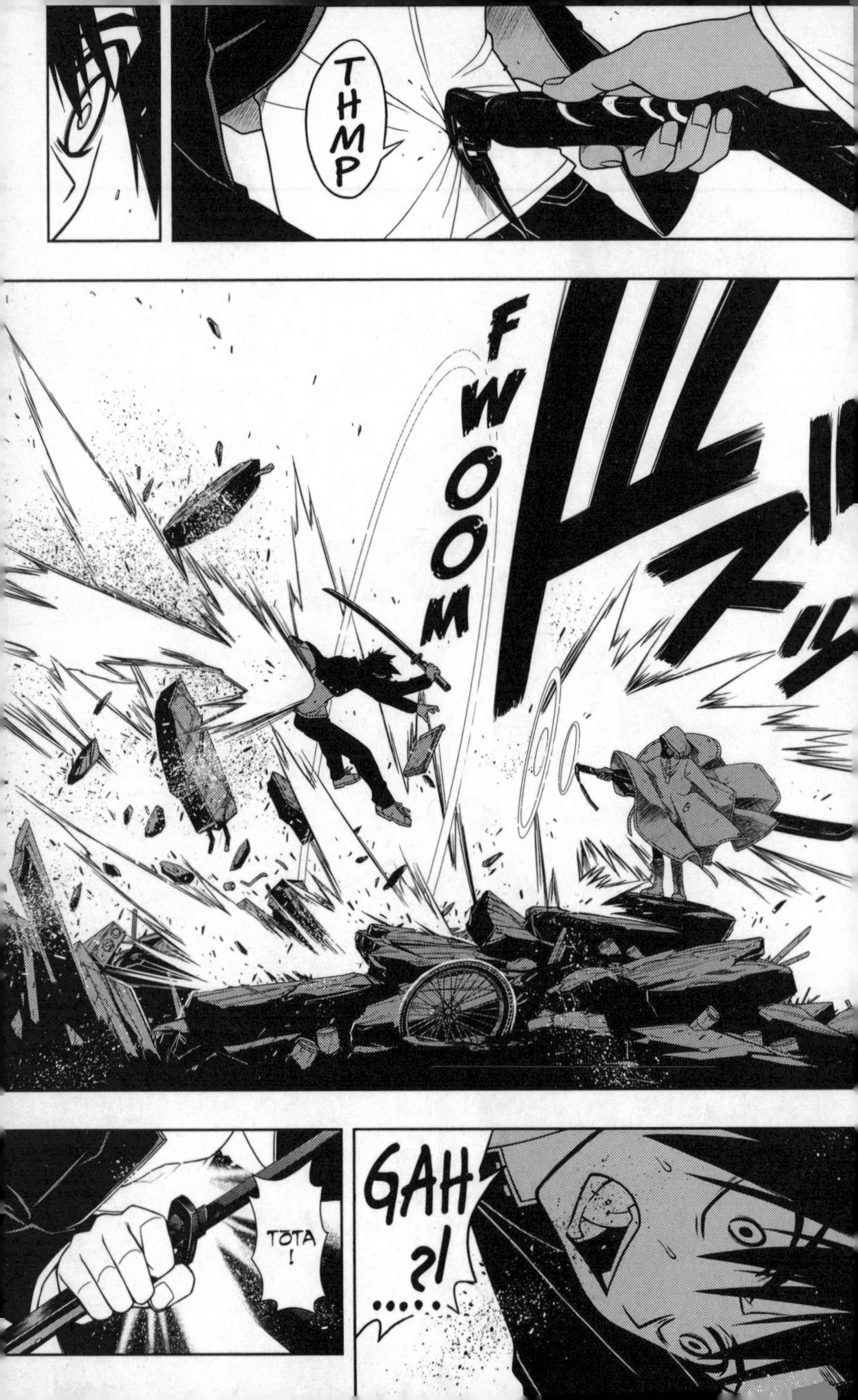
THMP
FWOOOM
GAH ?!
......
TŌTA!

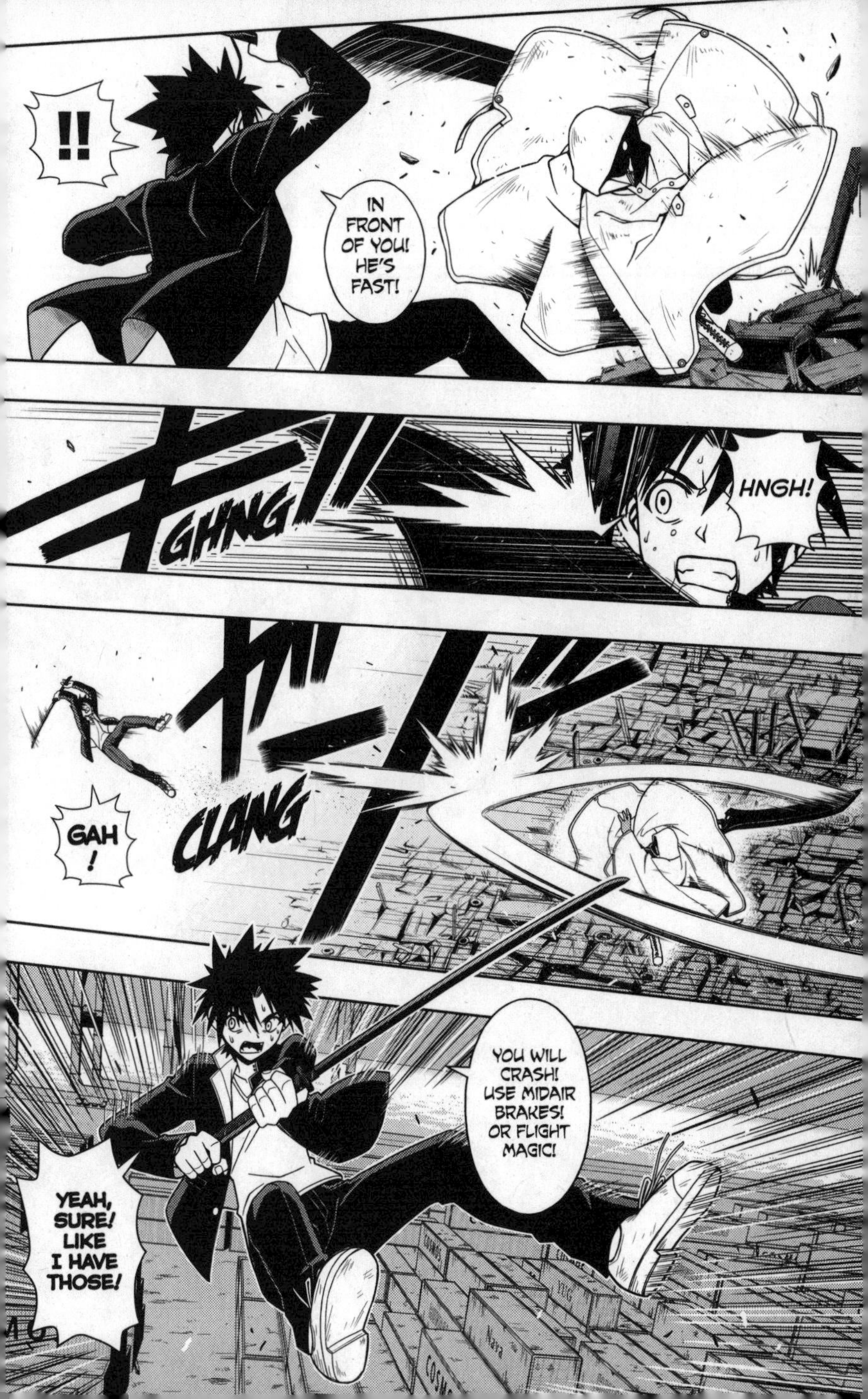
IN FRONT OF YOU! HE'S FAST!
!!
HNGH!
GHNG
CLANG
GAH!
YOU WILL CRASH! USE MIDAIR BRAKES! OR FLIGHT MAGIC!
YEAH, SURE! LIKE I HAVE THOSE!

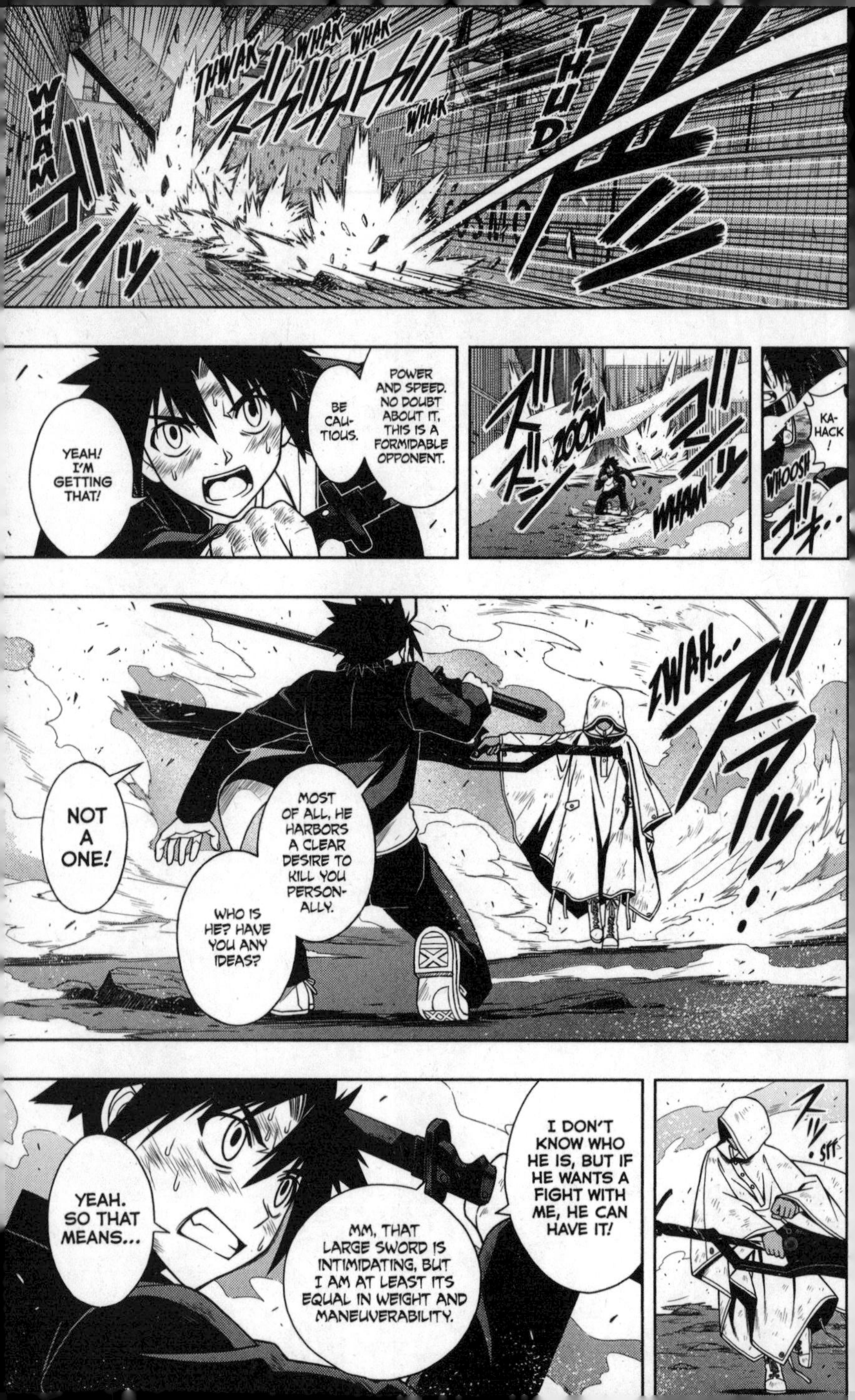
THUD
WHAK
WHAK
WHAK
THWAK
WHAM
KA-HACK!
WHOOSH
ZOOM
WHAM
POWER AND SPEED. NO DOUBT ABOUT IT, THIS IS A FORMIDABLE OPPONENT.
BE CAU-TIOUS.
YEAH! I'M GETTING THAT!
ZWAH...
MOST OF ALL, HE HARBORS A CLEAR DESIRE TO KILL YOU PERSON-ALLY.
WHO IS HE? HAVE YOU ANY IDEAS?
NOT A ONE!
SFT
MM, THAT LARGE SWORD IS INTIMIDATING, BUT I AM AT LEAST ITS EQUAL IN WEIGHT AND MANEUVERABILITY.
YEAH. SO THAT MEANS...
I DON'T KNOW WHO HE IS, BUT IF HE WANTS A FIGHT WITH ME, HE CAN HAVE IT!

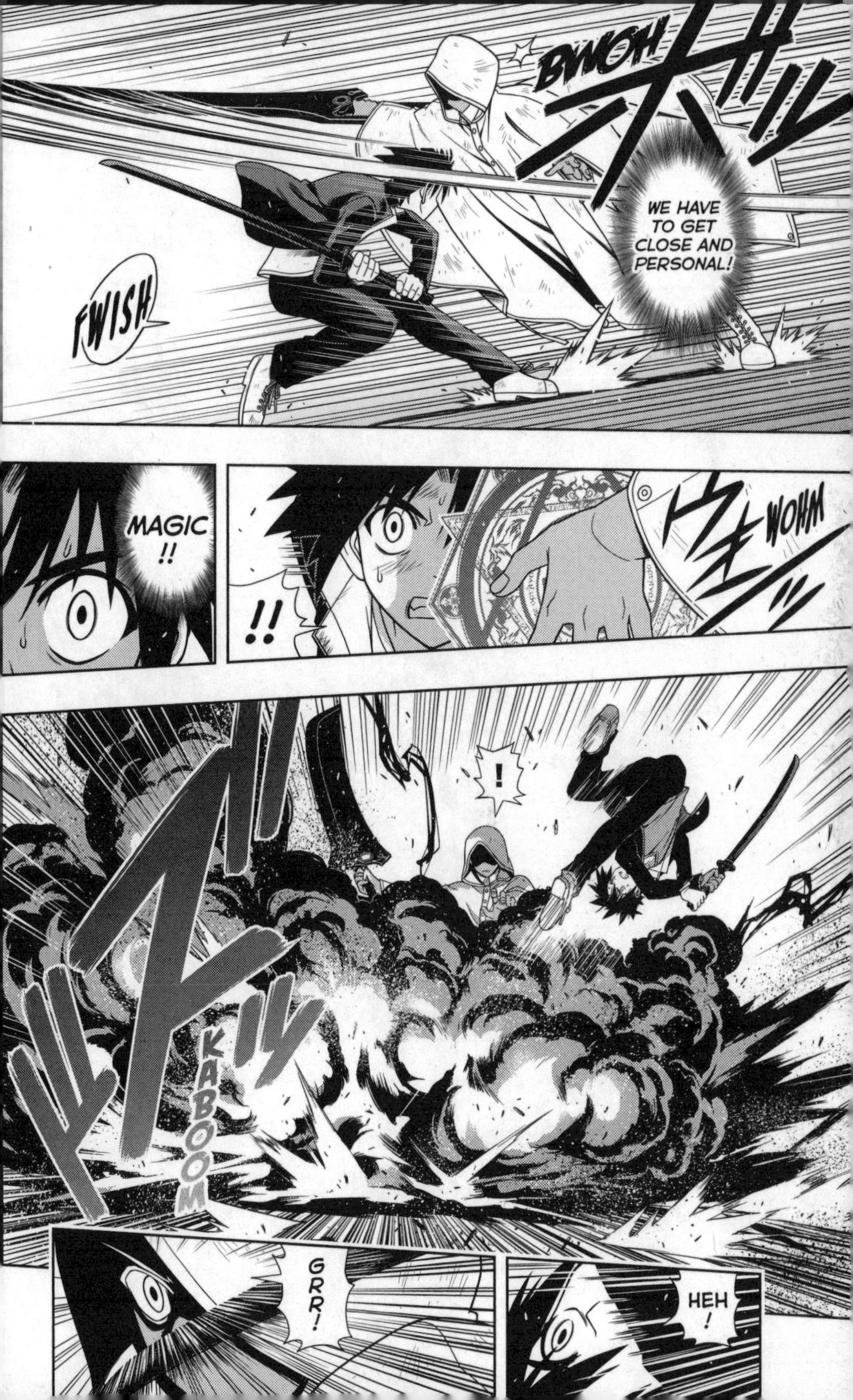
BWOH
WE HAVE TO GET CLOSE AND PERSONAL!
FWISH
WOHM
!!
MAGIC !!
!
KABOOM
HEH!
GRR!

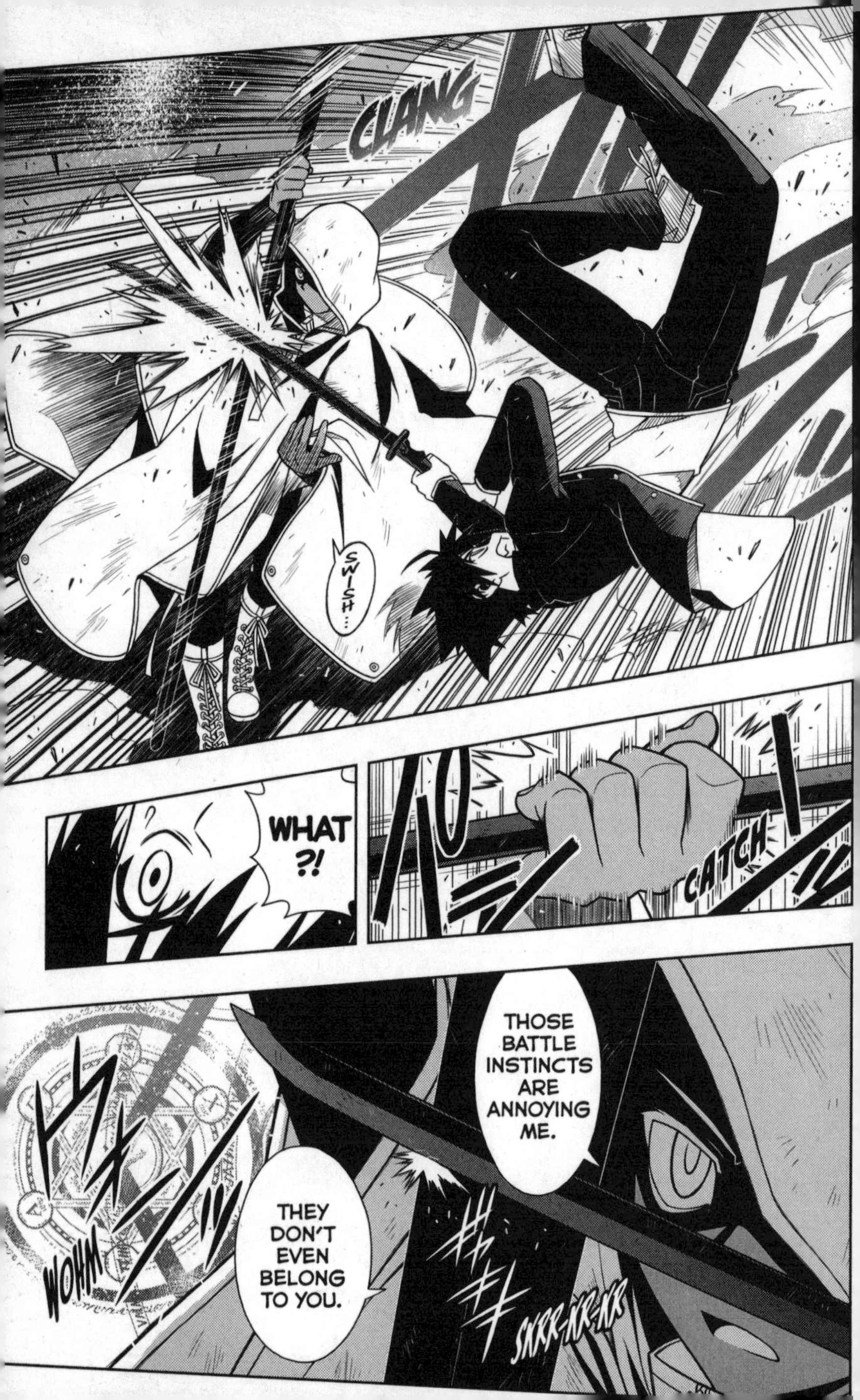
CLANG
SWISH...
CATCH
WHAT ?!
THOSE BATTLE INSTINCTS ARE ANNOYING ME.
THEY DON'T EVEN BELONG TO YOU.
SKRR-KR-KR
WOHM

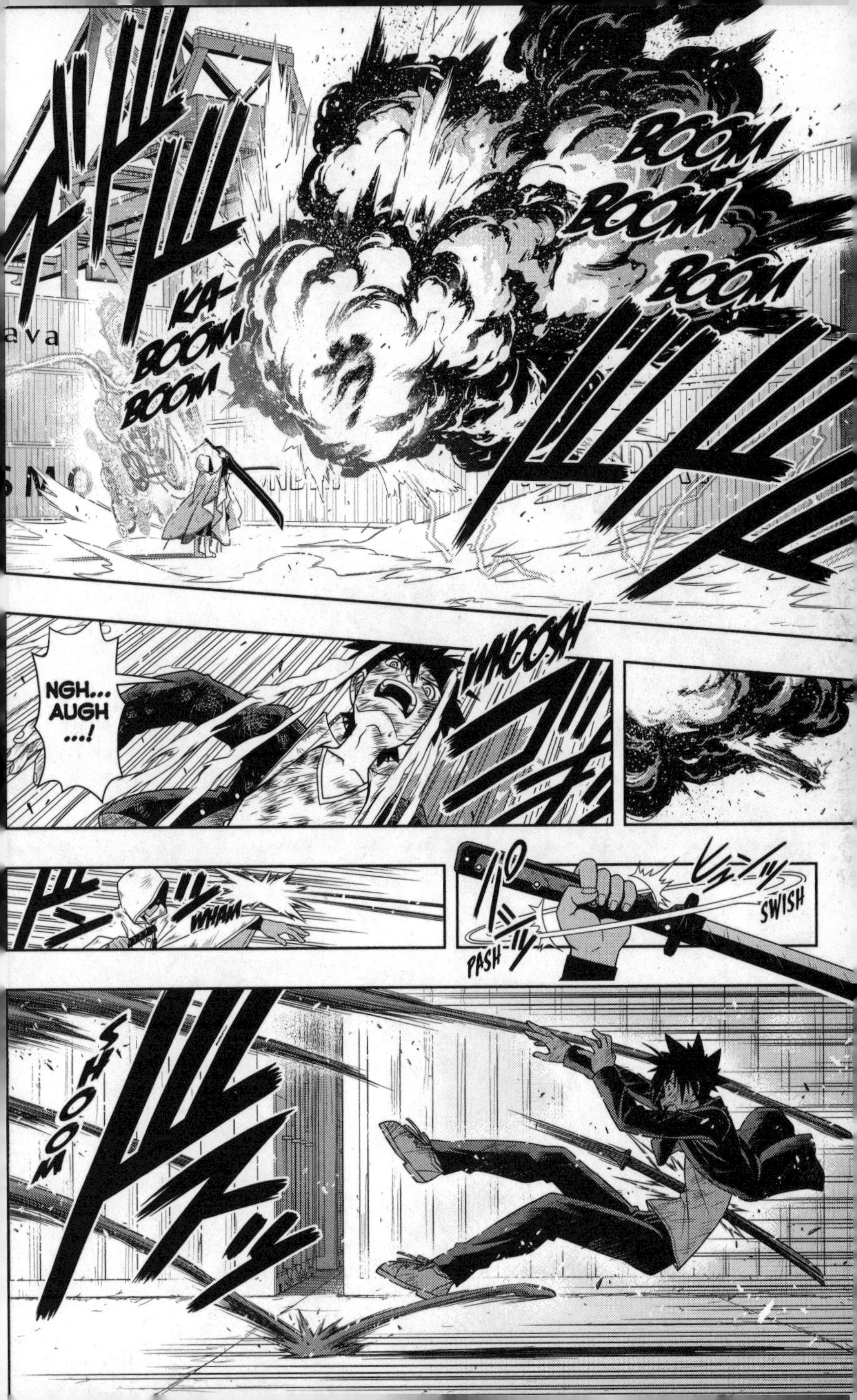
BOOM
BOOM
BOOM
KA-
BOOM
BOOM
WHOOSH
NGH... AUGH ...!
SWISH
PASH
WHAM
SHOOOM

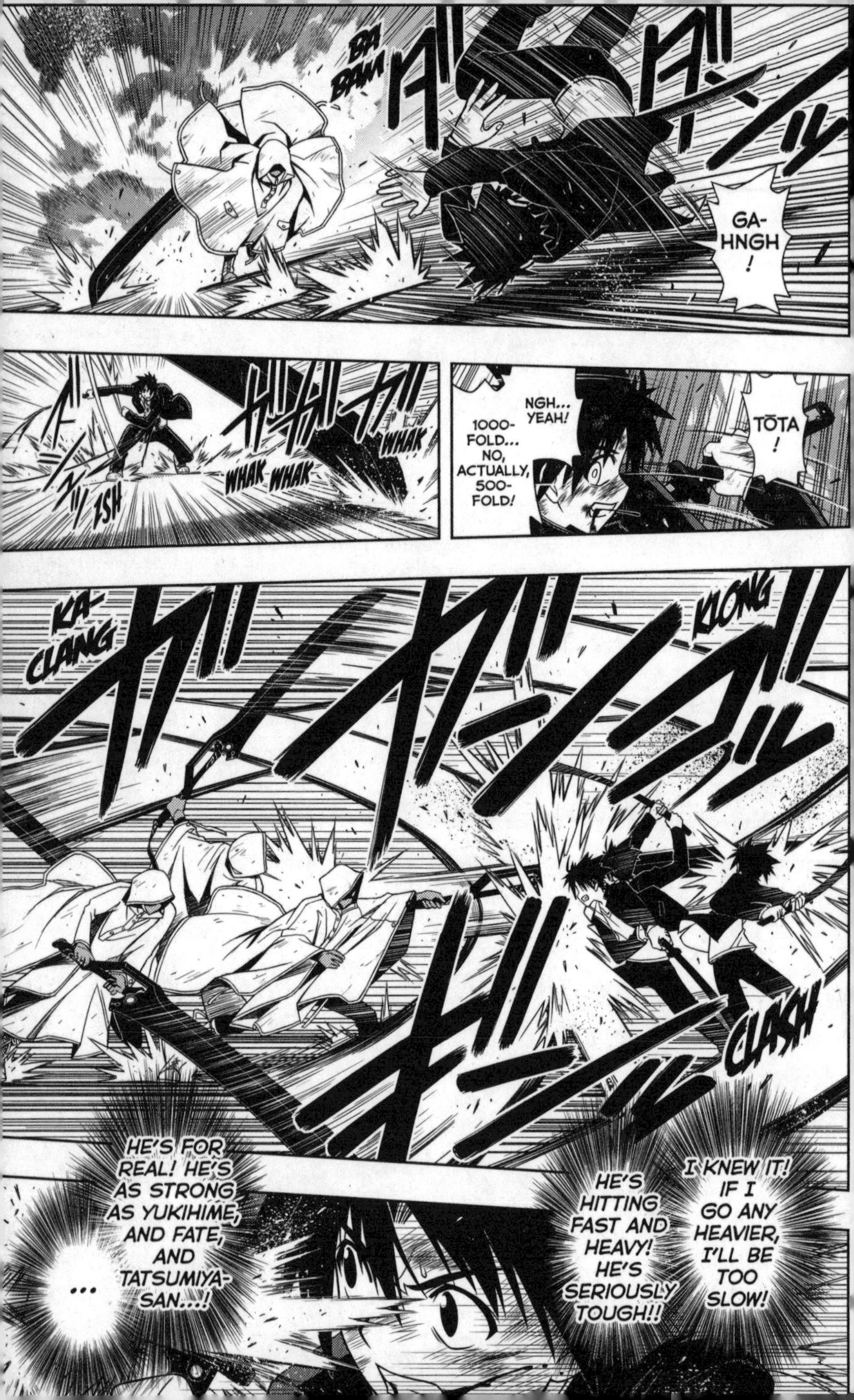
BA BAM
GA-HNGH!
TŌTA!
NGH... YEAH!
1000-FOLD... NO, ACTUALLY, 500-FOLD!
WHAK
WHAK WHAK
ZSH
KLONG
KA-CLANG
CLASH
I KNEW IT! IF I GO ANY HEAVIER, I'LL BE TOO SLOW!
HE'S HITTING FAST AND HEAVY! HE'S SERIOUSLY TOUGH!!
HE'S FOR REAL! HE'S AS STRONG AS YUKIHIME, AND FATE, AND TATSUMIYA-SAN...!
...

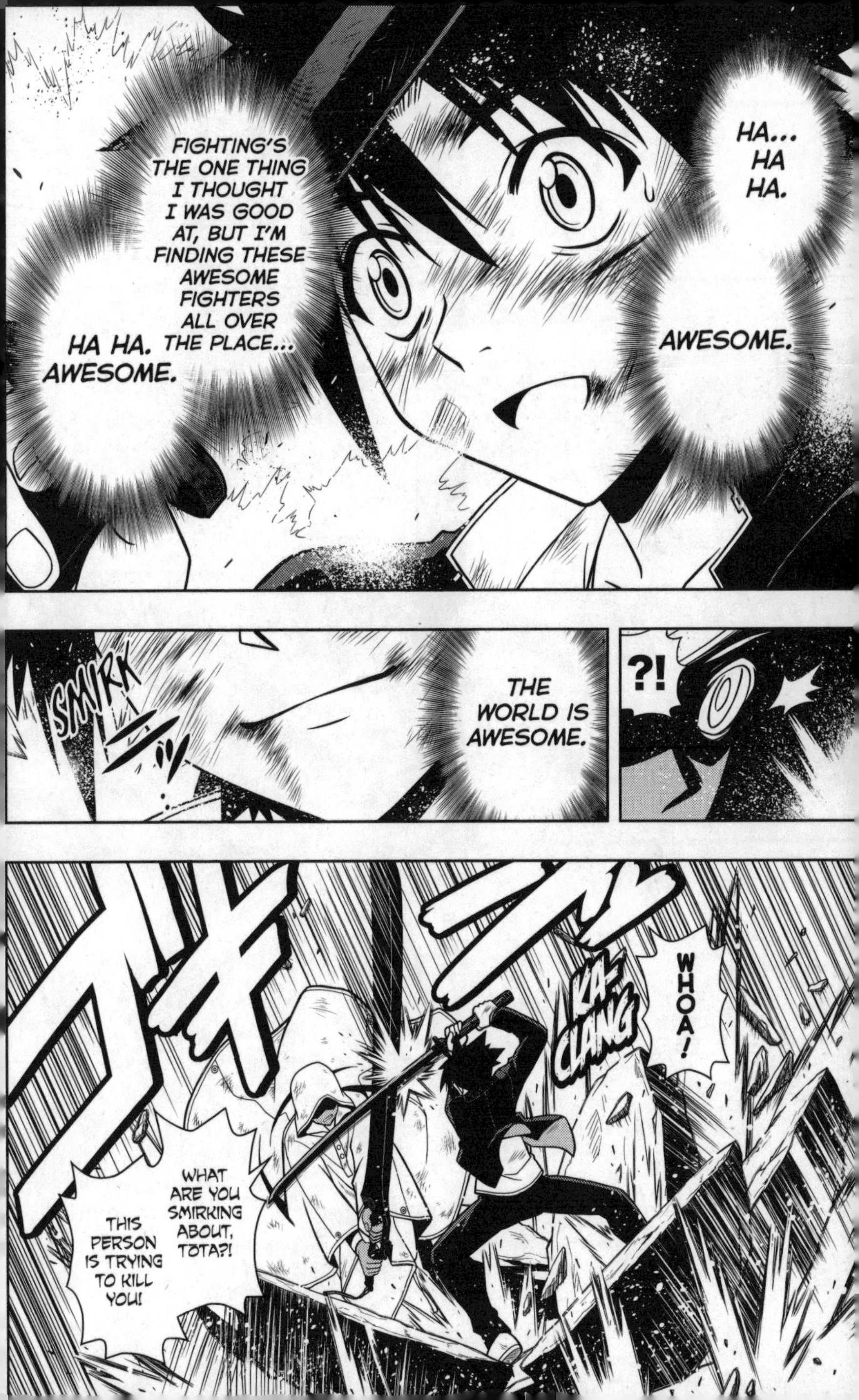
HA... HA HA.
AWESOME.
FIGHTING'S THE ONE THING I THOUGHT I WAS GOOD AT, BUT I'M FINDING THESE AWESOME FIGHTERS ALL OVER THE PLACE...
HA HA. AWESOME.
?!
THE WORLD IS AWESOME.
SMIRK
WHOA!
KA-CLANG
WHAT ARE YOU SMIRKING ABOUT, TŌTA?!
THIS PERSON IS TRYING TO KILL YOU!

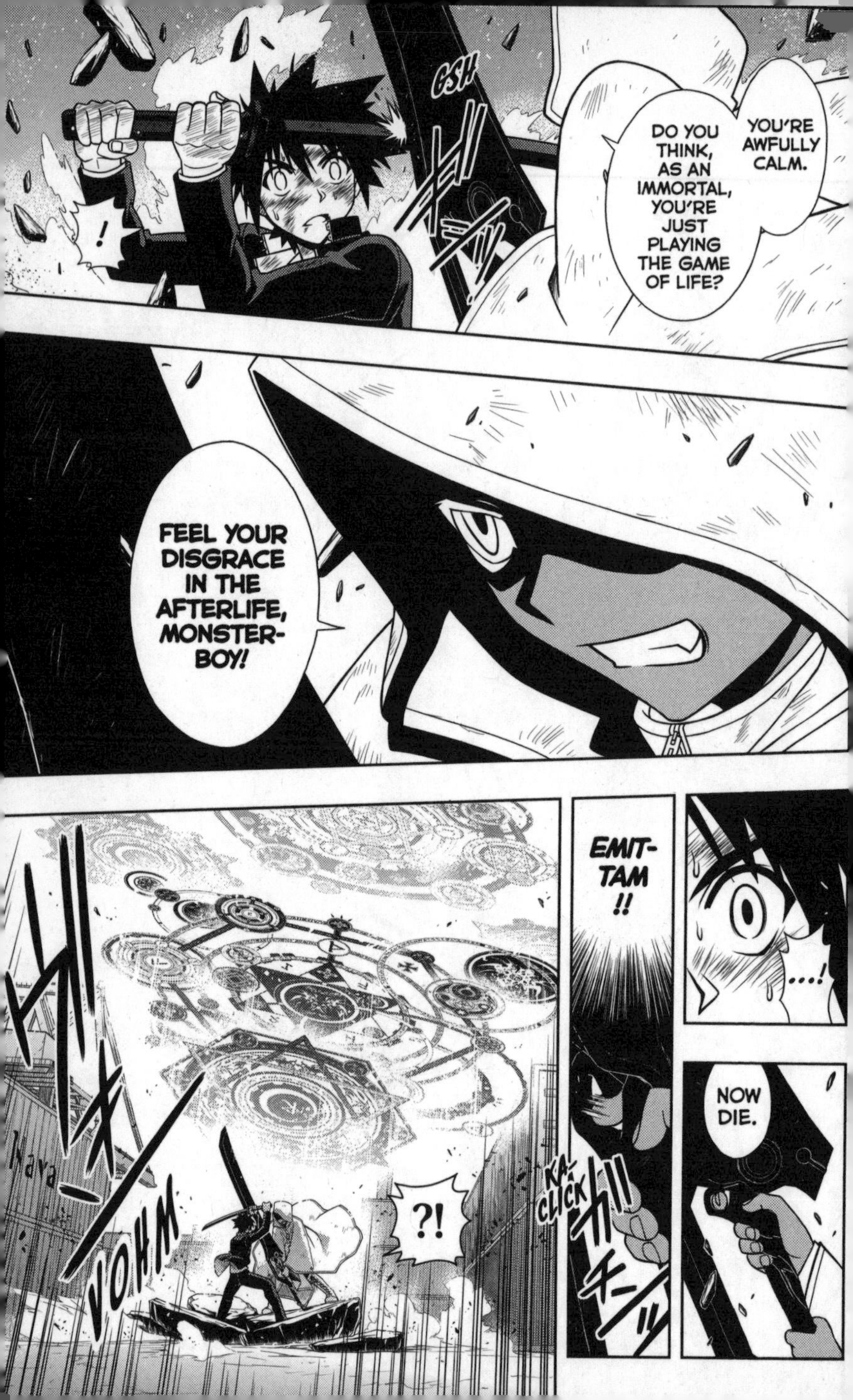
YOU'RE AWFULLY CALM.
DO YOU THINK, AS AN IMMORTAL, YOU'RE JUST PLAYING THE GAME OF LIFE?
GSH
!
FEEL YOUR DISGRACE IN THE AFTERLIFE, MONSTER-BOY!
....!
NOW DIE.
KA-CLICK
EMIT-TAM!!
?!
VOHM

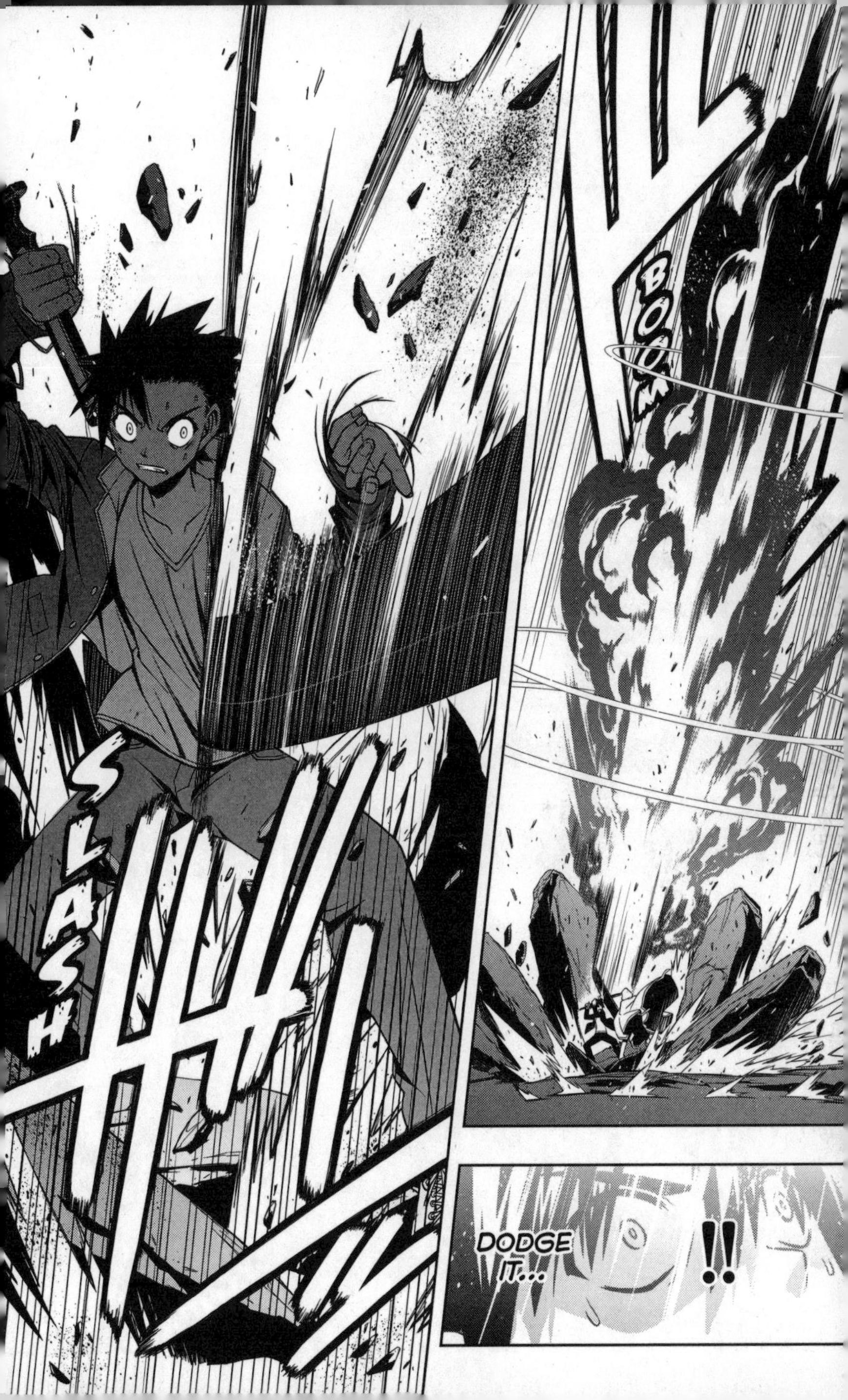
BOOM
DODGE IT...
!!
SLASH

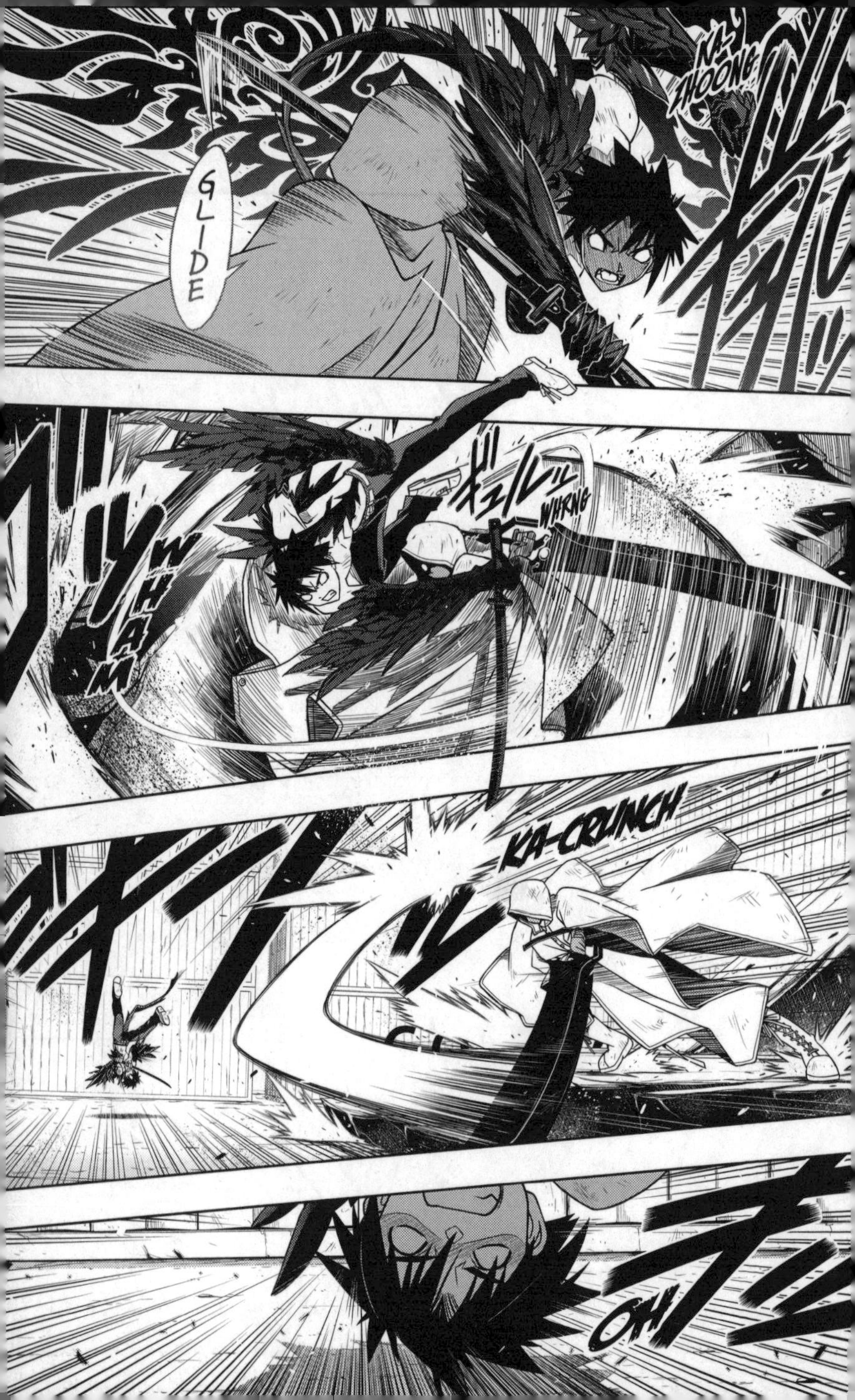
KA-ZHOONG
GLIDE
WHRNG
WHAM
KA-CRUNCH
OH

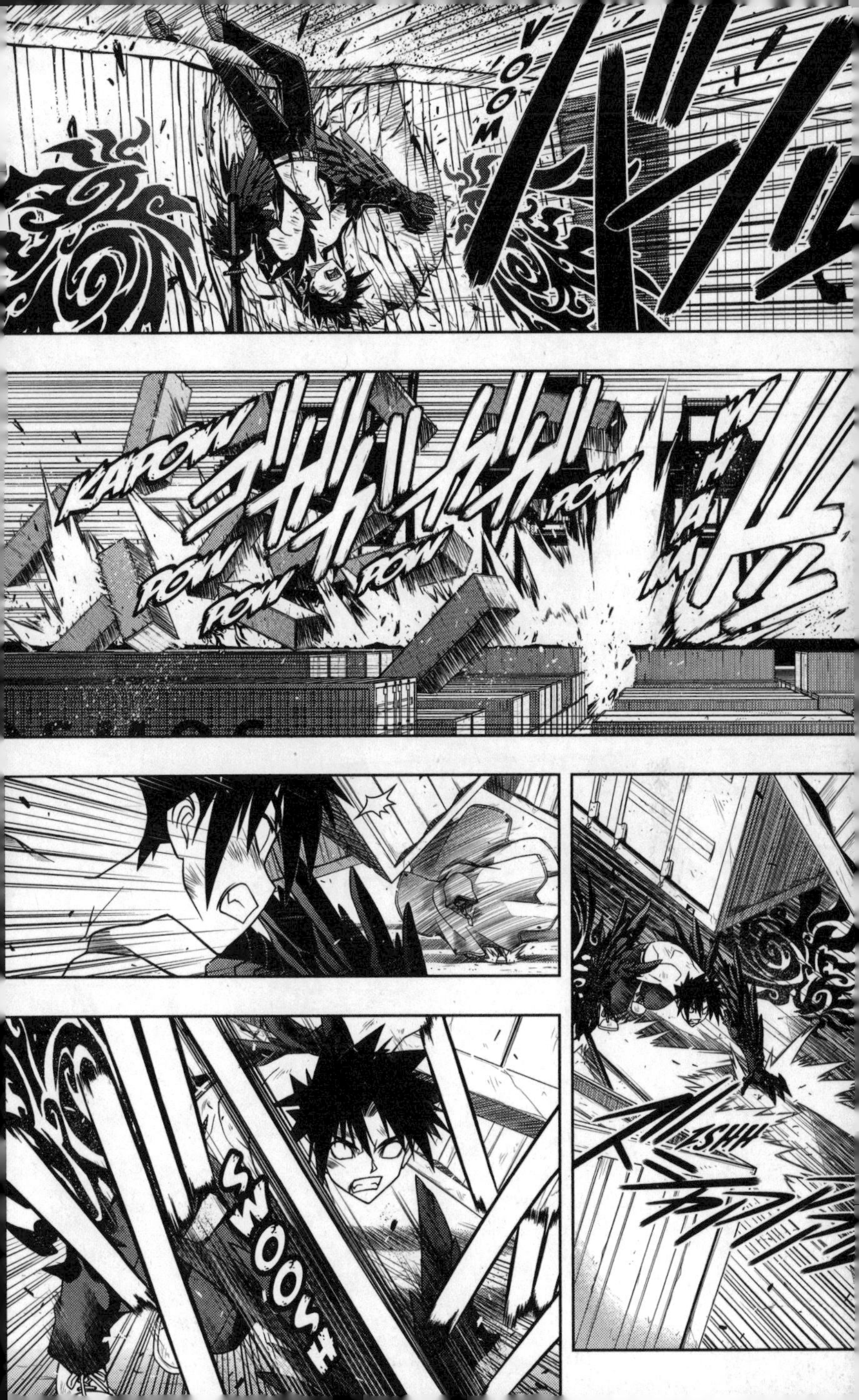
VOOOM
WHAM
POW
POW
POW
POW
POW
KAPOW
SWOOSH

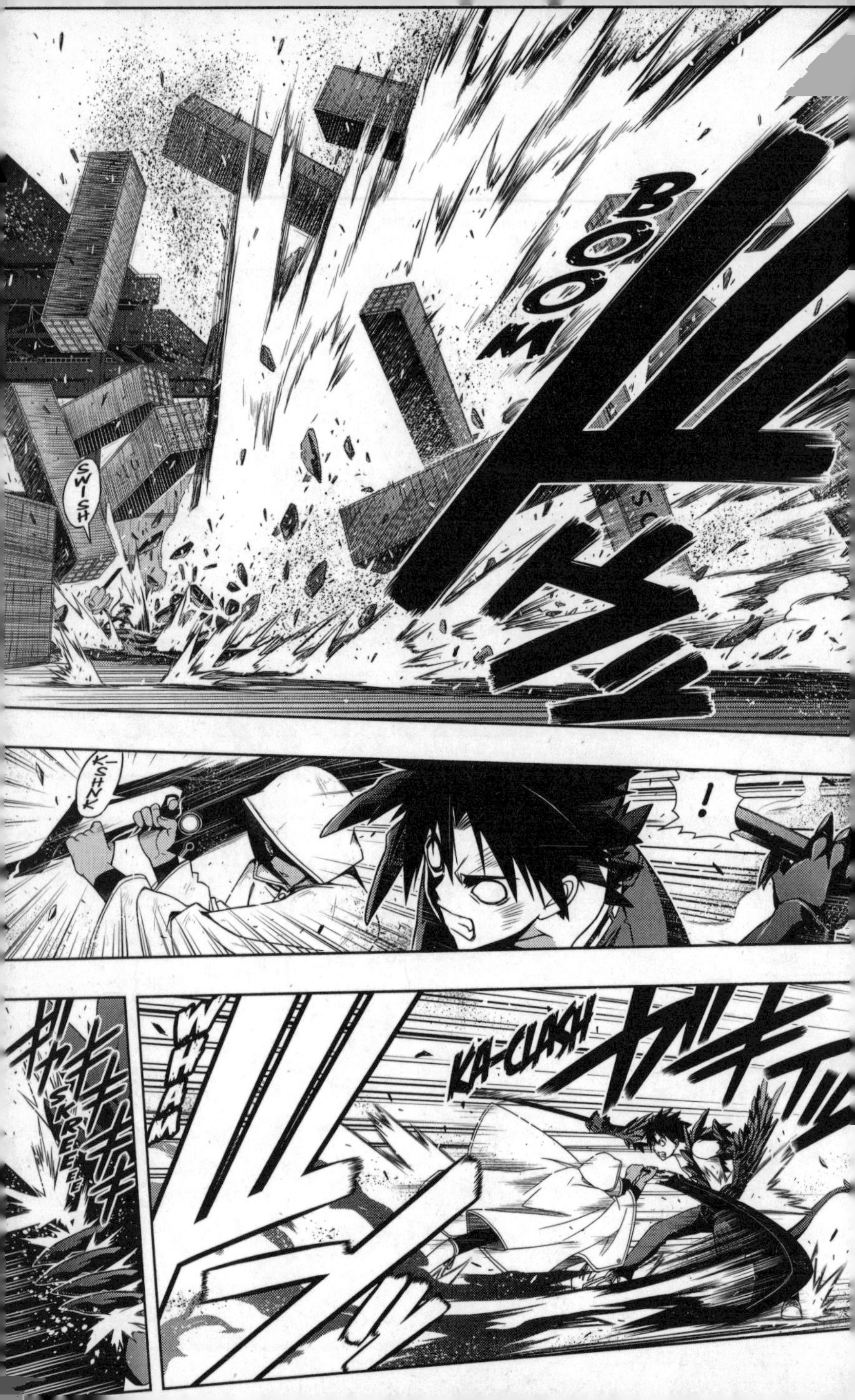
BOOM
SWISH
!
K-SHNK
KA-CLASH
WHAM
SKREEEE

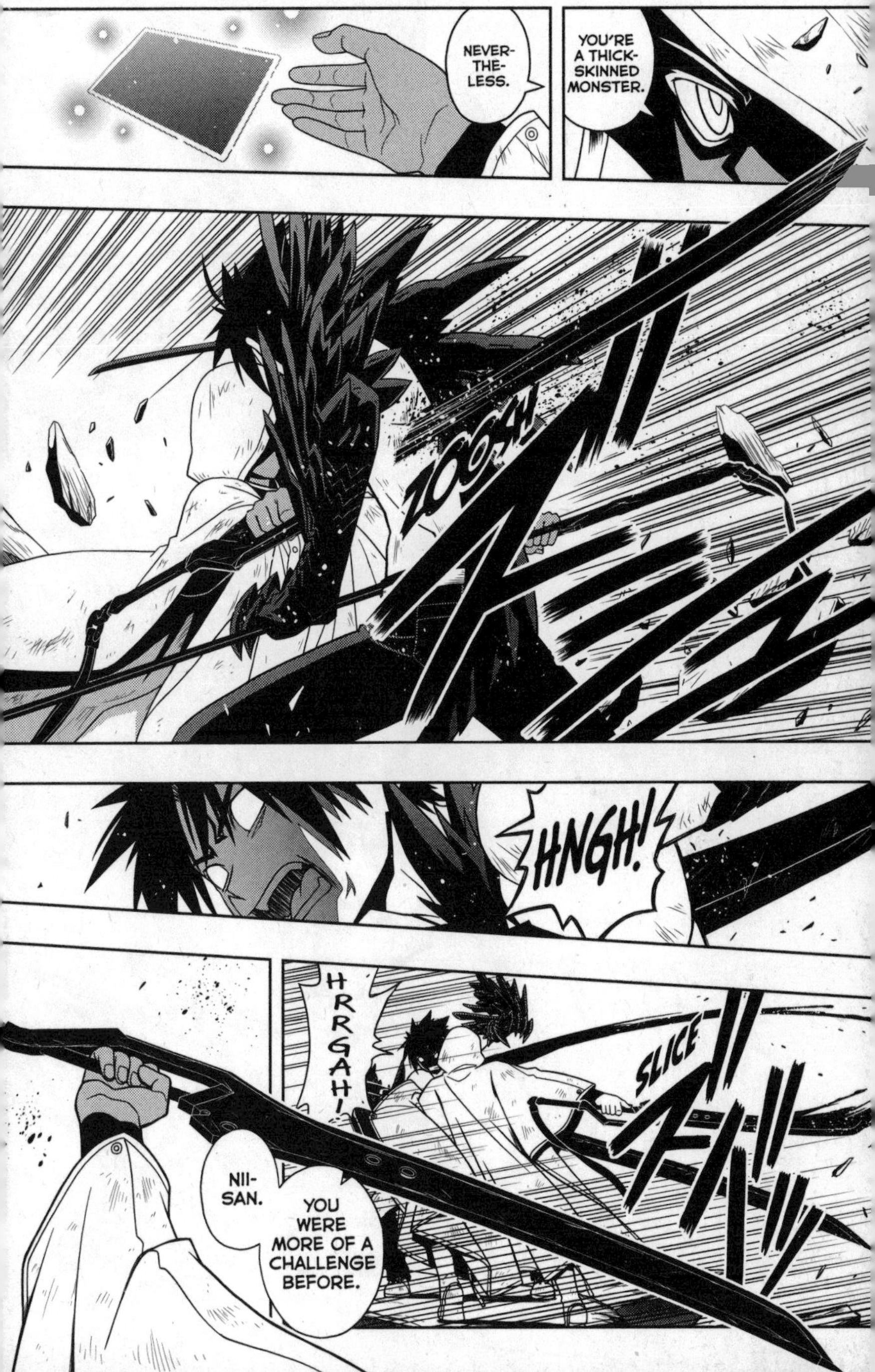
YOU'RE A THICK-SKINNED MONSTER.
NEVER-THE-LESS.
ZOOSH
HNGH!
SLICE
HRRGAH!
NII-SAN.
YOU WERE MORE OF A CHALLENGE BEFORE.

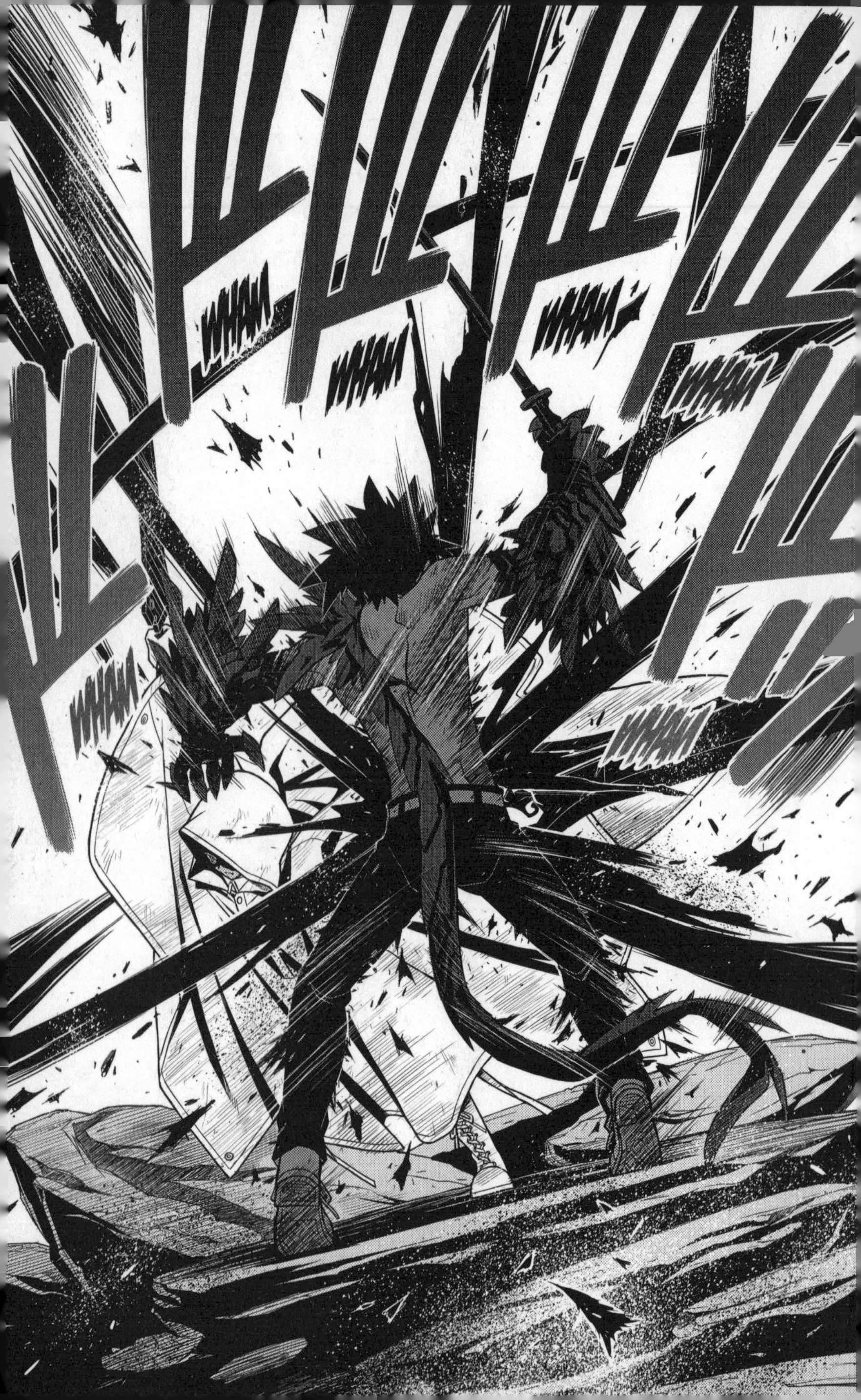
WHAM
WHAM
WHAM
WHAM
WHAM
WHAM

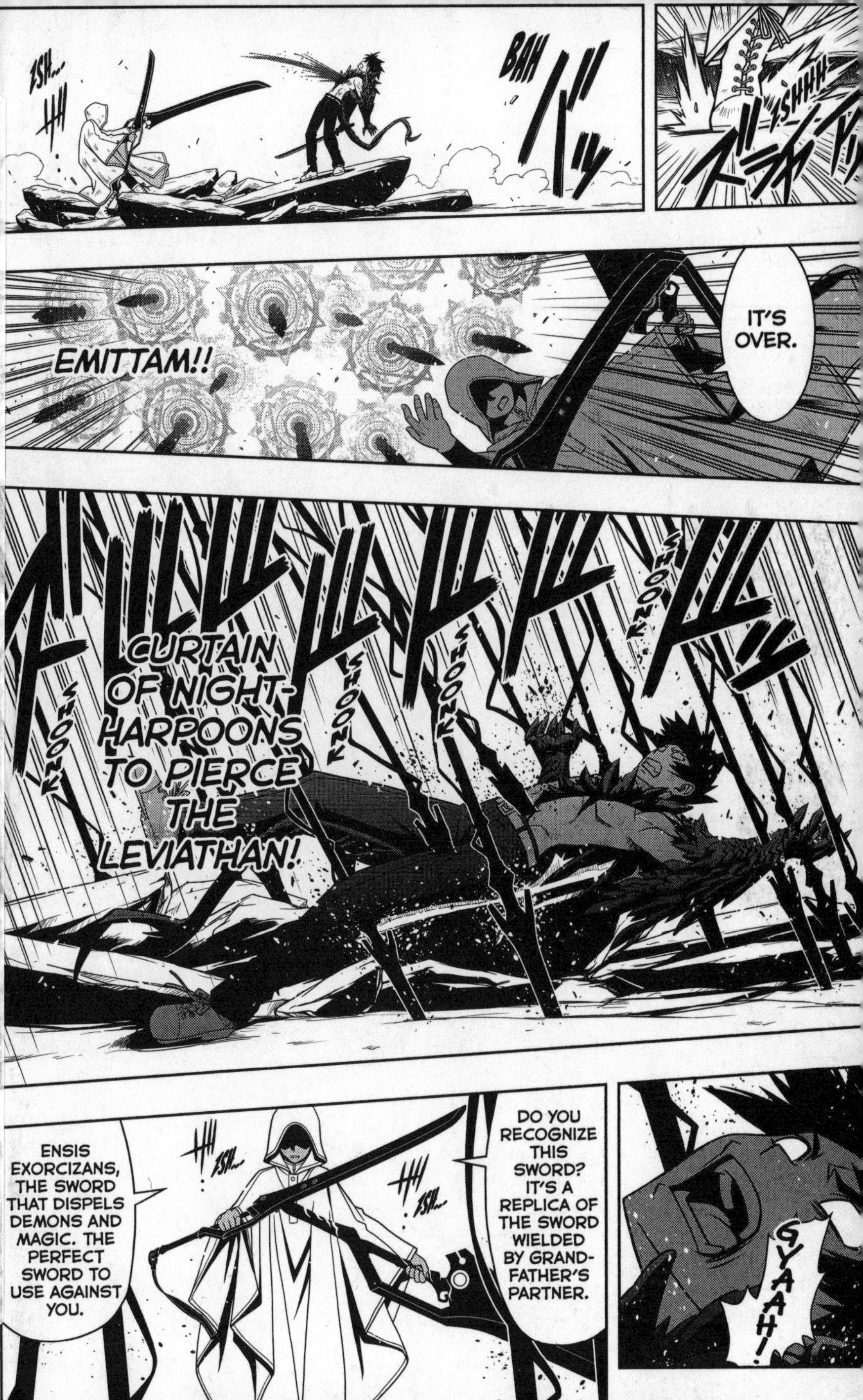
ZSHHH
BAH
ZSH...
IT'S OVER.
EMITTAM!!
SHOONK
SHOONK
SHOONK
SHOONK
CURTAIN OF NIGHT-HARPOONS TO PIERCE THE LEVIATHAN!
GYAAAH!
DO YOU RECOGNIZE THIS SWORD? IT'S A REPLICA OF THE SWORD WIELDED BY GRAND-FATHER'S PARTNER.
ZSH...
ZSH...
ENSIS EXORCIZANS, THE SWORD THAT DISPELS DEMONS AND MAGIC. THE PERFECT SWORD TO USE AGAINST YOU.

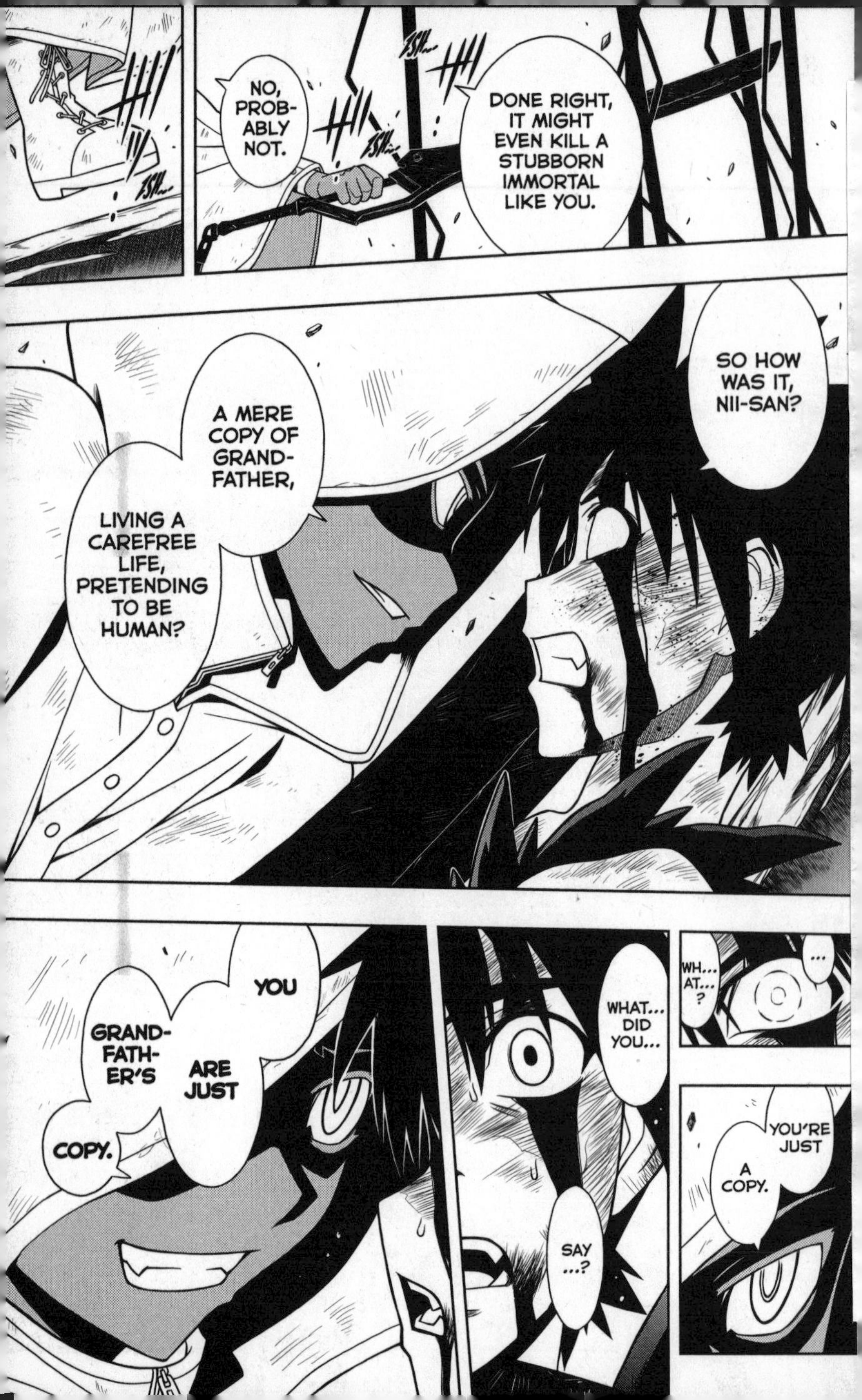
TSH...
TSH...
DONE RIGHT, IT MIGHT EVEN KILL A STUBBORN IMMORTAL LIKE YOU.
NO, PROBABLY NOT.
TSH...
SO HOW WAS IT, NII-SAN?
A MERE COPY OF GRANDFATHER,
LIVING A CAREFREE LIFE, PRETENDING TO BE HUMAN?
...
WH... AT...?
YOU'RE JUST A COPY.
WHAT... DID YOU...
SAY ...?
YOU ARE JUST GRANDFATHER'S COPY.

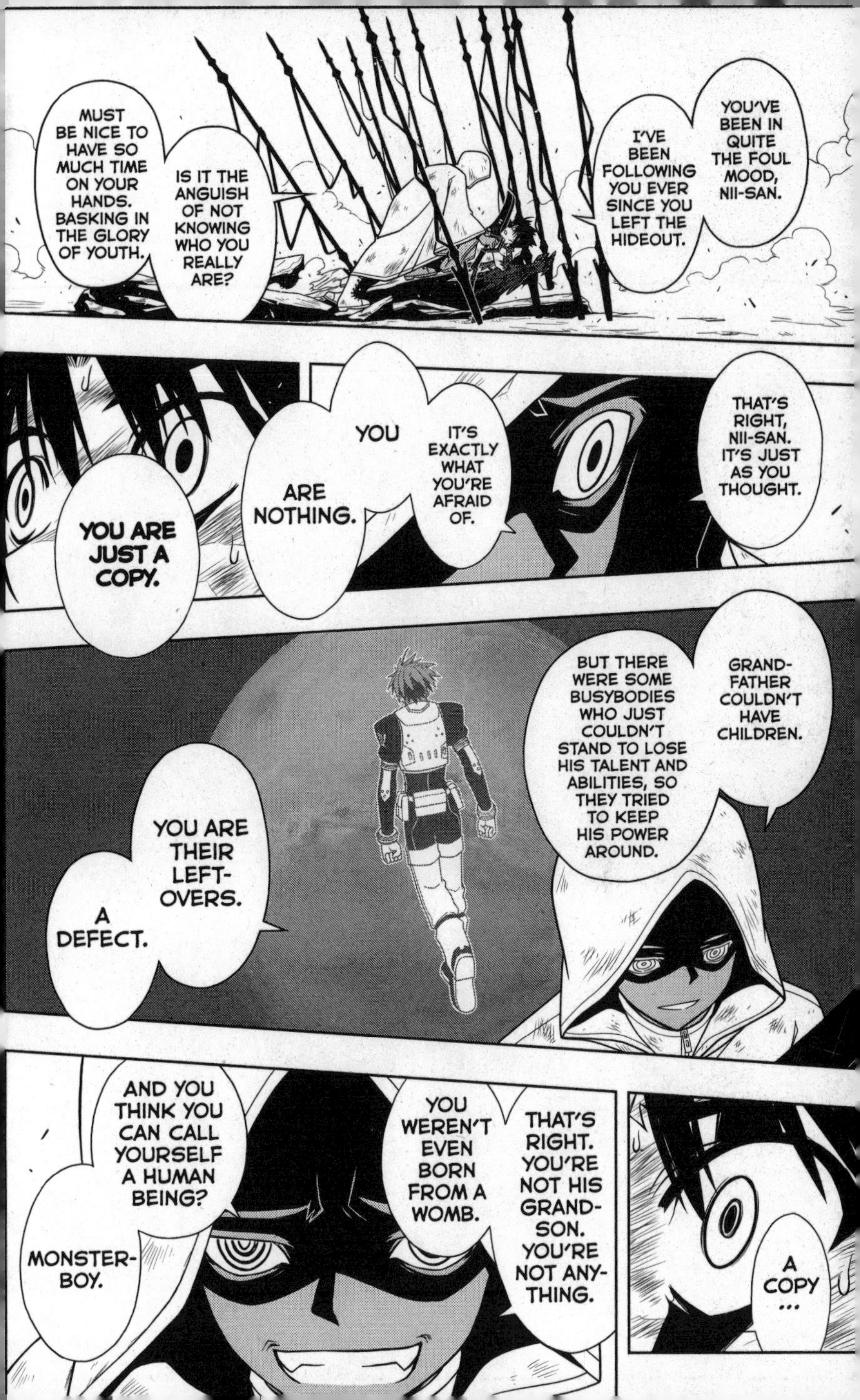
YOU'VE BEEN IN QUITE THE FOUL MOOD, NII-SAN.
I'VE BEEN FOLLOWING YOU EVER SINCE YOU LEFT THE HIDEOUT.
IS IT THE ANGUISH OF NOT KNOWING WHO YOU REALLY ARE?
MUST BE NICE TO HAVE SO MUCH TIME ON YOUR HANDS. BASKING IN THE GLORY OF YOUTH.
THAT'S RIGHT, NII-SAN. IT'S JUST AS YOU THOUGHT.
IT'S EXACTLY WHAT YOU'RE AFRAID OF.
YOU ARE NOTHING.
YOU ARE JUST A COPY.
GRAND-FATHER COULDN'T HAVE CHILDREN.
BUT THERE WERE SOME BUSYBODIES WHO JUST COULDN'T STAND TO LOSE HIS TALENT AND ABILITIES, SO THEY TRIED TO KEEP HIS POWER AROUND.
YOU ARE THEIR LEFT-OVERS. A DEFECT.
A COPY ...
THAT'S RIGHT. YOU'RE NOT HIS GRAND-SON. YOU'RE NOT ANY-THING.
YOU WEREN'T EVEN BORN FROM A WOMB.
AND YOU THINK YOU CAN CALL YOURSELF A HUMAN BEING?
MONSTER-BOY.

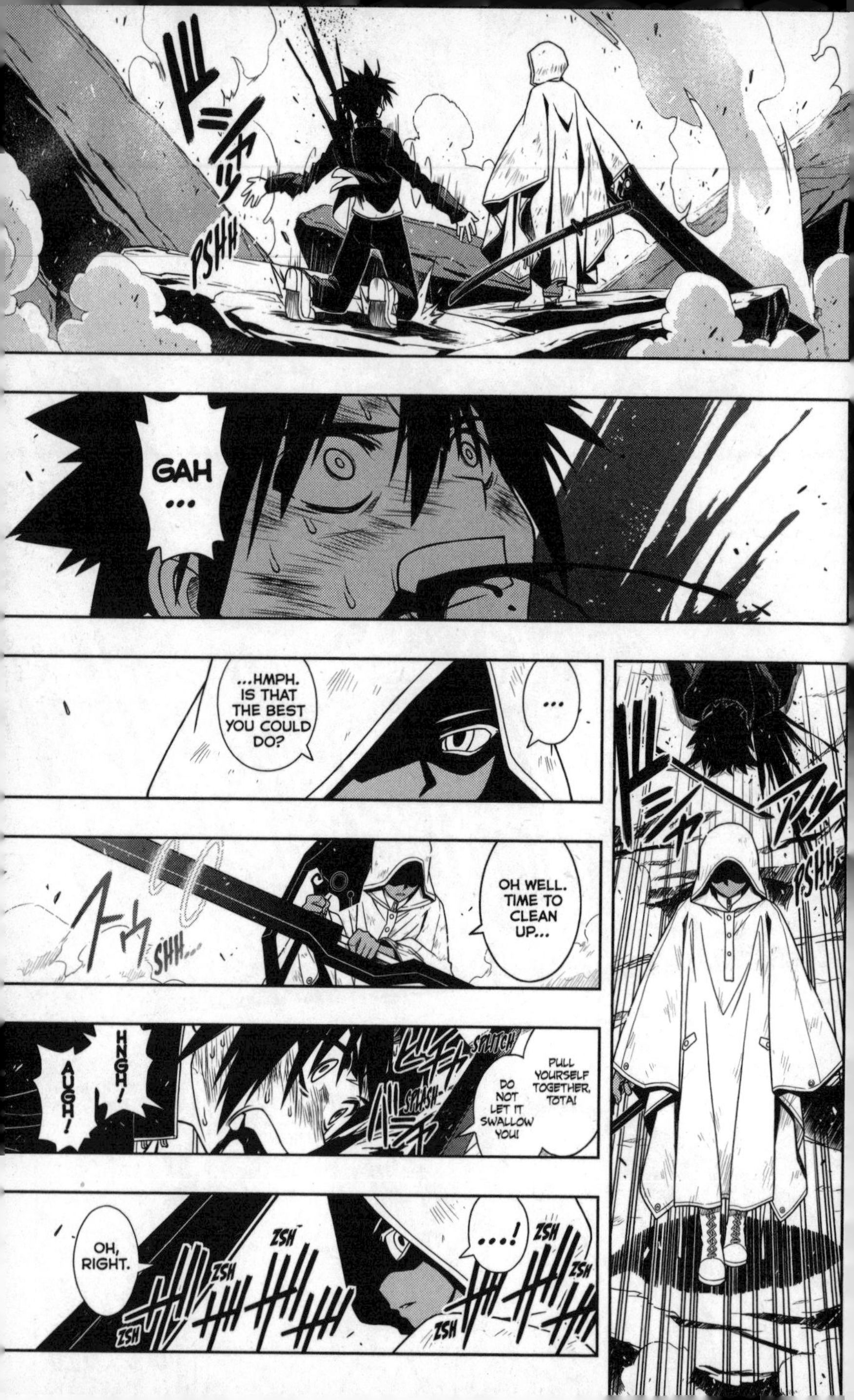
PSHH
GAH ...
PSHH
...
...HMPH. IS THAT THE BEST YOU COULD DO?
OH WELL. TIME TO CLEAN UP...
SHH...
PULL YOURSELF TOGETHER, TOTA!
DO NOT LET IT SWALLOW YOU!
SPLITCH
SPLASH
HNGH!
AUGH!
...!
ZSH
ZSH
ZSH
ZSH
ZSH
OH, RIGHT.

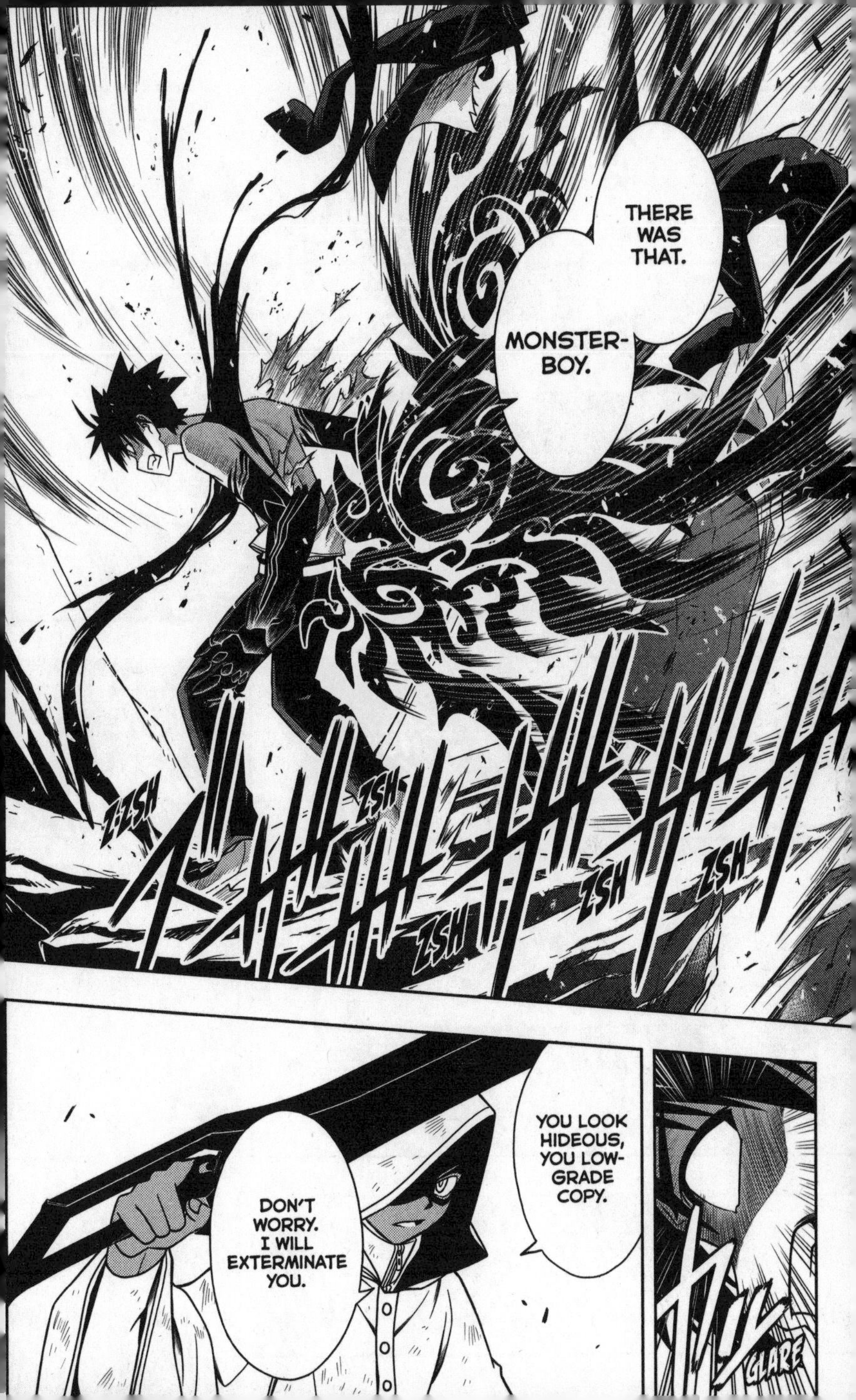
THERE WAS THAT.
MONSTER-BOY.
ZSH
ZSH
ZSH
ZSH
Z-ZSH
GLARE
YOU LOOK HIDEOUS, YOU LOW-GRADE COPY.
DON'T WORRY. I WILL EXTERMINATE YOU.

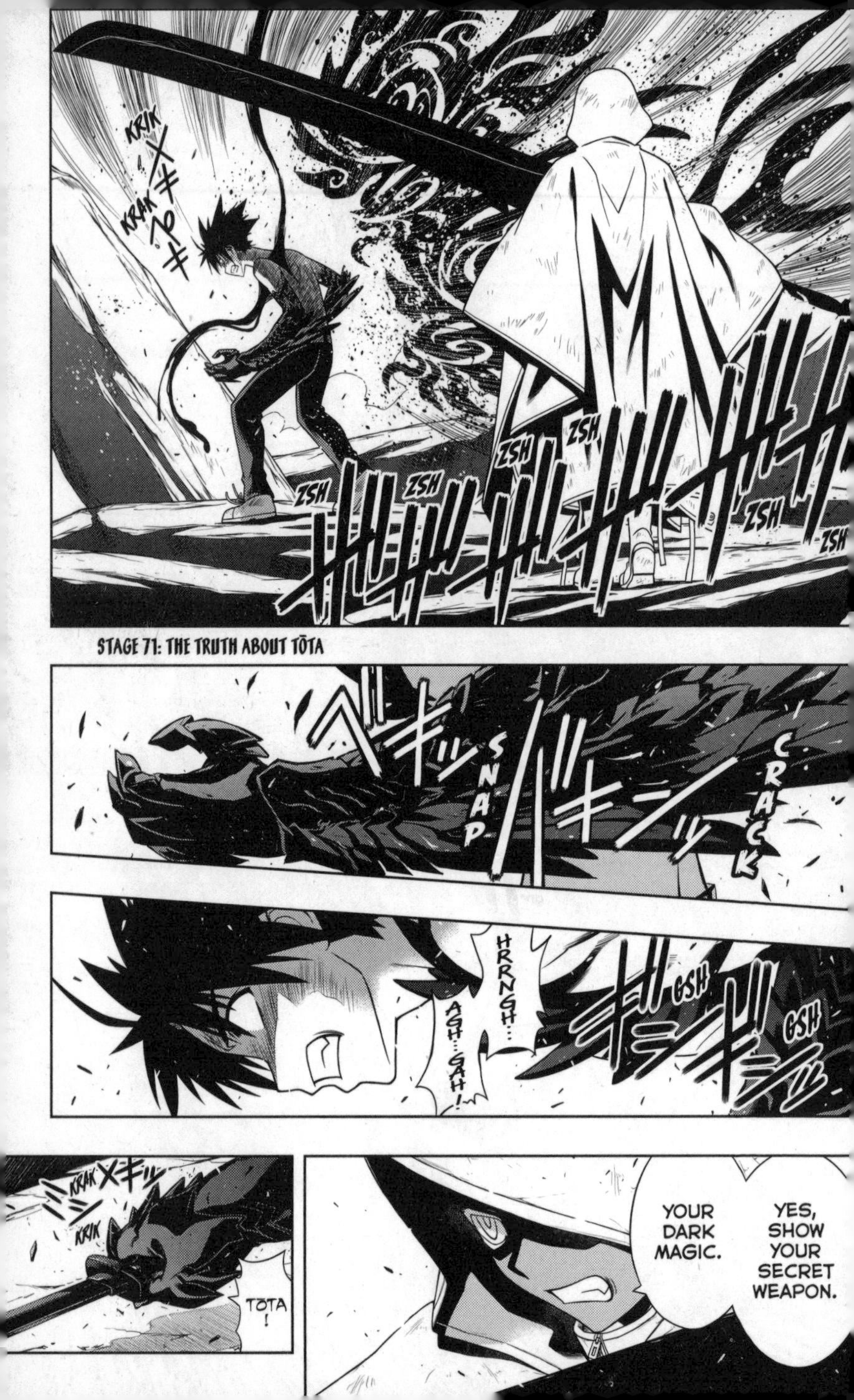
KRIK
KRAK
ZSH
ZSH
ZSH
ZSH
ZSH
ZSH
STAGE 71: THE TRUTH ABOUT TŌTA
SNAP
CRACK
HRRNGH...
AGH... GAH!
GSH
GSH
YES, SHOW YOUR SECRET WEAPON.
YOUR DARK MAGIC.
KRAK
KRIK
TŌTA!

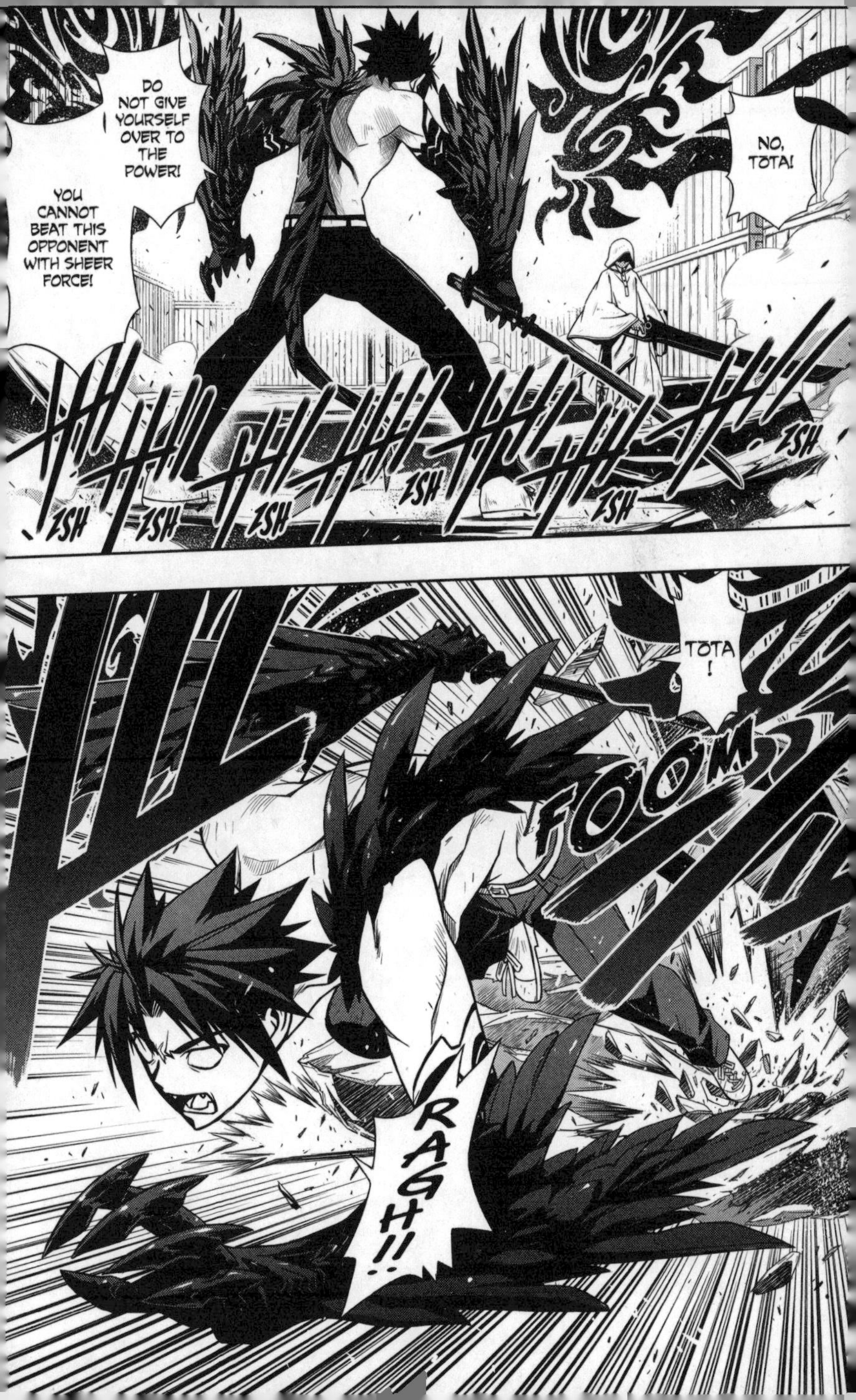
NO, TŌTA!
DO NOT GIVE YOURSELF OVER TO THE POWER!
YOU CANNOT BEAT THIS OPPONENT WITH SHEER FORCE!
ZSH ZSH ZSH ZSH ZSH ZSH
TŌTA!
FOOM
RAGH!!

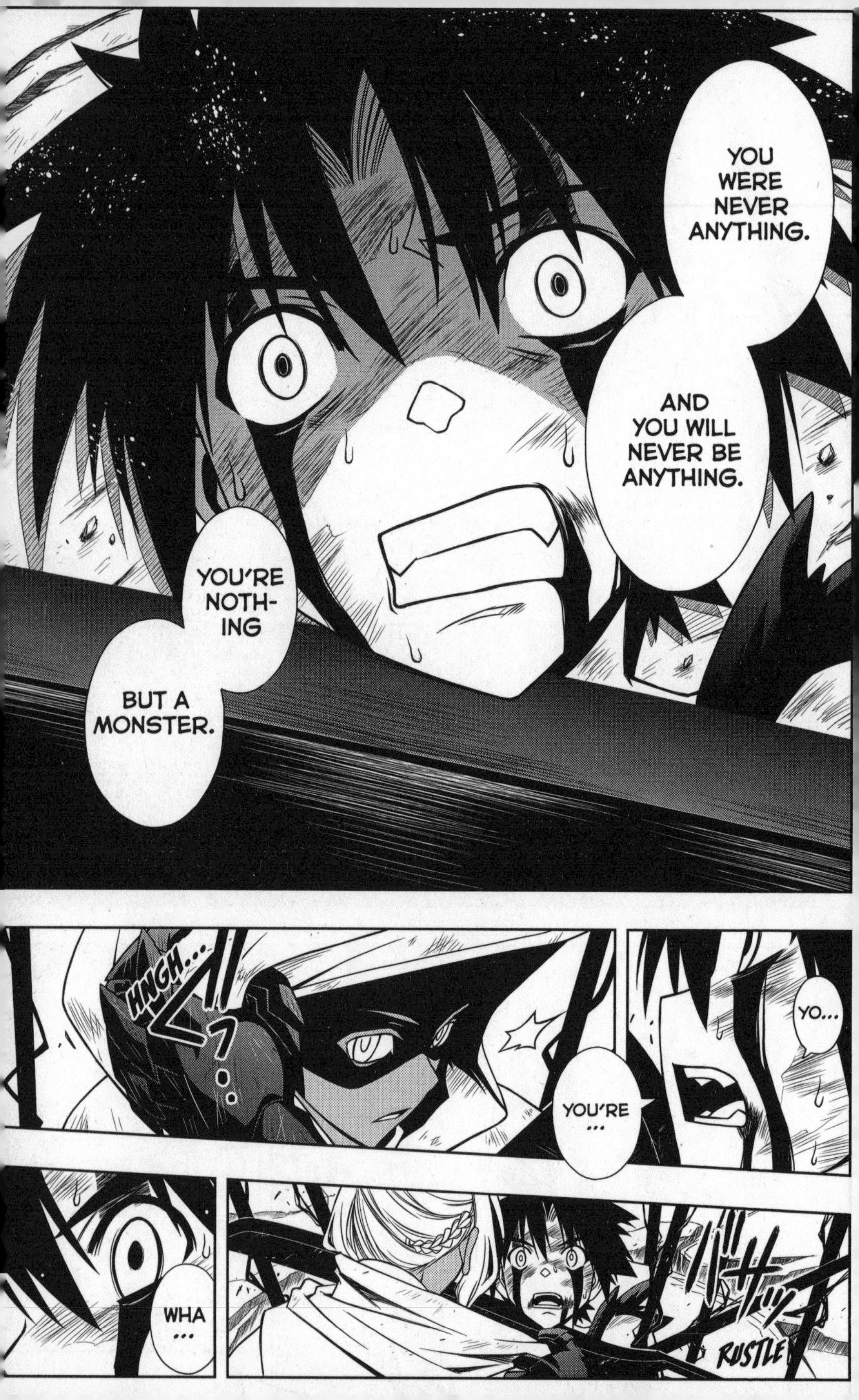
YOU WERE NEVER ANYTHING.
AND YOU WILL NEVER BE ANYTHING.
YOU'RE NOTHING
BUT A MONSTER.
YO...
YOU'RE ...
HNGH...
RUSTLE
WHA ...

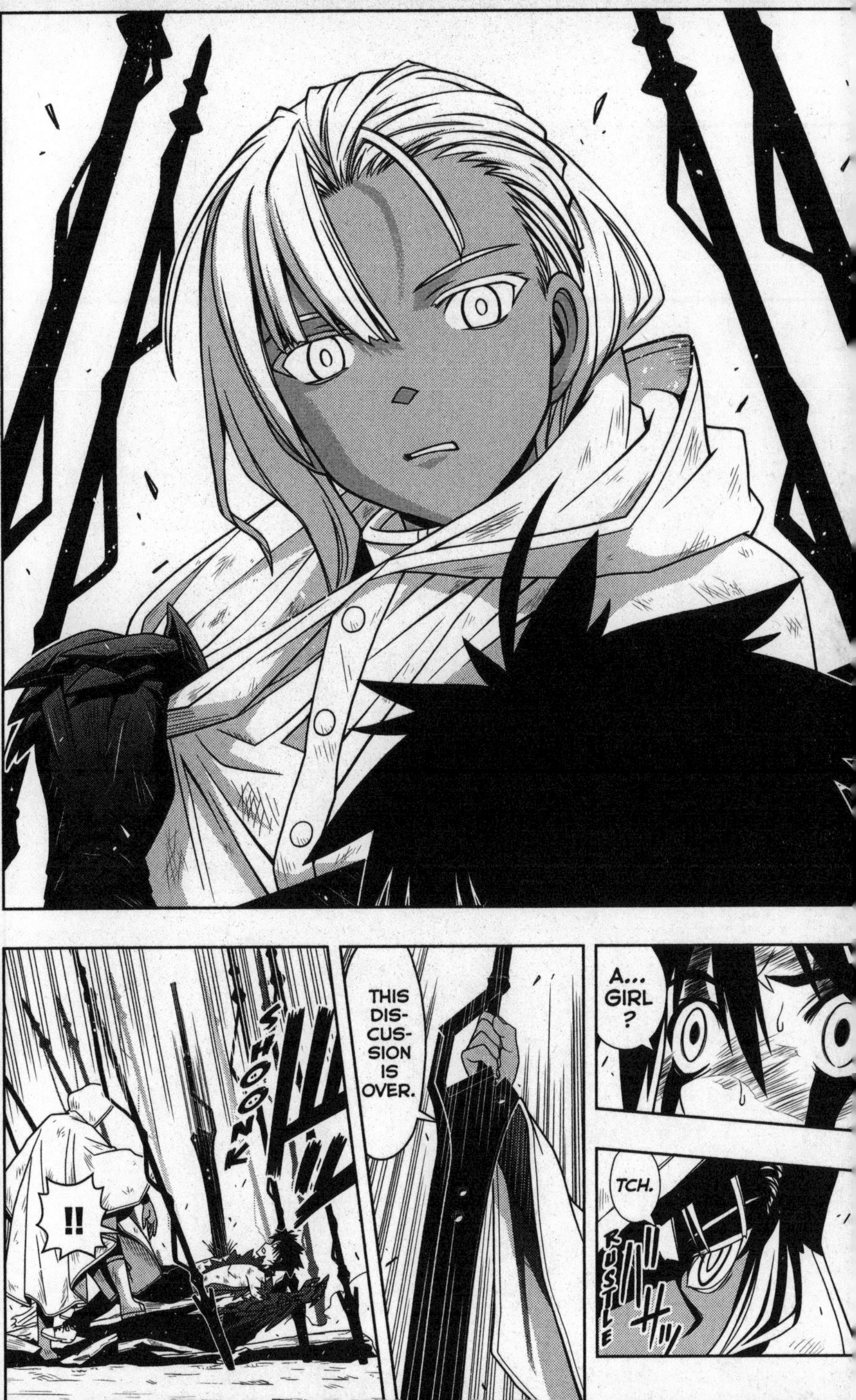
A... GIRL?
TCH.
RUSTLE
THIS DISCUSSION IS OVER.
SHOONK
!!

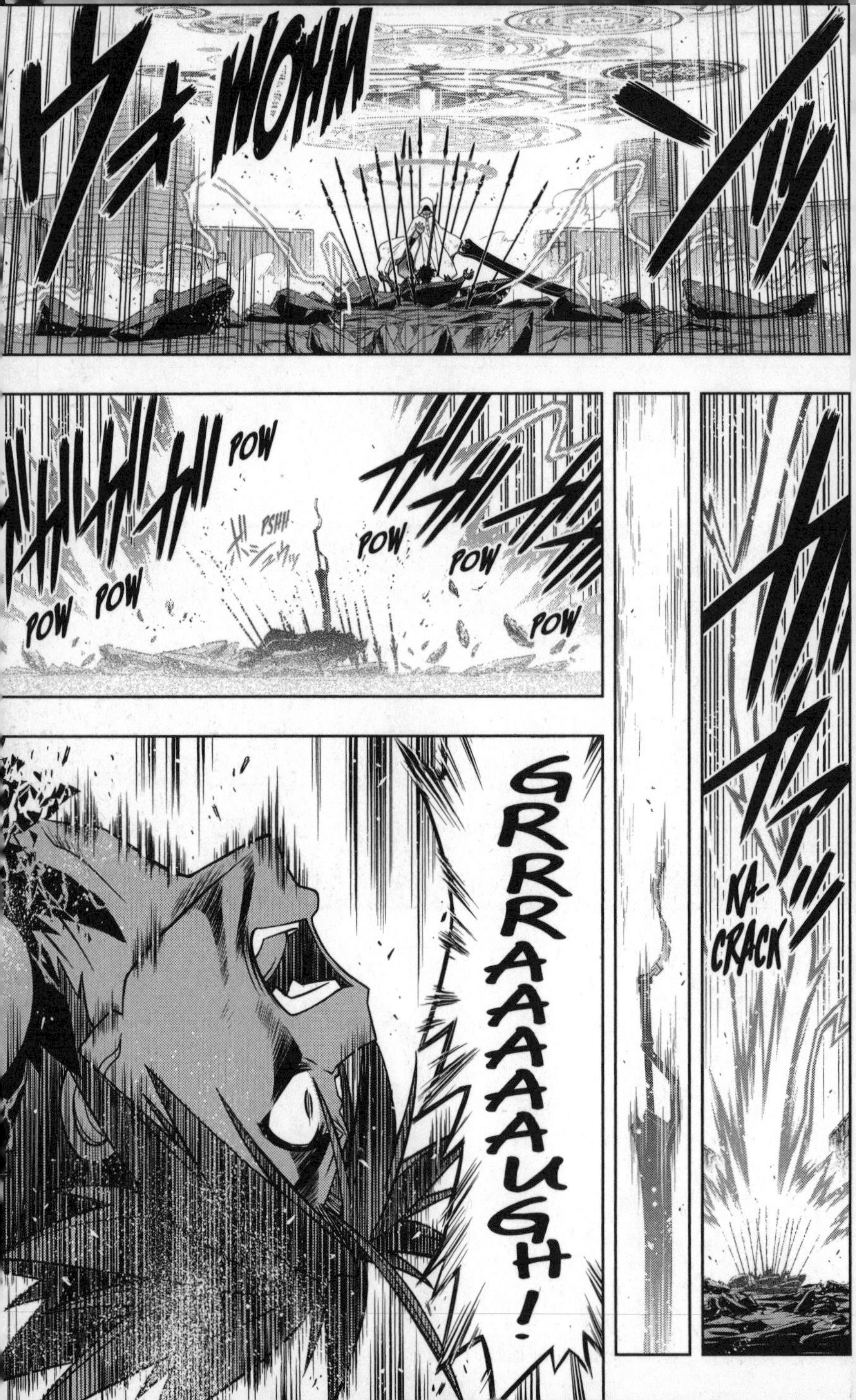
WOHM
KA-CRACK
POW
POW
POW
PSHH
POW
POW
POW
GRRRAAAAAAUGH!

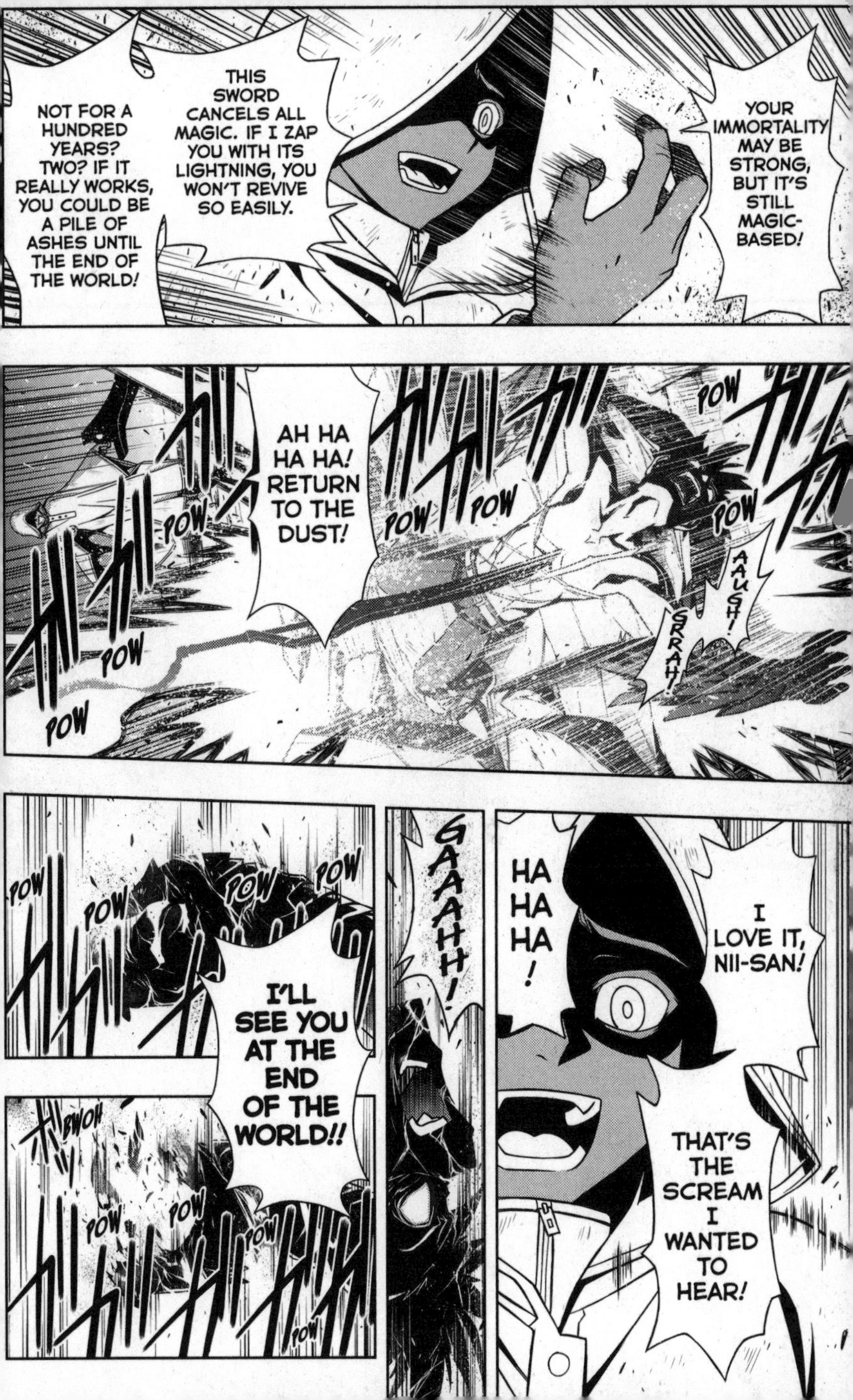
YOUR IMMORTALITY MAY BE STRONG, BUT IT'S STILL MAGIC-BASED!
THIS SWORD CANCELS ALL MAGIC. IF I ZAP YOU WITH ITS LIGHTNING, YOU WON'T REVIVE SO EASILY.
NOT FOR A HUNDRED YEARS? TWO? IF IT REALLY WORKS, YOU COULD BE A PILE OF ASHES UNTIL THE END OF THE WORLD!
POW
POW
AAUGH!
GRRAH!
POW
POW
AH HA HA HA! RETURN TO THE DUST!
POW
POW
POW
I LOVE IT, NII-SAN!
HA HA HA!
THAT'S THE SCREAM I WANTED TO HEAR!
GAAAAHH!
POW
POW
POW
POW
I'LL SEE YOU AT THE END OF THE WORLD!!
BWOH
POW
POW
POW
POW

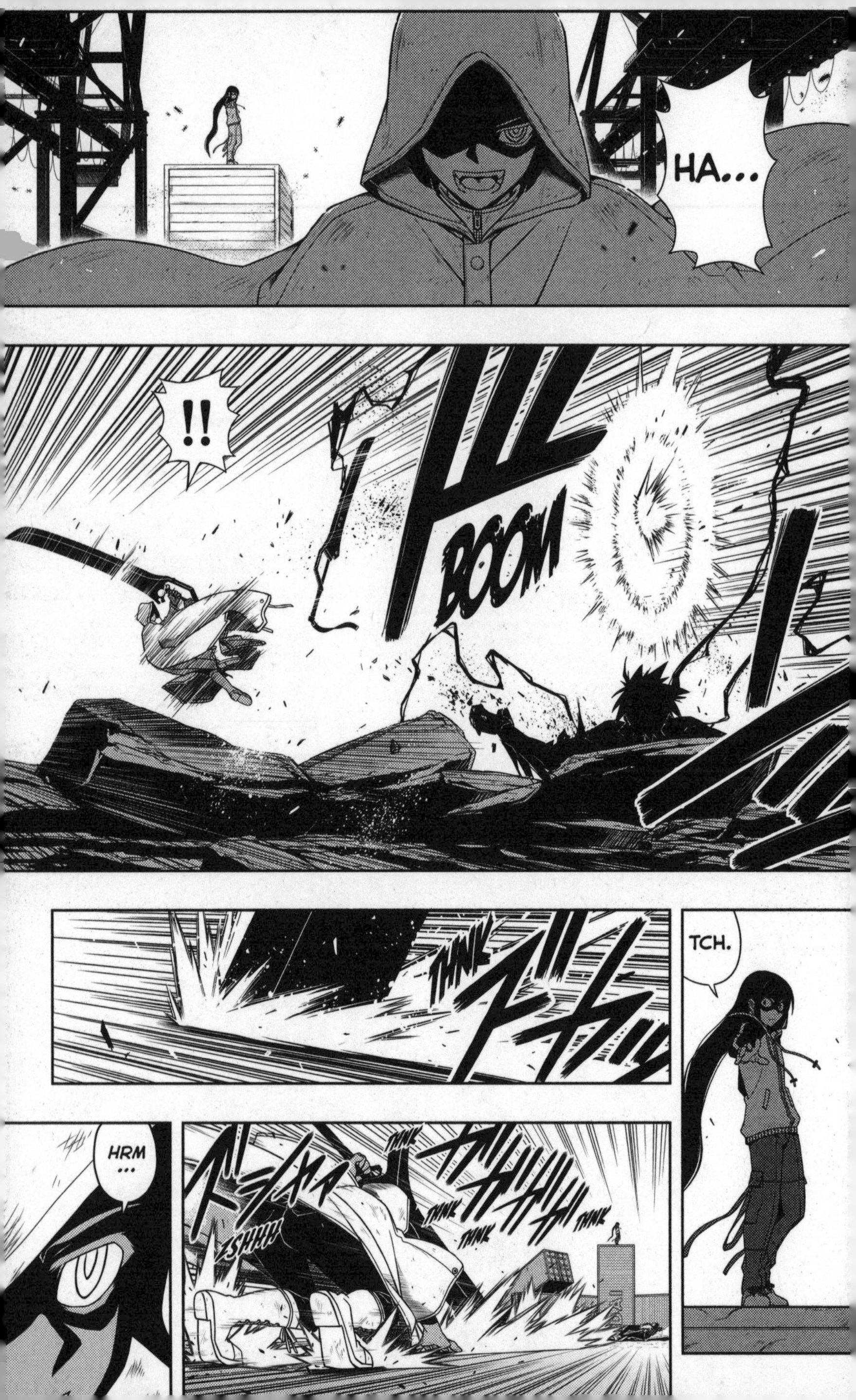
HA...
!!
BOOM
TCH.
THUNK
THUNK
THUNK
THUNK
THUNK
THUNK
SHHH
HRM ...

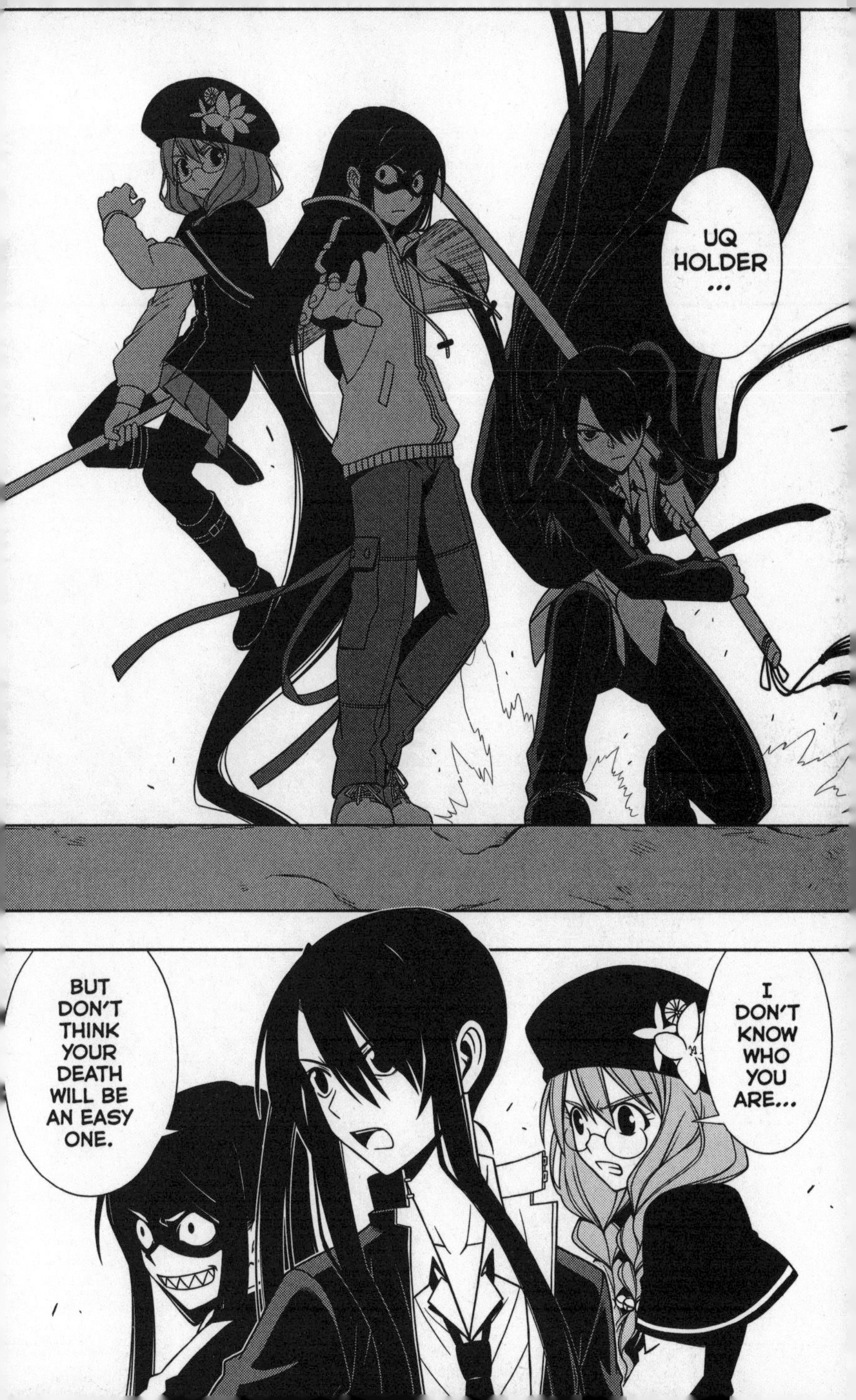
UQ HOLDER ...
I DON'T KNOW WHO YOU ARE...
BUT DON'T THINK YOUR DEATH WILL BE AN EASY ONE.

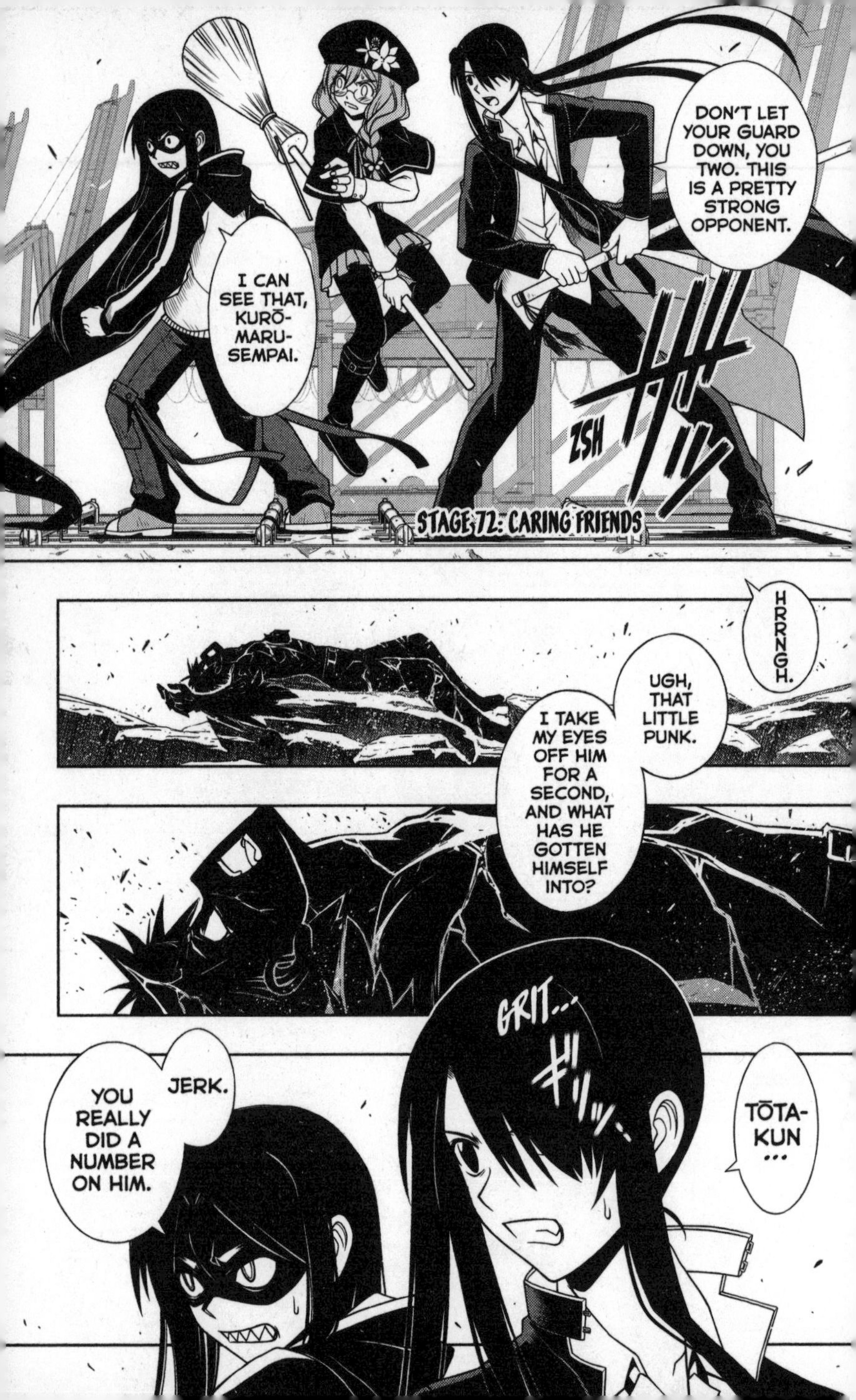
DON'T LET YOUR GUARD DOWN, YOU TWO. THIS IS A PRETTY STRONG OPPONENT.
I CAN SEE THAT, KURŌ-MARU-SEMPAI.
ZSH
STAGE 72: CARING FRIENDS
HRRNGH.
UGH, THAT LITTLE PUNK.
I TAKE MY EYES OFF HIM FOR A SECOND, AND WHAT HAS HE GOTTEN HIMSELF INTO?
TŌTA-KUN...
GRIT...
JERK.
YOU REALLY DID A NUMBER ON HIM.

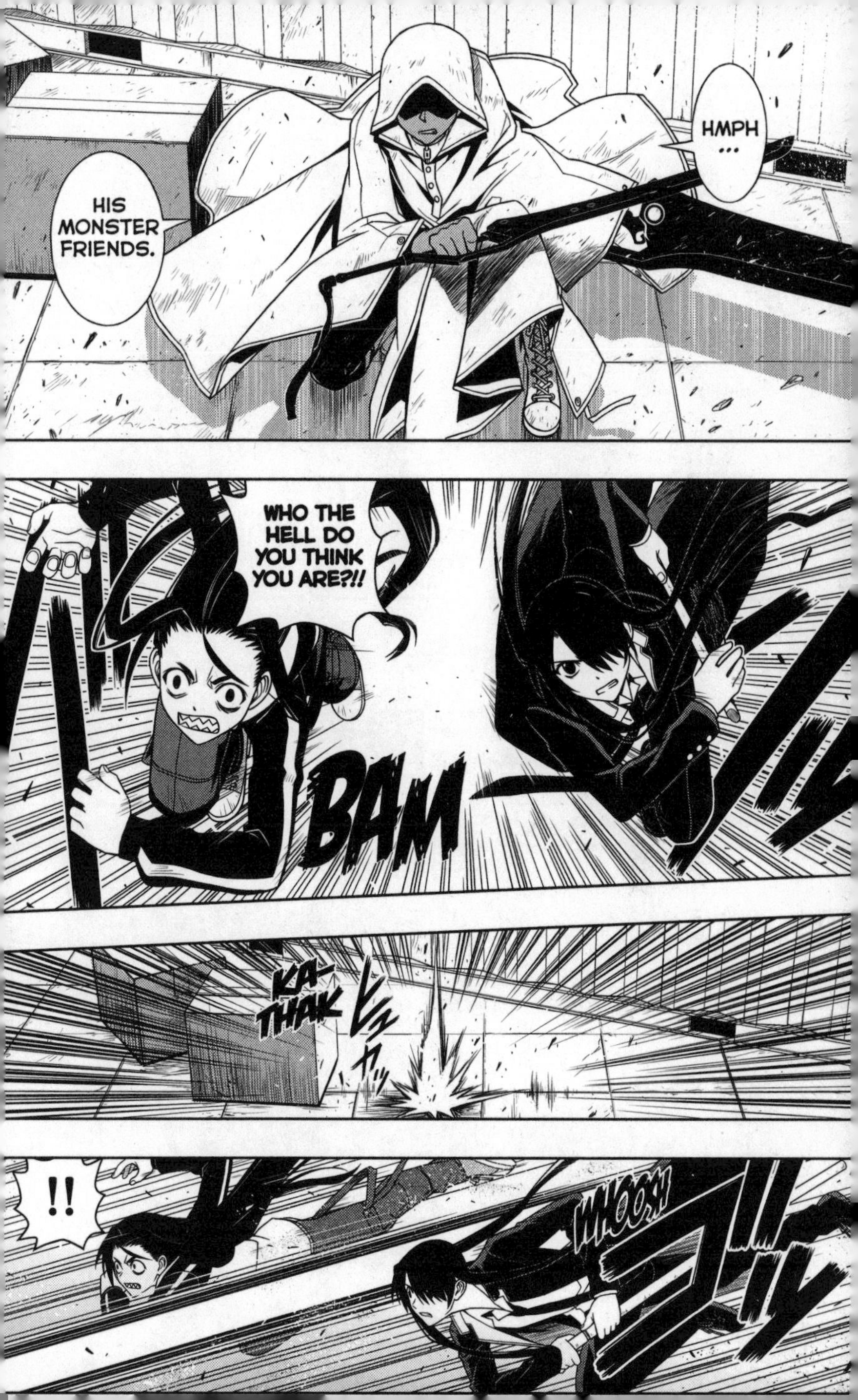
HMPH ...
HIS MONSTER FRIENDS.
WHO THE HELL DO YOU THINK YOU ARE?!!
BAM
KA-THAK
WHOOSH
!!

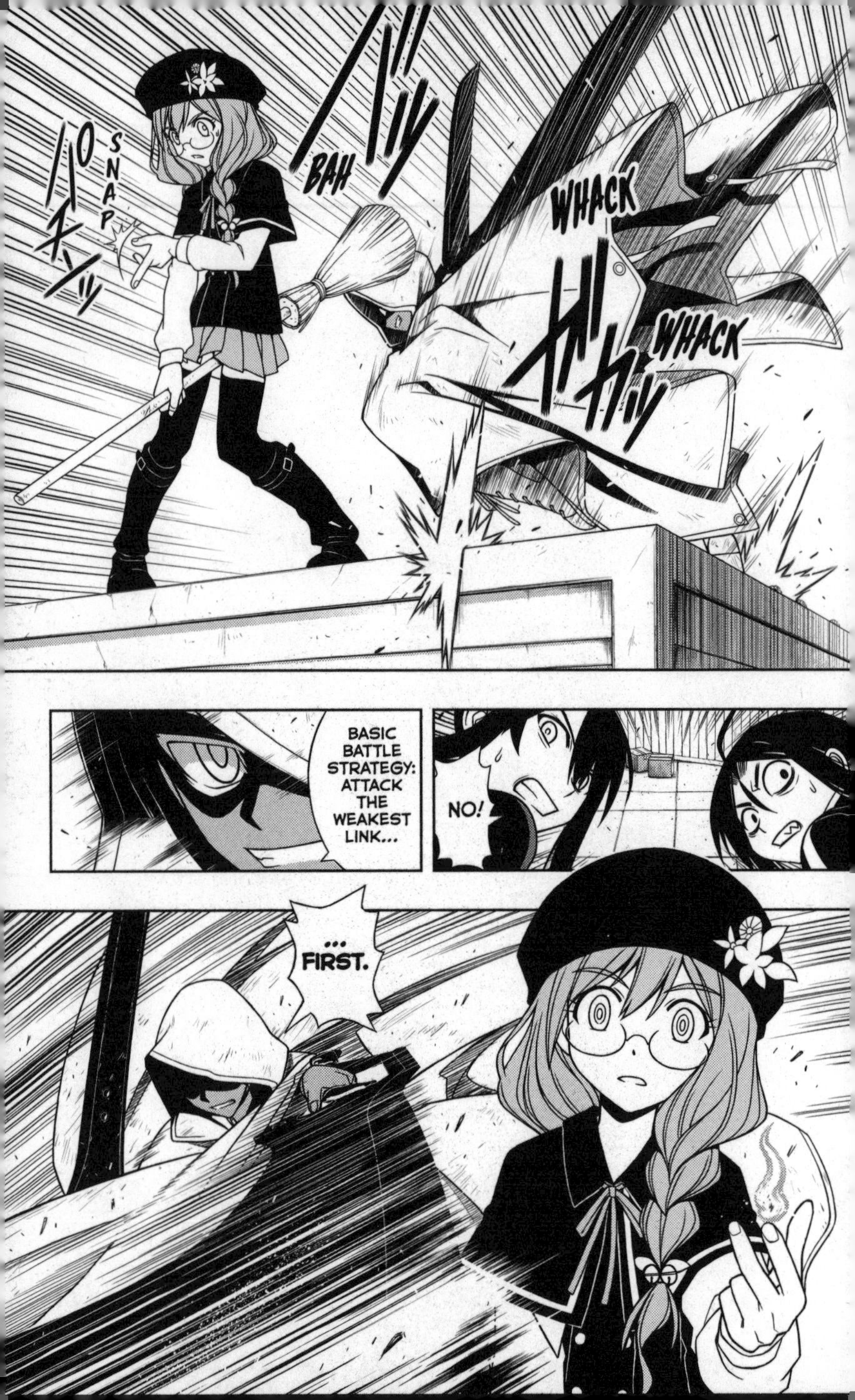
WHACK
WHACK
BAH
SNAP
NO!
BASIC BATTLE STRATEGY: ATTACK THE WEAKEST LINK...
...FIRST.

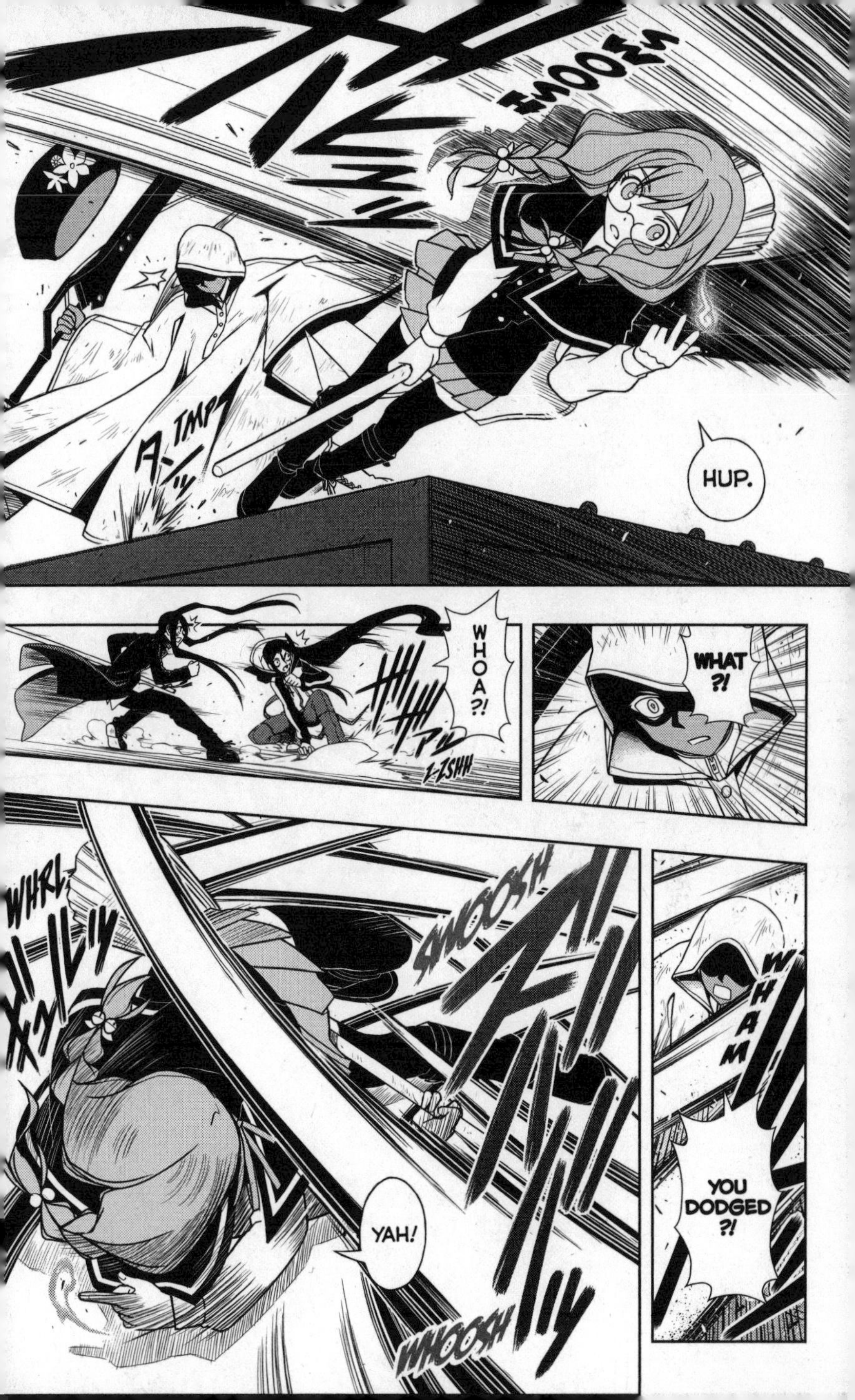
SWOOSH
HUP.
TMP
WHAT ?!
WHOA ?!
Z-ZSHH
WHAM
YOU DODGED ?!
WHRL
SWOOSH
YAH!
WHOOSH

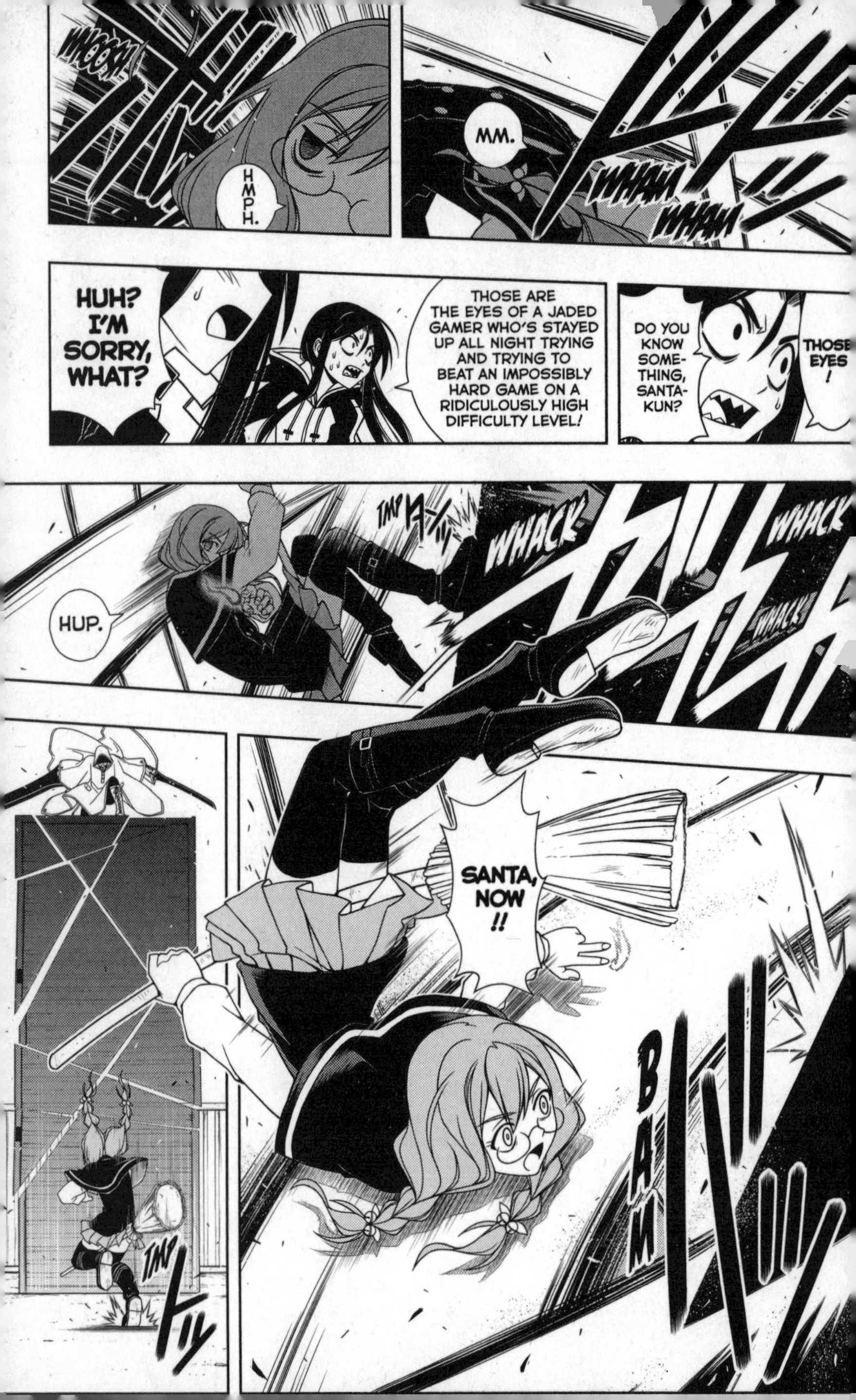
MM.
WHAM
WHAM
WHOOSH
HMPH.
THOSE EYES!
DO YOU KNOW SOMETHING, SANTA-KUN?
THOSE ARE THE EYES OF A JADED GAMER WHO'S STAYED UP ALL NIGHT TRYING AND TRYING TO BEAT AN IMPOSSIBLY HARD GAME ON A RIDICULOUSLY HIGH DIFFICULTY LEVEL!
HUH? I'M SORRY, WHAT?
WHACK
WHACK
WHACK
TMP
HUP.
SANTA, NOW!!
BAM
TMP

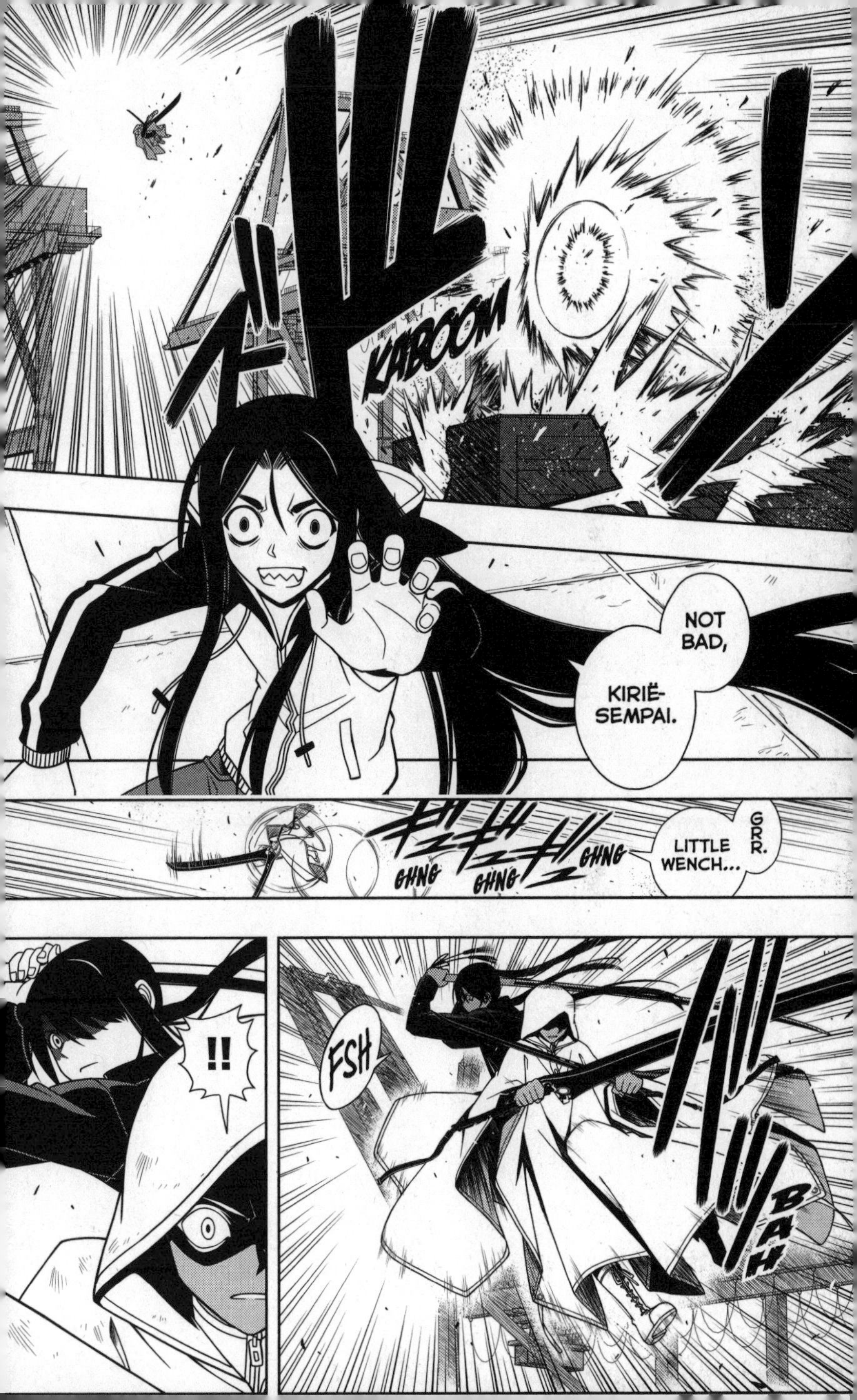
KABOOM
NOT BAD,
KIRIË-SEMPAI.
GRR.
LITTLE WENCH...
GHNG
GHNG
GHNG
BAH
FSH
!!

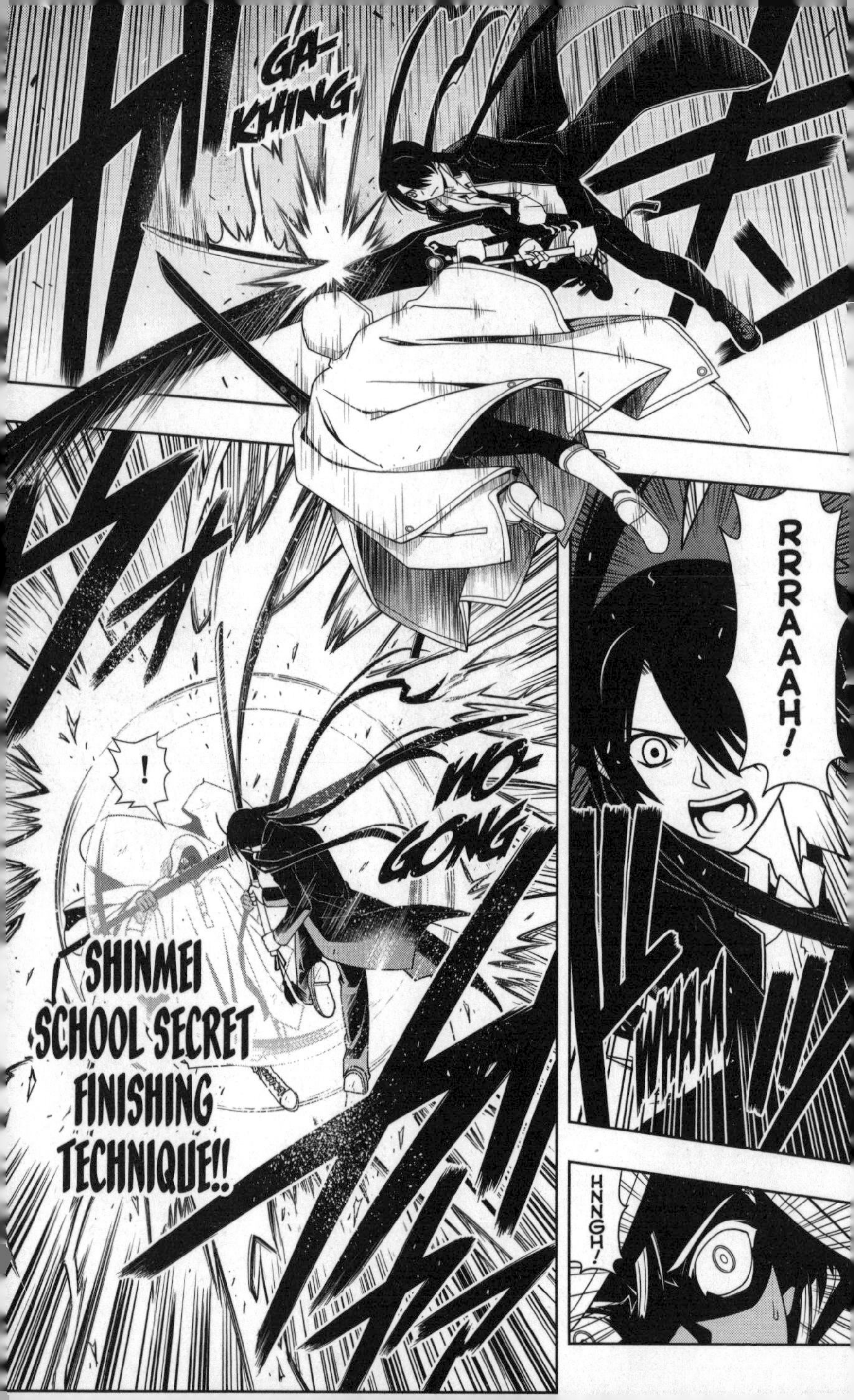
GA-KHING
RRRAAAH!
WO-GONG
!
SHINMEI SCHOOL SECRET FINISHING TECHNIQUE!!
WHAM
HNNGH!

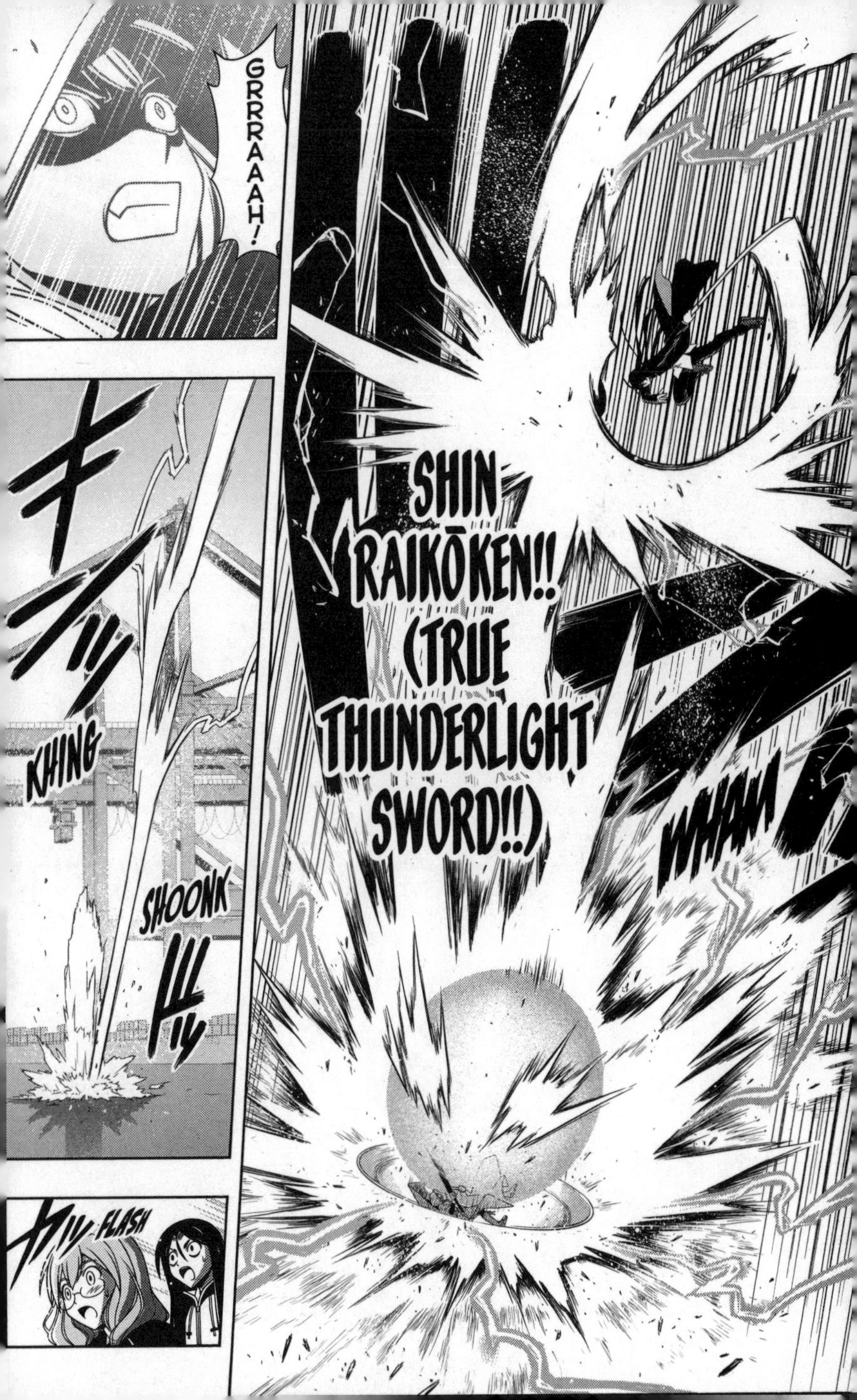
SHIN RAIKŌKEN!! (TRUE THUNDERLIGHT SWORD!!)
WHAM
GRRRAAAH!
KHING
SHOONK
FLASH

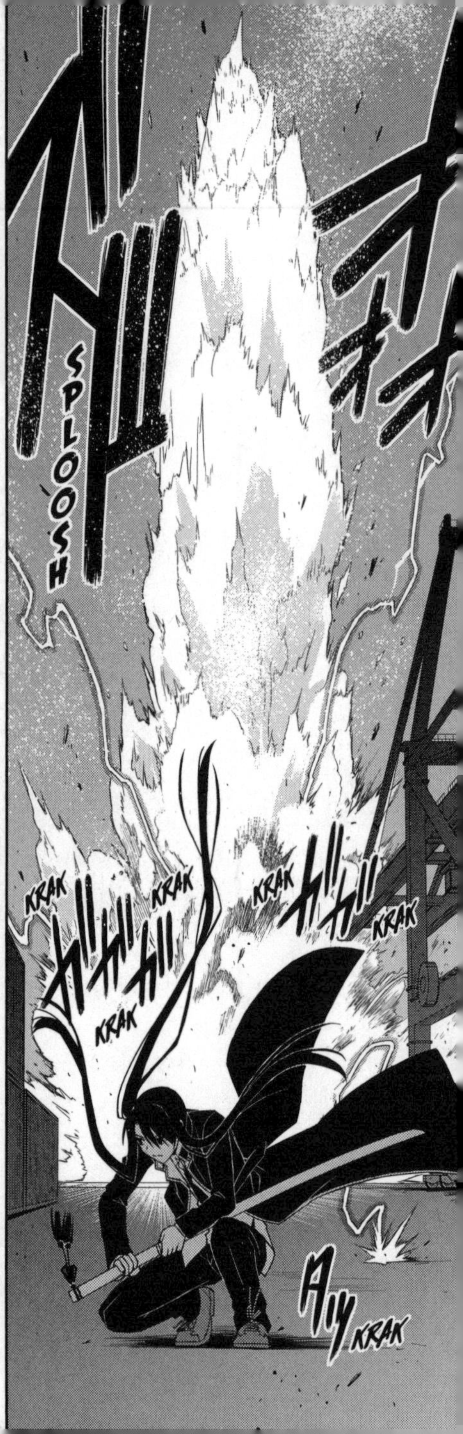
SPLOOOSH
KRAK
KRAK
KRAK
KRAK
KRAK
KRAK
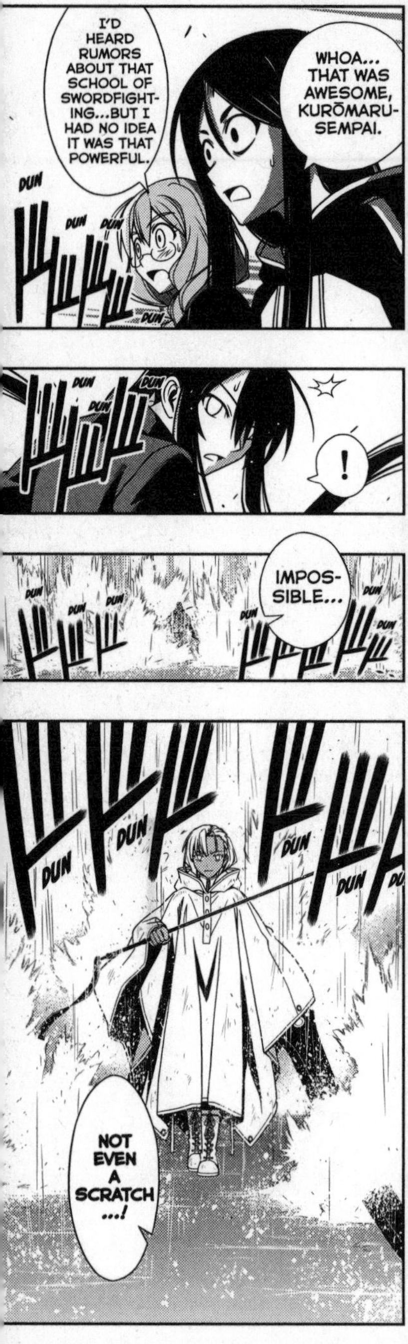
WHOA... THAT WAS AWESOME, KURŌMARU-SEMPAI.
I'D HEARD RUMORS ABOUT THAT SCHOOL OF SWORDFIGHTING...BUT I HAD NO IDEA IT WAS THAT POWERFUL.
DUN DUN DUN DUN
DUN DUN DUN
!
IMPOSSIBLE...
DUN DUN DUN DUN DUN DUN
DUN DUN DUN DUN DUN DUN
NOT EVEN A SCRATCH...!

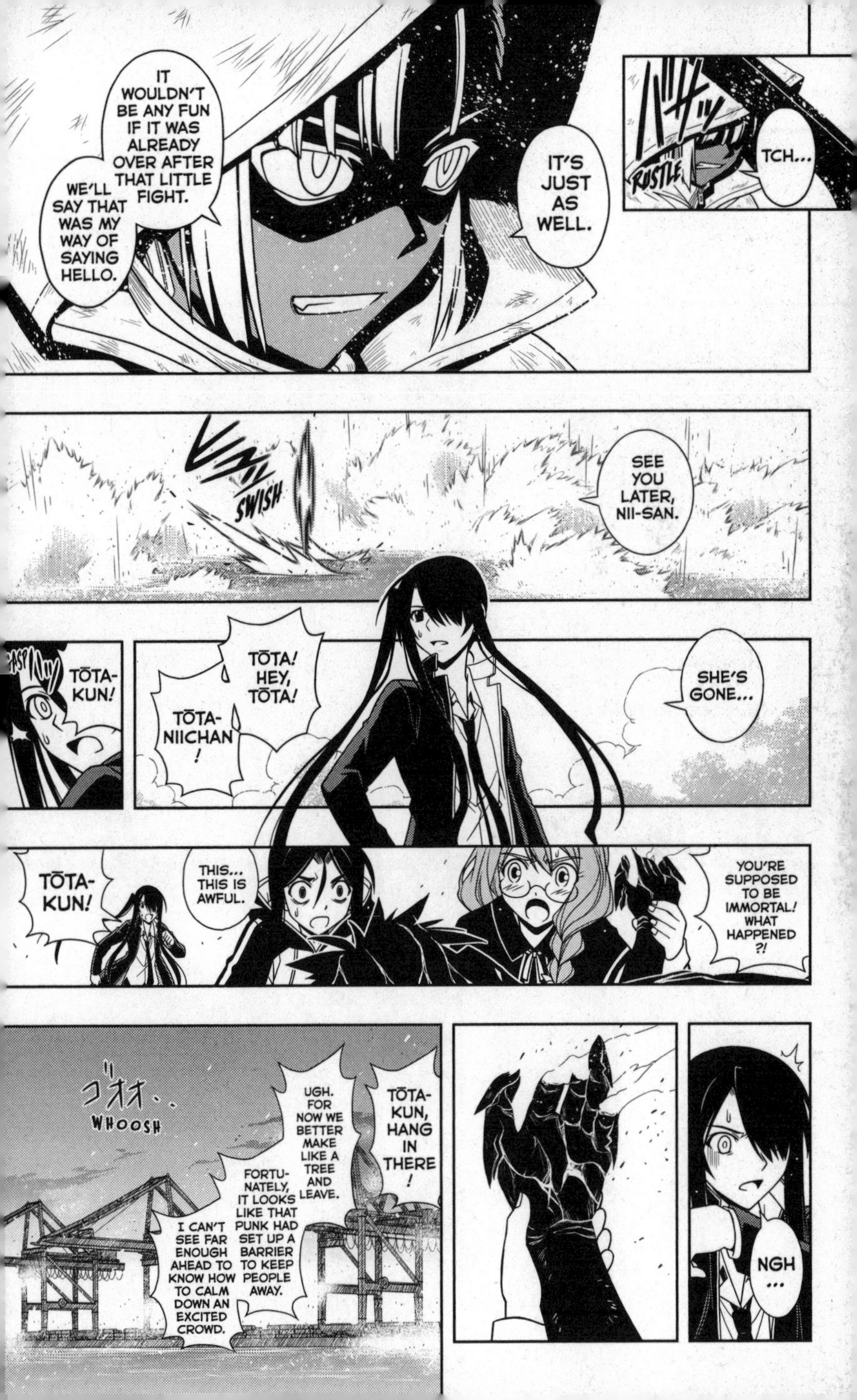
TCH...
RUSTLE
IT'S JUST AS WELL.
IT WOULDN'T BE ANY FUN IF IT WAS ALREADY OVER AFTER THAT LITTLE FIGHT.
WE'LL SAY THAT WAS MY WAY OF SAYING HELLO.
SEE YOU LATER, NII-SAN.
SWISH
SHE'S GONE...
TŌTA! HEY, TŌTA!
TŌTA-NIICHAN!
GASP
TŌTA-KUN!
YOU'RE SUPPOSED TO BE IMMORTAL! WHAT HAPPENED?!
THIS... THIS IS AWFUL.
TŌTA-KUN!
NGH...
TŌTA-KUN, HANG IN THERE!
UGH. FOR NOW WE BETTER MAKE LIKE A TREE AND LEAVE.
FORTUNATELY, IT LOOKS LIKE THAT PUNK HAD SET UP A BARRIER TO KEEP PEOPLE AWAY.
I CAN'T SEE FAR ENOUGH AHEAD TO KNOW HOW TO CALM DOWN AN EXCITED CROWD.
ゴオオ..
WHOOSH

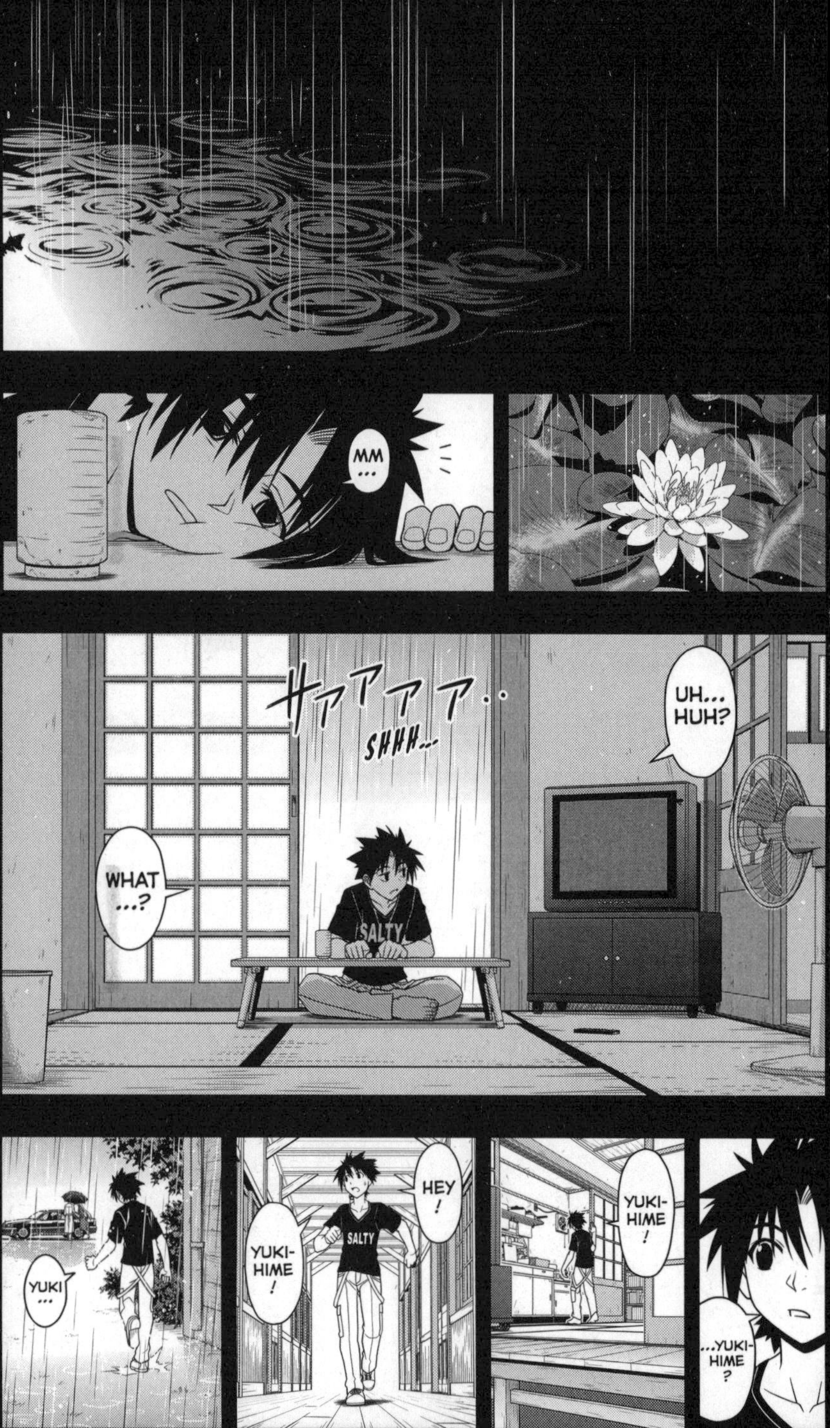
MM ...
UH... HUH?
サァアアア..
SHHH...
WHAT ...?
...YUKI-HIME ?
YUKI-HIME !
HEY !
YUKI-HIME !
YUKI ...

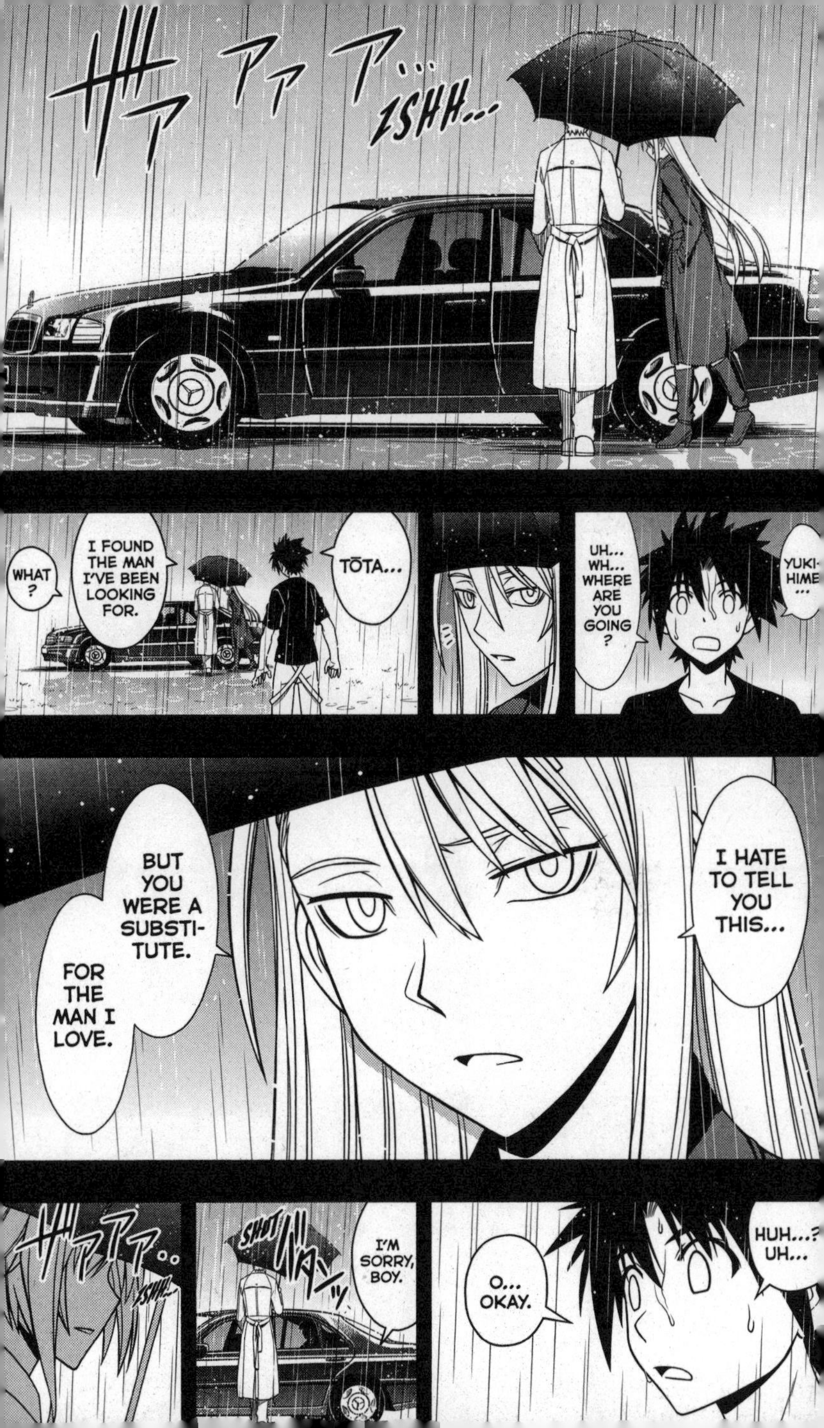
ZSHH...
YUKI-HIME ...
UH... WH... WHERE ARE YOU GOING ?
TŌTA...
I FOUND THE MAN I'VE BEEN LOOKING FOR.
WHAT ?
I HATE TO TELL YOU THIS...
BUT YOU WERE A SUBSTI-TUTE.
FOR THE MAN I LOVE.
HUH...? UH...
O... OKAY.
I'M SORRY, BOY.
SHUT
ZSHH...

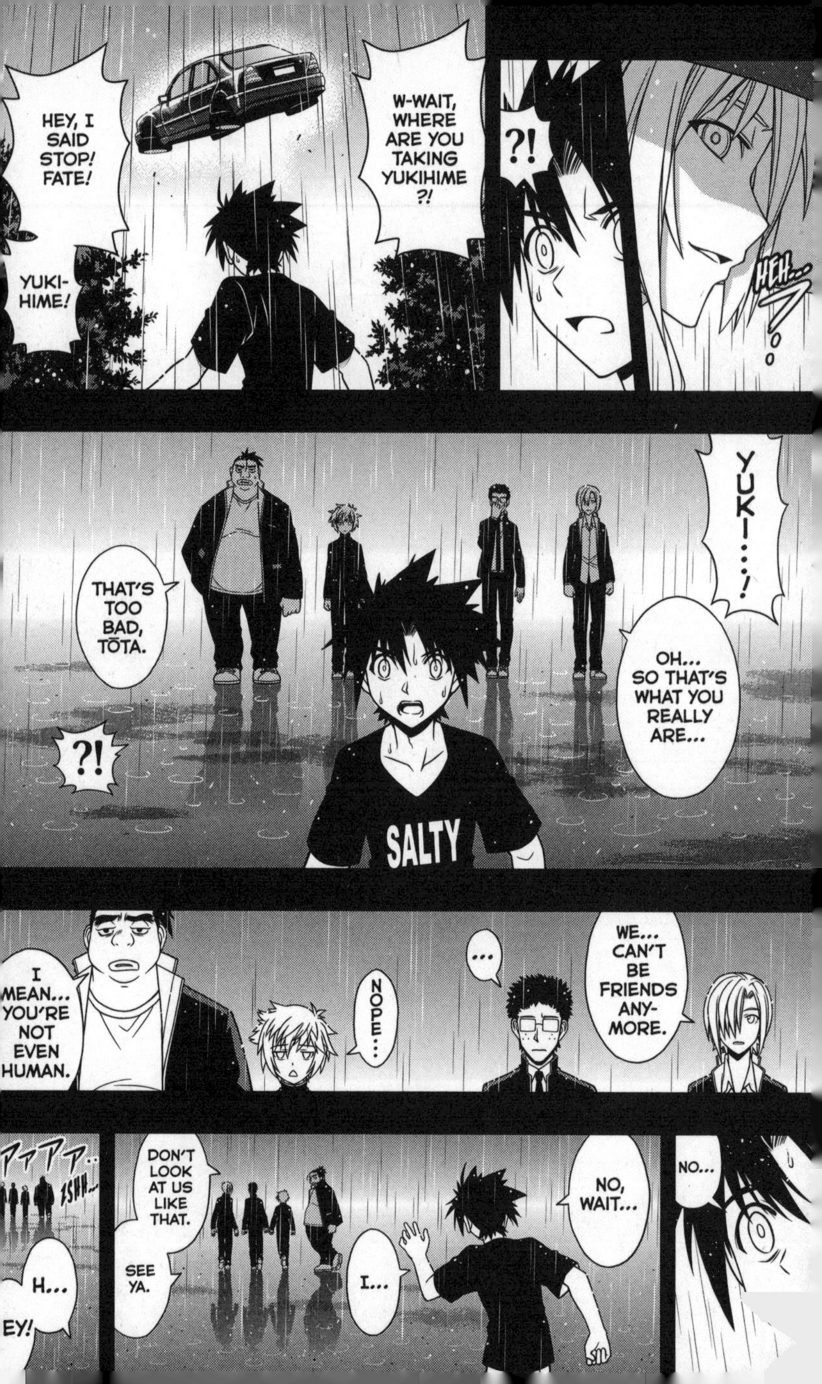
?!
HEH...
W-WAIT, WHERE ARE YOU TAKING YUKIHIME ?!
HEY, I SAID STOP! FATE!
YUKI-HIME!
YUKI...!
OH... SO THAT'S WHAT YOU REALLY ARE...
THAT'S TOO BAD, TŌTA.
?!
WE... CAN'T BE FRIENDS ANYMORE.
...
NOPE...
I MEAN... YOU'RE NOT EVEN HUMAN.
NO...
NO, WAIT...
I...
DON'T LOOK AT US LIKE THAT.
SEE YA.
ZSHH...
H...
EY!

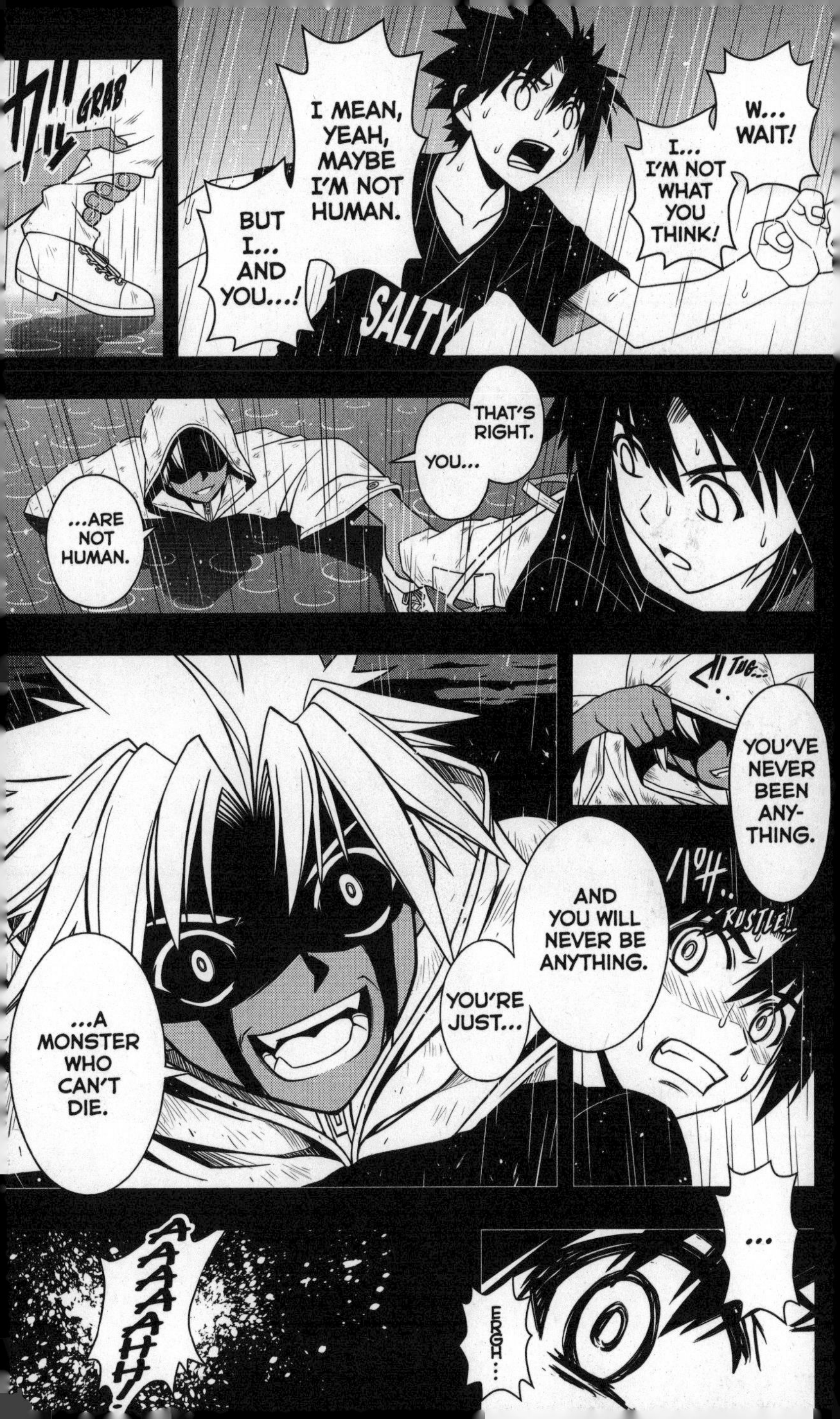
W... WAIT!
I... I'M NOT WHAT YOU THINK!
I MEAN, YEAH, MAYBE I'M NOT HUMAN.
BUT I... AND YOU...!
GRAB
THAT'S RIGHT.
YOU...
...ARE NOT HUMAN.
TUG...
YOU'VE NEVER BEEN ANY-THING.
RUSTLE...
AND YOU WILL NEVER BE ANYTHING.
YOU'RE JUST...
...A MONSTER WHO CAN'T DIE.
...
ERGH...
AAAAAHH!

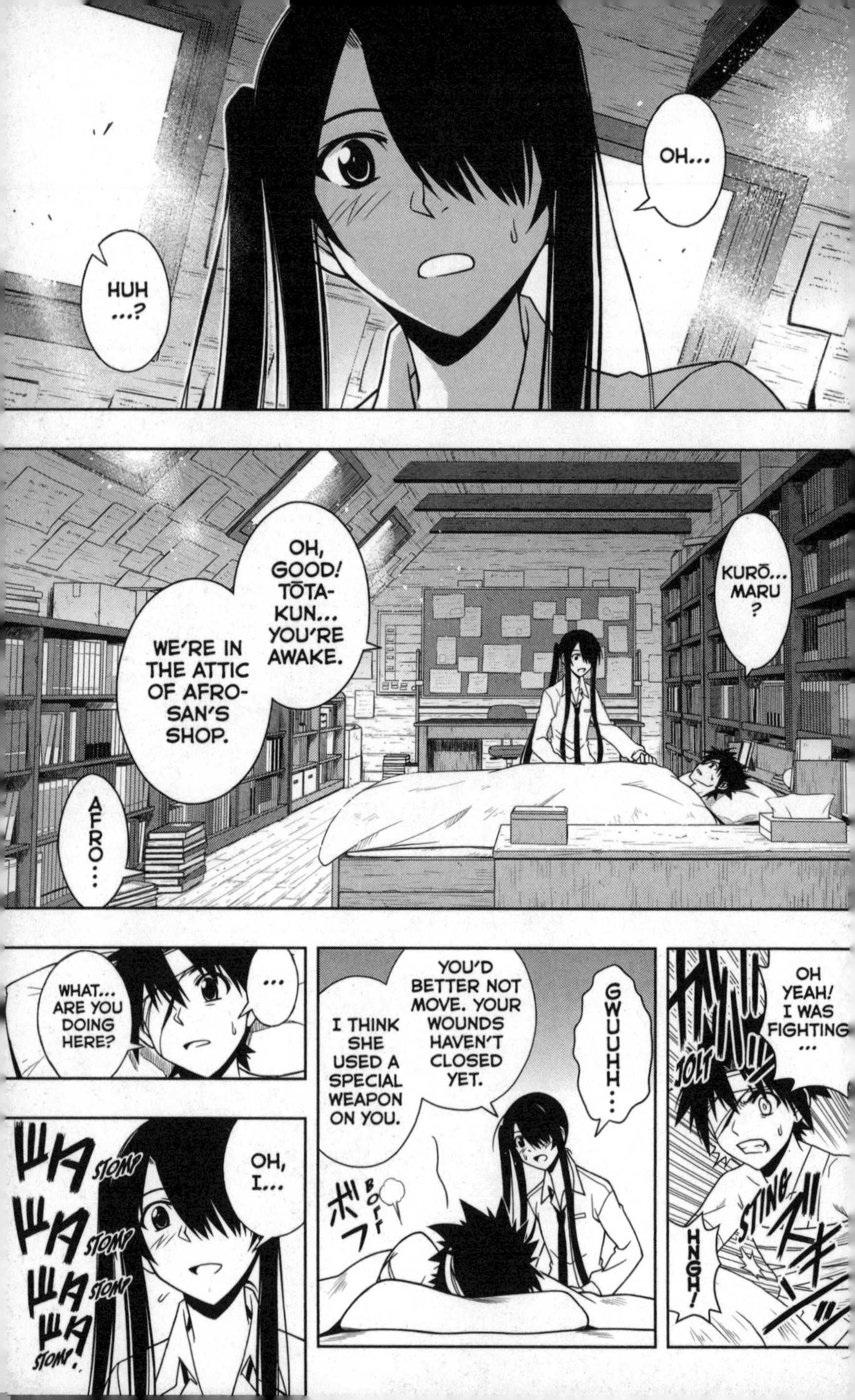
OH...
HUH ...?
KURŌ... MARU ?
OH, GOOD! TŌTA-KUN... YOU'RE AWAKE.
WE'RE IN THE ATTIC OF AFRO-SAN'S SHOP.
AFRO...
OH YEAH! I WAS FIGHTING ...
JOLT
STING
HNGH!
GWUUHH...
YOU'D BETTER NOT MOVE. YOUR WOUNDS HAVEN'T CLOSED YET.
I THINK SHE USED A SPECIAL WEAPON ON YOU.
BOFF
...
WHAT... ARE YOU DOING HERE?
OH, I...
STOMP
STOMP
STOMP
STOMP

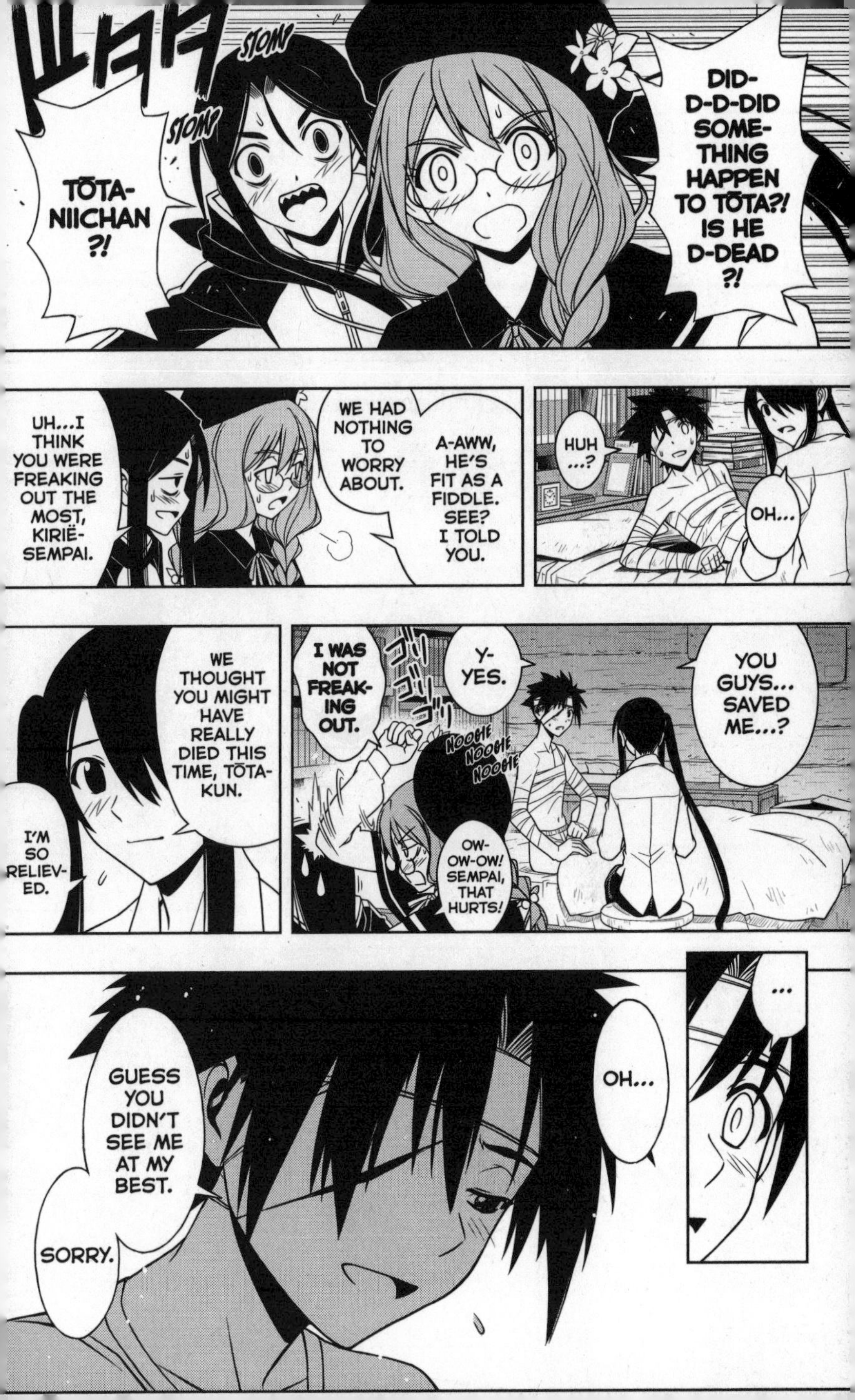
DID-D-D-DID SOMETHING HAPPEN TO TŌTA?! IS HE D-DEAD?!
STOMP
STOMP
TŌTA-NIICHAN?!
HUH...?
OH...
A-AWW, HE'S FIT AS A FIDDLE. SEE? I TOLD YOU.
WE HAD NOTHING TO WORRY ABOUT.
UH...I THINK YOU WERE FREAKING OUT THE MOST, KIRIË-SEMPAI.
YOU GUYS... SAVED ME...?
Y-YES.
I WAS NOT FREAKING OUT.
NOOGIE
NOOGIE
NOOGIE
OW-OW-OW! SEMPAI, THAT HURTS!
WE THOUGHT YOU MIGHT HAVE REALLY DIED THIS TIME, TŌTA-KUN.
I'M SO RELIEVED.
...
OH...
GUESS YOU DIDN'T SEE ME AT MY BEST.
SORRY.

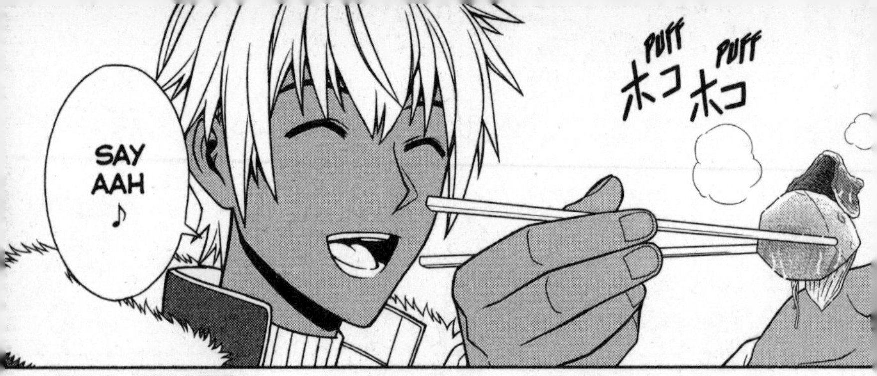
ホコ PUFF
ホコ PUFF
SAY AAH ♪

STAGE 73: RECOGNITION

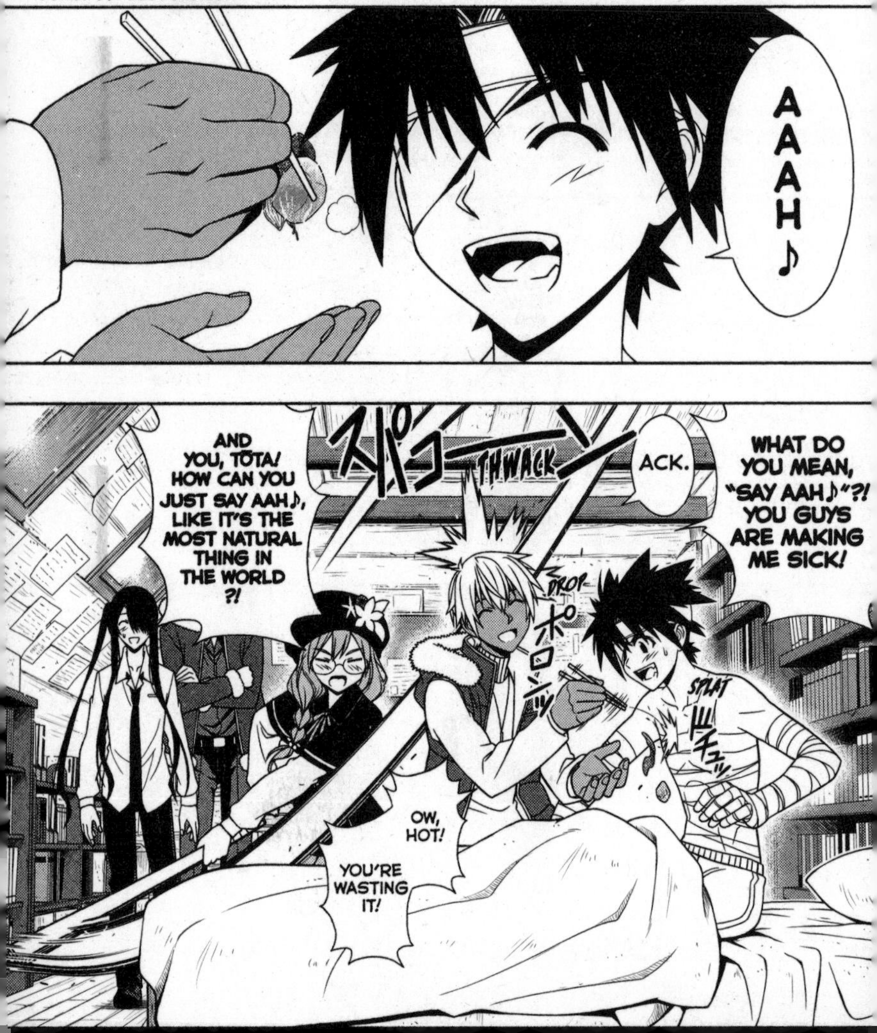
AAAH♪
WHAT DO YOU MEAN, "SAY AAH♪"?! YOU GUYS ARE MAKING ME SICK!
ACK.
スパコーン THWACK
AND YOU, TŌTA! HOW CAN YOU JUST SAY AAH♪, LIKE IT'S THE MOST NATURAL THING IN THE WORLD ?!
ボロンッ DROP
ビチュッ SPLAT
OW, HOT!
YOU'RE WASTING IT!

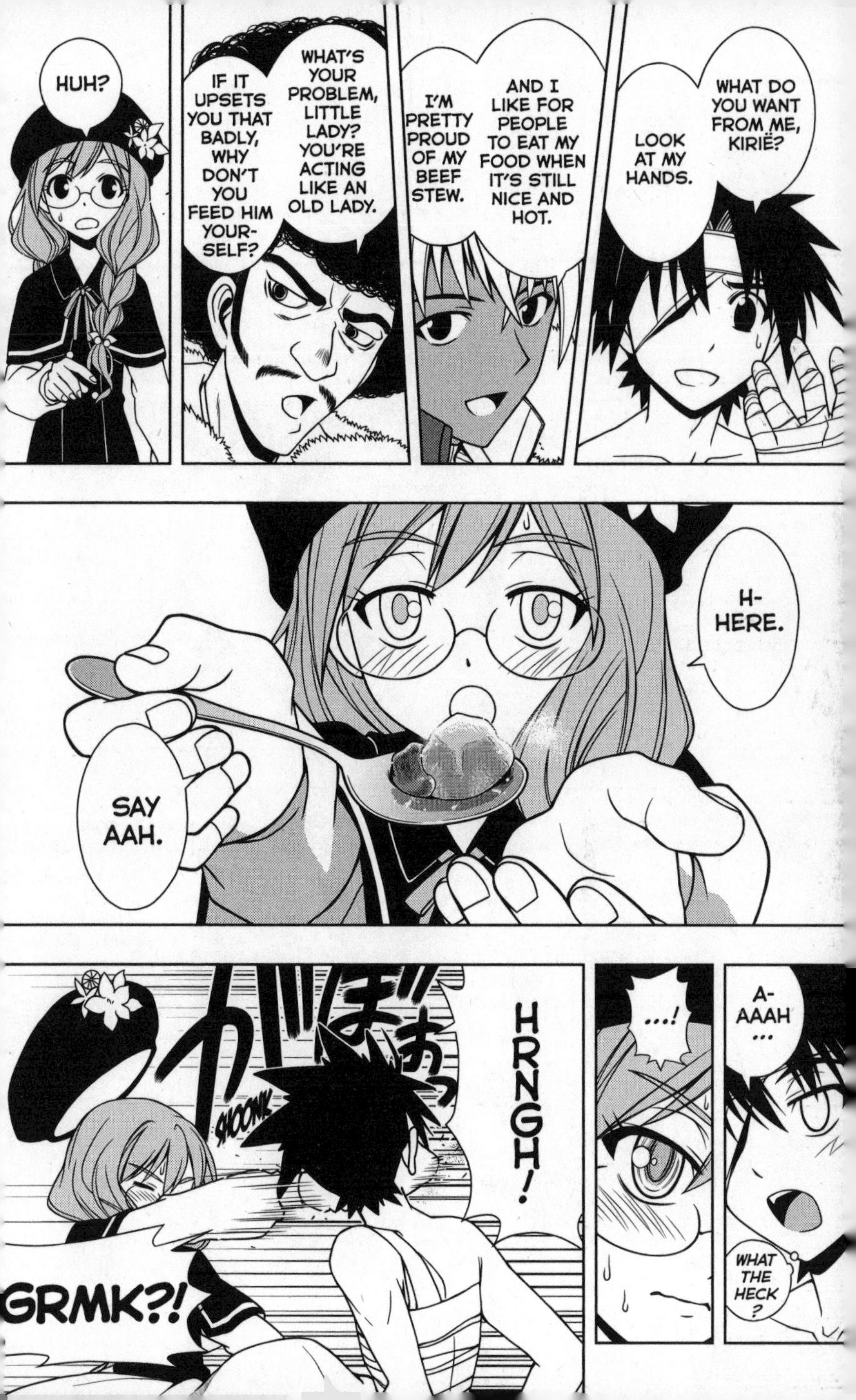
WHAT DO YOU WANT FROM ME, KIRIË?
LOOK AT MY HANDS.
AND I LIKE FOR PEOPLE TO EAT MY FOOD WHEN IT'S STILL NICE AND HOT.
I'M PRETTY PROUD OF MY BEEF STEW.
WHAT'S YOUR PROBLEM, LITTLE LADY? YOU'RE ACTING LIKE AN OLD LADY.
IF IT UPSETS YOU THAT BADLY, WHY DON'T YOU FEED HIM YOURSELF?
HUH?
H- HERE.
SAY AAH.
A- AAAH ...
WHAT THE HECK ?
...!
HRNGH!
SHOONK
GRMK?!

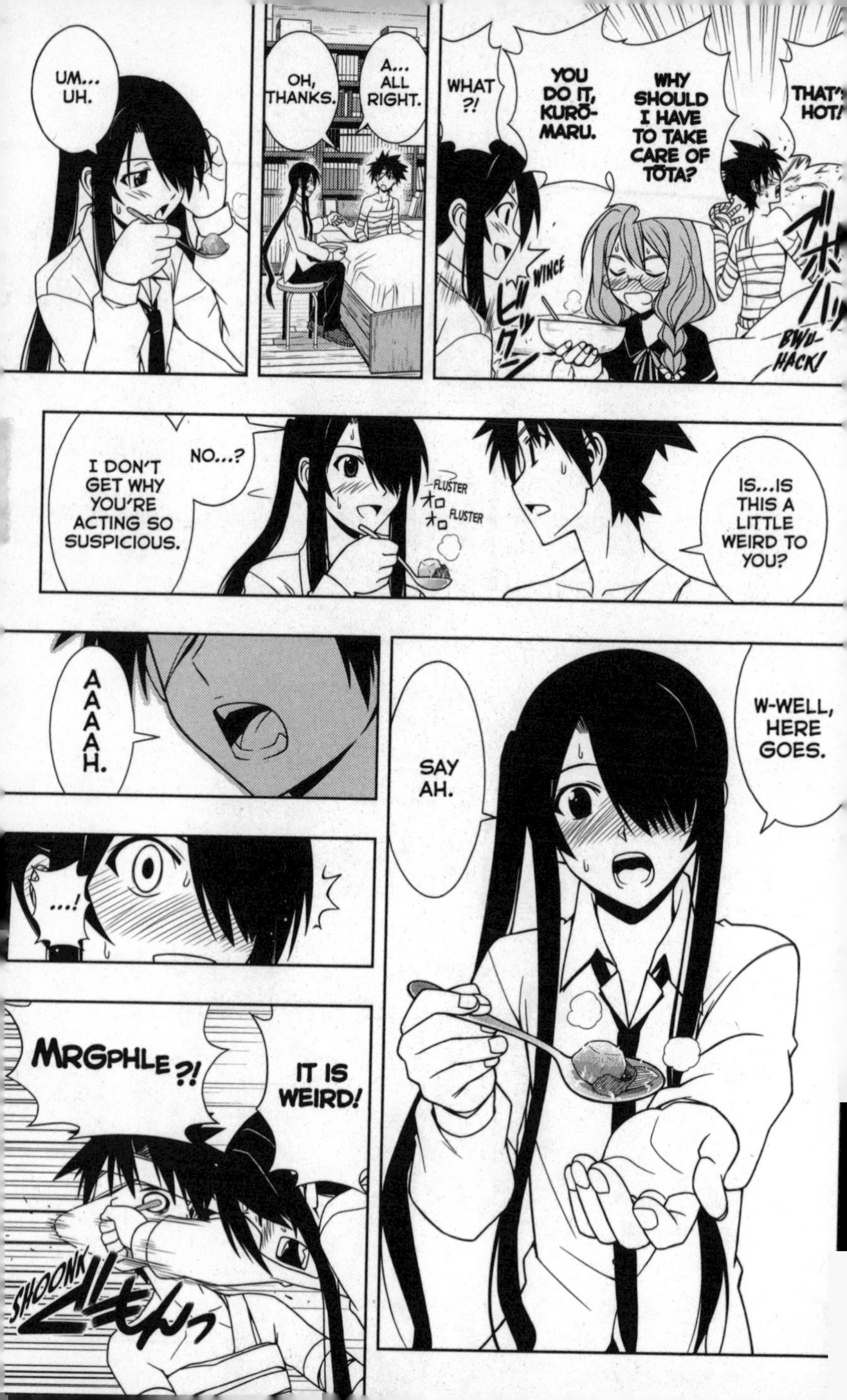
THAT'S HOT!
BWU-HACK!
WHY SHOULD I HAVE TO TAKE CARE OF TŌTA?
YOU DO IT, KURŌ-MARU.
WINCE
WHAT ?!
A... ALL RIGHT.
OH, THANKS.
UM... UH.
IS...IS THIS A LITTLE WEIRD TO YOU?
FLUSTER
FLUSTER
NO...?
I DON'T GET WHY YOU'RE ACTING SO SUSPICIOUS.
W-WELL, HERE GOES.
SAY AH.
AAAAAH.
...!
IT IS WEIRD!
MRGPHLE ?!
SHOONK

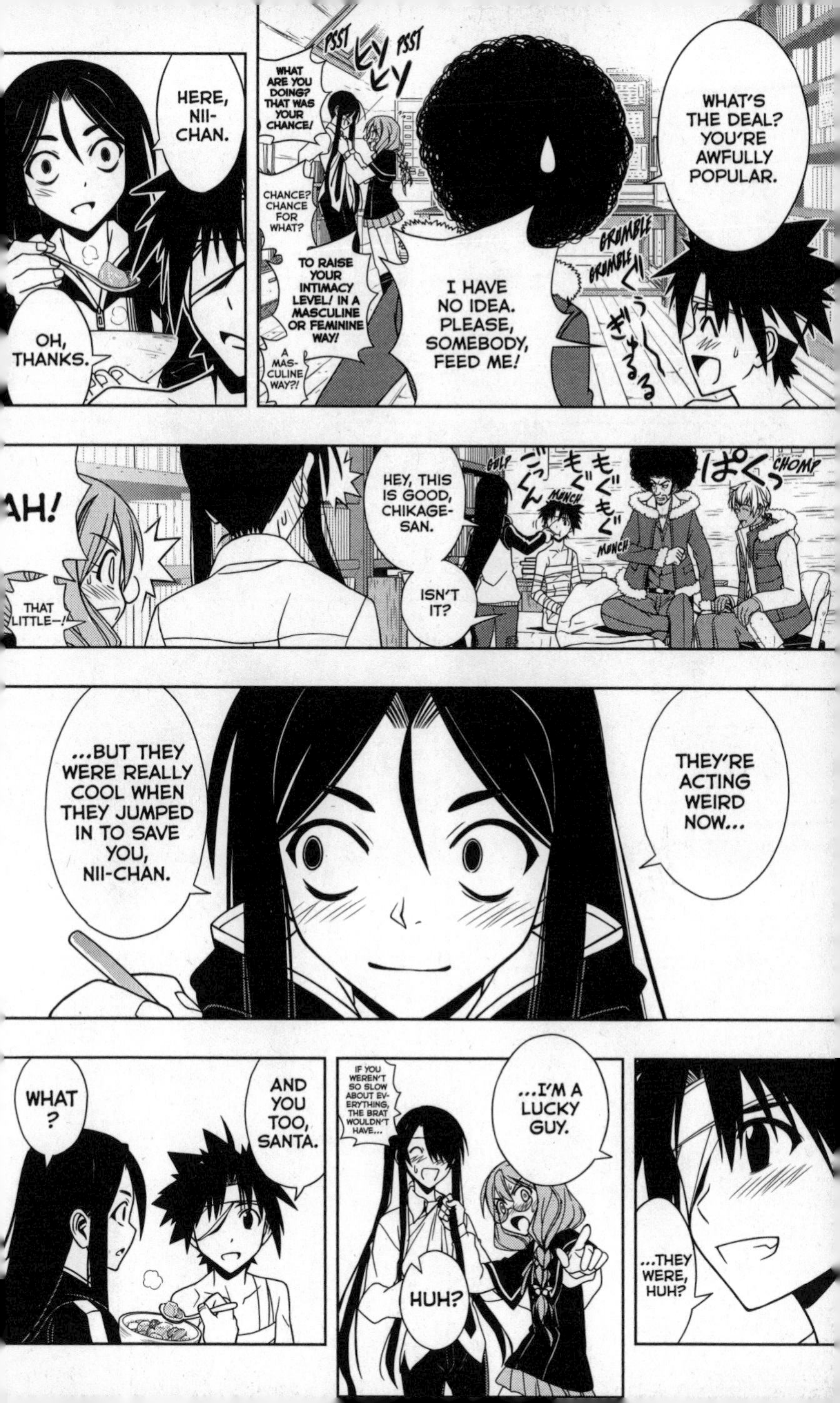
WHAT'S THE DEAL? YOU'RE AWFULLY POPULAR.
GRUMBLE GRUMBLE ぐぅ～ぎゅるる
I HAVE NO IDEA. PLEASE, SOMEBODY, FEED ME!
PSST ヒソ PSST ヒソ
WHAT ARE YOU DOING? THAT WAS YOUR CHANCE!
CHANCE? CHANCE FOR WHAT?
TO RAISE YOUR INTIMACY LEVEL! IN A MASCULINE OR FEMININE WAY!
A MAS-CULINE WAY?!
HERE, NII-CHAN.
OH, THANKS.
ぱくっ CHOMP
もぐもぐ MUNCH MUNCH
ごっくん GULP
HEY, THIS IS GOOD, CHIKAGE-SAN.
ISN'T IT?
AH!
THAT LITTLE—!
THEY'RE ACTING WEIRD NOW...
...BUT THEY WERE REALLY COOL WHEN THEY JUMPED IN TO SAVE YOU, NII-CHAN.
...THEY WERE, HUH?
...I'M A LUCKY GUY.
IF YOU WEREN'T SO SLOW ABOUT EV-ERYTHING, THE BRAT WOULDN'T HAVE...
HUH?
AND YOU TOO, SANTA.
WHAT?

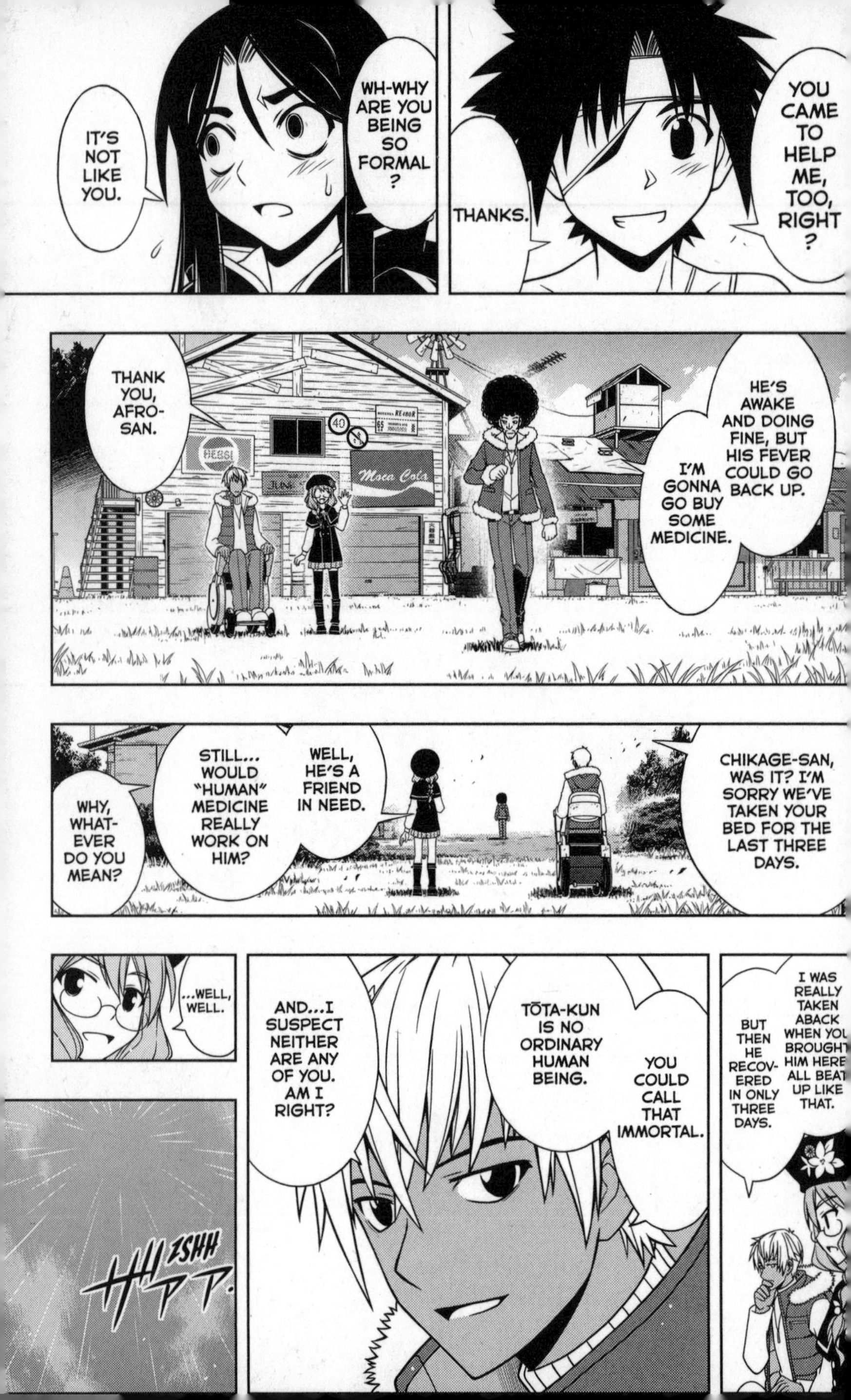
YOU CAME TO HELP ME, TOO, RIGHT?
THANKS.
WH-WHY ARE YOU BEING SO FORMAL?
IT'S NOT LIKE YOU.
HE'S AWAKE AND DOING FINE, BUT HIS FEVER COULD GO BACK UP.
I'M GONNA GO BUY SOME MEDICINE.
THANK YOU, AFRO-SAN.
CHIKAGE-SAN, WAS IT? I'M SORRY WE'VE TAKEN YOUR BED FOR THE LAST THREE DAYS.
WELL, HE'S A FRIEND IN NEED.
STILL... WOULD "HUMAN" MEDICINE REALLY WORK ON HIM?
WHY, WHATEVER DO YOU MEAN?
I WAS REALLY TAKEN ABACK WHEN YOU BROUGHT HIM HERE ALL BEAT UP LIKE THAT.
BUT THEN HE RECOVERED IN ONLY THREE DAYS.
TŌTA-KUN IS NO ORDINARY HUMAN BEING.
YOU COULD CALL THAT IMMORTAL.
AND...I SUSPECT NEITHER ARE ANY OF YOU. AM I RIGHT?
...WELL, WELL.
ZSHH

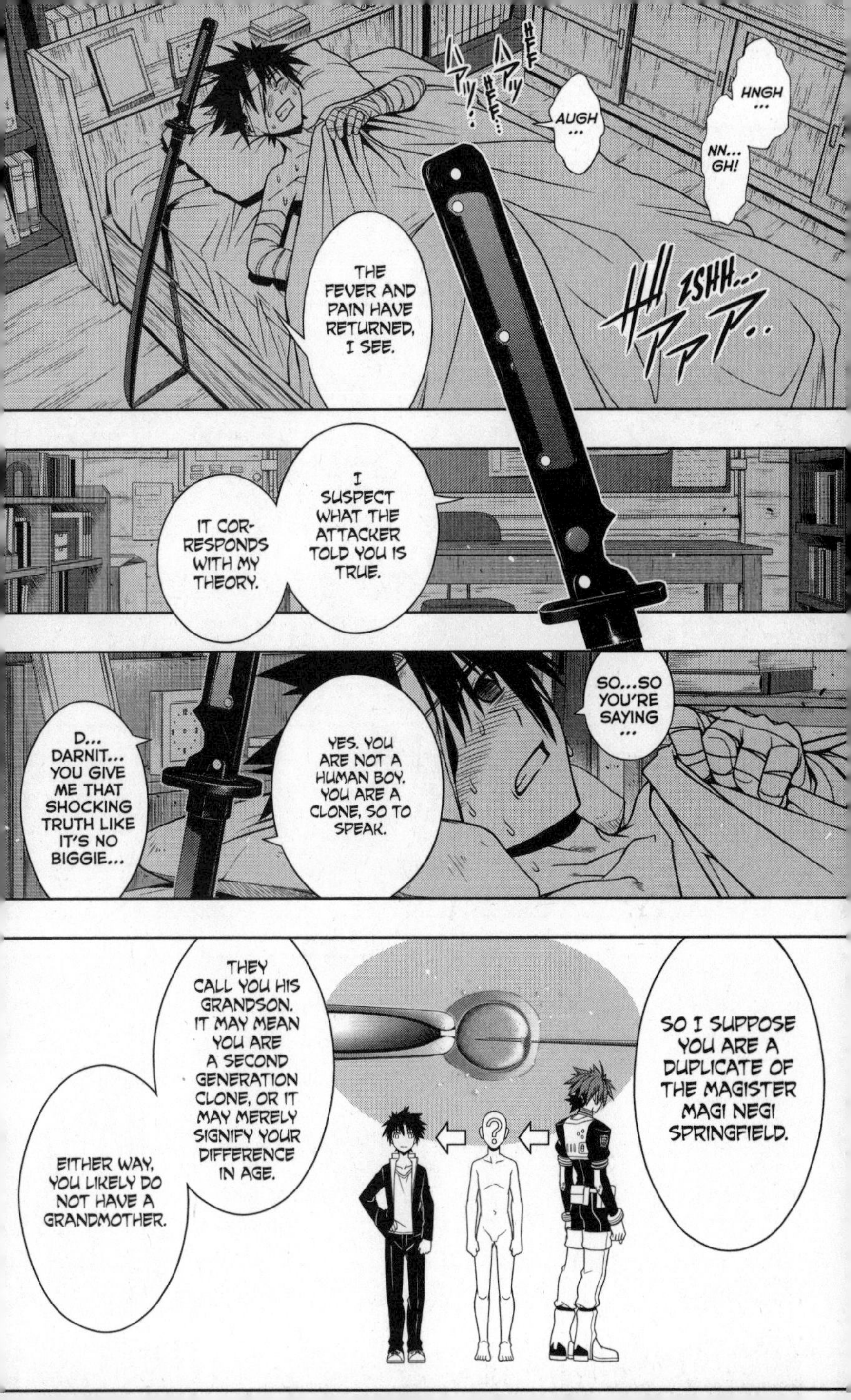
HNGH ...
NN... GH!
HEFF
HEFF...
AUGH ...
ZSHH...
THE FEVER AND PAIN HAVE RETURNED, I SEE.
I SUSPECT WHAT THE ATTACKER TOLD YOU IS TRUE.
IT COR- RESPONDS WITH MY THEORY.
SO...SO YOU'RE SAYING ...
YES. YOU ARE NOT A HUMAN BOY. YOU ARE A CLONE, SO TO SPEAK.
D... DARNIT... YOU GIVE ME THAT SHOCKING TRUTH LIKE IT'S NO BIGGIE...
SO I SUPPOSE YOU ARE A DUPLICATE OF THE MAGISTER MAGI NEGI SPRINGFIELD.
THEY CALL YOU HIS GRANDSON. IT MAY MEAN YOU ARE A SECOND GENERATION CLONE, OR IT MAY MERELY SIGNIFY YOUR DIFFERENCE IN AGE.
EITHER WAY, YOU LIKELY DO NOT HAVE A GRANDMOTHER.

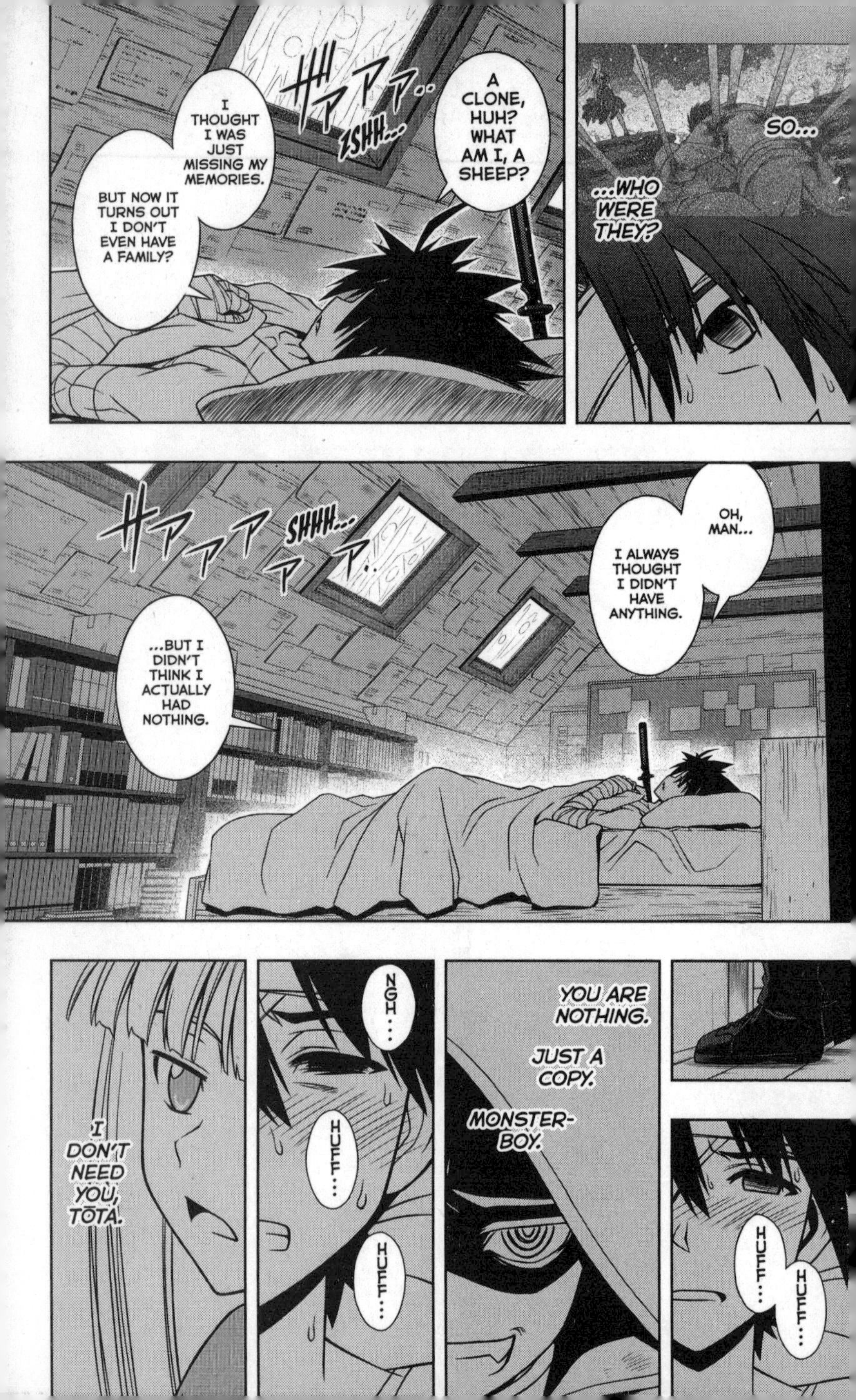
SO...
...WHO WERE THEY?
ZSHH...
A CLONE, HUH? WHAT AM I, A SHEEP?
I THOUGHT I WAS JUST MISSING MY MEMORIES.
BUT NOW IT TURNS OUT I DON'T EVEN HAVE A FAMILY?
OH, MAN...
I ALWAYS THOUGHT I DIDN'T HAVE ANYTHING.
SHHH...
...BUT I DIDN'T THINK I ACTUALLY HAD NOTHING.
HUFF...
HUFF...
YOU ARE NOTHING.
JUST A COPY.
MONSTER-BOY.
NGH...
HUFF...
HUFF...
I DON'T NEED YOU, TŌTA.

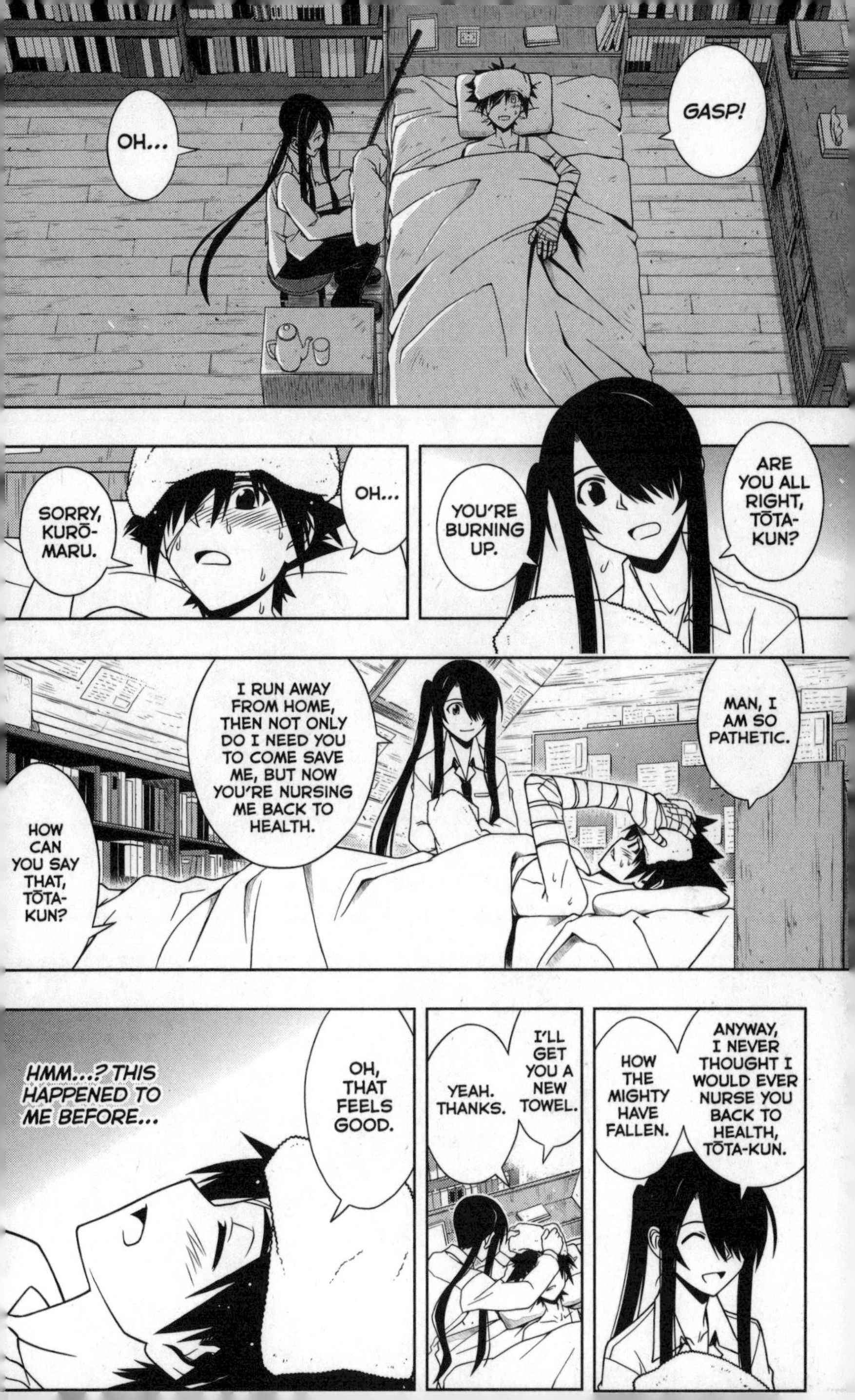
GASP!
OH...
ARE YOU ALL RIGHT, TŌTA-KUN?
YOU'RE BURNING UP.
OH...
SORRY, KURŌ-MARU.
MAN, I AM SO PATHETIC.
I RUN AWAY FROM HOME, THEN NOT ONLY DO I NEED YOU TO COME SAVE ME, BUT NOW YOU'RE NURSING ME BACK TO HEALTH.
HOW CAN YOU SAY THAT, TŌTA-KUN?
ANYWAY, I NEVER THOUGHT I WOULD EVER NURSE YOU BACK TO HEALTH, TŌTA-KUN.
HOW THE MIGHTY HAVE FALLEN.
I'LL GET YOU A NEW TOWEL.
YEAH. THANKS.
OH, THAT FEELS GOOD.
HMM...? THIS HAPPENED TO ME BEFORE...

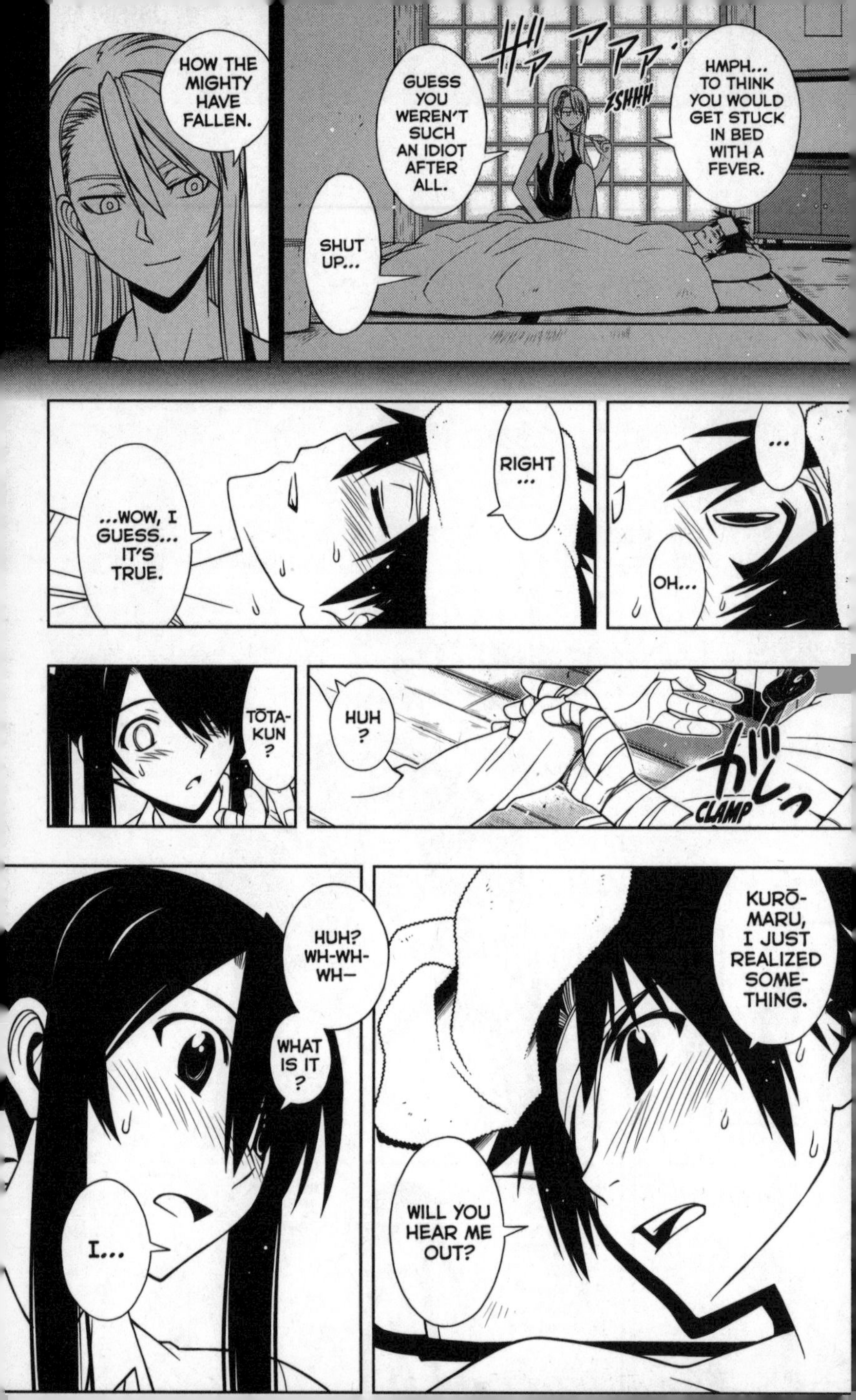
HMPH... TO THINK YOU WOULD GET STUCK IN BED WITH A FEVER.
ZSHHH
GUESS YOU WEREN'T SUCH AN IDIOT AFTER ALL.
SHUT UP...
HOW THE MIGHTY HAVE FALLEN.
...
OH...
RIGHT...
...WOW, I GUESS... IT'S TRUE.
HUH?
CLAMP
TŌTA-KUN?
KURŌ-MARU, I JUST REALIZED SOME-THING.
WILL YOU HEAR ME OUT?
HUH? WH-WH-WH—
WHAT IS IT?
I...

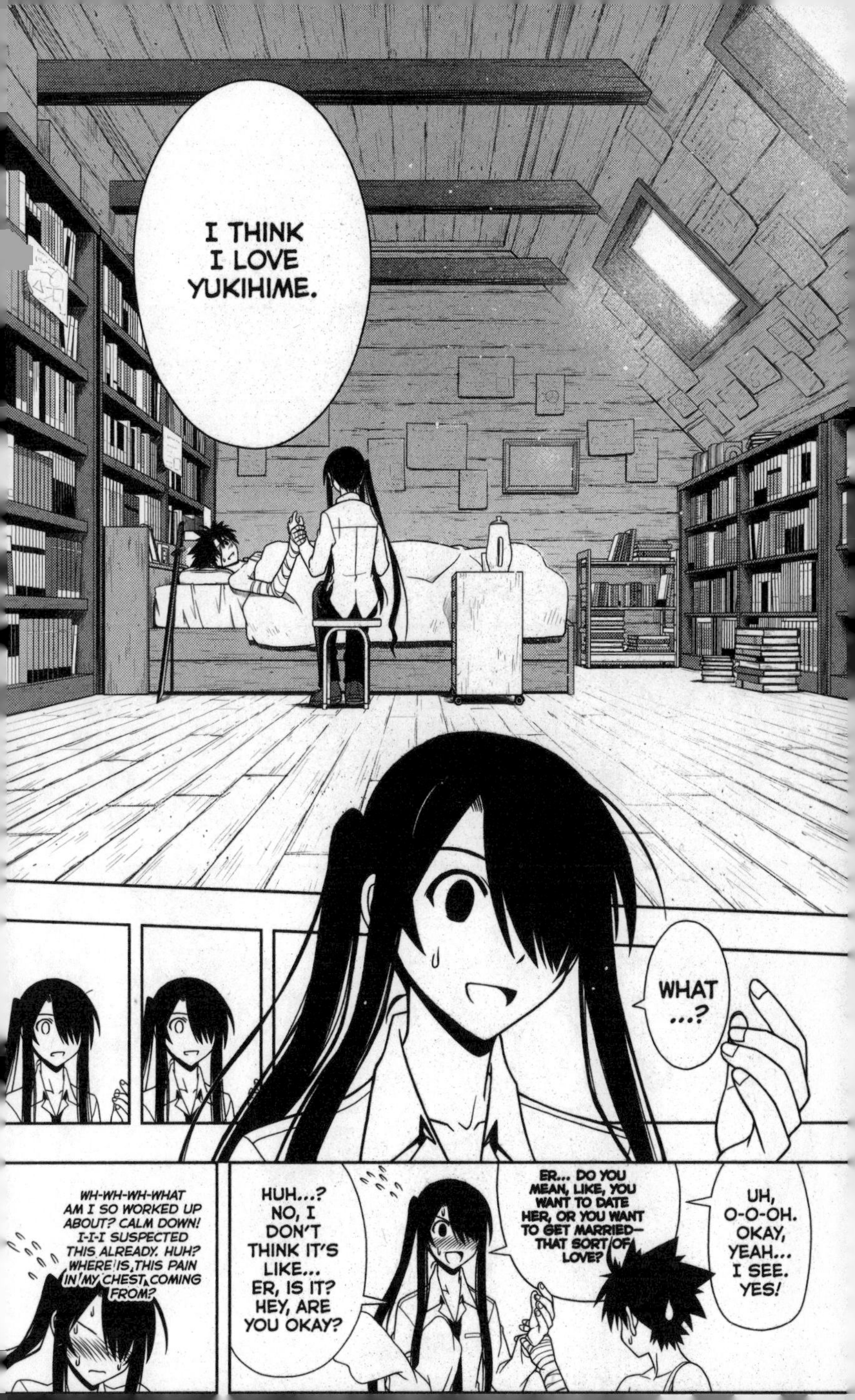
I THINK I LOVE YUKIHIME.
WHAT ...?
UH, O-O-OH. OKAY, YEAH... I SEE. YES!
ER... DO YOU MEAN, LIKE, YOU WANT TO DATE HER, OR YOU WANT TO GET MARRIED—THAT SORT OF LOVE?
HUH...? NO, I DON'T THINK IT'S LIKE... ER, IS IT? HEY, ARE YOU OKAY?
WH-WH-WH-WHAT AM I SO WORKED UP ABOUT? CALM DOWN! I-I-I SUSPECTED THIS ALREADY. HUH? WHERE IS THIS PAIN IN MY CHEST COMING FROM?

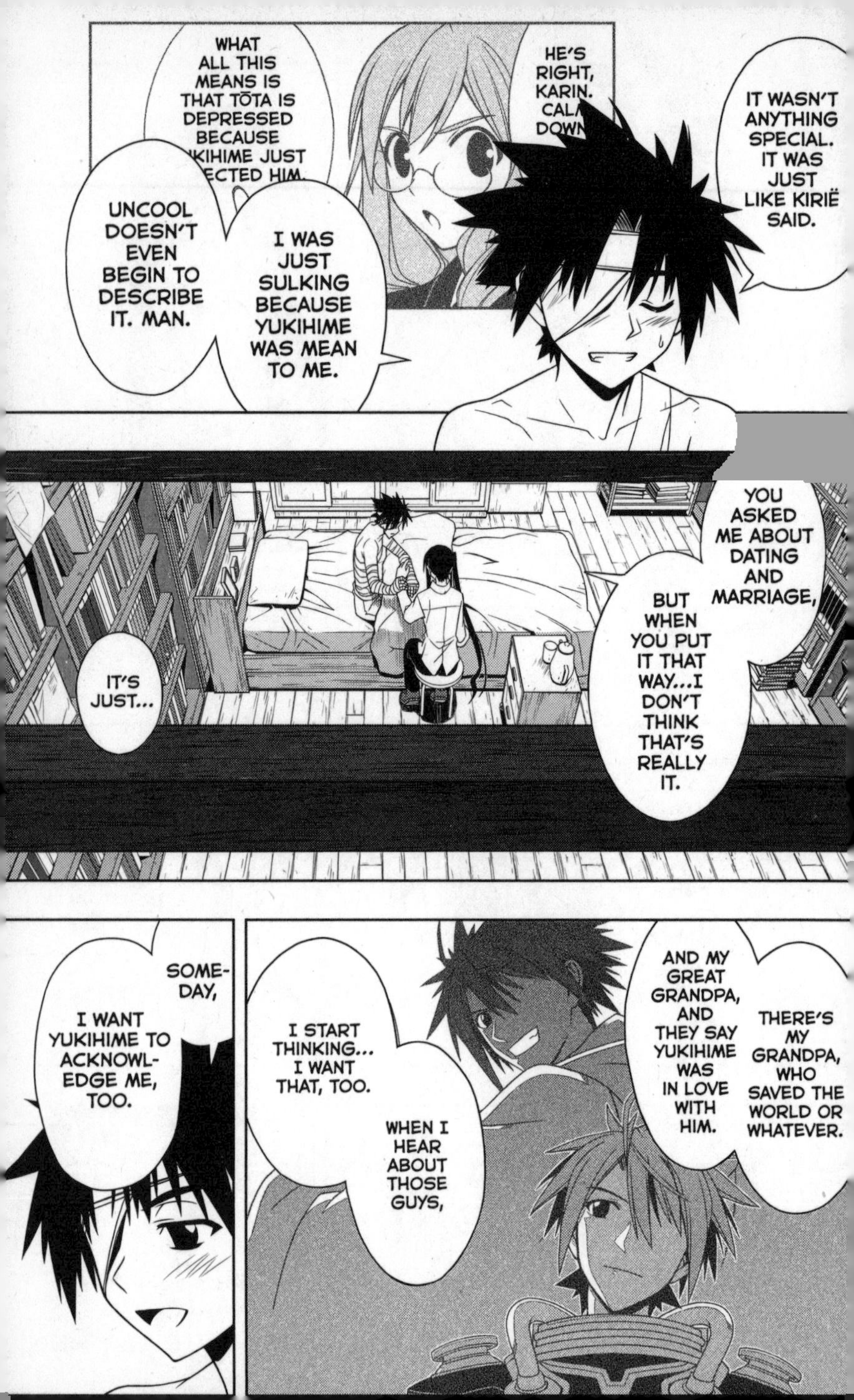
IT WASN'T ANYTHING SPECIAL. IT WAS JUST LIKE KIRIË SAID.
HE'S RIGHT, KARIN.
WHAT ALL THIS MEANS IS THAT TŌTA IS DEPRESSED BECAUSE
I WAS JUST SULKING BECAUSE YUKIHIME WAS MEAN TO ME.
UNCOOL DOESN'T EVEN BEGIN TO DESCRIBE IT. MAN.
YOU ASKED ME ABOUT DATING AND MARRIAGE,
BUT WHEN YOU PUT IT THAT WAY...I DON'T THINK THAT'S REALLY IT.
IT'S JUST...
THERE'S MY GRANDPA, WHO SAVED THE WORLD OR WHATEVER.
AND MY GREAT GRANDPA, AND THEY SAY YUKIHIME WAS IN LOVE WITH HIM.
WHEN I HEAR ABOUT THOSE GUYS,
I START THINKING... I WANT THAT, TOO.
SOME-DAY,
I WANT YUKIHIME TO ACKNOWL-EDGE ME, TOO.

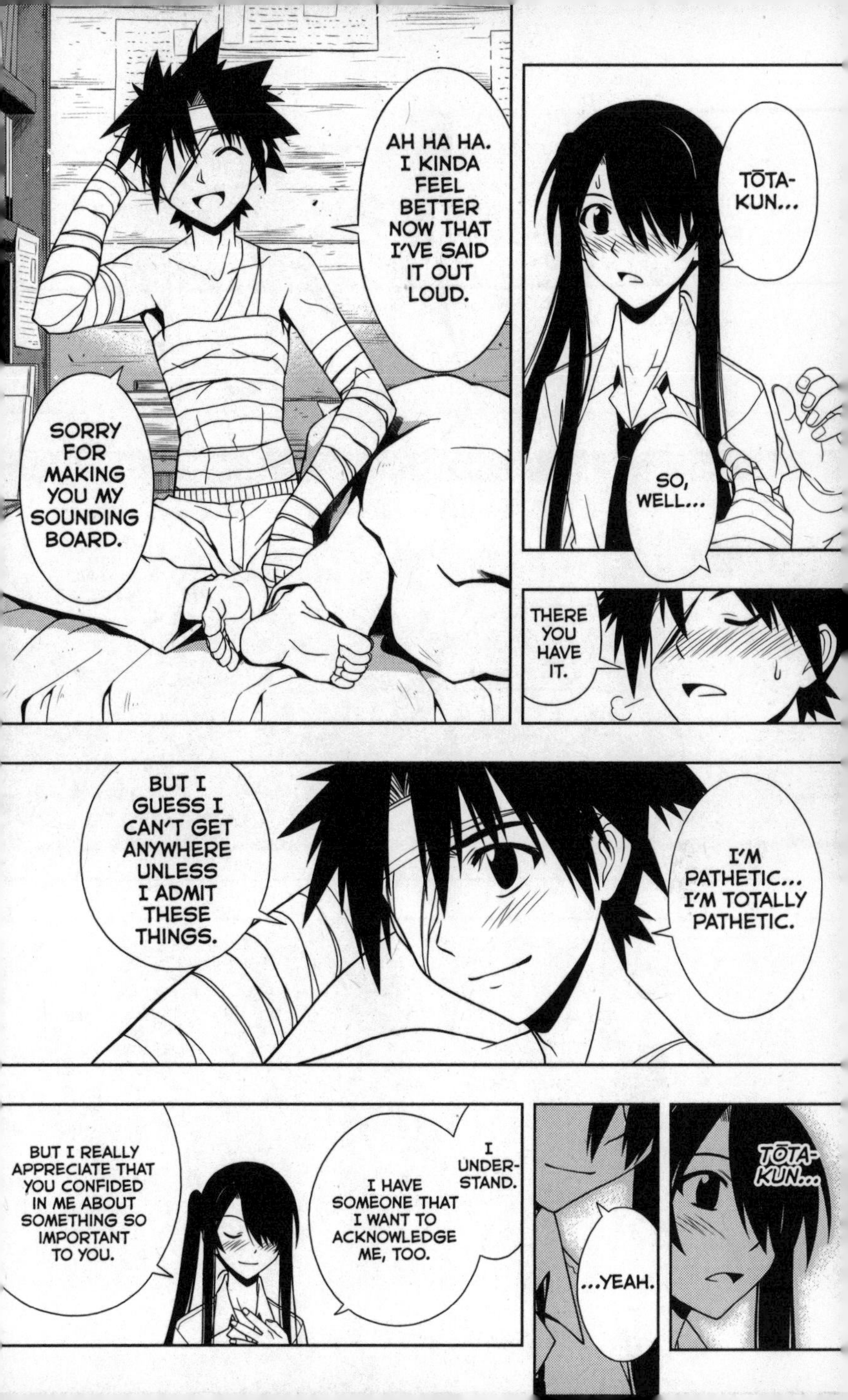
TŌTA-KUN...
SO, WELL...
THERE YOU HAVE IT.
AH HA HA. I KINDA FEEL BETTER NOW THAT I'VE SAID IT OUT LOUD.
SORRY FOR MAKING YOU MY SOUNDING BOARD.
I'M PATHETIC... I'M TOTALLY PATHETIC.
BUT I GUESS I CAN'T GET ANYWHERE UNLESS I ADMIT THESE THINGS.
TŌTA-KUN...
...YEAH.
I UNDERSTAND.
I HAVE SOMEONE THAT I WANT TO ACKNOWLEDGE ME, TOO.
BUT I REALLY APPRECIATE THAT YOU CONFIDED IN ME ABOUT SOMETHING SO IMPORTANT TO YOU.

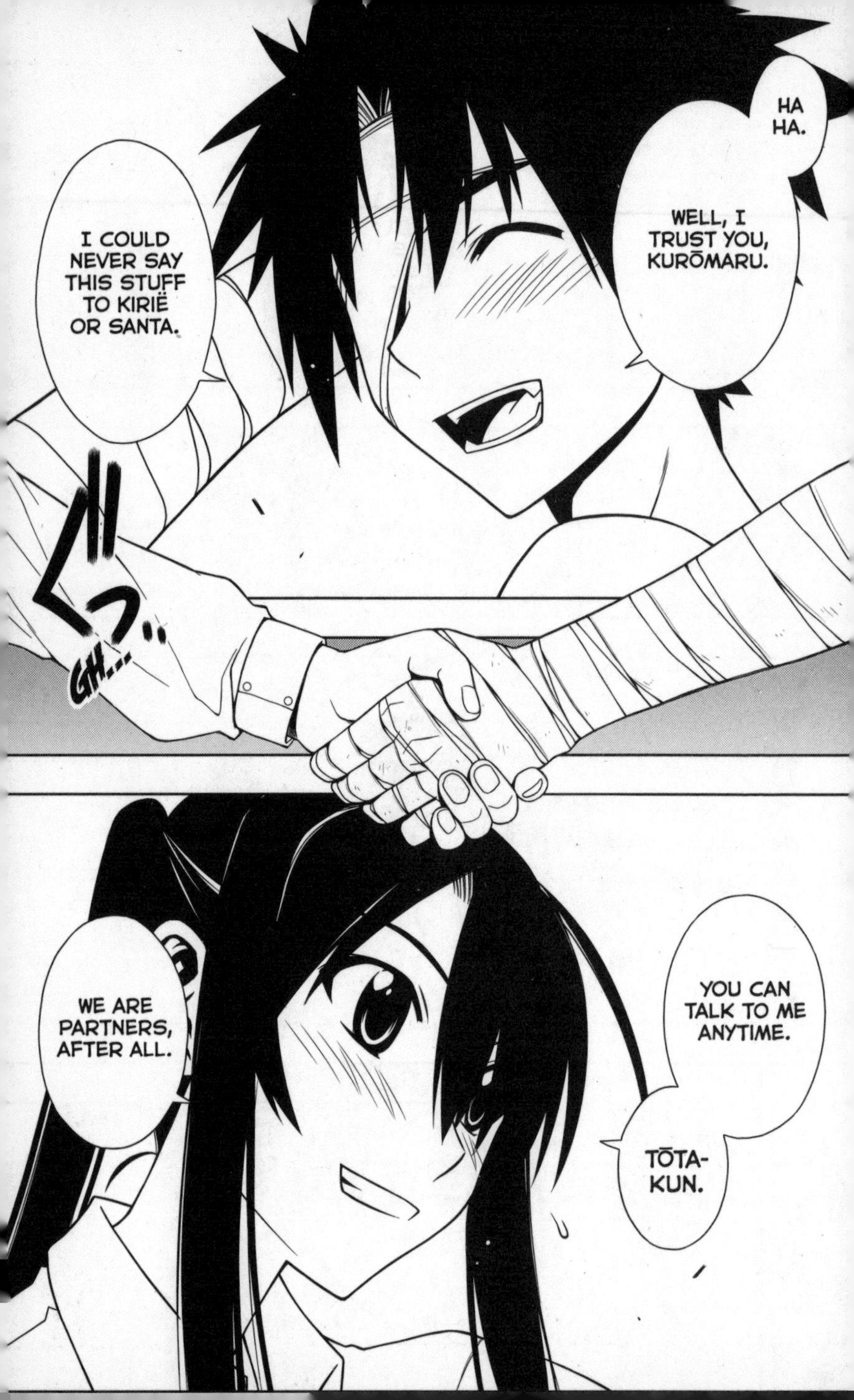
HA HA.
WELL, I TRUST YOU, KURŌMARU.
I COULD NEVER SAY THIS STUFF TO KIRIË OR SANTA.
GH...
YOU CAN TALK TO ME ANYTIME.
TŌTA-KUN.
WE ARE PARTNERS, AFTER ALL.

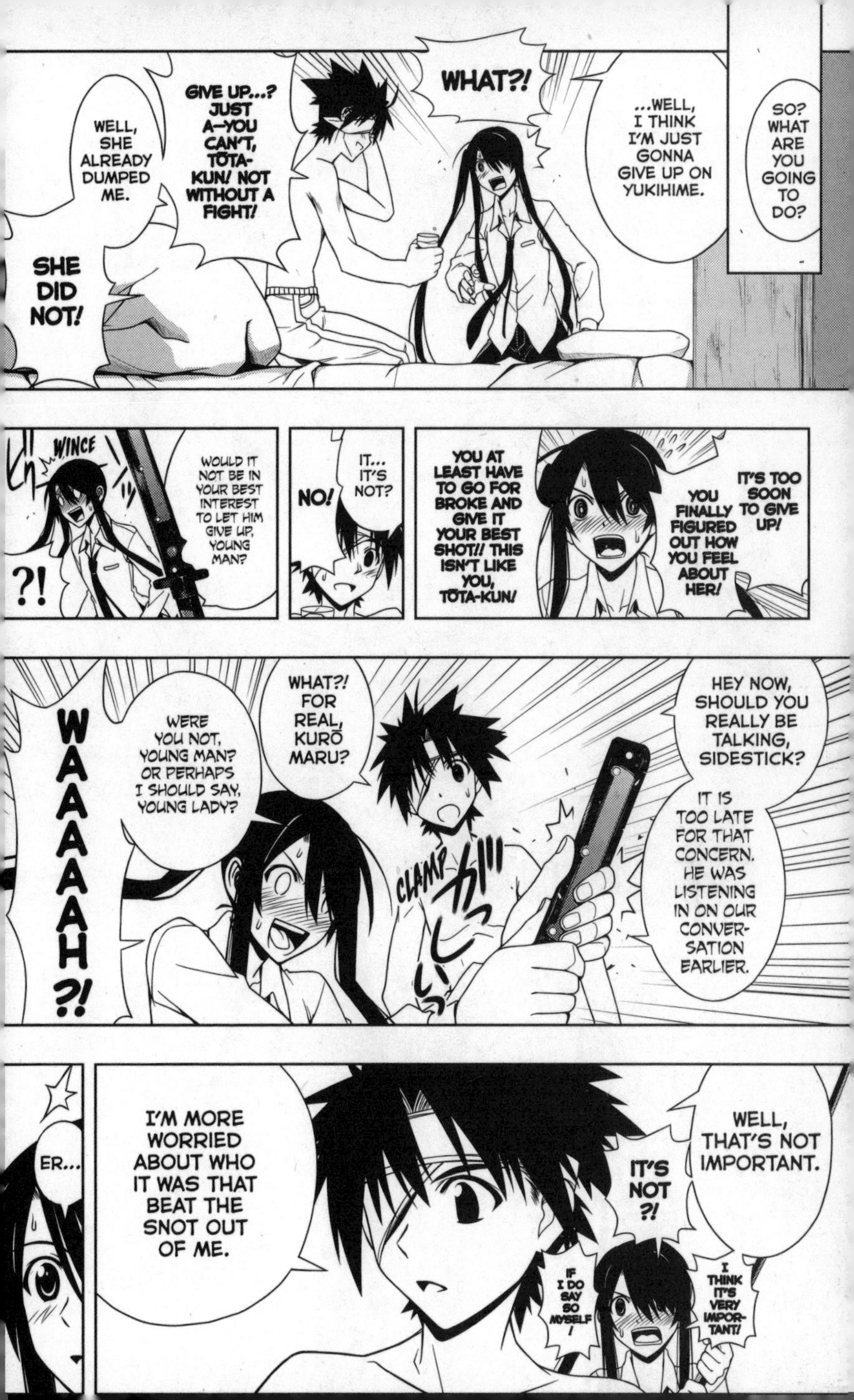
SO? WHAT ARE YOU GOING TO DO?
...WELL, I THINK I'M JUST GONNA GIVE UP ON YUKIHIME.
WHAT?!
GIVE UP...? JUST A—YOU CAN'T, TŌTA-KUN! NOT WITHOUT A FIGHT!
WELL, SHE ALREADY DUMPED ME.
SHE DID NOT!
IT'S TOO SOON TO GIVE UP!
YOU FINALLY FIGURED OUT HOW YOU FEEL ABOUT HER!
YOU AT LEAST HAVE TO GO FOR BROKE AND GIVE IT YOUR BEST SHOT!! THIS ISN'T LIKE YOU, TŌTA-KUN!
IT... IT'S NOT?
NO!
WOULD IT NOT BE IN YOUR BEST INTEREST TO LET HIM GIVE UP, YOUNG MAN?
WINCE
?!
HEY NOW, SHOULD YOU REALLY BE TALKING, SIDESTICK?
IT IS TOO LATE FOR THAT CONCERN. HE WAS LISTENING IN ON OUR CONVERSATION EARLIER.
CLAMP
WHAT?! FOR REAL, KURŌMARU?
WERE YOU NOT, YOUNG MAN? OR PERHAPS I SHOULD SAY, YOUNG LADY?
WAAAAAAH?!
WELL, THAT'S NOT IMPORTANT.
IT'S NOT?!
I THINK IT'S VERY IMPORTANT!
IF I DO SAY SO MYSELF!
I'M MORE WORRIED ABOUT WHO IT WAS THAT BEAT THE SNOT OUT OF ME.
ER...

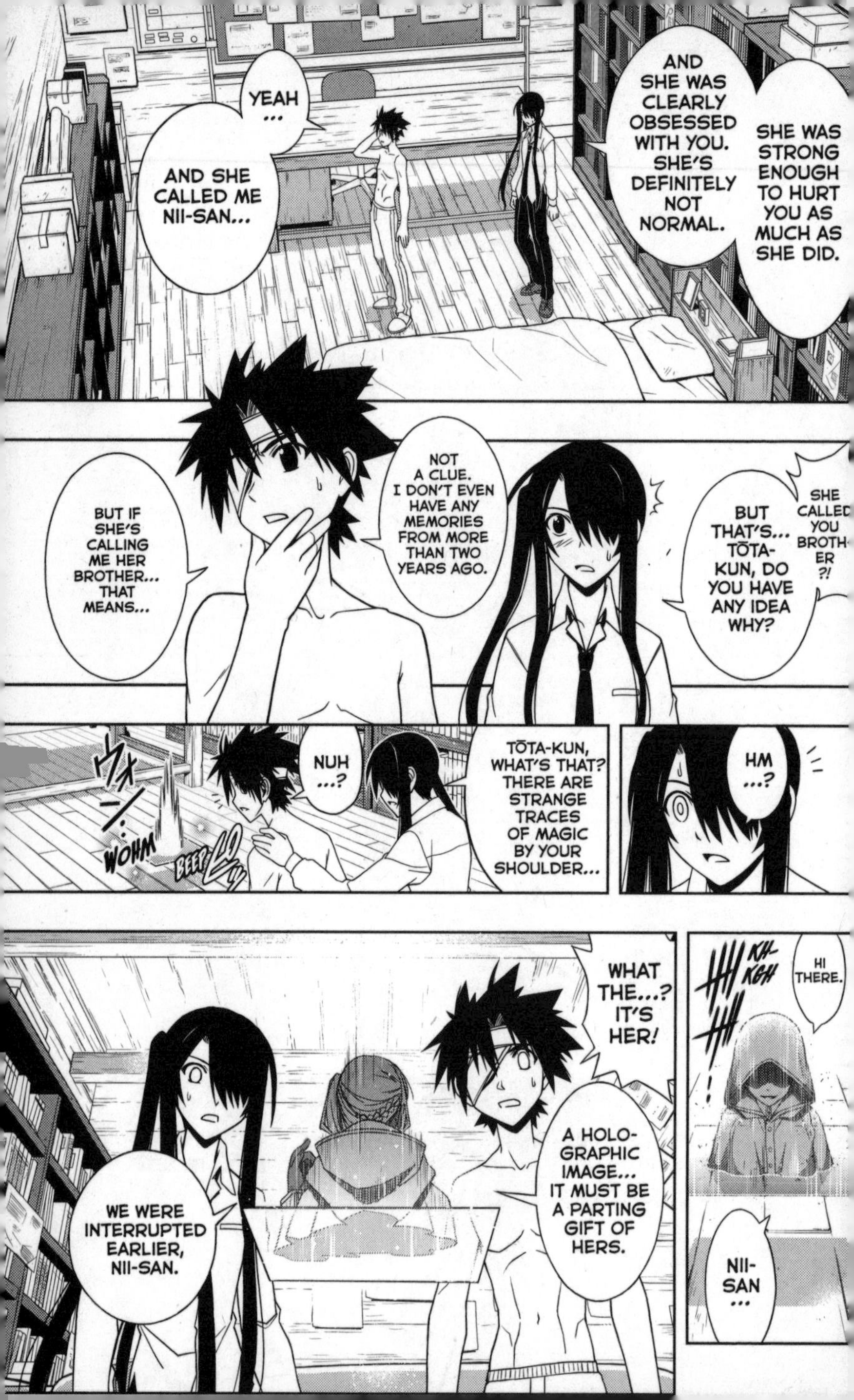
SHE WAS STRONG ENOUGH TO HURT YOU AS MUCH AS SHE DID.
AND SHE WAS CLEARLY OBSESSED WITH YOU. SHE'S DEFINITELY NOT NORMAL.
YEAH...
AND SHE CALLED ME NII-SAN...
SHE CALLED YOU BROTHER?!
BUT THAT'S... TŌTA-KUN, DO YOU HAVE ANY IDEA WHY?
NOT A CLUE. I DON'T EVEN HAVE ANY MEMORIES FROM MORE THAN TWO YEARS AGO.
BUT IF SHE'S CALLING ME HER BROTHER... THAT MEANS...
HM...?
TŌTA-KUN, WHAT'S THAT? THERE ARE STRANGE TRACES OF MAGIC BY YOUR SHOULDER...
NUH...?
BEEP
WOHM
HI THERE.
KH-KGH
NII-SAN...
WHAT THE...? IT'S HER!
A HOLOGRAPHIC IMAGE... IT MUST BE A PARTING GIFT OF HERS.
WE WERE INTERRUPTED EARLIER, NII-SAN.

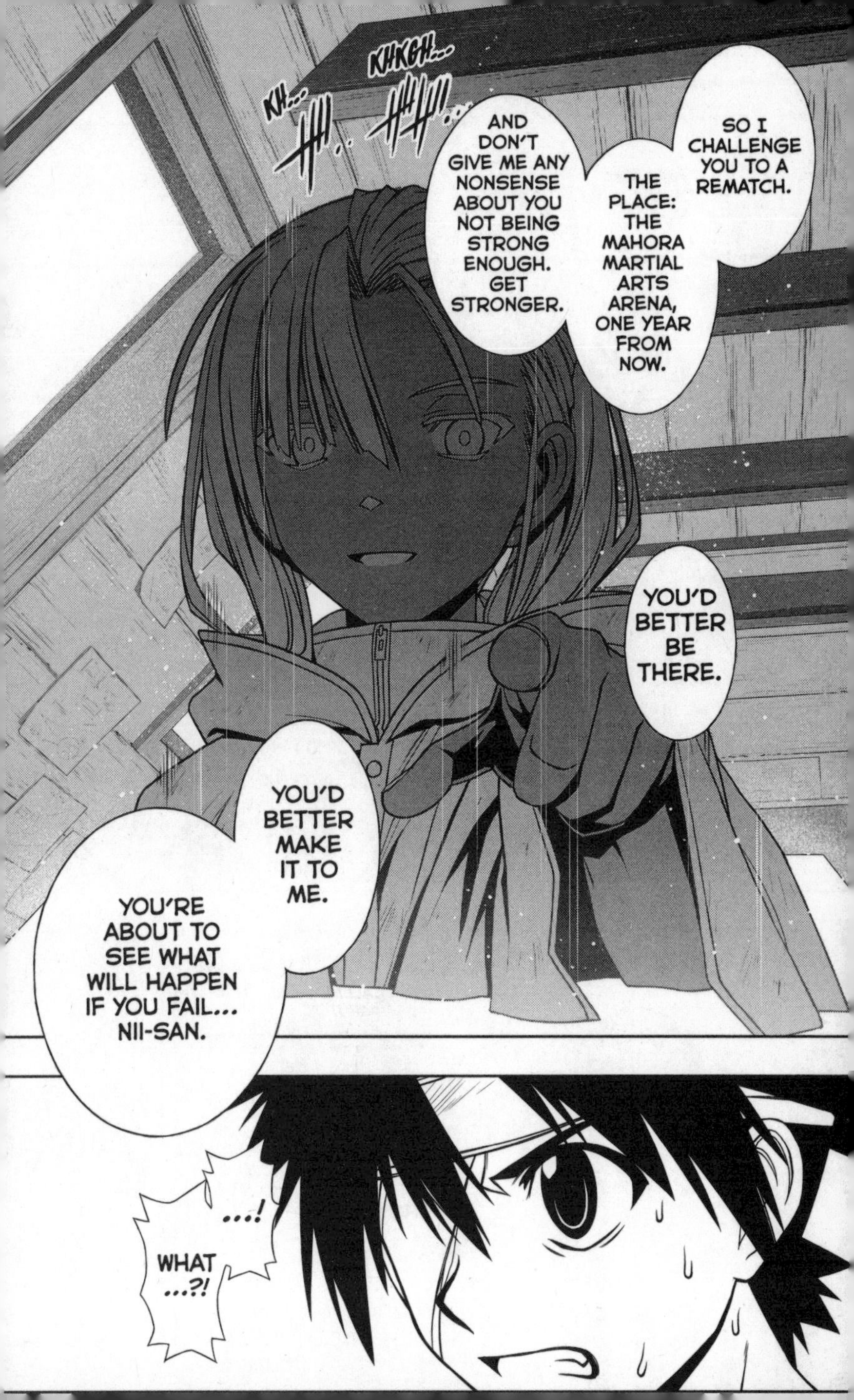
SO I CHALLENGE YOU TO A REMATCH.
THE PLACE: THE MAHORA MARTIAL ARTS ARENA, ONE YEAR FROM NOW.
AND DON'T GIVE ME ANY NONSENSE ABOUT YOU NOT BEING STRONG ENOUGH. GET STRONGER.
KHKGH...
KH...
YOU'D BETTER BE THERE.
YOU'D BETTER MAKE IT TO ME.
YOU'RE ABOUT TO SEE WHAT WILL HAPPEN IF YOU FAIL... NII-SAN.
...!
WHAT ...?!

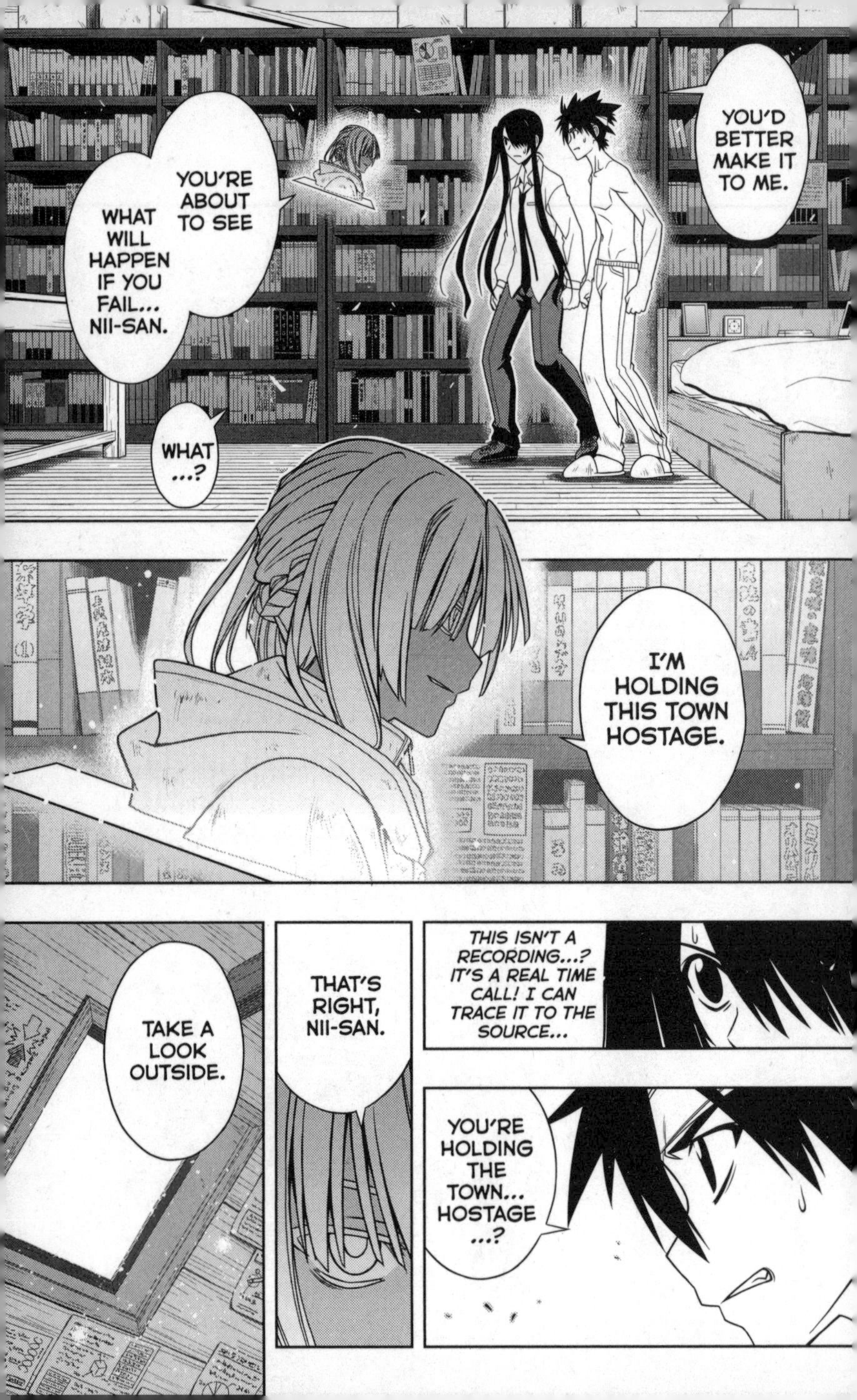
YOU'D BETTER MAKE IT TO ME.
YOU'RE ABOUT TO SEE WHAT WILL HAPPEN IF YOU FAIL... NII-SAN.
WHAT...?
I'M HOLDING THIS TOWN HOSTAGE.
THIS ISN'T A RECORDING...? IT'S A REAL TIME CALL! I CAN TRACE IT TO THE SOURCE...
YOU'RE HOLDING THE TOWN... HOSTAGE...?
THAT'S RIGHT, NII-SAN.
TAKE A LOOK OUTSIDE.

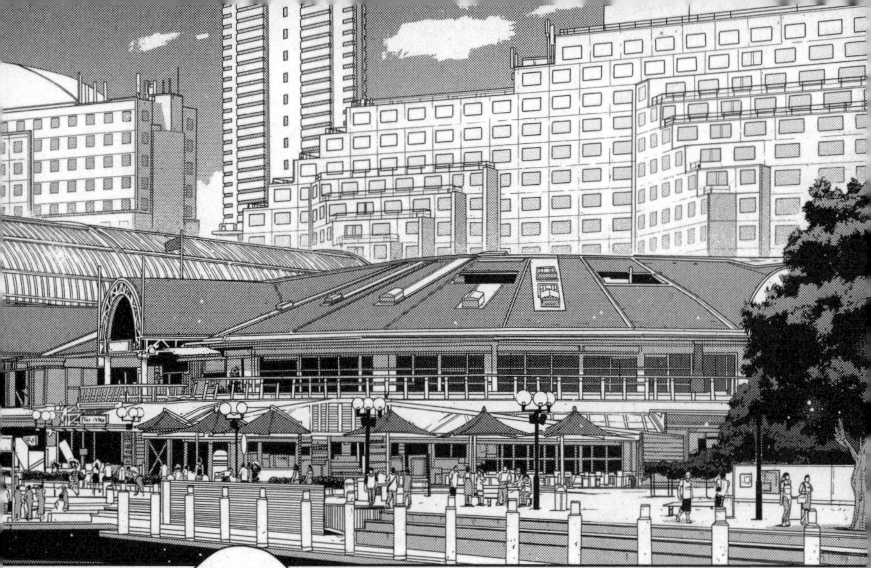

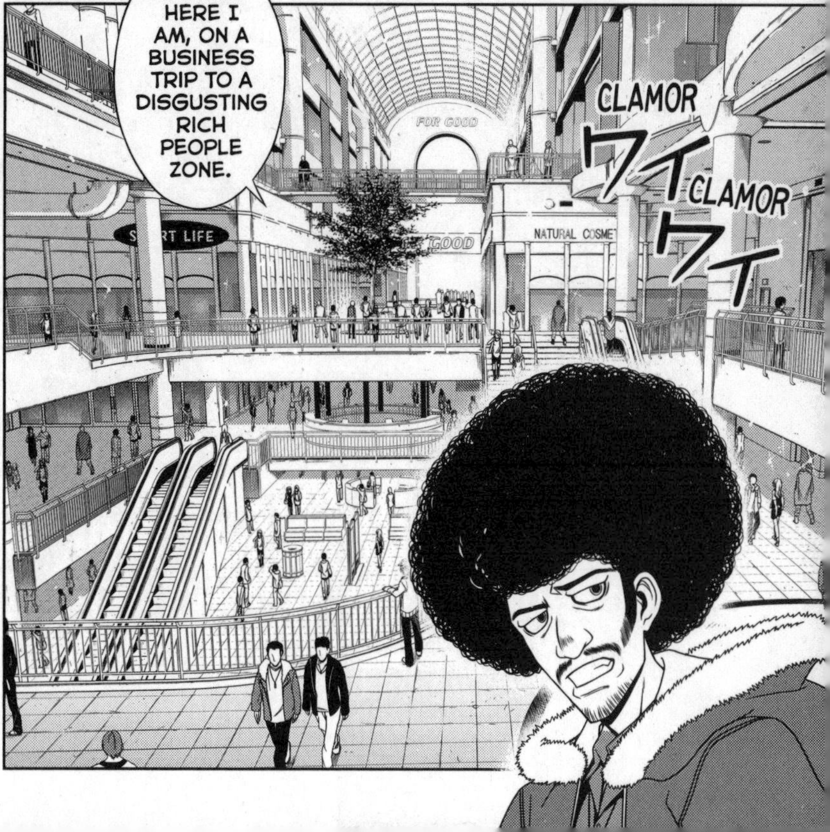
AND NOW HERE I AM, ON A BUSINESS TRIP TO A DISGUSTING RICH PEOPLE ZONE.
CLAMOR
ワイ
CLAMOR
ワイ
FOR GOOD

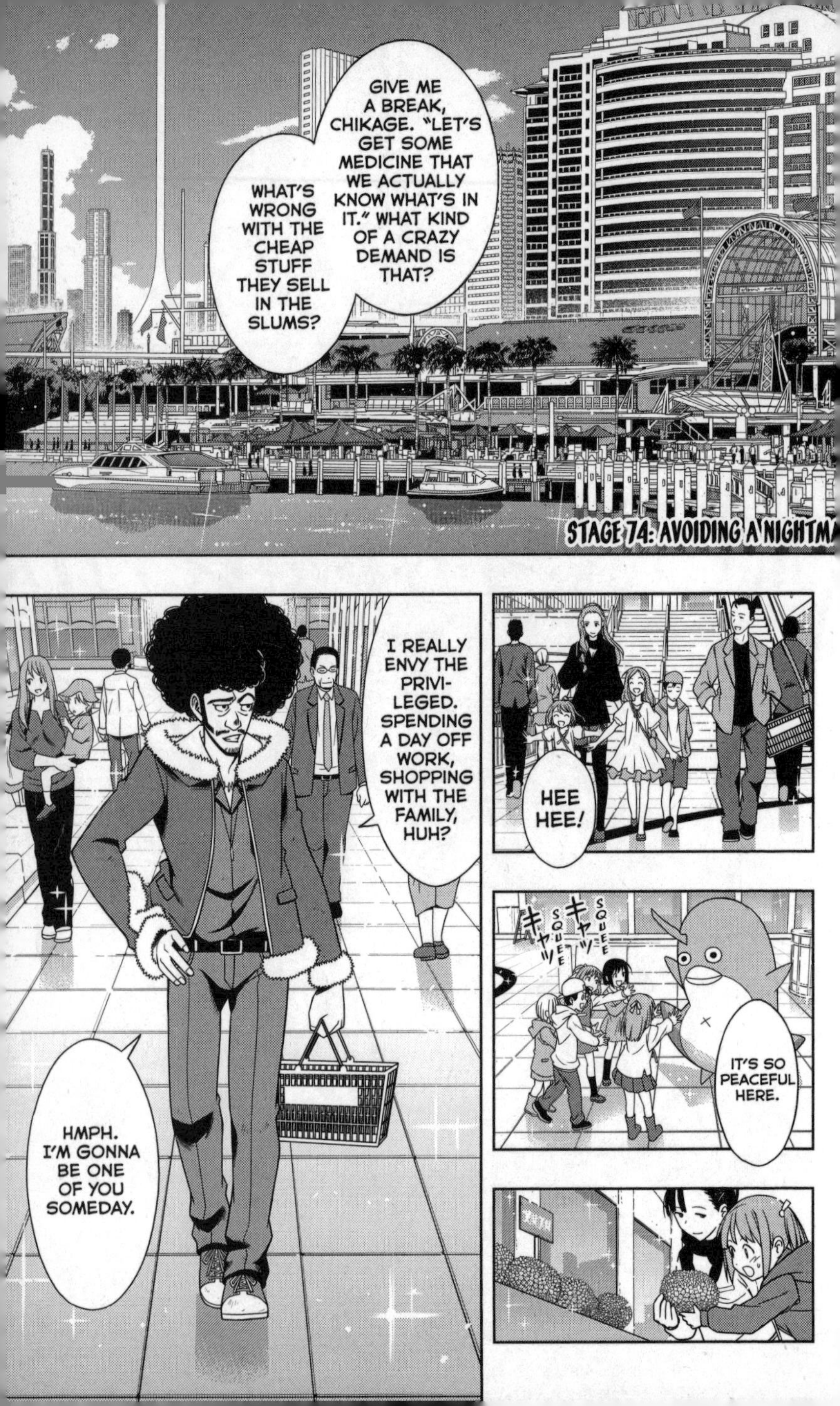
GIVE ME A BREAK, CHIKAGE. "LET'S GET SOME MEDICINE THAT WE ACTUALLY KNOW WHAT'S IN IT." WHAT KIND OF A CRAZY DEMAND IS THAT?
WHAT'S WRONG WITH THE CHEAP STUFF THEY SELL IN THE SLUMS?
STAGE 74: AVOIDING A NIGHTM
HEE HEE!
キャッ SQUEE
キャッ SQUEE
IT'S SO PEACEFUL HERE.
I REALLY ENVY THE PRIVI-LEGED. SPENDING A DAY OFF WORK, SHOPPING WITH THE FAMILY, HUH?
HMPH. I'M GONNA BE ONE OF YOU SOMEDAY.

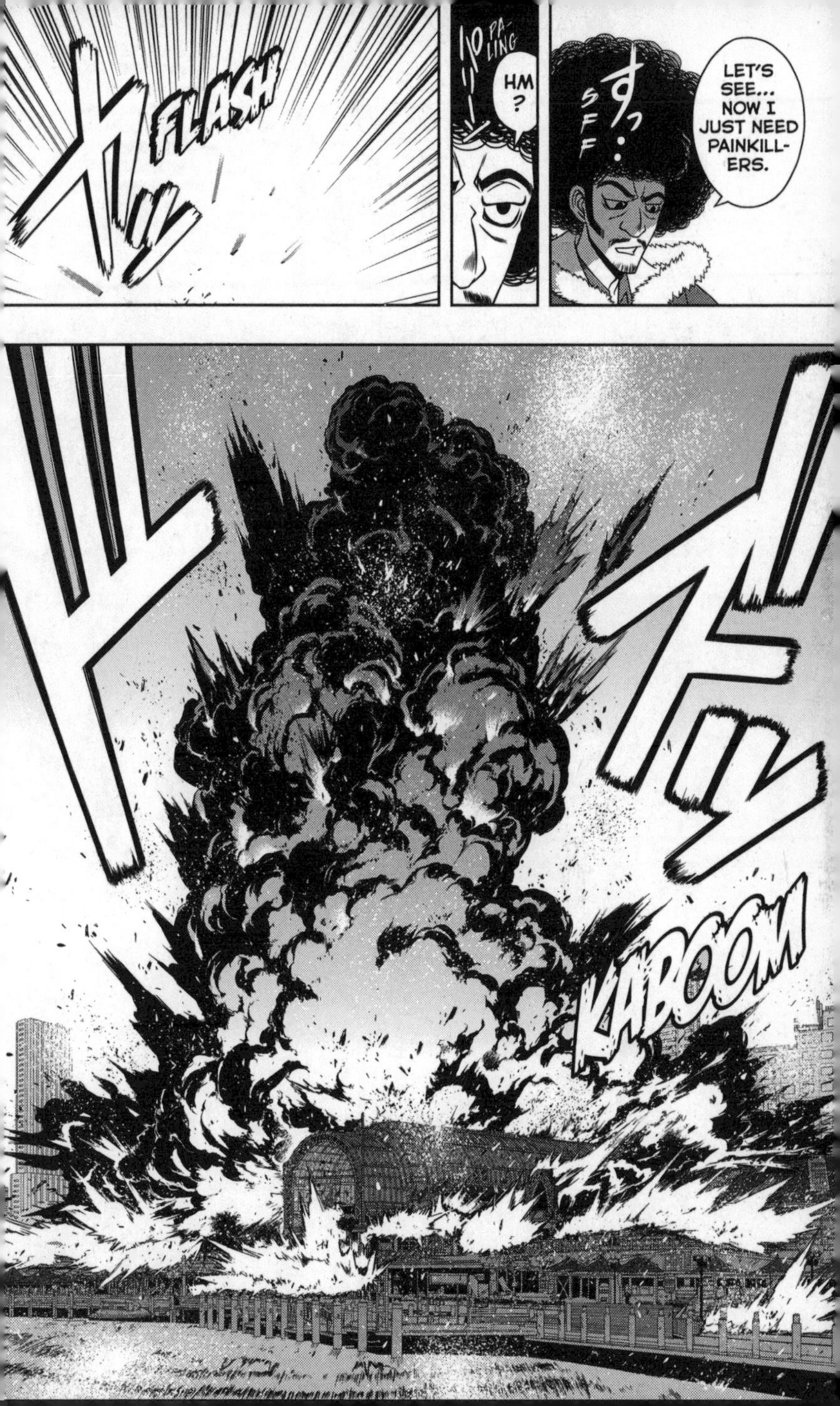
LET'S SEE... NOW I JUST NEED PAINKILL-ERS.
SFF
PA-LING
HM?
FLASH
KABOOM

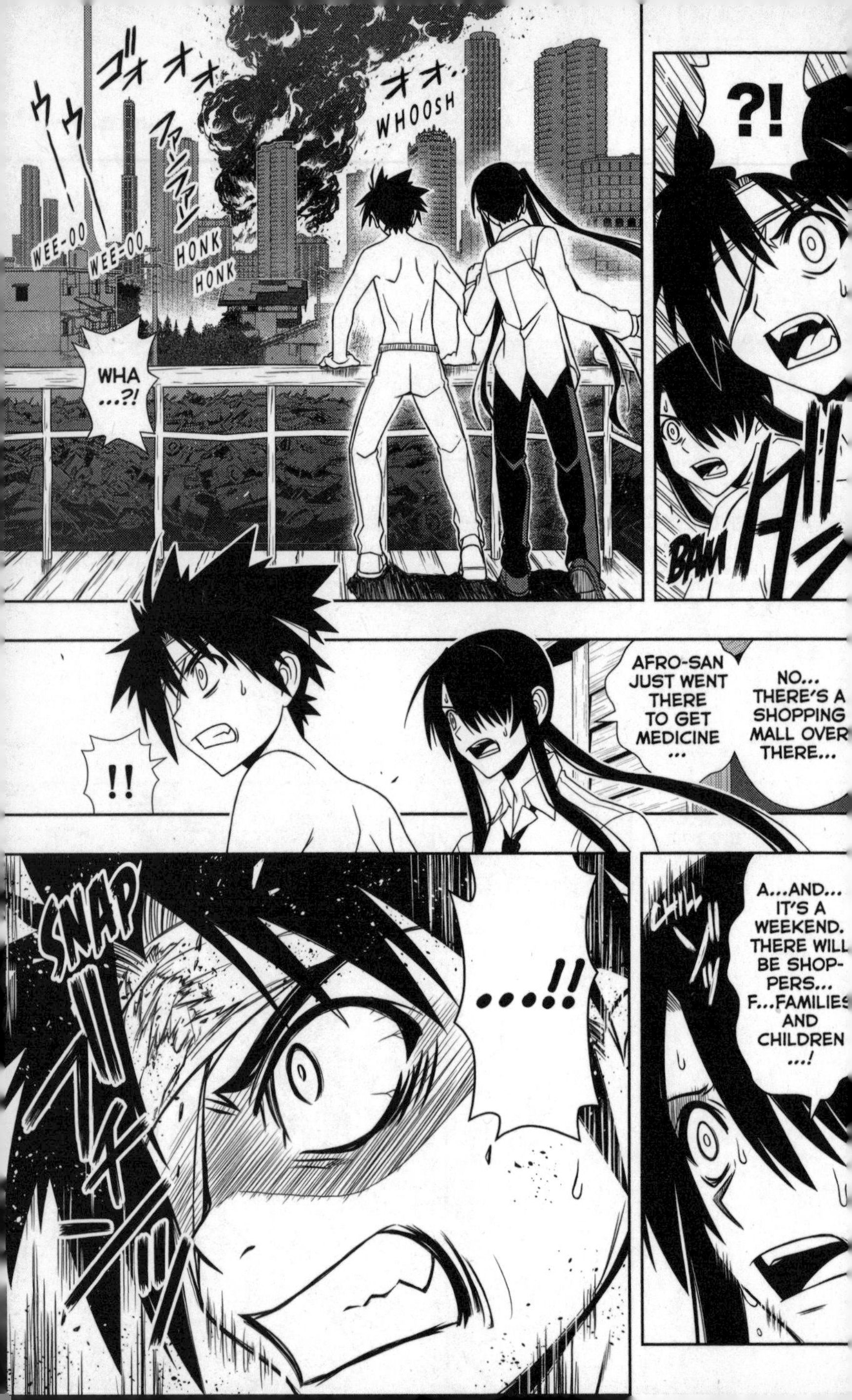
?!
BAM
WEE-OO
WEE-OO
HONK
HONK
WHOOSH
WHA ...?!
NO... THERE'S A SHOPPING MALL OVER THERE...
AFRO-SAN JUST WENT THERE TO GET MEDICINE ...
!!
CHILL
A...AND... IT'S A WEEKEND. THERE WILL BE SHOP-PERS... F...FAMILIES AND CHILDREN ...!
...!!
SNAP

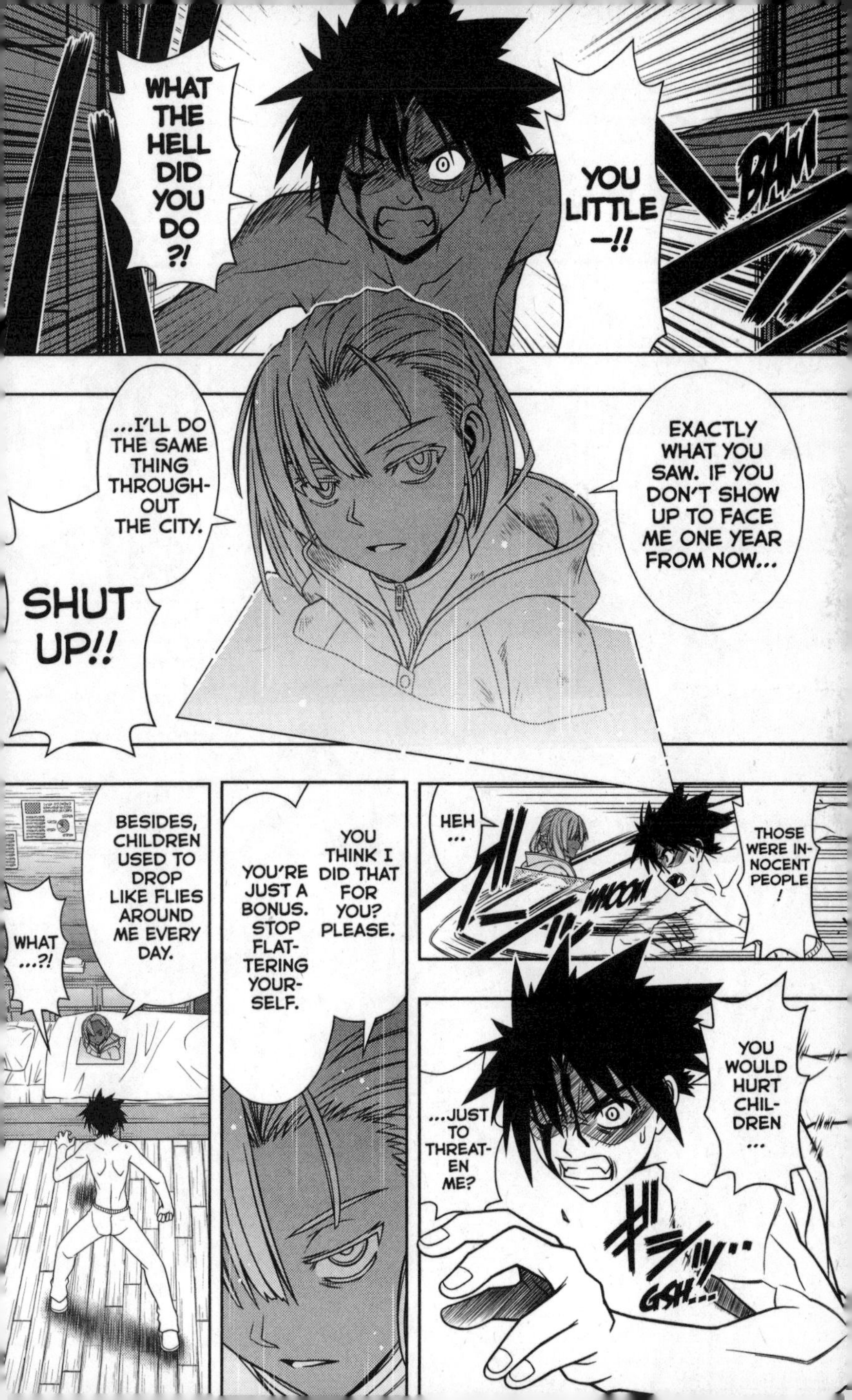
YOU LITTLE —!!
BAM
WHAT THE HELL DID YOU DO ?!
EXACTLY WHAT YOU SAW. IF YOU DON'T SHOW UP TO FACE ME ONE YEAR FROM NOW...
...I'LL DO THE SAME THING THROUGHOUT THE CITY.
SHUT UP!!
THOSE WERE INNOCENT PEOPLE!
HEH...
WHOOM
YOU WOULD HURT CHILDREN...
...JUST TO THREATEN ME?
GSH...
YOU THINK I DID THAT FOR YOU? PLEASE.
YOU'RE JUST A BONUS. STOP FLATTERING YOURSELF.
BESIDES, CHILDREN USED TO DROP LIKE FLIES AROUND ME EVERY DAY.
WHAT...?!

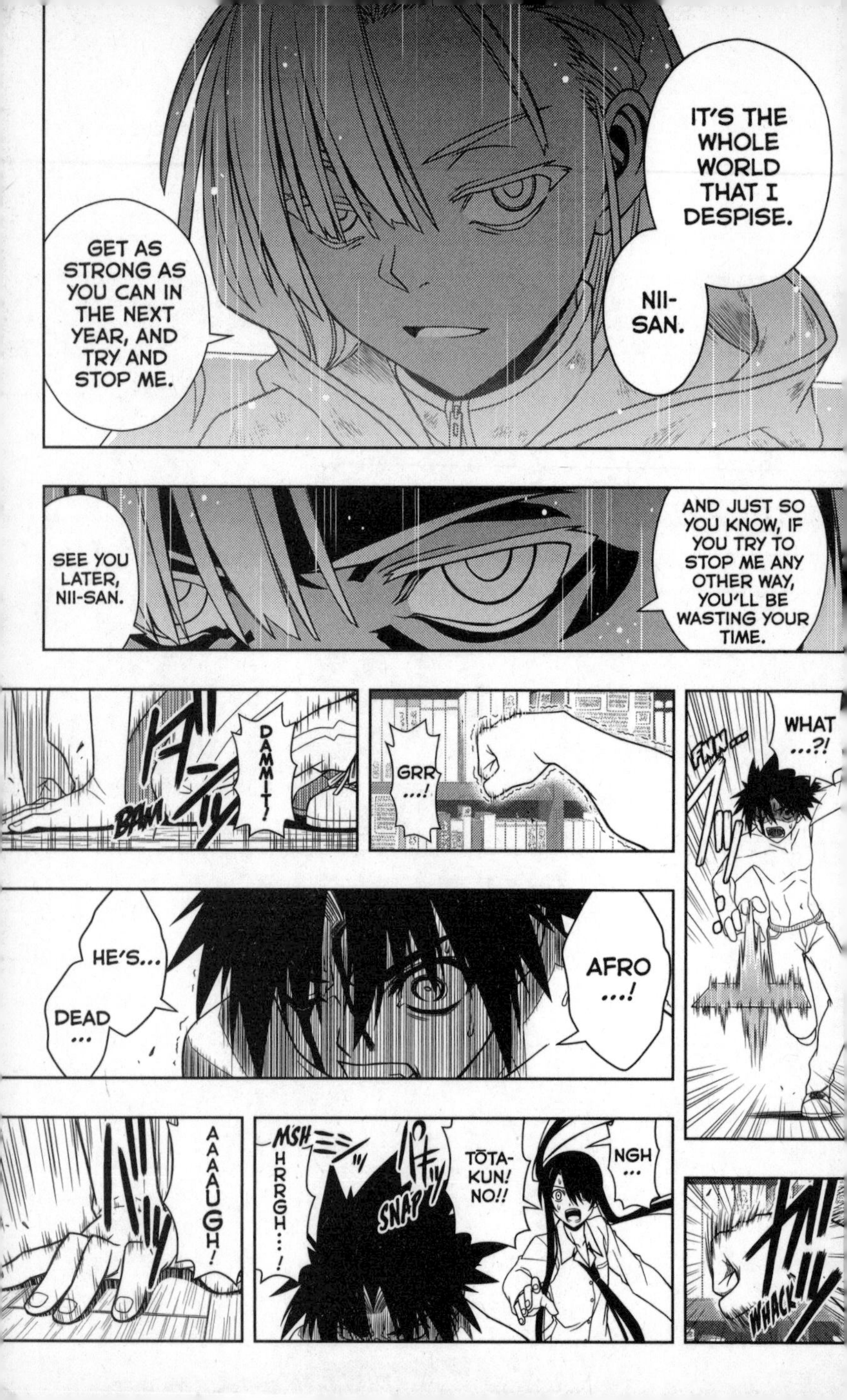
IT'S THE WHOLE WORLD THAT I DESPISE.
NII-SAN.
GET AS STRONG AS YOU CAN IN THE NEXT YEAR, AND TRY AND STOP ME.
AND JUST SO YOU KNOW, IF YOU TRY TO STOP ME ANY OTHER WAY, YOU'LL BE WASTING YOUR TIME.
SEE YOU LATER, NII-SAN.
WHAT ...?!
FNN...
GRR ...!
DAMMIT!
BAM
AFRO ...!
HE'S...
DEAD ...
WHACK
NGH ...
TŌTA-KUN! NO!!
SNAP
MSH
HRRGH...!
AAAAUGH!

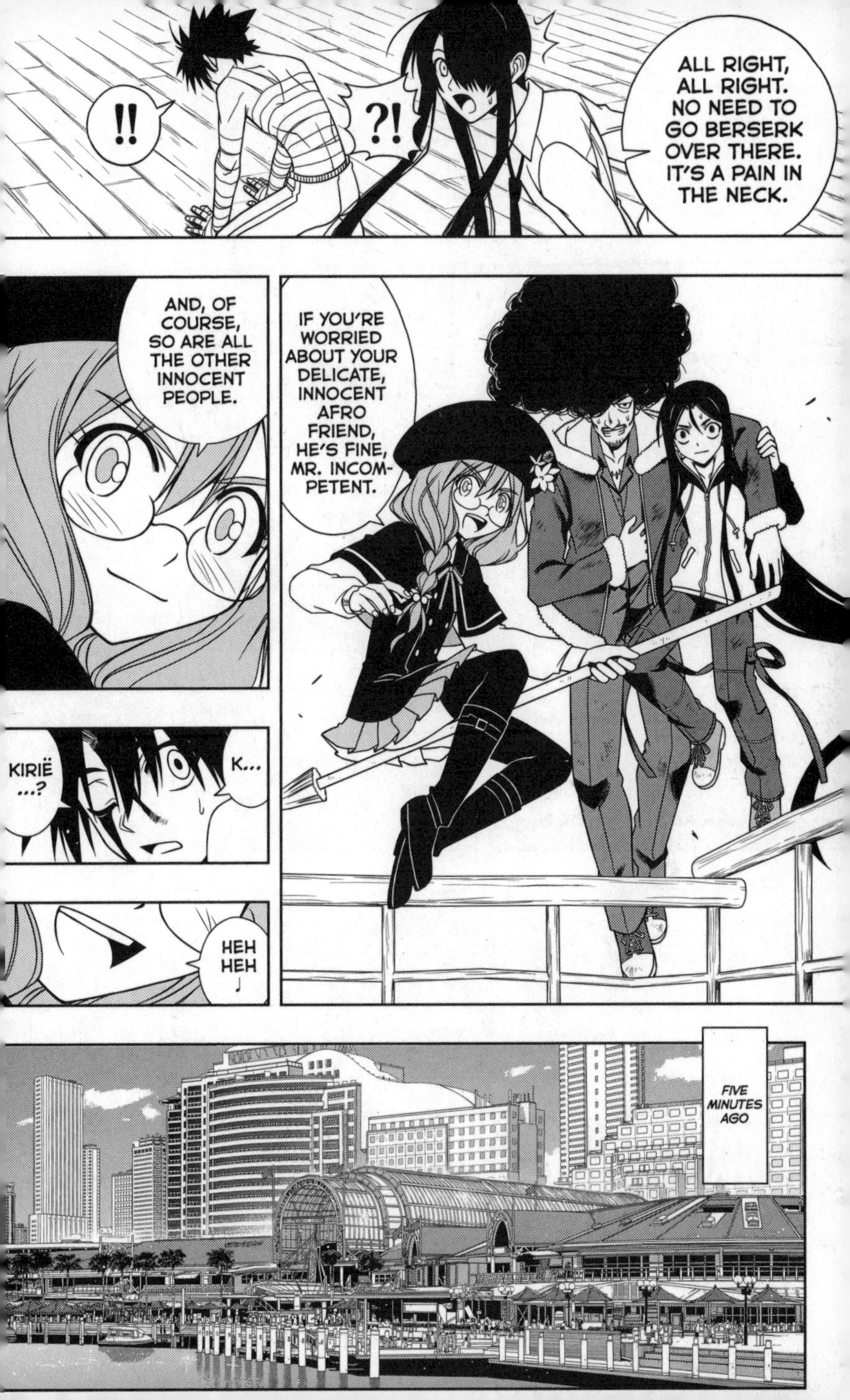
ALL RIGHT, ALL RIGHT. NO NEED TO GO BERSERK OVER THERE. IT'S A PAIN IN THE NECK.
?!
!!
IF YOU'RE WORRIED ABOUT YOUR DELICATE, INNOCENT AFRO FRIEND, HE'S FINE, MR. INCOM-PETENT.
AND, OF COURSE, SO ARE ALL THE OTHER INNOCENT PEOPLE.
K...
KIRIË ...?
HEH HEH ♪
FIVE MINUTES AGO

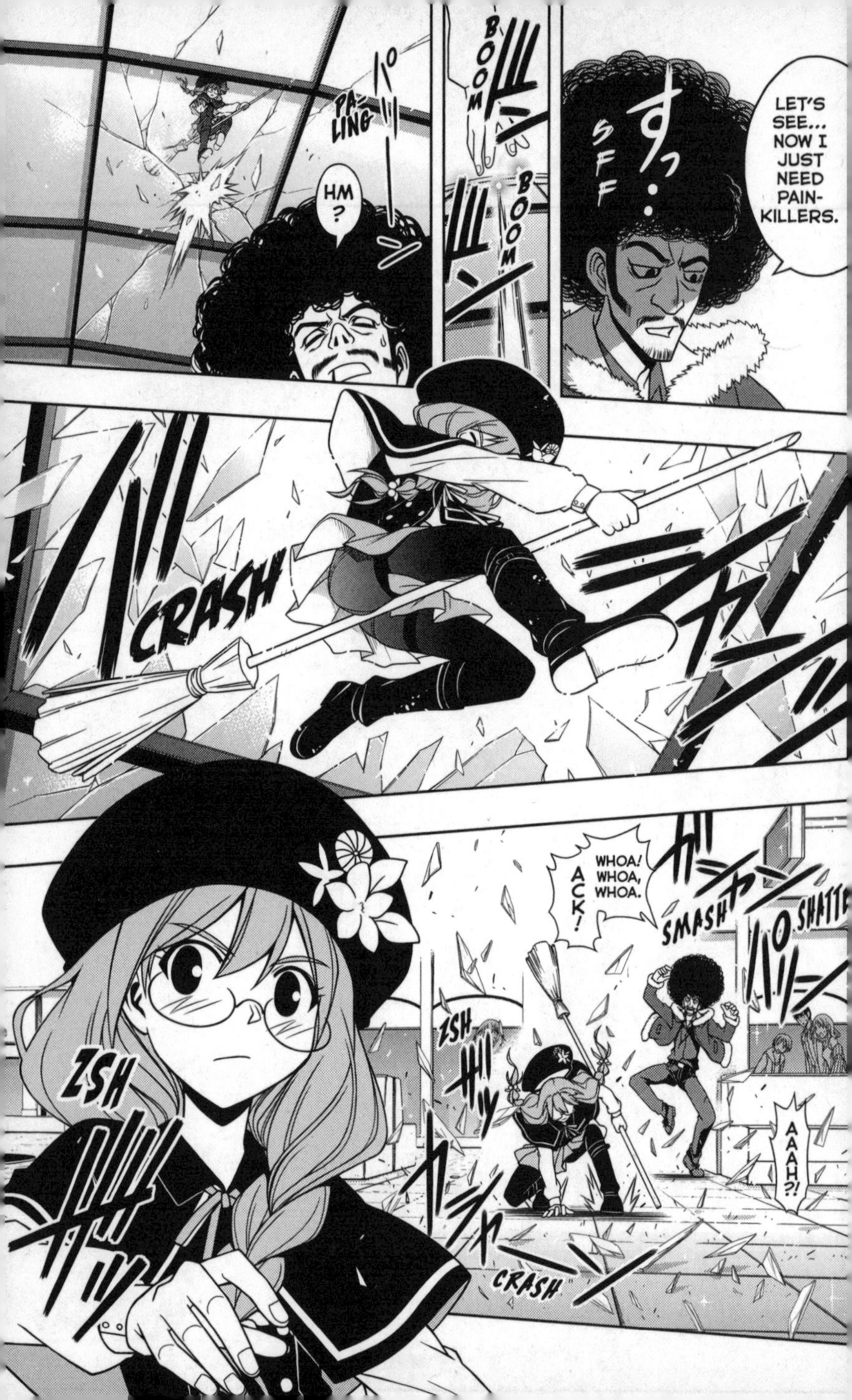
LET'S SEE... NOW I JUST NEED PAIN-KILLERS.
SFF
BOOM
BOOM
PA-LING
HM?
CRASH
WHOA! WHOA, WHOA.
ACK!
SMASH
SHATTE
AAAH?!
ZSH
CRASH
ZSH

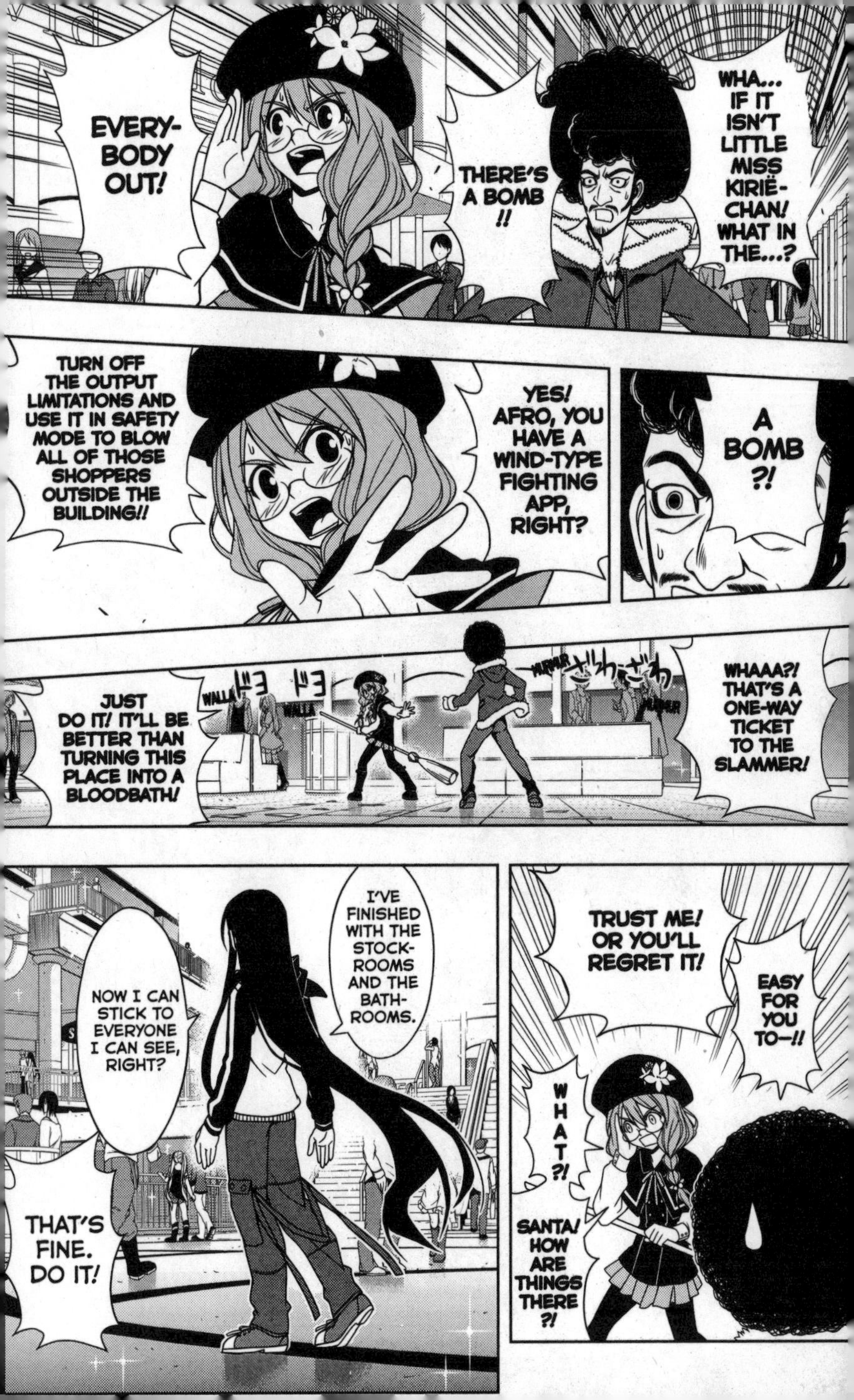

WHA... IF IT ISN'T LITTLE MISS KIRIË-CHAN! WHAT IN THE...?
THERE'S A BOMB !!
EVERY-BODY OUT!
A BOMB ?!
YES! AFRO, YOU HAVE A WIND-TYPE FIGHTING APP, RIGHT?
TURN OFF THE OUTPUT LIMITATIONS AND USE IT IN SAFETY MODE TO BLOW ALL OF THOSE SHOPPERS OUTSIDE THE BUILDING!!
WHAAA?! THAT'S A ONE-WAY TICKET TO THE SLAMMER!
MURMUR ざわざわ
MURMUR
ドヨ ドヨ
WALLA
WALLA
JUST DO IT! IT'LL BE BETTER THAN TURNING THIS PLACE INTO A BLOODBATH!
TRUST ME! OR YOU'LL REGRET IT!
EASY FOR YOU TO—!!
WHAT?!
SANTA! HOW ARE THINGS THERE ?!
I'VE FINISHED WITH THE STOCK-ROOMS AND THE BATH-ROOMS.
NOW I CAN STICK TO EVERYONE I CAN SEE, RIGHT?
THAT'S FINE. DO IT!

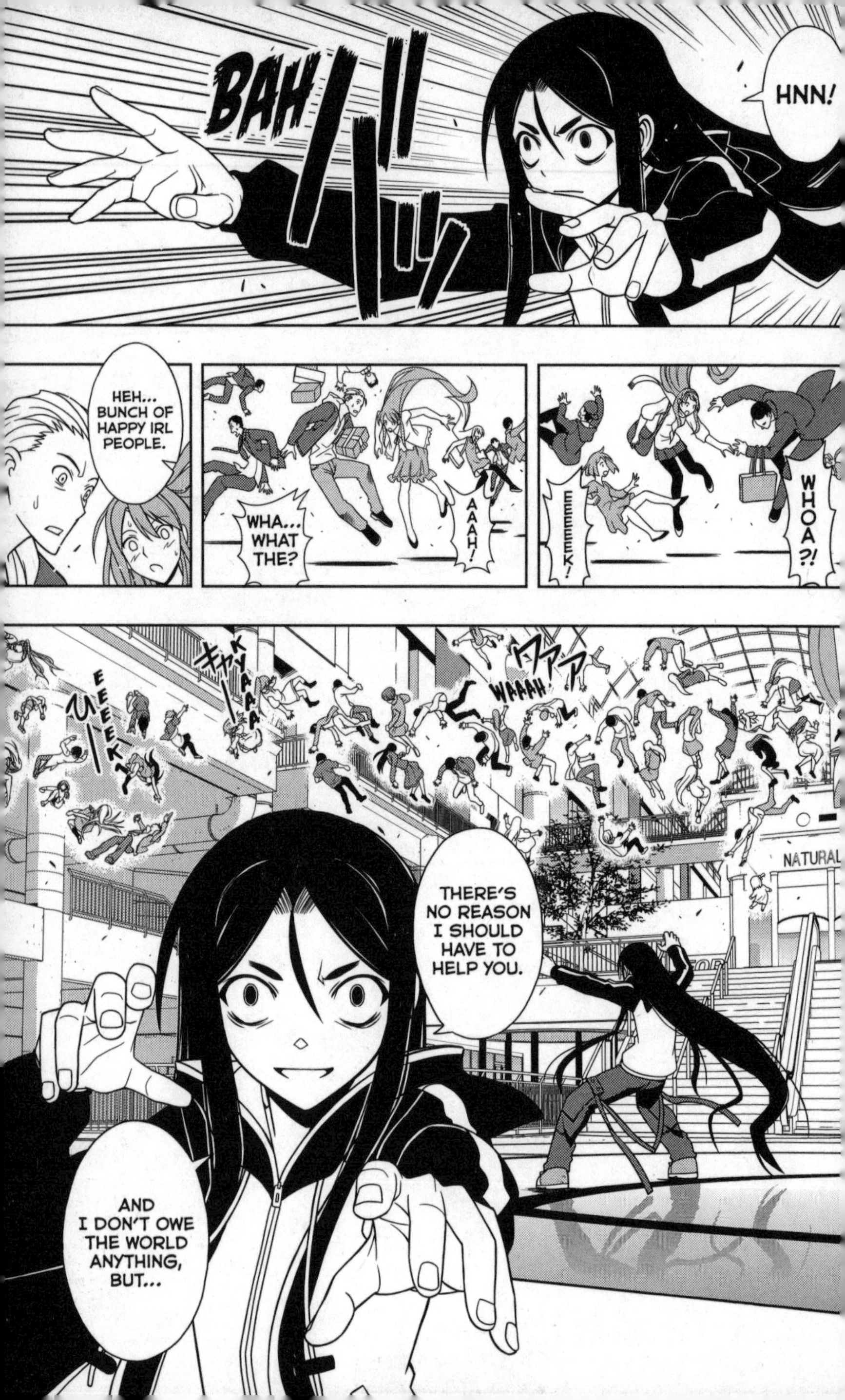
HNN!
BAH
WHOA?!
EEEEEK!
AAAH!
WHA... WHAT THE?
HEH... BUNCH OF HAPPY IRL PEOPLE.
NATURAL
ワァア WAAAH
キャー KYAAA
ひー EEEEK
THERE'S NO REASON I SHOULD HAVE TO HELP YOU.
AND I DON'T OWE THE WORLD ANYTHING, BUT...

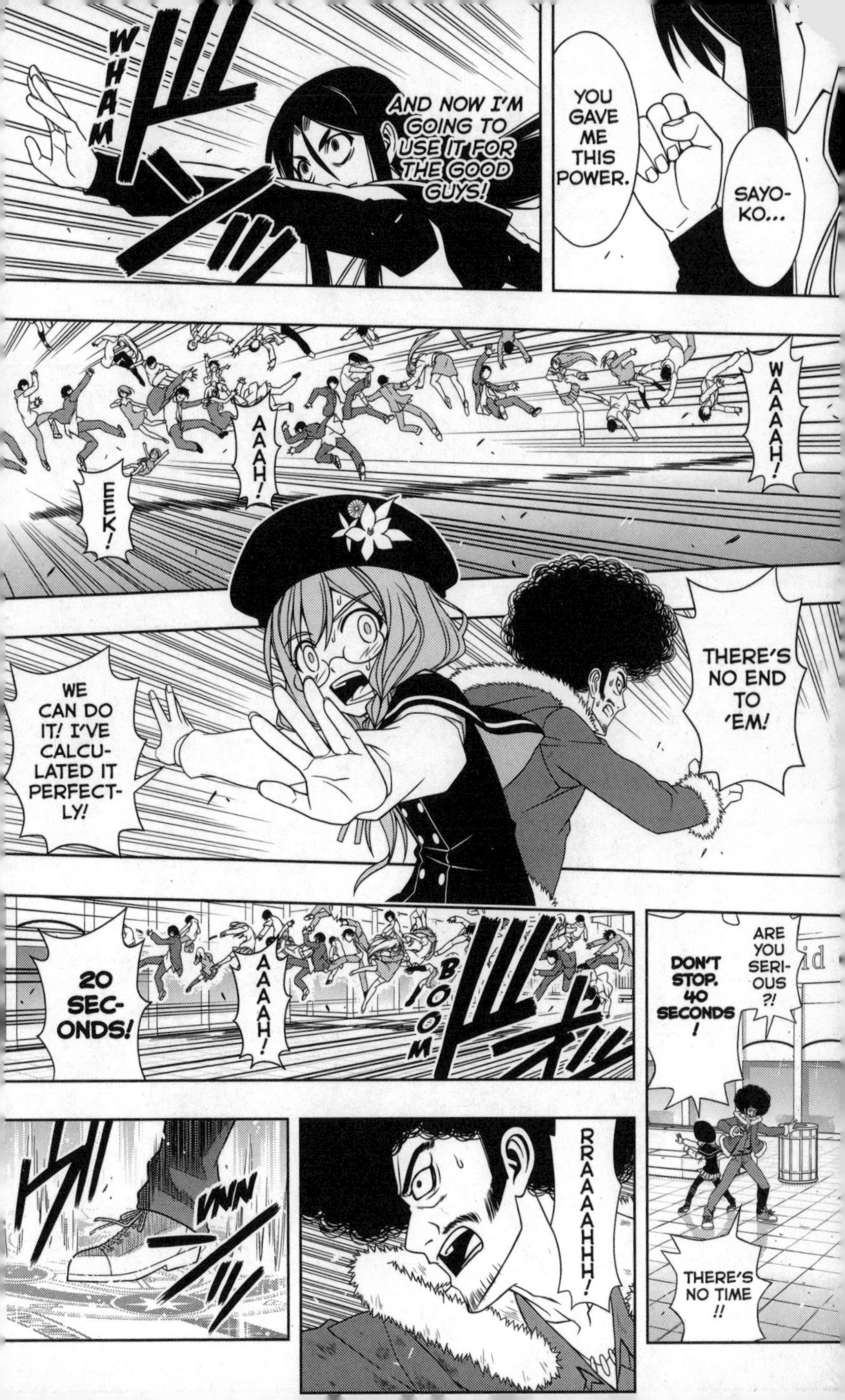
SAYO-KO...
YOU GAVE ME THIS POWER.
WHAM
AND NOW I'M GOING TO USE IT FOR THE GOOD GUYS!
WAAAAAH!
AAAH!
EEK!
THERE'S NO END TO 'EM!
WE CAN DO IT! I'VE CALCU-LATED IT PERFECT-LY!
ARE YOU SERI-OUS?!
DON'T STOP. 40 SECONDS!
THERE'S NO TIME!!
BOOM
AAAAH!
20 SEC-ONDS!
RRAAAAAHHH!
VNN

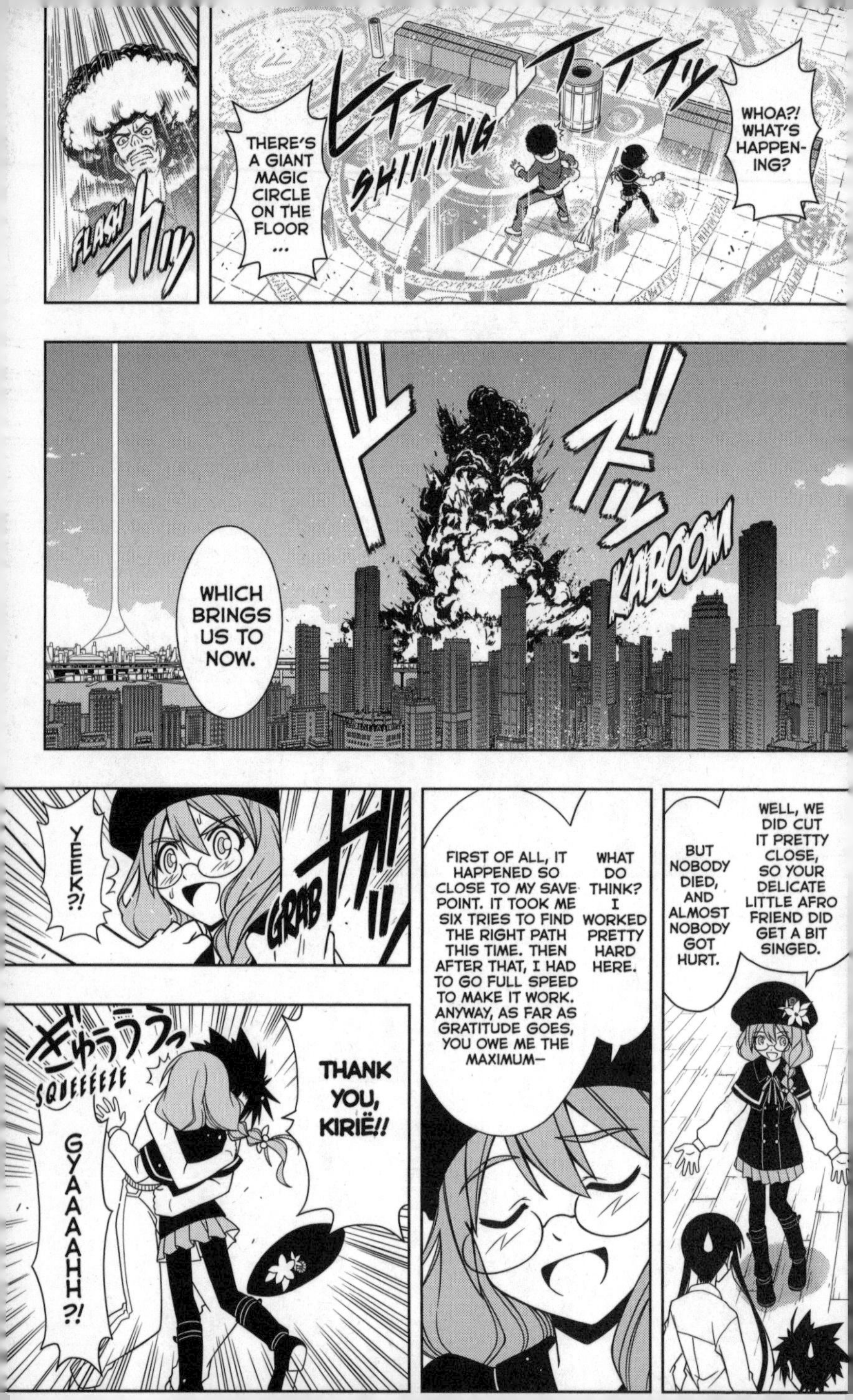
WHOA?! WHAT'S HAPPEN-ING?
SHIIIING
THERE'S A GIANT MAGIC CIRCLE ON THE FLOOR...
FLASH
KABOOM
WHICH BRINGS US TO NOW.
WELL, WE DID CUT IT PRETTY CLOSE, SO YOUR DELICATE LITTLE AFRO FRIEND DID GET A BIT SINGED.
BUT NOBODY DIED, AND ALMOST NOBODY GOT HURT.
WHAT DO THINK? I WORKED PRETTY HARD HERE.
FIRST OF ALL, IT HAPPENED SO CLOSE TO MY SAVE POINT. IT TOOK ME SIX TRIES TO FIND THE RIGHT PATH THIS TIME. THEN AFTER THAT, I HAD TO GO FULL SPEED TO MAKE IT WORK. ANYWAY, AS FAR AS GRATITUDE GOES, YOU OWE ME THE MAXIMUM—
GRAB
YEEK?!
THANK YOU, KIRIË!!
SQUEEEEZE
GYAAAAAHH?!

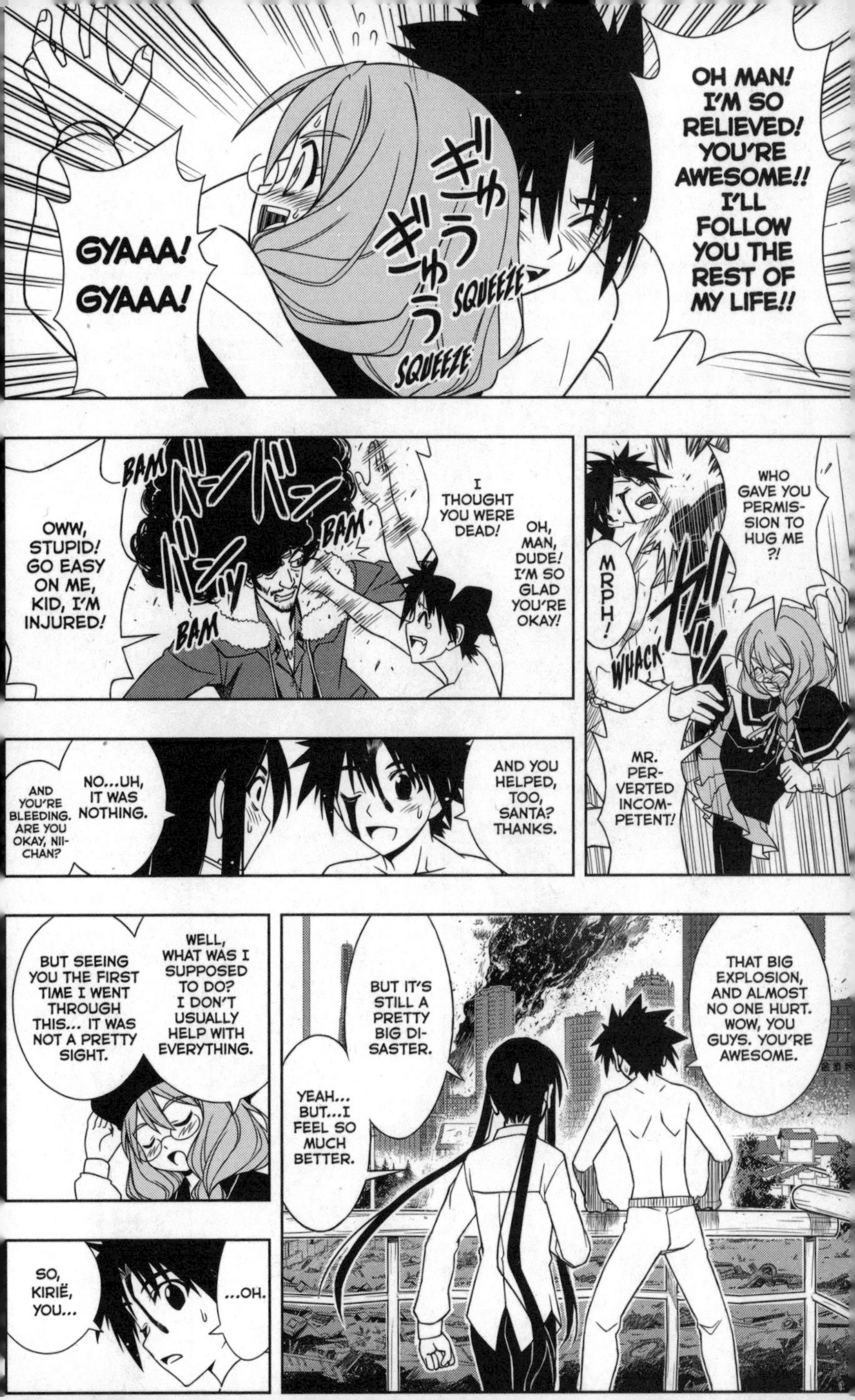
OH MAN! I'M SO RELIEVED! YOU'RE AWESOME!! I'LL FOLLOW YOU THE REST OF MY LIFE!!
ぎゅう
ぎゅう
SQUEEZE
ぎゅう
SQUEEZE
GYAAA! GYAAA!
WHO GAVE YOU PERMIS-SION TO HUG ME?!
MRPH!
WHACK
MR. PER-VERTED INCOMPE-TENT!
OH, MAN, DUDE! I'M SO GLAD YOU'RE OKAY!
I THOUGHT YOU WERE DEAD!
BAM
BAM
BAM
OWW, STUPID! GO EASY ON ME, KID, I'M INJURED!
AND YOU HELPED, TOO, SANTA? THANKS.
NO...UH, IT WAS NOTHING.
AND YOU'RE BLEEDING. ARE YOU OKAY, NII-CHAN?
THAT BIG EXPLOSION, AND ALMOST NO ONE HURT. WOW, YOU GUYS. YOU'RE AWESOME.
BUT IT'S STILL A PRETTY BIG DI-SASTER.
YEAH... BUT...I FEEL SO MUCH BETTER.
WELL, WHAT WAS I SUPPOSED TO DO? I DON'T USUALLY HELP WITH EVERYTHING.
BUT SEEING YOU THE FIRST TIME I WENT THROUGH THIS... IT WAS NOT A PRETTY SIGHT.
...OH.
SO, KIRIË, YOU...

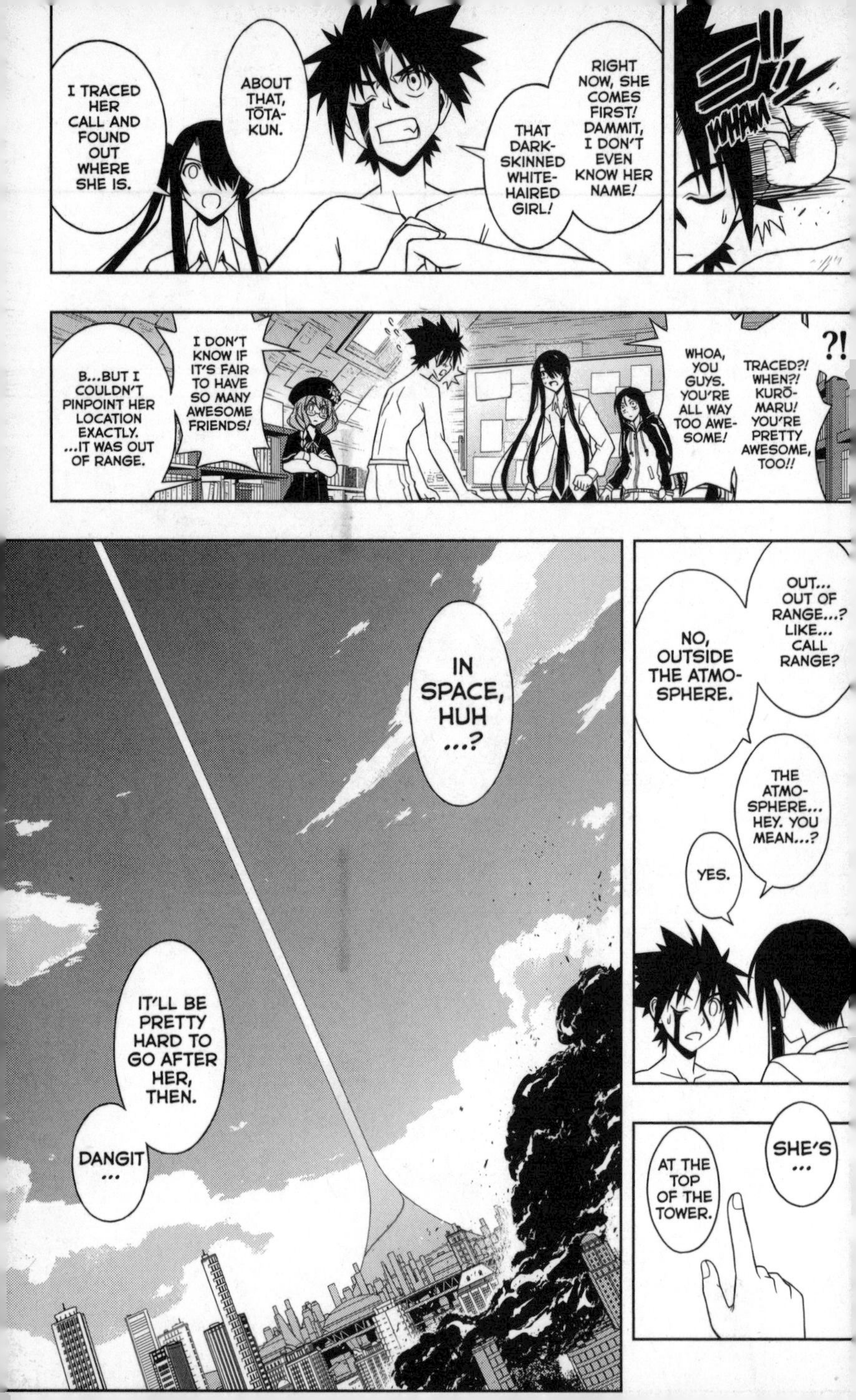

WHAM
RIGHT NOW, SHE COMES FIRST! DAMMIT, I DON'T EVEN KNOW HER NAME!
THAT DARK-SKINNED WHITE-HAIRED GIRL!
ABOUT THAT, TŌTA-KUN.
I TRACED HER CALL AND FOUND OUT WHERE SHE IS.
?!
TRACED?! WHEN?! KURŌ-MARU! YOU'RE PRETTY AWESOME, TOO!!
WHOA, YOU GUYS. YOU'RE ALL WAY TOO AWE-SOME!
I DON'T KNOW IF IT'S FAIR TO HAVE SO MANY AWESOME FRIENDS!
B...BUT I COULDN'T PINPOINT HER LOCATION EXACTLY. ...IT WAS OUT OF RANGE.
OUT... OUT OF RANGE...? LIKE... CALL RANGE?
NO, OUTSIDE THE ATMO-SPHERE.
THE ATMO-SPHERE... HEY. YOU MEAN...?
YES.
SHE'S...
AT THE TOP OF THE TOWER.
IN SPACE, HUH ...?
IT'LL BE PRETTY HARD TO GO AFTER HER, THEN.
DANGIT ...

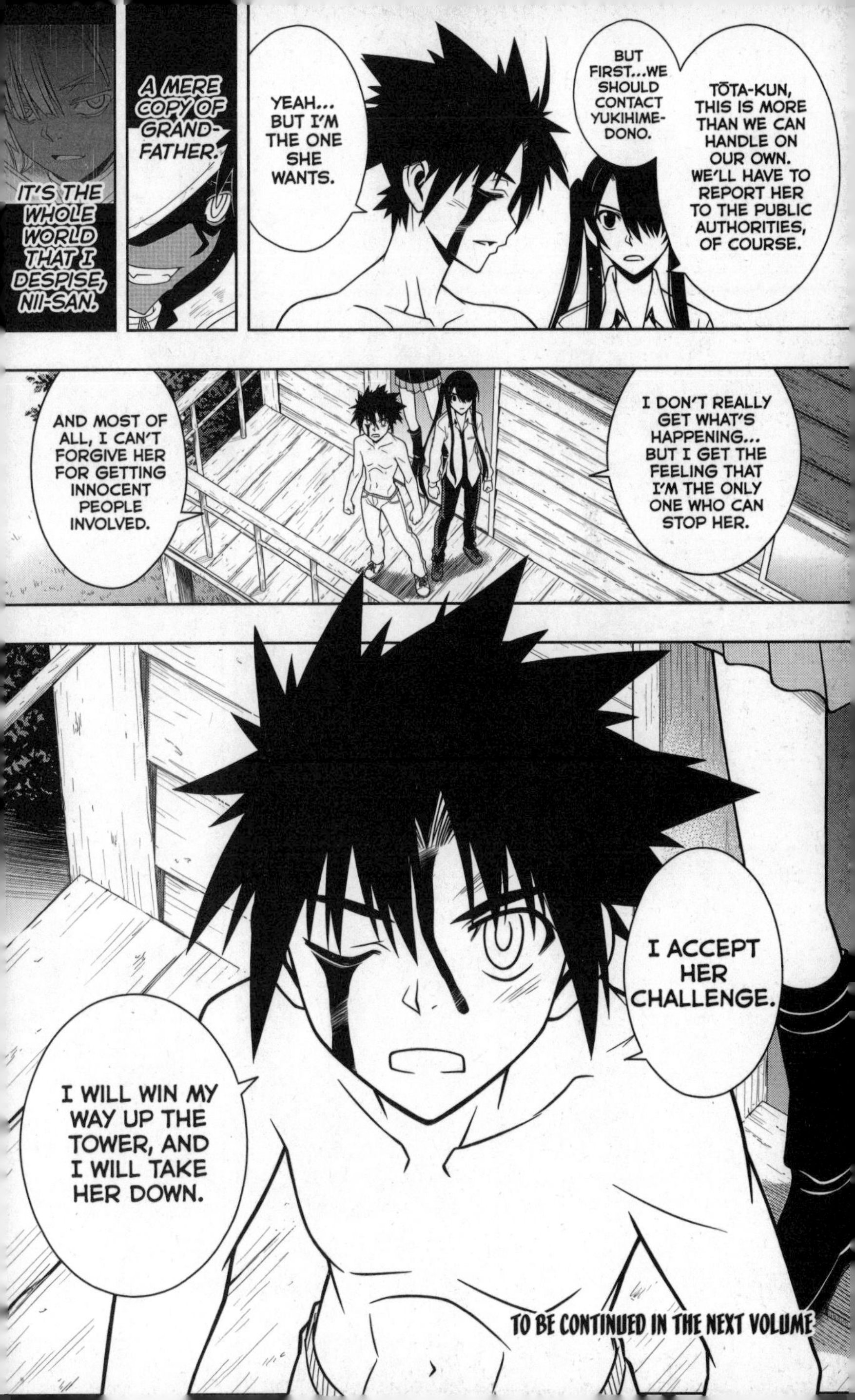
TŌTA-KUN, THIS IS MORE THAN WE CAN HANDLE ON OUR OWN. WE'LL HAVE TO REPORT HER TO THE PUBLIC AUTHORITIES, OF COURSE.
BUT FIRST...WE SHOULD CONTACT YUKIHIME-DONO.
YEAH... BUT I'M THE ONE SHE WANTS.
A MERE COPY OF GRAND-FATHER.
IT'S THE WHOLE WORLD THAT I DESPISE, NII-SAN.
I DON'T REALLY GET WHAT'S HAPPENING... BUT I GET THE FEELING THAT I'M THE ONLY ONE WHO CAN STOP HER.
AND MOST OF ALL, I CAN'T FORGIVE HER FOR GETTING INNOCENT PEOPLE INVOLVED.
I ACCEPT HER CHALLENGE.
I WILL WIN MY WAY UP THE TOWER, AND I WILL TAKE HER DOWN.
TO BE CONTINUED IN THE NEXT VOLUME

UQ HOLDER!

STAFF

Ken Akamatsu
Takashi Takemoto
Kenichi Nakamura
Keiichi Yamashita
Tohru Mitsuhashi
Susumu Kuwabara
Yuri Sasaki

Thanks to Ran Ayanaga

DEVIL SURVIVOR
デビルサバイバー

AFTER DEMONS BREAK THROUGH INTO THE HUMAN WORLD, TOKYO MUST BE QUARANTINED. WITHOUT POWER AND STUCK IN A SUPERNATURAL WARZONE, 17-YEAR-OLD KAZUYA HAS ONLY ONE HOPE: HE MUST USE THE *"COMP,"* A DEVICE CREATED BY HIS COUSIN NAOYA CAPABLE OF SUMMONING AND SUBDUING DEMONS, TO DEFEAT THE INVADERS AND TAKE BACK THE CITY.

BASED ON THE POPULAR VIDEO GAME FRANCHISE BY *ATLUS!*